D0206026

Pitt Series in

Russian and East European Studies

Origins of the
Czech
National Renascence

Hugh LeCaine Agnew

University of Pittsburgh Press
Pittsburgh and London

Pitt Series in Russian and East European Studies no. 18.
Published by the University of Pittsburgh Press, Pittsburgh, Pa., 15260
Copyright © 1993, University of Pittsburgh Press
All rights reserved
. Manufactured in the United States of America
Printed on acid-free paper

Library of Congress Cataloging-in-Publication Data

Agnew, Hugh LeCaine.
   Origins of the Czech national renascence / Hugh LeCaine Agnew.
p.   cm. — (Pitt series in Russian and East European studies ;
   no. 18)
   Includes bibliographical references and index.
   ISBN 0-8229-3742-5 (alk. paper)
   1. Czech Republic (Czechoslovakia)—Intellectual life—18th
century.   2. Czech Republic (Czechoslovakia)—Intellectual life—19th
century.   3. Nationalism—Czechoslovakia—Czech Republic.
I. Title. II. Series: Series in Russian and East European studies ; no. 18.
DB2168.A34   1993
943.7—dc20
                                    92-36909
                                        CIP

A CIP catalogue record for this book is available from the British Library.
Eurospan, London

Contents

Preface

This book began life, as so many first books do, as my doctoral dissertation at Stanford University. Unlike some of those dissertations, however, it has been a long time in the transformation from thesis to book. When I began looking into the origins of the Czech nationalist movement of the nineteenth century, contemporary Czechoslovakia was stultifying under "normalization" and Gustáv Husák was president and first secretary of the Communist party. If someone had offered to wager that Czechoslovakia would be transformed into a multiparty democracy and Václav Havel would be occupying the presidential office in the Hrad before my thesis appeared in book form, I would have thought it absurd. What a useful reminder that to most contemporaries the status quo seems permanent simply because it exists! From this perspective, the struggles of the Chartists and other dissidents under Communism reflect the same willingness to swim against the stream as those of the early Czech "awakeners." Perhaps that is one reason why at times of crisis, Czechs (and Slovaks, but this book is concerned only with the Czechs) keep returning to their history and the traditions of their nation, reexamining the past to understand its "meaning."

In this "dialogue with the past" (as E. H. Carr once defined history), I hope this book can take a part. It is based on both the secondary literature on this theme and the original primary sources left behind by its subjects. There is very little else that deals with this topic in the English language, and this book may help introduce it to the nonspecialist reader. Though not a Czech myself (by anything other than interest and inclination), I hope also that I can contribute in some small way to the ongoing discussions among the Czechs over this important phase in their history. An outsider can perhaps bring a different perspective simply because he is an outsider. If I have accomplished that, I shall be content.

Many people deserve recognition for their assistance in bringing this project to fruition. My parents, Jeanne LeCaine Agnew and Theodore Agnew, gave me a good example of the academic life. Two outstanding teachers shaped my interest in Eastern Europe: Lucien Karchmar of Queen's University, Kingston, Ontario, and Wayne S. Vucinich of Stanford University. That the latter's warm sense of *slovanská vzájemnost* led him to take on a student interested in Czech history is something I shall always appreciate.

The original dissertation took shape during an academic year in Prague made possible by a fellowship from the International Research and Exchanges Board in 1978–1979. Support from Stanford University, including a Harris Fellowship and a dissertation writing grant from the Weter Fund, helped see the project through. Revision and expansion of the dissertation was made easier by a summer research fellowship at the Indiana University Russian and East European Studies Institute in 1985, and participation in the University of Illinois Summer Research Laboratory in 1989 helped fill in a few details. Return visits to Prague in the summers of 1990 and 1991 were supported by research funds granted to the George Washington University by the American Council of Learned Societies.

Many other people in Singapore, Czechoslovakia, and the United States also contributed to the successful conclusion of this project. I am grateful to the History Department at the National University of Singapore, especially the late Professor Wong Lin Ken, his successor, Associate Professor Ernest C. T. Chew, and a congenial group of colleagues, especially Andrew Major, Frank Cibulka, and Malcolm Murfett.

Among Czech and Slovak scholars I have benefited greatly from the conversation and advice of Jan Havránek, Miroslav Hroch, and Jiří Kořalka. Less formal consultations with Roman Krasnický, Petr Čornej, and Vladimír Macura have also proved enlightening. A special place in our entire family's relationship with Czechoslovakia is held by our friends Věroslav Hába and Dana Hábová, Jiří Berger and Irena Bergerová, and Roman Krasnický and Irena Krasnická. It is a pleasure to be able now to thank them by name for kindnesses dating back to 1978.

In the United States, my friends and colleagues in the History Department and Elliott School of International Affairs at the George Washington University have been very supportive, especially Sharon Wolchik and Muriel Atkin. Stanley Winters, past president of the Czechoslovak History Conference, saw to it that I never lost touch with my fellow Czech and Slovak specialists during my time in Singapore. Joseph F. Zacek and Josef Anderle both read and commented on the manuscript, and if I have not always taken their advice in every case, I certainly appreciated receiving it.

In Prague I am indebted to the staff of the former Státní a univerzitní knihovna (the Clementinum), especially the Manuscripts and Old Prints reading room; the Historický kabinet, Katedra obecných dějin a pravěku, Filosofická fakulta Univerzity Karlova; and the Strahovská knihovna. Their colleagues at the Literární archiv Památníku národního písemnictví, the Archiv Národního muzea, and the Státní ústřední archiv also deserve my gratitude. To their number should be added their counterparts in the Österreichische Nationalbibliothek, Vienna; the British Library and the School of Slavonic and East European Studies, London; and of course the libraries of the National University of Singapore, Indiana University, and the University of Illinois. Thanks also to my editor, Jane Flanders, and others on the University of Pittsburgh Press staff who worked on this project.

Finally, I would like to thank my wife, Nancy MacLachlan, and our children, Robert, Colin, and Fiona, for sharing my time and attention with this book for so long.

Origins of the

Czech

National Renascence

Introduction

The Czech national renascence of the nineteenth century is one of those historical themes to which Czechs return again and again in their search for meaning in their past. In the aftermath of the revolution of 1989, as so many times before, the problems of national identity and the historical heritage were again being actively debated. Some observers have pointed out, however, the danger of refighting old battles over the meaning of Czech history with the findings and attitudes of an earlier generation.[1] This danger threatens if one simply expunges the historical work of the communist period from the argument and returns to the precommunist period. In the joyous moment of liberation from an enforced "Marxist" orthodoxy, one loses sight of the extent to which the official ideology of the former regime simply took over attitudes and ideas developed during the last half of the nineteenth century (though instead of black and white, it saw the Czech past in the colors black and red). Its basic view of Czech history is vividly summarized by Petr Čornej:

> All of us surely know from our schoolrooms, history text-books, and artistic images that picture of the Czech past whose apogee is formed by Hussitism and the period of the national renascence. Between them lies an epoch of decline, indeed of outright "darkness," gradually dispersed by

3

> the glimmers of the Enlightenment and the first awaken-
> ers. We all learned about the treacherous, morally corrupt,
> and, in the final analysis, alien nobility, treading down the
> morally pure country people, who toiled in the sweat of
> their brows and suffered cruelly for each rebellion, and
> nevertheless preserved in their breasts the flames of de-
> fiance. We have all heard and read about the brave and
> persecuted members of the Unity of Brethren and the in-
> famous Catholic church, throttling every sign of progress.[2]

Such views were propagated by all the means available to the
state, including a series of screen epics directed by Otakar
Vávra.[3] But instead of being the result of "Marxist" science,
these attitudes have roots deeper in the past.

The prevailing nationalist interpretation of Czech history,
including the national renascence, emerged out of the romantic historiography of the first half of the nineteenth century and was widely popularized by the use made of it,
especially by the Young Czechs, in arguing for greater political independence for Bohemia. František Palacký gave this
historiographical tradition an important element when he elevated the Hussite period to the status of key epoch in Czech
history. A Protestant himself, Palacký did not deny the Catholic church an important role in shaping Czech culture; but
his ideas were further developed and used in the political
struggle by historians and popularizers close to the Young
Czechs. Their liberal anticlericalism made them see the Catholic church as a pillar of the Austrian establishment, and they
used Palacký's history to support an interpretation of the
Czech past aimed at undermining the Catholic influence and
emphasizing the link between the Hussite past, the traditions
of the Unity of Czech Brethren, and the national renascence
of the nineteenth century. Though at odds with the Young
Czechs over many issues, Tomáš G. Masaryk shared their hostility to the Catholic church, and in his many works on the
meaning of Czech history helped further establish this orientation to the past in the popular mind.[4] The newly inde-

pendent Czechoslovak state after 1918 took over much of this interpretation into its official ideology.[5]

While these attitudes became widely accepted through popular belles-lettres and patriotic art, professional historians were developing different approaches. The historical seminar established at the Czech University by Jaroslav Goll (1846–1929) became the training ground for a new, positivistic attitude to the Czech past. Goll was suspicious of Palacký's broad, general approach and the involvement of romantic historiography in political affairs. He emphasized history for its own sake and concentrated on the critical scholarly monograph rather than the broad, sweeping general histories of the earlier generation. But it was from among Goll's students that the leading figures in the continuing debate over the meaning of Czech history would emerge.[6]

In reaction to the influence of Masaryk's ideas on the meaning of Czech history, but especially during the years immediately before and during the First World War, two main tendencies began to emerge in Goll's school. In them questions of historical interpretation were also influenced by differing political beliefs. One tendency, represented by Václav Novotný (1869–1932), was more sympathetic to Masaryk's point of view and supported his struggle for independence during the war. The other, led by the man who was probably Goll's most outstanding pupil, Josef Pekař (1870–1937), remained hostile to the Masaryk conception and supported autonomy within Austria-Hungary until the final days of the war. It is with the name of Josef Pekař that the most powerful criticism of the prevailing orientation toward the meaning of Czech history is connected. Already before the war, he had published important polemical works attacking Masaryk's views. In his own major monographs, he contributed vitally to a reevaluation of the period of "darkness" (*doba temna*) of the seventeenth and early eighteenth centuries, and to a critical assessment of the life of the Hussite war leader Jan Žižka.[7]

Another Goll pupil, Kamil Krofta (1876–1945), though he had participated in the polemic with Masaryk before World

War I, eventually moved closer to the views of Masaryk and Novotný. His works concerned in particular the history of the Hussite period and the era before the defeat of the Bohemian Estates' rebellion at the Battle of the White Mountain in 1620, an era which he viewed much more positively than did Pekař.[8]

Thus by the mid-twentieth century two distinct traditions in viewing the Czech past, including the national renascence, had emerged and established themselves. Each agreed that the beginnings of the national renascence could be placed in the later part of the eighteenth century, but they differed on what factors were important in understanding it. On the one hand, the traditional nationalist view lauded the value of the Hussite period and Protestantism in Bohemia, and asserted a link between them and the national renascence. This approach emphasized the importance of the religious policies of Joseph II, especially his Patent of Toleration (1781) and other reforms undermining the position of the Catholic church. The other view, represented by Pekař and his followers, along with certain other scholars not quite in either camp, insisted instead on the continuity of Czech culture after the White Mountain, the role of Catholicism in the Czech national identity, and the connections between the national renascence and the traditions of the Czech Catholic baroque. This tradition tended to emphasize the reaction of elements in Bohemian society to Josephinism, especially its centralism and Germanization, and saw the role of Bohemia's traditional nobility in a more positive light.[9]

After the Communist takeover in 1948, Marxist historiography dominated official historical writing in Czechoslovakia, and official interpretations of the renascence. At its worst, Marxist writing was a crude caricature of the traditional nationalist interpretation, seen through the blood-red glasses of the class war. At its best (and, especially for earlier periods, much valuable work was still done) it added other concerns to the search for the meaning of Czech history. The economic determinist bent in Marxism increased the importance of economic development as a topic for study (already begun by some historians before the war), and the focus in the history of the renascence shifted to the industrial revolution and the rise of capitalism in the Czech lands. For this approach, it was above all the economic and social policies of Joseph II which occupied the foreground in evaluating the beginnings of the renascence, especially the Leibeigenschaft Patent of 1781 and the attempted urbarial reform of his later years.[10]

More than forty years ago, on the eve of the Communist takeover of his homeland, the literary historian Albert Pražák called for historians of the renascence to seek a synthetic approach, which would avoid the extremes of either of the two dominant lines of interpretation developed in the nineteenth and first half of the twentieth centuries.[11] Instead, a new dominant interpretation was enthroned, at least officially, and the argument could still be made that a new synthetic interpretation is necessary. Pražák's own great work on the renascence, *České obrození* (1947) is now quite dated, and since it was largely written under the shadow of the Nazis it has a strongly patriotic-defensive tone.[12] In addition, its focus is almost exclusively on literary history. The standard synthesis published during the Communist period, Josef Kočí's *České národní obrození* (most recent edition, 1978), though it makes an admirable attempt to place the Czech developments into the wider context of European political, social and economic history, is marred by its overly schematic Marxist framework, and those elements of the Marxist version of the nationalist view that do not take account of the arguments of Pekař's school. Both Pražák and Kočí deal with the national renascence up to the middle of the nineteenth century, which takes them beyond the phase of its origins and into the active patriotic struggle.

A valuable study with more limited aims is Bedřich Slavík's *Od Dobnera k Dobrovskému* (1975), which focuses on the Enlightenment in Bohemia, looking largely at literary and intellectual history. Although forced to pay lip service to the Marxist categories, it brings an interesting argument to the interpretation of the origins of the renascence and the role of the Enlightenment and Josephinism in it. Slavík distinguishes between a Viennese form of Enlightenment and Josephinism, and two local Bohemian variants, a territorial one (*zemské osvícenství, zemské Josefinismus*), and a Czech one. While this approach allows one to recognize the differences among members of the intellectual and official strata at the time, it seems to me to be an unnecessarily complicated scheme, on the one hand, and to restrict the human capacity to be self-contradictory on the other. A later, more overtly "Marxist" work on the Czech Enlightenment is Josef Haubelt's *České osvícenství* (1986). Haubelt argues, quite correctly, that previous historians have overconcentrated on the humanist disciplines and literature in particular, and that the Enlightenment had a great and important impact on natural and exact sciences as well. The value of this corrective, however, is reduced by the rigidly schematic approach that insists on a dialectical opposition of Enlightenment to the previous baroque culture and its values, and sees the Enlightenment, predictably, as the ideology of the "bourgeoisie." Haubelt savages earlier interpretations which he sees as overvaluing the baroque, without acknowledging the other tradition in which his work fits (short of a citation to a late article by Zdeněk Nejedlý). After a ten-year delay, the Czechoslovak Academy of Sciences finally published in 1990 a collective volume, *Počátky českého národního obrození, 1770–1791* under the general editorship of Josef Petráň. This work ranges widely over its limited chronological span, including encyclopedic chapters looking at economic and social conditions, the reform program of enlightened absolutism, popular culture, the social activity and "ideology" of the common people, and only one chapter devoted to the language, culture, science, and the Enlightenment. In many ways this work, too, looks rather like a fly in amber—a delicately preserved example of the best of something that is gone. The Marxist schematic framework, reflected in its insistence that the most important aspects of the period lie in the struggle for citizenship and freedoms by the lower classes and the development of the economic conditions leading to the growth of capitalist relations, betrays the fact that most of its contributions were still prepared "za totáče" (under totalitarianism), as the Czechs say today.

Since the collapse of Communism, Czech scholarly life has been freed from restrictions imposed by the state in the name of a political ideology. With the continued interest in the meaning of the Czech past, including the renascence, the possibility now exists for the development of a new approach such as the one Pražák called for so long ago. Standing in the way, however, are other problems of a different nature. There are so many other pressing needs, from writing new textbooks for all levels of public schools, to working out how the universities will function now that their academic autonomy has been returned to them, that it seems unlikely that major new syntheses will be forthcoming for some time. Until that becomes possible, I hope that this book can fill the gap to some extent. It may also help to provide to an English-speaking audience an introduction to a fascinating and important part of Czech history that also has a wider significance as a part of the general development of nationalism in Europe in the nineteenth century.

Let us turn, then, to the national renascence: what is it, and where did it come from? The nineteenth-century patriots, when they described their national movement, turned initially to metaphors of rebirth, awakening, or resurrection (*znovuzrození, probuzení, vzkříšení*). The prevailing interpretation, as we have seen, saw the Czech nation as a community with a long and glorious past that had somehow fallen asleep or even died during the period of "darkness" that had descended upon it after the defeat of the Bohemian Estates' revolt in 1620. Now it had, perhaps miraculously, awakened, come to life, and begun to demand its rightful place among other European nations. Toward the threshold of the twentieth century, the less emotionally charged term "renascence" (*obrození*) began to replace the earlier, less accurate terms and is now in general use. Nevertheless, the patriots of the first two generations are still usually called "awakeners" (*bu-diteé*).[13] Even these revised expressions still imply the existence of certain major characteristics of the renascence. In the first place, they imply continuity, since that which undergoes a revival or renascence must have existed before. Second, they imply change or transformation, since waking is a changed state in comparison with sleeping. Finally, these terms raise the question of agency, for if the nation was roused by "awakeners," then human will must have played a role. Embedded in the very terminology used to describe the national renascence, then, are several questions, including these three: What existed before the emergence of the modern nation? What happened to bring about this emergence? What was the part played by individual human choice?

The first of these questions raises the problem of whether nations and nationalism should be seen as distinctly modern features of human society, or whether they also existed in the past.[14] Certainly one can find evidence of attitudes among at least some levels of society, even a long way back in the past, that resemble those of modern nationalism. A good example of this from the Czech past would be the *Kronika Boleslavská*, once attributed to a certain Dalimil. In it the chronicler not only expresses a clear idea of the separate status of the Kingdom of Bohemia, but also of the Slavic community of the Czechs. It also includes strong expressions of anti-German sentiment.[15] Yet even if we accept that "the ability to distinguish between one's own national community and other national communities was unimpaired, unambiguous, supra-social, and—one might add—remarkably accurate long before modern nationalism," this does not mean that modern nationalism is the same thing as this earlier awareness of national community.[16] If we term this awareness of community *national consciousness* and keep it separate from modern nationalism, then we can argue that while national consciousness can exist, and has done so quite happily in the past, without modern nationalism, modern nationalism cannot exist without national consciousness. Thus the spectacle of "nation building" in the modern world includes efforts to create and inculcate national consciousness.[17]

The attitudes of national consciousness can be, however, both ancient and deeply rooted. Civilizational patterns such as those characteristic of nomad or sedentary ways of life, universal religions granting fundamental legitimacy to the basic attitudes of societies, the impact of religious organizations and political structures on the basic driving myths that give societies meaning and cohesion, the patterns of influence from town to countryside and back; all these elements help create a framework within which narrower factors of culture, language, history and religious experience can contribute to the national identity.[18] The interplay of these narrow factors has attracted the attention of several Czech scholars. František Graus devoted several works to analyzing the problems of premodern national consciousness in Eastern and Central Europe in which he points to the crucial importance of the ninth and tenth centuries, when the state forms that eventually became national states first emerged, and the fourteenth and fifteenth centuries, by which time attitudes were expressed that can undoubtedly be characterized as national. In his view, premodern national consciousness in this region is characterized by a general sense of linguistic community, which eventually becomes identified as a *Schicksalgemeinschaft*. A dynastic tradition about the origins and importance of the ruling dynasty and "tribe" emerges, followed by the territorialization of originally personal relationships between ruler and subjects, culminating in the abstraction of the territory to symbols (*regnum, corona*). Religious practices such as the veneration of patron saints can build up an identification between patron and land, or even people, that could sink roots deep into society. An example of this would be the Czech veneration of Saint Václav (the "good King Wenceslas" of the Christmas carol), which was well established at least by the twelfth century.[19] Finally, groups emerge who see themselves as speaking for wider elements in their societies, and eventually are accepted as such (originally clerics, later urban elements).[20]

The effect of the Hussite revolution on the specific case of Bohemia, according to Graus, was to create a special situation with a wider social base, the complete separation of national consciousness from the person of the monarch, and the exceptionally clear conviction of a special mission granted to the linguistic community.[21] Other scholars interested in the Hussite period have also pointed to its importance for premodern Czech national consciousness. Since most Germans in Bohemia (except the Waldensian heretics) did not join the Hussite movement, the original sense of being chosen to recognize and spread God's word fused with the old Czech anti-German aversion. Most of the anti-Hussite crusades came from German-speaking Europe, and this fact only added to the strength of the national element, giving to Hussite national consciousness its precociously modern appearance.[22]

During the roughly two centuries between the martyrdom of Hus and the defeat of the Bohemian Estates' revolt in 1620, the religious divisions in Bohemia—Catholic, Utraquist, Unity of Czech Brethren, and increasingly Lutheran and Calvinist groups all competed with each other—led to the development of competing versions of Czech identity. After the Thirty Years' War, only the Catholic version could be officially reflected in Bohemia, but it produced its own distinct forms of Czech consciousness (as reflected in such Catholic baroque authors as Bohuslav Balbín, discussed in chapter 1).[23] When modern nationalism emerged in the lands of the Czech crown, these earlier traditions were there, available for use, as it were, in the new conditions.[24]

But how does one get from ethnic communities with their distinct forms of self-awareness to nations and modern nationalism? What were the forces that led to the emergence of Czech nationalism and its counterparts elsewhere in Europe? The emergence of modern nationalism is closely bound up with the modern transformation of European society, a transformation so profound that the temptation to call it a revolution is well-nigh irresistible. This Western revolution was a threefold one, involving economic and social life, military and administrative organization, and religious and cultural thinking, and it shaped modern, industrial society in Europe and the world over.[25] The growth of capitalism increased economic links among the states of Europe, with the rise of a core of strong states controlling weaker, peripheral areas and maritime mercantile empires; but it also intensified contacts within individual states between urban and economic elites, linking them in a common economic fate and wearing down regional differences. In the process the wealth at the disposal of the state increased, and methods of military and administrative control changed in keeping with this development. The rise of professional military forces, coupled with technological developments in the art of warfare, increased the power of the state, and the development of professional administrative bureaucracies staffed by a trained intelligentsia created a new kind of "rational state" that was superior to previous types of state formation.[26] This bureaucratic, "rational" state proceeded to play a central part in a cultural and educational revolution, aimed at ending the authority of the church and ancient traditions and substituting itself and the community of citizens and equals that it created for the earlier forms of religious or traditional community. In the process, it promoted cultural standardization by spreading secular education and adopting uniform administrative languages, allowing the "imagining" of a limited, sovereign community to which all educated citizens belonged.[27]

Each of the three aspects of this Western revolution involved a strengthened and centralized state. As these transformations affected existing communities, then, it was not surprising that resistance to state power, and then achieving and using it, became the major goals of the social movements called forth by the changed conditions, and nationalism a major means to those goals. This apparent link between the rise of the modernizing, centralizing state and modern nationalism, including the Czech variety, gives the latter a distinct political coloration that helps differentiate it from earlier forms of national self-awareness.[28] The consciousness of national community developed in earlier times is now elaborated in a national ideology that plays an important part in the threefold task of nationalist politics: coordinating various elites in resisting the demands of the centralizing state and struggling for control over it, mobilizing support from wider levels of society, and gaining legitimacy for nationalist claims, or, where successful, the new nation-states.[29] This is not to limit modern nationalism solely to the status of a political movement, narrowly defined, but to suggest that in modern, industrial, mass-based societies the political consequences of the "all-inclusive penetration of national consciousness into every going pursuit" are inescapable.[30]

The Czech scholar Miroslav Hroch has described three stages in the development of modern nationalist movements among Europe's "small nations" such as that of the Czechs. In the first stage, a small group of intellectuals begins to study the language and history of the national community; in the second, a wider group of active patriots, having elaborated a national ideology, undertakes active agitation in the name of the nation; and in the final, mass-based stage the movement reaches its peak.[31] This study focuses on the earliest phase of the Czech national renascence, before the emergence of a fully fledged nationalist movement.[32] The state within which this Czech renascence developed was the multiethnic Habsburg monarchy, where from the mid-eighteenth century a feudal conglomeration of territories was undergoing a cultural shift from the universal Catholicism of the Counter-Reformation to the no less cosmopolitan outlook of the Enlightenment. At the same time, Maria Theresa and Joseph II, under the impact of that same Enlightenment and developments in statecraft elsewhere in Europe, attempted to do away with the mediated authority of the feudal order and reorganize their possessions on rational, enlightened principles.[33]

Coinciding roughly with the period of Maria Theresa's

and Joseph II's reforms were the beginnings of a remarkable Czech cultural and linguistic revival in Bohemia, initially the work of a small group of intellectuals—members of that intelligentsia whose emergence plays an important, if not indispensable, role in the development of modern nationalism.[34] Like their counterparts elsewhere in Europe, these Bohemian intellectuals were largely of non-noble background, educated according to Western standards, and earned a living in one way or another through their intellectual labor. Although certain representatives of the nobility acted as patrons to these scholars and shared some of their intellectual interests, the direct involvement of members of the nobility in their activities was small.[35] The very cosmopolitanism of Enlightenment culture forced the Bohemian intelligentsia to confront the issue of their self-image, their differences and similarities with other peoples in Europe. In the process, they articulated a complex of attitudes and ideas about the Czech language, culture, and nation that would provide important material for later nationalist ideologies and suggests the importance of culture in the formation and expression of national consciousness.[36]

The exact relationship between the cultural developments of eighteenth-century Bohemia (especially the Enlightenment), the reform program of enlightened absolutism, and the emerging national renascence is complicated and many-sided. While it is no longer acceptable to dismiss the baroque and rococo periods in Bohemia as a time of "darkness" (*temno*), the Enlightenment did open up new possibilities for the intelligentsia with its emphasis on the ability of human reason, critically applied, to reach truths about the past and present. In Bohemia especially, the emphasis on the freedom of individual conscience and inquiry struck deep resonances.[37]

Simultaneously these attitudes, coupled with reforms undertaken by "enlightened absolutist" monarchs (inspired in part by the same culture), suggested a "private" conception of society in which other forms of cohesion and relationship to authority would have to be sought than traditional, feudal ones. Enlightened absolutism, especially in the form of Josephinism, evoked both support and resistance from the intelligentsia in this period.[38] Support, because many of the goals of the reforms chimed well with those of the intelligentsia, notably the loosening of censorship, proclamation of religious toleration, and the educational reforms. Many intellectuals also supported some of the economic goals of enlightened absolutism, including even the Leibeigenschaft Patent of 1781. Resistance, because enlightened absolutism challenged the privileges of the established institutions of the church and nobility, to which many of the intellectuals were connected in one way or another. Also, the drive to adopt a single language of state (German) for the new, "rational," centralized monarchy ran counter to the linguistic diversity of Bohemia and other parts of the Habsburg realm.

Resistance to the centralizing, reforming state, when it first began, was not national in the modern sense. While contemporaries did recognize in Bohemia the existence of two peoples, "both ... Bohemians by birth and country, but otherwise in many respects very different," and even conceded that "one must distinguish the actual Bohemians, the Czechs, as the main nation (*Hauptnation*) from the German-Bohemians,"[39] they were still far from a modern, ethnolinguistic concept of nation, either Czech or German.

The leaders of the resistance to the centralizing reforms of "enlightened absolutism" were the nobility, and they based their resistance on historical and territorial rights. The primary example of this early resistance is, of course, the Hungarian nobility's near revolt during Joseph's reign, which had its paler echo among the nobility of Bohemia.[40] Reflected in both movements was a concept of nation limited to the groups with political rights—primarily the nobility—and a patriotism based on an historical and territorial attachment to the Crown of Saint Stephen or Saint Václav. In Bohemia, where following the Thirty Year's War the old Bohemian nobility had been almost entirely destroyed by confiscation and emigration, the descendants of the rewarded imperial servants who replaced it paraded a distinct Bohemian *Landespatriotismus* in the face of the centralizing ambitions of Vienna.[41] That it was less genuine than the Hungarian version also made this noble "nationalism" less effective, but the privileged groups' example was eventually to prove contagious. It required, nevertheless, a shift in its basic supports, a shift away from defense of historic privilege and toward a resistance to the demands of the modernizing state based on something else. The historical tradition of the Bohemian nobility was common to both old Czech and old German noble families; but it was not easily translated into something shared by wider social groups whose support was eventually to be mobilized for the national movement.[42] As a concept of nation defined culturally and linguistically replaced the older, political concept, *Landespatriotismus* ceased to be sufficient as a foundation for "national" resistance to Vienna. It was replaced by Czech nationalism.[43]

During the cultural and linguistic revival mentioned above, many of the attitudes of Czech national consciousness, taken up by later nationalists, were elaborated. For clarity's sake, we will follow this process of elaborating a modern Czech national consciousness thematically, rather than purely chronologically. It is important to remember that these developments often took place simultaneously, and that individual patriots were active in more than one area of cultural work at the same time. The combination of their historical research, literary scholarship, and linguistic reform during this opening phase of the national renascence, as well as their halting efforts to create contemporary culture in Czech, provided the raw materials for redefining the Czech community in terms of modern nationalism. These raw materials would be built with during the second phase of the renascence, until with the 1848 revolutions Czech nationalism first produced an outright political program.[44] What follows is the story of the development of these attitudes during the generation between the Enlightenment and romanticism.

1

The Presence of the Past

*H*istorians like to believe that their craft is not only rewarding, but also important. In this they are no doubt like any other professionals, but it is not owing to such considerations alone that this discussion of the origins of the Czech national renascence begins by considering the changes taking place in the craft of history in eighteenth-century Bohemia. These changes, in particular the rise of the critical method in history, were closely related to other developments that together helped lay the ideological foundation for the national movement of the nineteenth century.

The year 1761 provides a convenient watershed, for it was then that a Piarist monk and scholar named Gelasius Dobner (1719–1790) published the first volume of his life's work, a critical commentary to a Latin translation of Václav Hájek z Libočan's *Kronyka česká*. Hájek had been a favorite source for historians since the sixteenth century, and Dobner's critical comments on his veracity, especially his questioning of the story of the founding of the Czech kingdom, made him something of a celebrity among German and Bohemian historians. In fact he was lionized by some, largely as a result of this project, as the "father of Czech critical historiography."[1] What was it about this work that earned its author such a resounding title? And why was it, and the critical method it helped spread, so important to the development of Czech national consciousness? To understand the impact of Dobner's commentary of Hájek, it helps to go back more than a century, to survey the condition of historical writing in Bohemia after the Thirty Years' War.[2]

The Establishment of Critical History in Bohemia

With the defeat of the rebellious Bohemian Estates at the Battle of the White Mountain in 1620 and the establishment of a new internal regime institutionalized in the Verneuerte Landesordnung of 1627, the cultural development of Bohemia was diverted into channels it might not otherwise have entered. The victorious Counter-Reformation harbored suspicions about the Czech language and culture, since they had produced Jan Hus and were connected with the Protestant Reformation.[3] Under these conditions, the traditions of Czech humanist historiography could only be carried on in exile by such scholars as Jan Amos Komenský (Comenius) (1592–1670), last bishop of the Czech Brethren, or the Neo-Utraquist Pavel Stránský (1589–1657). Robbed of the polemical opponents with whom they had coexisted during the sixteenth century, Catholic writers were free to interpret their past according to their own lights, but even they had to cope with the taint of heresy that clung to Bohemian history. This could only gradually be removed, as Bohemia was brought back ever more firmly into the Catholic fold.[4]

During the century and a half following the White Mountain, the cultural and educational life of Bohemia was largely dominated by the Jesuit order, which returned in 1624 to lead the reconversion of the kingdom of heretics. Historical writing in the first decades consisted mainly of collections of saints' lives, the only framework in which anything good about the Bohemian past could be said. This extremely negative approach did not last, however, and toward the end of the century a school of historical writing began to develop within the Jesuit order itself (as it absorbed the best minds it found among its pupils) which attempted to be both loyally Catholic and positive in its attitude to at least some aspects of Czech history. The Czech Jesuit Bohuslav Balbín (1621–1688) gave his name to this stream of Czech historiography,[5] in which the regional tradition of Catholicism was combined with the patriotic tradition kept alive for a time by exiled Czech Brethren and Protestants.[6] The subjects of Balbín's earlier works were the lives of the Bohemian and Moravian saints and the veneration of the Virgin Mary at places of pilgrimage in the Czech lands. His apologetic theme was evident, as he attempted to prove that Bohemia had been the land of many true Catholics, as well as giving birth to Hus. Such themes appeared even more clearly in his later works, such as the *Vita venerabilis Arnesti, primi archiepiscopi Pragensis* (1644). He was also an indefatigable collector, gathering material for a massive *Miscellanea historica regni Bohemiae,* of which the first part appeared in 1679. In this work collecting documentary sources, Balbín reflected newer methods further developed by succeeding generations. It also reflected his attempt to preserve and defend his fatherland, the Kingdom of Bohemia.[7] Sometimes, in fact, Balbín's patriotism went further than his superiors would allow. One of the most influential and clearly patriotic of his writings, an elegy on the former greatness and present decline of the Czech language after the White Mountain, usually known as *Dissertatio apologetica pro lingua slavonica, praecipue bohemica,* was published only in 1775.[8]

The influence of this "Balbín school" reached down to the revival period in the works of such historians as Tomáš Pešina z Čechorodu (1629–1680), Jiří Středovský (1670–1713), František Beckovský (1658–1725) and eventually Johann Adalbert Berghauer (1684–1760), in whose lifetime the new trends of critical historiography connected with the Enlightenment began to assert themselves.[9] In their works these men followed the example set by the Jesuit Bollandist fathers, who began publishing their massive edition of the lives of the saints, *Acta sanctorum,* in France in 1643. These Czech and Slovak scholars' studies of the lives of the saints and the history of the church and religious orders in their homelands were quite in the spirit of the Bollandists.[10] During the eighteenth century, however, the Bollandist tradition in Bohemia began to be supplanted by the Maurist school, which had more advanced methodological principles.

Even at the height of the Counter-Reformation, Bohemia had not been entirely cut off from the historiography of the German Reformation or humanism,[11] but it was especially through the spread of Maurist historical methods by way of German and, above all, Austrian historians that historiography in Bohemia absorbed the new, critical approach. The Benedictine monks of the Congrégation de Saint-Maur, who developed this approach in France during the seventeenth century, differed from their predecessors mainly in their diligent cultivation of the auxiliary sciences, especially diplomatics. Their methods were ably set out by the leading Maurist scholar, Mabillon, in his *De re diplomatica* (1681).[12] The Maurists stressed the importance of proper sources and the need for a critical approach to them, which accounts for their efforts to make complete collections of sources for the periods of history in which they were interested. In their insistence on a careful, exact reading of the document, they also broke with the aesthetic conventions of the humanist historians, who had not hesitated to improve the texts of their sources to suit their own taste.[13]

The ideas of the Maurists quickly spread among their fellow Benedictines in other countries. In the Austrian lands, their leading representative was the Benedictine historian Bernard Pez (1683–1735), who had traveled widely in Austria, Bavaria, Belgium, and France, where he met Mabillon himself. His less well-known brother, Hieronymous Pez (1685–1762), also applied the new methods to his work, especially in his three-volume collection of documents, *Scriptores rerum Austriacarum veteres ac genuini* (1721–1745).[14] Both brothers influenced another Benedictine historian who concerned himself with the history of the Bohemian lands, Magnoald Ziegelbauer (1689–1750).[15]

Ziegelbauer was a Swabian by birth, but spent much of his active life in Vienna, Prague, and Olomouc, where by his scholarly endeavors he made a significant contribution to the development of his adopted homeland. He was encouraged by the example of Bernard Pez to attempt a literary history of the Benedictines, *Historia rei litterariae Ordinis S. Benedicti,* but the manuscript did not see print until 1754, and then it had to be published outside of Austria.[16] From Vienna, Ziegelbauer was called to Prague by the abbot of the Benedictine monastery of Břevnov to begin a history of that foundation. The fruit of his sojourn there of several months was his *Epitome historica . . . Monasterii Brevnoviensis,* which appeared in Cologne in 1740. This history of Břevnov was highly prized by later historians in Bohemia, above all for its sections of documents.[17] Another important consequence of Ziegelbauer's stay in Prague was his acquaintance with Count Phillip Joseph Kinský (1700–1749), a leading Czech nobleman of wide education and interests.[18] Among these interests was a plan to establish an academy for the children of nobles in Prague, which would be placed under the direction of the Benedictines. Ziegelbauer was approached about becoming one of the instructors at the academy, but the plan came to naught, due to the outbreak of war with Prussia in 1744 and the strenuous objections of the Jesuit order to losing its monopoly over higher education in the kingdom.[19]

The other great undertaking that Kinský urged upon Ziegelbauer, the preparation of a collection of documents of Czech history on the model of Hieronymus Pez's collection of Austrian sources, met with a similar fate. Ziegelbauer began work on this collection in 1745, and by virtue of diligence and considerable expense, the manuscript of his *Scriptorum rerum Bohemicarum Bibliotheca* was ready to be submitted to the censor for approval sometime late in the year. Approval, however, was not forthcoming, and the manuscript languished in Vienna while Ziegelbauer was unable to secure its return.[20] In the meantime, though, another representative of the educated aristocracy had invited him to Olomouc in Moravia, where a society of scholars interested in propagating the new approaches to learning had been organized.

This nobleman was the Freiherr Joseph von Petrasch (1714–1772), the son of an Austrian general of Croatian background. He was well and widely educated, had traveled in the Low Countries, England, France, Switzerland, and Italy, served as an adjutant in Prince Eugene's armies, and eventually married and settled down in Olomouc, where he dedicated himself to the support of learning. Here he became one of the prime movers in the establishment of a learned society modelled after those of Western Europe, which took the name Societas Incognitorum Litteratorum.[21]

The Olomouc Societas Incognitorum represented the first organized attempt to cultivate scholarly study in the critical spirit of the Enlightenment, not only in the Czech lands, but in the Habsburg territories as a whole.[22] Petrasch was able to use his contacts at court to such good effect that the society's existence was given official recognition and confirmation on 16 March 1747. Its membership included some of the most illustrious names in the Austrian monarchy and abroad, such as van Swieten, Muratori, Gottsched and Jordan; but the most active members were those who lived and worked in the Czech lands, notably Ziegelbauer, his fellow Benedictine Oliver Legipont, and Count Franz Giannini.[23] The society used its periodical publication, *Monathliche Auszüge alt- und neuer Gelehrten Sache,* to spread information about the latest discoveries of modern science through excerpts and extensive reviews. Subjects covered in the *Monathliche Auszüge* were not confined to any one branch of learning, but the contributors to the journal especially welcomed advances in the natural sciences and history.[24]

It was in its reviews and comments on historical works that the *Monathliche Auszüge* made its major contribution to the spread of the critical method. For example, a review of a book by the Göttingen professor Simonetti on the character of a historian served as a platform from which to preach such professional virtues as: a thorough knowledge of the sources and subject of enquiry; a mastery of the auxiliary disciplines of paleography, chronology, numismatics, and heraldry; and an ability to make use of the findings of philology and linguistics for historical research. A true historian should also approach his sources critically, separating truth from falsehood—a task for which he would need to cultivate a wise and rational skepticism.[25]

In addition to spreading such ideas about a historian's qualities, the *Monathliche Auszüge* informed its readers about the latest publications in history, especially collections of primary sources. On these it placed great importance. The example of Schwandtner's *Scriptores rerum Hungaricum* elicited the hope that a similar work could be published for the Czech lands; and indeed the Societas Incognitorum attempted to use its contacts to get approval for the publication of Ziegelbauer's *Scriptorum rerum Bohemicarum Bibliotheca,* but to no avail.[26] This failure was part of an ongoing struggle between the Societas Incognitorum and elements in the church hierarchy in Olomouc who opposed it, notably the Jesuits. Because of this opposition, the third volume of the *Monathliche Auszüge* (1750) had to be published in Frankfurt and Leipzig—that is, not only outside Moravia, but beyond the Habsburg dominions altogether. In the same year, Ziegelbauer, the leading historian of the Societas Incognitorum, died (rumor whispered of an unnatural demise), and when its founder and patron, Petrasch, left Olomouc in 1751 the society ceased to function.[27]

Although its active life was short, the Olomouc Societas Incognitorum was an important focal point for introducing and propagating the critical methods of the Enlightenment in many fields of learning. In history in particular, the Societas Incognitorum served as a bridge and meeting place for the native Balbín tradition and the Maurist approach, a role symbolized by the presence among the society's members of conservative representatives of the native school like J. A. Berghauer and supporters of the new trends like Ziegelbauer.[28] The wide scope of the society's membership also united the leading scholars of the Habsburg monarchy with the foremost representatives of learning in other lands, and its inclusion of both Catholic and Protestant gave a working example of scholarly toleration in practice, even though the views expressed in the *Monathliche Auszüge* remained firmly Catholic. By including such Protestant scholars as Matěj Bél, a Slovak, the Societas Incognitorum also linked up with the unbroken tradition of Protestant historiography that had been kept alive in Slovakia.[29]

Finally, the Societas Incognitorum represented a trend that would continue well into the nineteenth century, the coming together of the historical and political interests of members of the Bohemian aristocracy with the scholarly concerns of the non-noble intelligentsia. Bohemian nobles had frequently patronized or protected individual scholars before this. The organization of the Societas Incognitorum was a natural continuation of this private support into a more public sphere, and it pointed the way to such future joint efforts as the Royal Bohemian Society of Sciences and even the Bohemian National Museum. Historical research could, after all, provide the Czech nobility with proof of the ancient rights and privileges of the kingdom of Bohemia, and thus strengthen their position vis-à-vis a centralizing court in Vienna. At the same time, patronage of newer trends in learning was in keeping with the cultural and ethical ideals of the Enlightenment and its concept of patriotism, which had gained a firm foothold in the upper levels of Bohemian society by this time.[30]

The demise of the Societas Incognitorum did not mean an end to the spread of critical methods in history in the Czech lands. The society's interests and ideals continued to influence Bohemian historians, such as Josef Bonaventura Piter (1708–1764), prior of the monastery of Rájhrad. A Benedictine like Ziegelbauer, Piter attempted to use the same critical approach to remove the fables of ages past from the chronicles of Czech history. His views were moderately enlightened, recognizing the importance of sources and the regrettable effects of the Counter-Reformation policies in destroying or suppressing them. Characteristically, Piter was one of the first to succeed (in 1762) in obtaining a copy of

Balbín's banned work on Czech history, a collection of short biographies of famous learned Bohemians entitled *Bohemia docta*.[31] Piter's work was, however, still heavily influenced by the authority of tradition, and his greatest importance probably lies in the influence he had on another Bohemian historian, Gelasius Dobner.[32]

Piter and other scholars in Prague helped stimulate Dobner's interest in history during the 1750s. At first, he approached the study of history quite within the Balbín tradition, collecting material for a universal Czech historical, geographical, and biographical dictionary on the model of *Bohemia docta*. He based his research for this work largely on Balbín and other traditional sources, including Hájek's chronicle, but he also consulted the works of such non-Catholic chroniclers as Daniel Adam z Veleslavína and Prokop Lupáč z Hlaváčova.[33] When Dobner showed the material he had gathered to Antonín Vokoun (Wokaun), suffragan bishop and general vicar in Prague, the latter "convinced Dobner that he should preferably spend his energies on a truly critical history of Bohemia, which, deformed by the most ridiculous fables, adventures, and numerous chronological and historical errors, to the shame of the nation, had not up to now been properly treated by anyone."[34] Before he was able to begin a systematic treatment of Czech history, however, he became involved in the Piarists' plan to publish a Latin translation of Hájek's *Kronyka česká*. When he read the translation, Dobner found "that P. Victorin [the translator] had followed Hájek step by step, retaining all his fables and mistakes, and in fact defending most of them in the face of all healthy criticism."[35] He decided to accompany the publication with his own editorial comments, a critical apparatus that quickly grew larger than the text itself and was to involve Dobner's time and energies for over twenty years.

It would have been difficult to find a more prominent work on which to exercise the new critical historical methods than Hájek's chronicle. A convert to Catholicism from a Utraquist family, Václav Hájek z Libočan (died 1553) undertook his great historical work with the support of the Catholic lords in the Bohemian Estates and the king. His *Kronyka česká* was published in 1541 after having been approved by a special commission, so it may be considered to represent official Catholic views.[36] Hájek collected a voluminous amount of material, but (as was common enough during the humanist sixteenth century) he did not apply critical methodology to evaluating it. On the one hand, he sought to please his noble patrons by presenting their ancestors in the best possible light, and on the other he strove for a work that would be a success as literature, not scrupling to place literary considerations above those of historical accuracy. Its appealing style made the *Kronyka česká* accessible and popular; but above all the fact that it was both a major work of Czech history, and written from the Catholic viewpoint, ensured that it was practically the only historical reading widely available after the White Mountain. Hájek's *Kronyka česká* remains a great work of Czech literature, but Dobner's critical commentary called into question its validity as history.[37]

Dobner attacked Hájek's authority directly, beginning with the first volume of his edition, which (as we have seen) appeared in 1761. He insisted on exposing the lack of historical grounds for some of the most cherished fables about the early years of Czech history, including the one that involved him in the most repercussions, the story of the "national fathers" of the Slavs, Čech, Lech, and Rus'. These three brothers were supposed to have left their homeland (according to tradition, Croatia)[38] and wandered northwards with their tribal followers. Each eventually became the "primal father" (*Urvater, praotec*) of one of the Slavic nations. Čech led his band into present-day Bohemia, where he established a kingdom and people both of which supposedly derived their name from him (Čechy, Češi). Lech established the Polish state and nation, while Rus' fathered the Russians. The traditional legend had presented these patriarchs as medieval princes complete with bands of feudal retainers, but Dobner denied that there was any historical evidence for the existence of the three, that the picture of the social organization of the early Slavs was incorrect, and that the origin of the Czechs was quite otherwise. In doing so, he unleashed storms of protest, not least from historians closer to the Bohemian aristocracy, many of whom counted Čech's retainers among their ancestors. Not surprisingly, the Bohemian Estates preferred to make Dobner's more conservative opponent, František Pubička, their official historiographer.[39] Dobner was drawn into bitter polemical discussions at home and abroad, with his opponents accusing him of lack of patriotism for daring to question the existence of Praotec Čech. He answered them with a clear formulation of a different concept of patriotism, linked to the Enlightenment idea of love of truth for its own sake: "It is the foremost duty of the historian that out of love for his fatherland and for knowledge he should wipe away everything that was invented by later ages, and thus rescue his nation from the ridicule of foreigners."[40]

Thus the emergence of critical history in Bohemia could be dated from the publication of the six volumes of Dobner's *Wenceslai Hagek a Liboczan Annales Bohemorum* (1761–1782). This is not to say that Dobner's views were immediately accepted (indeed, Hájek remained popular reading outside the rarefied atmosphere of scholarship well into the nineteenth century), nor did Dobner proceed beyond the task of critical destruction to the new, synthetic treatment of Czech history in the light of modern methods, which his patron had requested. Nevertheless his successors were now able to study Czech history unbound by the fetters of tradition. Dobner's edition marked the "end of Hájeking" (*konec Hájkování*) in Czech history, as Palacký later phrased it.[41]

If Dobner's edition of Hájek spelled the end of the uncritical approach to history in the Czech lands, it was the Royal Bohemian Society of Sciences that provided an institutional framework for the organized cultivation of critical historical writing. Here again the development of history as a discipline in Bohemia is closely connected to the Enlightenment. With its confident assertion of the ability of human reason to reach the truth, the Enlightenment called for the freeing of that reason to pursue its inquiries without regard to religious orthodoxy or political expediency. Associations, like the Royal Society in Britain, the Academy in France, and their like-minded counterparts elsewhere, provided support for the freedom of inquiry and a forum in which to conduct it.[42] The lasting Bohemian version of the enlightened learned society was to be the Royal Bohemian Society of Sciences (Königliche böhmische Gesellschaft der Wissenschaften, Královská česká společnost nauk).

Like the Olomouc Societas Incognitorum, its forerunner, the Bohemian Society of Sciences owed its formation largely to the activities of a patriotic member of the nobility. Ignatz von Born had first come to Prague in 1760 and quickly adopted Bohemia as his homeland.[43] Here he had taken an active part in the unofficial groups of scholars who gathered around certain literary periodicals and noble salons in Prague. These unofficial groups gave rise to the more organized (but still private) Society in Bohemia for the Development of Mathematics, Patriotic History and Natural History (Privatgesellschaft in Böhmen zur Aufnahme der Mathematik, vaterländischen Geschichte, und der Naturgeschichte), sometime around 1774.[44]

The Private Society established a journal, the *Abhandlungen einer Privategesellschaft in Böhmen* (the first volume appeared in 1775), and it continued to grow and solidify its position. In 1784 it was granted public status by Joseph II, and by 1790 began using the attribute *Royal*.[45] Again, like the Societas Incognitorum, the Bohemian Society of Sciences did not limit its interest to history. It was concerned also with the physical sciences, mathematics, and other fields of inquiry; but the philological and historical interests of some of its leading members meant that until well into the nineteenth century most of the critical history written in Bohemia appeared in the pages of its *Abhandlungen*.

Thus by the beginning of the final quarter of the eighteenth century, the conditions for organized, critical research into Bohemia's past were much better than they had been some 150 years before. The approach to history developed by the Maurists in France had been spread to Bohemia through the Benedictines and others, and in the work of Gelasius Dobner had become established as the most fruitful method of conducting historical research. In the process it had progressed far beyond the confines of the Maurists' original interest in church history and the lives of the saints to encompass secular subjects as well. The *Abhandlungen* of the Royal Bohemian Society of Sciences gave enlightened and patriotic scholars a forum for publishing their work, mutually encouraging and criticizing each other, and supporting and spreading the Maurist methods.[46]

Bohemian Historical Writing in the Late Eighteenth Century

This support for the critical method emerges clearly from the historical articles published in the society's journal.[47] Dobner, who was so closely involved in the propagation of critical methods, was a frequent contributor among the more senior Bohemian historians. In the articles he published in the *Abhandlungen,* Dobner expressed again and again his desire to uncover the truth, "which should be the soul of all history," and without which "history ceases to be history and becomes a flight of fancy (*Hirngespinst*)."[48] He also stressed the need for collections of source documents, and linked the task of producing them to his enlightened idea of patriotism, hoping that someone would produce the needed compilations "out of love for his fatherland."[49] His work reflected Dobner's own familiarity with auxiliary sciences such as numismatics and also gave him an opportunity to continue his polemics with opponents of his views.[50]

For all his critical approach to sources, at times Dobner showed a weakness in approaching the historical past. This is probably most clear in his argument with a younger colleague, Josef Dobrovský, about the relative age of the Czech translation of the Bible. Dobner maintained that the Czechs must have begun it no later than the beginning of the thirteenth century:

> In any case it would be strange and infamous for the earlier times, especially for the bishops and the entire clergy . . . if they were so dilatory that from the end of the ninth to the beginning of the thirteenth century, that is for more than four hundred years, they did not translate the Word of God into our mother tongue. . . . Who can easily believe that this work, so necessary and beneficial, could have been left to such a late date?[51]

This, as Dobrovský pointed out to a friend, was to expect the men of the Middle Ages to share the attitudes of the Enlightenment.[52] Dobner and Dobrovský also disagreed on such issues as the historical existence of Saint John of Nepomuk. When Dobner published a fervent defense of this Catholic martyr for the confessional seal,[53] Dobrovský included it in a review article in his *Litterarisches Magazin von Böhmen und Mähren*, vol. 3 (1787). Dobrovský's view was that there was no historical evidence for the existence of this saint so dear to the Counter-Reformation, and that the historical John of Pomuk may have died a martyr for the immunity of the church from secular power, but not for the secrecy of the confessional. In Dobner's work "the otherwise customary thoroughness of the author [was] completely absent."[54] Yet in spite of its limitations, Dobner's example inspired a generation of scholars, and his participation could not but add to the prestige of the *Abhandlungen* and the Society of Sciences.

Another frequent contributor to the *Abhandlungen* during its earlier years was Mikuláš Adaukt Voigt (1733–1787). Voigt's interests ranged more widely than Dobner's, but his mastery of the critical method was not as great. To the *Abhandlungen* he contributed an essay on the introduction of writing and the alphabet to Bohemia, one on the use of vocal music in the church (which included the text and music of the famous Czech medieval hymn, "Hospodině, pomiluj ny"), a sketch of the history of Prague university, an essay on the calendar of the early Slavs, and a study of Bohemian patrons of the arts and learning.[55] Voigt concentrated his main efforts on literary history, through which he attempted to prove, as Pelcl noted, "that Czech soil had supported and produced learned fruit even in earlier centuries."[56] His major works in this field were published elsewhere, but even in his articles in the *Abhandlungen,* a certain patriotic attitude stands out. Where his less critical predecessors had claimed the achievements of foreigners for the Czechs, if they only published in Bohemia, Voigt confidently proclaimed: "We Czechs do not find it necessary to appropriate famous men who belong to other countries."[57]

Voigt expressed his patriotic attitudes even more clearly in a work he submitted in a competition sponsored by the Bohemian Society of Sciences. Though Voigt's *Über den Geist der Böhmischen Gesetze in den verschiedenen Zeitaltern* was not exactly what the Society was looking for, it did publish it in 1788, as a sort of memorial to its newly deceased member. In it, Voigt defended the early Slavs, including the Czechs, from the prejudiced pictures painted of them by other, especially German, historians.

> It is an unforgivable injustice of certain German writers of the Middle Ages and later eras, that they deny the ancient Slavic peoples all cultivation, order, and political organization, and present them as the most unintelligent and uncivilized barbarians. This is a result of the historically wellknown national hatred of the Germans for the Czechs.[58]

Voigt's picture of the early Slavs was no doubt rather idealized; and the same might be said of his description of the constitutional system of the Kingdom of Bohemia as it developed before 1627. His final work was, in fact, a sort of panegyric of the Bohemian *Ständestaat,* emphasizing the importance of the Bohemian Estates to the political life of the kingdom: "One can see that the Estates at that time [1526] had a great say in legislation. The kings could command nothing; levy no new taxes; make no important changes in the state system, without the consent of the three estates."[59] The implied contrast with the situation of Bohemia under Joseph II would have been clear to Voigt's readers.[60]

The librarian of the Clementinum in Prague, Karel Raphael Ungar (1743–1807), also betrayed an interest in literature and the history of education in his contributions to the *Abhandlungen*. He dealt with his own profession in an essay on the history of libraries in Bohemia and added another on the early history of book printing among the Czechs.[61] In an article on Jan Žižka's military organization, Ungar expressed a surprisingly positive attitude to the Hussite leader, especially for an ex-Jesuit. In the introduction to the main body of this essay, which was a reprinting of two letters by Žižka on the problem of military organization, Ungar did not even mention the religious issue and wrote of Žižka instead as a national hero and a military genius.[62]

Another contributor to the *Abhandlungen* who was a supporter of Dobner in the Čech-Lech polemics, and a proponent of the critical method, was František Martin Pelcl (1734–1801). Pelcl, a layman among so many Piarists and ex-Jesuits, was tutor from 1761 to the young counts Joachim and Johann Sternberg, and after 1769 he held a similar post in the Nostitz household.[63] He showed a real appreciation of the necessity of proper documentation and frequently followed his articles with the texts of the documents on which they were based. "Documents," he maintained, "must be the soul of history, the supports of truth, the surest refuge of the critic and the most trustworthy witness of chronology."[64] Of course, even documents needed to be interpreted, and errors could creep in through copying and recopying. A case in point was provided by Pelcl's article about a decree of Emperor Charles IV against heretics in Bohemia. Pelcl pointed out the many historical inaccuracies in the text of the document, still widely accepted by his own contemporaries as genuine, and demonstrated how it had been taken from Hájek's chronicle, translated into German, and included in several histories and collections of sources until it had been reprinted eight times without ever having its accuracy tested.[65]

Of all the historians who contributed to the *Abhandlungen*, the most consistently and strictly critical was Josef Dobrovský (1753–1829). He united the ideals of the Enlightenment and the critical method of the Maurists with a rigorous philological training, thus bringing to history the critical tools developed by the Göttingen theologian Michaelis for biblical criticism.[66] It is typical that one of the earlier contributions Dobrovský made to the *Abhandlungen* should be concerned with the use of documentary sources for national history. In this article, Dobrovský reiterated the frequently expressed wish of the critical historians for a collection of sources for Czech history: "What a service it could render to the enlightening of our fatherland's history!"[67]

Dobrovský later worked on a whole series of articles for the journal of the Society of Sciences discussing the problems involved in separating fact from fiction in the old legends that were frequently the only sources for early Bohemian history. In the three articles that actually appeared in his time, Dobrovský dealt with the legends of Bořivoj's baptism, Ludmila and Drahomír, and Václav and Boleslav. A fourth article, on the legend of Prokop, remained in manuscript.[68] Dobrovský defined the methodological principle of all his work as "to accept nothing without adequate witnesses, and always to go back to the earliest source."[69] Since he did not always have the necessary tools to establish the validity of certain documents, not all of Dobrovský's conclusions have withstood the test of time; but his championship of critical methods in general was far more important than the validity of any particular result.

Other articles which Dobrovský wrote for the *Abhandlungen* reflected his general interest in the earliest history of the Slavs, and the question of the Czech Bible. He also devoted two articles to aspects of the history of the Hussite period in Bohemia. In a work on the Czech Adamites and Picards, Dobrovský demolished some of the worst distortions of a previously accepted authority, Eneas Sylvio Piccolomini, and wrote quite sympathetically about Hus and Jerome of Prague, "the two Czech martyrs."[70] The other work, which appeared in a later number, dealt with the use of the chalice in Bohemia.[71] Dobrovský approached the Hussite period not only with a critical regard for the truth, but also with the Enlightenment's dislike for religious intolerance and superstition. As he wrote elsewhere, "one must be ashamed of earlier times, when such mischief was carried on in the name of religion."[72]

The fact that the new ideal of a historian included a skeptical approach to tradition and the application of rational criticism to the documents did not mean that the new history was fundamentally unpatriotic, as some traditionalists charged. We have seen how Dobner and Dobrovský, to name but two, linked the critical treatment of their country's history with patriotic love of the fatherland. The subjects the historians in the Society of Sciences chose to treat in their articles concerned areas of Bohemia history such as the early history of the Slavs, the foundation of the Czech state, and aspects of its cultural development and its constitutional relationship to the German Reich. The fact that these themes, which stressed the uniqueness and historical tradition of the Czech kingdom, could serve the interests of the Bohemian nobility in their competition with the aims of a centralizing court in Vienna was not coincidental. Many of the members of the Society of Sciences were leading representatives of the nobility, and the scholars making up the patriotic intelligentsia depended to a great extent on noble patronage, as did the earlier members of the Societas Incognitorum.

This bread-and-butter explanation of the historian's attitudes, however, is not by itself entirely convincing. The intellectuals were probably also influenced in their attitudes to their past, and the themes they chose to study, by the traditional, corporate view of the Estates as the nation. This view was reinforced by the way in which the development of absolutism in East Central Europe had tended to erode the power and independence of the towns, rather than the aristocracy. Thus the Estates, dominated by the nobility, provided the only entrenched, institutional expression of the separate statehood and national existence of Bohemia.[73] In such a case, the historical themes to which scholars would be drawn would also not be unaffected. In addition, these historians, for all their commitment to the critical method, the search for truth, and skepticism, were not always successful in maintaining detachment, and they sometimes expressed openly patriotic attitudes just as representatives of the less critical Balbín school had. In fact, in some areas of Czech history it was precisely the development of critical historiography that opened the way for more positive assessments, notably for the Hussite period. The honor and reputation of some of the national heroes, especially Charles IV, were also staunchly defended by these historians.

Even Dobner, the "father" of the critical method in Bohemia, was not immune from patriotic attitudes. He took issue with a contemporary historian in Hungary who claimed that the borders of the Great Moravian Empire had not included the territory of present-day Moravia—a view Dobner felt to be an insult to the memory of Saint Methodius and the Moravian rulers Mojmir and Rastislav.[74] On the problem of the introduction of Christianity into Moravia, Dobner opposed Dobrovský and Ungar on one side, arguing that Saint Methodius had actually traveled to Moravia himself and that his Slavic liturgy had been in fairly wide use there. On the other side, he denied an assertion by an anonymous author that it was Christianity according to the Greek rites that had been introduced into the Czech lands and that the Hussite movement had its roots in the survival of this tradition. Dobner maintained that the liturgy had been in the Slavic language, but in conformity with the teachings of Rome, and that the pope had not forbidden the Slavic rite as such, but its use contrary to the beliefs of the Latin church.[75]

Pelcl also struck a patriotic attitude with his article on Samo, ruler of one of the earliest Slavic political entities in

Central Europe. Pelcl attempted to prove that Samo was a Slav, not a Frank, and a warrior, not a merchant. He also insisted that the boundaries of Samo's state included present-day Bohemia. Pelcl wanted to show that the Slavs had been capable of organizing their early political entities by themselves, without help from the Germanic Franks, and he was also trying to establish continuity between this early Slavic polity and the kingdom of Bohemia. Elsewhere, Pelcl maintained the Czech origin of the Hussite martyr Jacobellus de Misa (Jakoubek ze Stříbra), because even though he was a heretic, it was a matter of national honor to refute the claim that he came from Meissen in Saxony.[76] One historian whose contributions to the *Abhandlungen* were exclusively devoted to the careers of national heroes was the Prague professor Ignac Cornova (1740–1822).[77] Even a much larger nation than Bohemia, he claimed, would have difficulty in producing three such rulers as Přemysl Otakar II, Charles IV, and Jiří z Poděbrad. Cornova devoted an article to each. Přemysl Otakar II sealed his own fate when he ceased to play the role of willing tool of the pope in the empire; but before his downfall he had brought Bohemia great territorial expansion and a reputation for military prowess.[78] King Jiří was admirable because, although he was often forced to wage war, he attempted to create a league of rulers that would avoid conflicts; nor was he, as his enemies claimed, an atheist.[79] Cornova's highest praise was reserved for Charles IV, however. In fact, his words gave a clear picture of the status this greatest of Bohemia's medieval rulers enjoyed in the eyes of the patriotic scholars:

> Prejudice in favor of his own nation frequently stands in the way of the impartiality of the historian. Yet when a Czech (Böhme) finds, the more attentively he searches the historical documents of his fatherland, not only so many more proofs of Charles's talents as a ruler . . . but also of that high-mindedness, which certain writers wish to strip from him by force—then it is not just praiseworthy zeal for the national honor, not simply gratitude for the memory of

the Father of the Fatherland; then it is a holy duty to the truth to expose what is weak and based on unreliable sources in the accusations against Charles.[80]

One cannot help feeling that for Cornova, the critical method served patriotic ends to such an extent that true critical principles stood in danger of becoming obscured.

The central importance of the period of Charles IV and Jan Hus to the patriotic historians of this era is also reflected in the works of some historians who did not publish in the *Abhandlungen*. Of these, the most influential was probably Kaspar Royko, whose *Geschichte der grossen allgemeinen Kirchenversammlung zu Kostnitz* appeared in four volumes between 1781 and 1785. Though Royko was a Slovene by birth, and the first two volumes of his history appeared in Graz, he came to Prague to take up the chair of church history at the university, and the last two volumes of his work were published there. In some sense this made him a part of the Prague intellectual environment, and he had close ties of friendship and association with some of the leading patriotic historians. Also, his history, though concerned with the entire story of the Council of Constance, would of necessity have to deal with the problem of Jan Hus and the start of the Hussite movement. Thus his conclusions, which were remarkably sympathetic to Hus, had an immediate impact on the Bohemian environment. Royko's history stirred up resistance among the more conservative Catholics, but Dobrovský praised it for rescuing the reputation of Hus, his fellow countryman.[81]

Pelcl also returned to the Hussite period and its immediate antecedents in his biographies of Charles IV and Václav IV. In the latter work, Pelcl wrote what amounted to a defense of Hus against the charges for which he was burned at Constance, and he effectively described the outraged reaction of the Czech nobles and king upon hearing the news of the martyr's death.[82] He depicted Charles IV's reign in colors that glowed no less brightly than Cornova's. The Czechs under Charles "were the most learned nation, and the greatest statesmen; they possessed the greatest wealth and the highest regard in the eyes of other nations—in a word, the Czechs were at that time the ruling nation in Europe, and it was considered a special privilege to be a native Czech."[83]

Voigt also depicted Charles IV as a great ruler and model for patriots of all times in one of his important works, the four-volume *Beschreibung der bisher bekannten Böhmischen Münzen nach chronologischer Ordnung* (1771–1781). Voigt saw this collection as a vital contribution to critical historical research, but at the same time it was "love of [his] fatherland, and the desire to bring light into its history, and the longing to render a useful service to the state and [his] fellow countrymen," that motivated him.[84] Voigt's patriotism found clear expression when he described the role of Charles IV:

> In short, Charles was a true father, or to put it more accurately, a true mother of his fatherland; which he dearly loved, greatly enlarged, and, as far as he was able, made truly happy. The memory of this great Prince will remain unforgettable and blessed to all Czech patriots into the farthest future.[85]

Praise of the reign of Charles IV, and a defense against the Emperor Maximilian's charge that he had been a "stepfather" to the Reich, clearly constituted a common conclusion of these Bohemian scholars—a conclusion based on patriotic feeling as well as historical evidence.

If the supporters of critical history were not always able to maintain that "wise and reasonable skepticism" so desirable to a historian, neither were they able to sweep all their rivals and forerunners from the field immediately. Older tendencies such as the Balbín tradition continued to exert an influence on some writers, nor was every historical work of the same type as the specialized articles published in the *Abhandlungen*. There were attempts at more synthetic surveys of Czech history, not always from a consistently critical standpoint, and also works of a more popular nature, directed at a wider literate public, both German and Czech.

One general survey of Czech history influenced in part by the older, Balbín tradition was the *Chronologische Geschichte Böhmens unter den Slawen* by František Pubička (1722–1807). This mammoth work, which grew to stretch over ten volumes (issued between 1770 and 1801), earned for its author the title of official historiographer to the Bohemian Estates, a position later held by Palacký.[86] Yet he was by no means a consistent supporter of the critical approach pioneered by Dobner, as his participation in the polemics with the latter on the side of the "Čechists" shows. In the *Chronologische Geschichte*, Pubička continued to attack Dobner and his views wherever the opportunity presented itself, which made a bad impression on some of his contemporaries.[87] Supporters of critical history such as Dobrovský criticized Pubička for his failure to use his sources properly, especially in the matter of citation. Yet even as stern a critic as Dobrovský had some positive things to say about the *Chronologische Geschichte*, such as that in its treatment of the conflicts between the medieval papacy and the emperors, Pubička's work represented an improvement over what had been written only a short time earlier.[88]

Even so, contemporaries felt that such a work did not answer the need of the time for a concise history of Bohemia. Pelcl was one of the first to attempt to fill this need with his *Kurzgefasste Geschichte der Böhmen*, which appeared in 1774 and was received with such enthusiasm that it went through new editions in 1779, 1782, and posthumously in 1817. This publishing history testifies to the effectiveness with which the *Kurzgefasste Geschichte* met the desires of the reading public. Even its format made it more accessible than earlier works, with its octavo size and German language, and its author attempted to be pragmatic and not devote space to controversial polemics.

Pelcl's approach to the subject was also more suited than Pubička's to a concise, general history. As he wrote in his foreword, "I have followed more the affairs of the nation than the biographies of its rulers. In periods when the Czechs played an important role, for example during the Hussite Wars, or the reigns of Rudolph II, Matthias, Ferdinand I and II, I have been more detailed."[89] This promise was not entirely borne out by the text, however. Pelcl still divided his work into periods based on the reigns of the Bohemia rulers; and when the "nation" did play an important role, Pelcl wrote of the nation in the political sense, of the "first subjects," the Bohemian nobility. This may well reflect the close relationship Pelcl had, as tutor to the families of Sternberg and Nostitz-Rieneck, with some of the leading Bohemian aristocrats. The *Kurzgefasste Geschichte* was based on the course of study Pelcl prepared for his noble pupils, and he dedicated it to one of them, the young Count Friedrich Nostitz. Pelcl's history thus reflected to a large extent the attitude of the educated, enlightened nobles; but he also wrote his work with the conscious aim of encouraging the Czech patriotism of his highly placed pupils and readers. This can be seen especially clearly in the passages close to the end of the book dealing with the language. After pointing out the consequences for Czech of the school reforms of Maria Theresa, Pelcl commented that only a section of the burghers, the peasants, and the urban poor (*Pöbel*) still spoke Czech.

> Only at the coronation of the Czech king, at the opening of the sessions of the Estates, and a few other public occasions are certain sentences still spoken in Czech by the Highest Burggrave and the officials of the kingdom. This in itself . . . ought to direct the attention of our nobles more to their native language (*Landessprache*) and induce them to bring it back to life among themselves. At least thus they could effectively resist those who reproach us with the fact that we no longer form a separate nation.[90]

In the polemics over Čech and Lech, Pelcl had ranged himself on Dobner's side, but in the *Kurzgefasste Geschichte* he showed himself to be less critical than the ideal. Especially in his description of the early Slavs he continued to rely on the chronicles Dobner had called into question, and his picture of the early history of the Czechs was idealized.[91] In other respects, however, Pelcl's enlightened attitudes helped him to present a more balanced account than earlier historians. This can be seen most clearly in the sections dealing with the Hussite period and the Counter-Reformation in Bohemia.[92] As he wrote in the foreword,

> perhaps enthusiasm for my fatherland has frequently led me to an excessive admiration for the deeds of our ancestors; but may a Czech not be proud of the heroism of his Žižka or Prokop? To be sure, they were Hussites, but they still believed in Christ, and venerated his Holy Mother and Saint Václav. Žižka even ordered that mass be read daily in his encampments, and so in this way they are better than those pagan heroes whose deeds are praised to the skies without regard for their heathenness.[93]

In the body of the text, Pelcl's attitudes to Hus and the other figures of the Czech Reformation seem to swing between two poles: on the one hand, he admired them for their positive human characteristics, and on the other, he found the cruelties and religious fanaticism of the period offensive. He wrote of Hus with surprising sympathy, praised Žižka and Prokop as national heroes and military geniuses, and took the part of King Jiří z Poděbrad in his conflicts with the popes and the Catholic party in Bohemia. Nevertheless, he deplored the widespread destruction caused by the unrest of the time, since it could not but harm the nation.[94]

Although the *Kurzgefasste Geschichte* went through four editions, Pelcl was unable to take the time to revise his text thoroughly, so that the 1817 version is basically that of 1782 with certain additions. He carried out serious revision only in the Czech language *Nová kronyka česká*, of which three volumes appeared between 1791 and 1796. *Nová kronyka česká* was eagerly awaited by the active Czech patriots, and advertised widely among the common people, but the audience Pelcl seems to address remains the same—the nobility. This continuing connection with the nobility is reflected in the dedication to Countess Marie von Rottenhan, wife of the then Highest Burggrave, in which Pelcl flattered her for her love of her mother tongue, Czech.[95] It should be noted in this regard that *Nová kronyka česká* appeared at a time when the Bohemian Estates, presenting their complaints to the new ruler, Leopold II, had called for the support of Czech through the establishment of a chair of Czech language and literature at the university in Prague (see chapter 2).[96]

The three volumes of *Nová kronyka česká* that were published brought Czech history down to the end of the reign of Charles IV, and a fourth volume, covering the Hussite period, remained in manuscript. In the main, Pelcl did not alter his approach or conclusions, although he did include some new materials on Žižka, perhaps from the biography of the Czech hero that he was planning to write.[97] As a critical historian, Pelcl did not reach the level of either Dobner or Dobrovský, his elder and younger contemporaries. Those tendencies characterized by Albert Pražák as "the desire to be more an awakener than a historian" represented a departure from the critical ideal. Pelcl was, however, able to provide the synthetic treatment of his country's history that Dobner never accomplished and Dobrovský never attempted, and he avoided the latter's hypercriticism. His openly patriotic approach in his pragmatic histories was already qualitatively different from the patriotism of the Balbín school, and his very deviations from strict criticism made him more popular with the next generation. His historical works served as an important source for future Czech writers of historical fiction.[98]

Czech History in Czech

The influence of most of these efforts to write critical but patriotic history in Bohemia and the effects of all the scholarly polemics over method and results were limited to a certain level of Bohemian society because of their language. Only those who knew German or Latin could actively follow the course of the historiographical quarrels or read the latest findings of scholars. Yet during this period the beginnings of change in the historians' attitude toward their audience can be discerned. Strengthened by some of the Enlightenment attitudes toward the place of the citizen in the state, and especially reinforced by the educational reforms begun by Maria Theresa and carried on more forcefully under Joseph II, some historians, at least, began to see their audience in the lower social classes rather than the aristocracy or clerical intelligentsia. One symptomatic indication of this is the publication of Aleš Pařízek's *Versuch einer Geschichte Böhmens für den Burger* in 1783, a history addressed specifically to a non-noble readership and intended for use in the reformed school system.[99] Similarly, Dobner's rejection of the idea that the ancient Czechs had a feudal, aristocratic social organization may have widened the audience for history at least slightly, by making it the inheritance of all Czechs and not just those who had a family genealogy going back to Čech or one of his followers.[100] And if historical writing were to reorient itself more toward the lower classes, that meant toward an audience, a significant portion of which spoke and read in Czech.

Pelcl's *Nová kronyka česká* was the most important attempt to write a history of Bohemia in the native language that would take into account the new developments in historical writing; yet its aristocratic viewpoint may have limited its popularity among the common people. Other historical publications in Czech, such as the translations of Royko's history of the Council of Constance, the work of the Czech radical Josephinist, Václav Stach (1755–1831),[101] were occasional in nature and did not represent a concerted effort to write Czech history in Czech. There were, nevertheless, some writers who attempted to provide historical works aimed specifically at the common people and therefore written in the native language. Among the most prolific of these was Jan Nepomuk Josef Rulík (1744–1812).

Rulík was an active translator and writer, connected with the "popular awakeners" Kramerius and Tomsa,[102] who was characterized more by patriotic enthusiasm than by originality and literary talent. One of his earliest historical publications was his *Velmi užitečná historie o slovutném národu Českém,* which appeared in 1793. Though its title seems to promise a history of the Czech nation, actually Rulík's work was essentially a Czech version of M. A. Voigt's forewords to his *Effigies virorum eruditorum atque artificum Bohemiae et Moraviae,* a collection of biographies of Bohemian writers and artists (see chapter 3). In the forewords, now rendered into Czech by Rulík, Voigt surveyed aspects of Bohemia's cultural past, especially literary history.[103] Through Rulík's *Velmi užitečná historie* these patriotically defensive forewords were now available to a Czech audience, but the work was not professional history in the sense of the articles published in the *Abhandlungen* or Pelcl's *Kurzgefasste Geschichte der Böhmen.* Rulík did, however, help bridge the gap between the patriotic intellectuals who wrote in German and Latin and the Czech public, and his criticisms of his more scholarly colleagues for not publishing their works in Czech were echoed by other popular awakeners and even patriots of the next generation.[104] Rulík's other historical works are interesting not for their connection with the new, critical methods, but with the Catholicism and patriotic pathos of the Balbín tradition.

These traits were clearly expressed in Rulík's *Vypsání životů svatých patronů českých,* published in two volumes in 1801. Just as in some of the works of his predecessors in the Balbín school, the emphasis in Rulík's collection was on the loyalty of the Czechs to Catholicism, and he expressed his historical patriotism in terms of the saints' lives. This was not an original work, but a translation and reworking of a German volume by one Joseph Schiffner, also the author of another interesting work that Rulík translated and published between 1803 and 1810 under the title *Gallerie, aneb vyobrazenost nejslovutnějších a nejznamenitějších osob země České.* The material in the book was "selected from the most excellent and trustworthy Czech chroniclers" and presented an idealized picture of the early Slavs and their legendary leaders, largely based on the discredited Hájek.[105]

Most of Rulík's other historical works were also within this Catholic tradition. In places, he paid at least lip service to the new principles of critical history, referring to an account in Hájek's chronicle as "pure fable and hearsay," for example.[106] Yet the general tone of his work as well as his subject matter was largely foreign to the concerns of enlightened historiography, and his criticism was not systematically applied.

Lack of criticism was a complaint leveled at his most ambitious work, the *Kalendář historický*, which he published from 1797 to 1810. Rulík harked back consciously to the example of the Renaissance humanist Daniel Adam z Veleslavína in this attempt to provide his readers with a modern chronicle and at the same time a history of Bohemia from the beginning of the seventeenth century to the present.[107] In his labors on the *Kalendář historický*, and perhaps even in the formulation of the idea, he was influenced by František Jan Vavák (1741–1816). Vavák was a successful farmer of peasant origin who held a position of some authority in the local administration of his village, Milčice near Poděbrady (he was a *vesnický rychtář* or *Dorfrichter*, something like a justice of the peace). In addition to this responsibility, Vavák kept a chronicle of events in his locality and region, read Kramerius's Czech newspapers, and corresponded with some of the leading patriots of his day.[108]

Rulík enjoyed friendly relations with Vavák and did not hesitate to request his help in the *Kalendář historický*.[109] Both men shared a similar patriotism and historical background, based in each case on Catholicism and the Czech chroniclers, especially Hájek. Obviously, such attitudes would not have much in common with those of the critical historians like Dobrovský or Pelcl. Rulík's *Kalendář historický* was welcomed by most patriots as a praiseworthy effort, yet they had reservations about its value both because of its obsolete form and its methods.

This reviewer must admit [wrote Dobrovský] that this is one of the author's most successful works. But why has he not made the effort to give it the highest possible level of perfection? Why has he not given the Czechs through his activities a work that could properly stand beside those of his forerunners, and compete with the best works from abroad? . . . Veleslavín selected with intelligence and exactitude, but his disciple seems to have been somewhat more remiss.[110]

Men like Rulík and Vavák simply were not equipped for the task of uniting modern historical methods with the use of the Czech language. This achievement was left to future generations of historians.

✿ ✿ ✿

The history these intellectuals were cultivating was not yet national history in the modern sense—that is, the history of an ethnic nation. Yet the development of critical historical method in late eighteenth-century Bohemia was of crucial importance to the later elaboration of Czech nationalist attitudes. Common traditions about the past make up an important part of any nation's self-consciousness, so that most modern nations have demonstrated a link between the development of nationalism and the study of history, especially as historical conclusions are disseminated among wider levels of the population through mass schooling, the growth of literacy, historical fiction, and popular publicization of contemporary historical research.[111] This was especially so in the Bohemian context, where the continuous cultural development of the country had been diverted, and historical consciousness harnessed to the ends of the Counter-Reformation. In Bohemia the development of critical historical methods prepared the ground for the influence of attitudes toward the nation's history on the Czech national movement. The commanding position enjoyed during the nineteenth century by František Palacký's conception of the meaning of Czech history, as worked out in his monumental *Dějiny národa českého,* would be difficult to imagine without the work of his late eighteenth-century predecessors. Their lively interest in the history of their nation (even when this idea of nation was still understood in a primarily territorial, not ethnic, sense) and their desire to remove the legends of more credulous ages led to a new, critical appreciation of the Czech past, while at the same time stimulating interest in literary history, philology, and literary criticism.[112]

The critical, rationalistic approach that they applied was transmitted to Czech historians in part through the works of German and Austrian historians who themselves learned the principles from the French. In this process, the role played by the Benedictines in Austria and Bohemia in spreading the methods developed by their fellows in the Congrégation de Saint-Maur was especially valuable. Once the new methods had gained adherents among historians in Bohemia, they continued to be developed, reinforced by the example of historians abroad, notably the Göttingen school.[113]

These historians set themselves the task of bringing the history of Bohemia out of the age of reliance on tradition not only because they wanted to clear away the fables of the past and reach the truth. They also wanted to purify their country's history, so that Bohemia, its history, and its historians could all take their place beside other enlightened nations without feeling inferior. Voigt's comments in his forewords to the volumes of *Beschreibung der Böhmischen Münzen,* or Dobner's definition of the task of the historian, make this point clear. The latter quarter of the eighteenth century saw the critical method so firmly established in Bohemia that in 1804 Dobrovský could dismiss his predecessor's magnum opus, the critical edition of Hájek's chronicle, with a brief remark: "It was not even worth a commentary."[114] Eloquent testimony to the distance Czech historiography had traveled in only one generation!

By applying their critical methods to the earlier periods of Czech and Slavic history, these historians demonstrated the historical distinctness, state-forming abilities, and cultural accomplishments of the early Czechs. Such historical images could work against the attempts of the centralizing Habsburg state under Joseph II to break down the cultural and political distinctiveness of the various parts of the Habsburg dominions.[115] In their treatment of some subjects distorted by the Counter-Reformation, their skeptical approach paved the way for a reevaluation of aspects of the Czech past that had been denigrated or denied after the Battle of the White Mountain. In this their patriotism was qualitatively different from that of the Balbín school: they combined it with the ideals of the Enlightenment, while Balbín's patriotism was expressed in the context of the Catholic church of the Counter-Reformation. The older tradition continued to survive among certain sections of the public, but the coming generation would nevertheless bring the heritage of the eighteenth-century historians to its historical writing in Czech and to its Czech patriotism. Thus by cultivating the history and strengthening an awareness of the past of their land, these critical historical scholars laid an important foundation stone for the future. As yet their work was still the cultural property of all Bohemians, whether Czech or German; but already they had begun creating a self-consciousness that, when infused with newer ideas about language, would lead to the eventual separation of the two nations.

2

"Our Natural Language"

The rise of critical method in history stimulated and reinforced a growing concern for the condition of the Czech language. This concern was linked with historical inquiry through philology, one of the most important of the auxiliary sciences for the critical method. If, as Pelcl wrote, documents were "the soul of history,"[1] then the language in which they were written, its history, grammar, and present condition, were necessarily subjects of interest. The contrast between the Czech of their documents and the Czech of their own day, both in its social status and functional roles, was all too clear to the patriotic intellectuals. By the later eighteenth century, faced with a newly flourishing German language and culture in Bohemia, Czech seemed to be on its way to oblivion.[2] This possibility was poignantly captured by Pelcl, who wrote in his "Geschichte der Deutschen und ihrer Sprache in Böhmen":

> Thus the second generation will already be German, and in fifty years more German than Czech will be spoken in Kouřím and the other cities of Bohemia; yes, it will be difficult even to flush out a Czech. . . . One can easily conclude how far the German language must come in a hundred years, and how much Czech in contrast must lose, until it finally dies out altogether.[3]

These words might suggest that Pelcl and others had already given Czech up for lost; but a more accurate way of seeing them would be as an attempt to shock complacent or unaware contemporaries into doing something about its decline.[4]

In this attempt, Pelcl joined a number of other writers of his time who produced a stream of works defending Czech from its detractors and asserting its right to recognition as a fully developed language with a rich historical tradition. At the same time, scholars (including Pelcl) also published specialized philological works intended to stabilize the grammatical and lexical foundations of the language. German provided one of the most important stimuli to the defense and development of the language, while at the same time serving as a model to imitate. Many of the arguments in these Czech defenses resemble those used by German patriots in their support of German vis-à-vis French—yet the Czech authors were *resisting* German.[5] The visible influence of German on Czech in syntax and especially vocabulary provoked purist zeal among some Czech grammarians—yet it was German philology that was so important in helping Czech scholars such as Dobrovský establish an appropriate grammatical and lexical base for Czech.[6]

At a time when Czech had been practically driven from use in the public sphere and was viewed in most cultured circles as a debased peasants' jargon, the defenders of the language presented arguments for its support and cultivation. In time their ideas contributed to a changing concept of nation, moving from one based on the historical state and allegiance to the monarch to one based on an organic community of people using the same language, a community embracing all levels of society. Meanwhile the grammarians provided the practical foundation for the renewal of the Czech language that the defenders were advocating, and that was a prerequisite for the gradual extension of Czech into all spheres of cultural activity.

In Defense of the Mother Tongue

The "defense of the language" as a literary genre was nothing new in Czech history, or, indeed, in the history of other nations.[7] In the later eighteenth century, however, it did experience a flourishing development, usually considered to have begun in 1773 with the publication in Prague of an anonymous work entitled *Erinnerung über einen wichtigen Gegenstand, von einem Böhmen.* The author, Count Franz Joseph Kinský, was concerned with pedagogical method and not directly with the position of Czech; but in one passage he discussed how his pupils (assumed to be children of the nobility) should study languages.

It was Kinský's contention that a pupil could not learn Latin properly "as long as he is not perfectly fluent in his mother tongue."[8] He then continued:

> To the phrase "his mother tongue" I would add: namely, Czech. I confess that, as a good descendant of the Slavs, I have inherited the prejudice that if the mother tongue of a Frenchman is French, and of a German, German, then the mother tongue of a Czech (*Böhmen*) must also be Czech.[9]

Kinský's arguments for learning Czech followed two main lines: Czech was useful and it was beautiful.[10] A landowner who knew Czech would be able to speak directly with the peasants under his jurisdiction, thereby winning their trust. In a similar way, a military officer would almost be forced to learn Czech in order to communicate with his Slavic troops. Since both of these functions were likely occupations for young sons of noblemen, these utilitarian arguments were calculated to appeal to Kinský's audience.

Czech also had other, more prestigious qualities, however. Kinský compared it to Latin and Greek, since it distinguished between long and short syllables, and he claimed that a knowledge of Czech would therefore make learning these two classical languages easier. What was more, it sounded pleasant. "Let those of refined taste laugh if they will," Kinský wrote, "I still say that Czech is a harmonious language." To support this assertion, he claimed that during the Seven Years' War French soldiers in Bohemia found Czech far less offensive to their refined ears than German. This alleged harmony of Czech also accounted for the renown of Kinský's fellow countrymen as professional musicians.

All this support for Czech did not mean, however, that Kinský would not have his pupils study German. In fact, he called for them to learn both languages from childhood, and in later passages he defended German against the polite prejudice in favor of French, praising such German authors as Gellert, Klopstock, Lessing, Wieland, among others, and referring to German as his "own language."[11] This apparent inconsistency (which drove later nationalist historians to exasperation)[12] suggests the limits to Kinský's linguistic patriotism. On closer consideration, however, it does not really seem so inconsistent. The Kinský family was one of the few old Czech families that remained among the Bohemian nobility after the wholesale changes in its makeup following the defeat of the Estates in 1620. The family was conscious of its Czech origin and antiquity, especially among so many "newcomers," so the idea that he was "a good descendant of the Slavs" would have been part of Kinský's family pride.

Like most members of the upper classes at the time, however, Kinský would have had some education in Latin (and possibly Greek) and, among the modern languages, German and French. Czech would have been picked up for the utilitarian purposes mentioned in the *Erinnerung* rather than formally studied, though members of the Kinský family are known to have used it in correspondence into the eighteenth century.[13] Yet at the time Kinský wrote, it was German, not Czech, that was undergoing an exciting cultural revival, while the Czech language and Czech literature were still neglected. The latent territorial basis of Kinský's support for Czech (a native of Bohemia [*Böhmen*] should speak Czech [*böhmisch*] just as a native of France should speak French) fitted a time when the concepts of nation and patriotism had not yet become exclusively ethnolinguistic. Even though later patriots would take their attitudes toward the Czech language in that direction, thus moving away from Kinský's position, the fact that he was a member of the higher nobility and still spoke up in favor of Czech meant that Kinský's *Erinnerung* became a landmark work, and his contemporaries headed their lists of defenders of the language with his name.[14]

Further impetus to the renewed concern for Czech came from the publication in 1775 of Bohuslav Balbín's *Dissertatio apologetica pro lingua slavonica, praecipue bohemica.* This work was to prove very influential, with its effective coupling of humanistic rhetorical technique with the burning pathos and exaggerated imagery of baroque preaching style.[15] The love for his language and nation and the sorrow over their decline that suffused Balbín's manuscript were deemed suspect by his superiors in the Jesuit order, so it was never published during the author's lifetime. The edition of 1775, though limited in its appeal to readers able to understand Latin, was still considered dangerous; and although initial approval was given by the censor, it was later withdrawn and all the unsold copies were confiscated. Pelcl, who acted as editor and who gave the manuscript the Latin title by which it is usually known, was himself accused of being the author.[16] This attempt to continue to suppress Balbín's *Dissertatio* was not fully successful, however, and together with his work on the literary figures of Bohemian history, *Bohemia docta* (published in part beginning in 1776; see chapter 3), it helped establish Balbín in the esteem of the eighteenth-century patriots who saw themselves as in some measure his successors.[17]

Echoes of both Balbín and Kinský sound in later defenses of Czech. The utilitarian arguments adduced by Kinský were frequently repeated, as were judgments of taste, refinement, euphony, and historical value. After the relaxation of censorship under Joseph II, publishing restrictions were loosened enough that several works whose sole aim was the defense of the language appeared, even though written in the vernacular. In 1783, Johann Alois Hanke von Hankenstein, a Moravian in government service in Vienna, published his *Empfehlung der böhmischen Sprache und Litteratur*, which he dedicated to his "fatherland"—the Margraviate of Moravia. In spite of this echo of territorially based patriotism, Hanke's concern was the Czech language. He began by reviewing the support once given Czech by the foremost nobles in the land, including such monarchs as Charles IV. In recent years, the status of Czech, once spoken by kings and great aristocrats, had fallen to such an extent that proposals were being made to "root it out and introduce in its stead a general state language—namely, German."[18] It was to counter this threat that Hanke, otherwise an adherent of Josephinism, took up his cudgels.

Yet if Czech were threatened from without, there was also a threat from within. Too many Bohemians admired foreign languages so much that they hardly ever spoke Czech, and when they did, they spoke it badly. With a nice satirical touch, Hanke depicted the style of Czech used at various levels of society—the nobleman interlarding it with French, the cleric with Latin, and the government official with both Latin and German. The solution might be to impose, in the best mercantilist manner, a protective tariff on the import of foreign words![19]

Hanke's arguments in support of Czech against these threats echoed Kinský's in many respects. Czech's usefulness to anyone in a position of authority over Slavic subjects, its richness, expressiveness, and euphony, and its great historical tradition, going back to the ancient Slavic liturgical language, all made their appearance. In the spirit of Josephinism, with its belief that the duty of all citizens (including the emperor) was to serve the common good, Hanke railed against what he called fashionable ignorance, that desired to know only French, German, or the oriental languages:

> So that we have in place of Czechs or Moravians nothing but Greeks, Englishmen, or Frenchmen—enlightened

men! earnest patriots!—who are not even capable of translating a decent English or French book into their mother tongue for the good of their homeland.[20]

Karel Hynek Thám's *Obrana jazyka českého proti zlobivým jeho utrháčům,* published in Prague in the same year as Hanke's *Empfehlung,* also linked up with the ideas of its predecessors. It shared with Balbín both the patriotic pathos and baroque flourishes, as well as the concern for the condition of the nation and language, that made the *Dissertatio* so powerful.[21] Thám also denied that Czech was debased, stressing its euphony, brevity of expression, and natural way of forming words. He produced the familiar utilitarian arguments for learning Czech, while adding that a knowledge of Czech gave the key to communication with other Slavs. In several other respects, too, Thám's *Obrana* broke new ground. For one thing, it was written in Czech, not German or Latin. It thus provided tangible proof, to the best of Thám's abilities, of his claims for the language. Other arguments were colored by an emotional note not so clear in Kinský's or Hanke's defenses. Czech was, for Thám, the "natural language" of the Bohemians that in the past had been supported by people of all degrees, as the heritage of Czech literature showed. This was the example of the past: that "love for their natural language so strongly filled the hearts of our ancestors that, whenever the need arose to defend it, quickly seizing their weapons, they met their enemies in the field for its glory, with courage and heroism."[22]

In his own day, however, Thám saw the language fallen and degraded. In one moving passage he invoked the names of Jan Hus, Bohuslav Hasištejnský, Karel Žerotín, Veleslavín, Balbín, and others, imagining how they would lament to see the present condition of Czech. How had this come about? Thám pointed directly at the nobility. Through their indolence and carelessness they had extinguished the love for the fatherland that should be blazing in their hearts, and thus smothered it in the hearts of their compatriots. By their example, which should have encouraged Czechs to work for the good of the country and the glory of the language, the gentry led them instead to an appreciation of comfort and an indifference to the decay of the language, and dissuaded them from undertaking tasks useful to the fatherland.[23] Thám admitted that there were some honorable exceptions, but in this passage he criticized the nobility's contribution to the decline of the language for the first time. The strength of the concept of the nobility as the political nation, the *natio* in the technical sense, showed through here as Thám expressed the exasperation of many of the patriotic intelligentsia that the Bohemian nobility did not take a more important part in the support and revival of Czech culture. It would be some time before the intellectuals were willing to give up on the nobility: for the moment they concentrated on bringing them to their senses through such appeals as Thám's.

Thám was also among the first to condemn explicitly the policies of the Counter-Reformation in Bohemia, at least as far as they affected the Czech language. In his list of great Czech men of letters, Thám had already included the heretical Jan Hus himself; and he also attacked the activities of the missionaries charged with returning the countryside to its Catholic allegiance, especially for their destruction of Czech books. One could learn good Czech style from them even if they contained religious errors, he argued, and the missionaries would have been more effective polemicists if they had made themselves familiar with the arguments of their opponents. Thanks to these missionaries, more good Czech books were printed in the surrounding Protestant areas of Germany than in the Czech lands themselves.[24] This sort of attack on the church's cultural policies during the Counter-Reformation was easier now than it would have been a decade earlier, because of Joseph II's own desire to curb the power of the church and strengthen the state's control over it. To the patriotic intelligentsia, a return to the great works of Czech humanism was important both from the point of view of the professional philologists and those among the intelligentsia who wanted to prove that Czech could fill all the functional roles of a literary language. Thus Joseph II's prestige, at least in the earlier part of his reign, stood high with those who felt, as Thám did, that perhaps they could look to the emperor for support in their efforts on behalf of Czech.[25]

Contemporaries recognized the new note that Thám introduced into defenses of the language. Dobrovský wrote that *Obrana jazyka českého* was more than a mere defense, it was a clarion call for active measures to improve and cultivate Czech. "Whether we will ever achieve the standard of our forerunners," he cautioned, "or even can achieve it as it is here presented, is a question that can be answered without difficulty."[26] In spite of this implied skepticism about the future of the Czech language, Dobrovský proved to be one of the major figures in its grammatical stabilization and revival. And even he was not immune to the wave of enthusiasm for the language connected with the end of Joseph's reign and the coronation of his successor, Leopold II, as king of Bohemia in Prague.[27] Dobrovský was chosen to give an address to the emperor at a special session of the Royal Bohemian Society of Sciences in 1791, and, discarding his original intention of keeping to the more technical philological questions and of closing with an appeal for Leopold's support for a comprehensive Slavic dictionary, he spoke instead about the importance of Austria's Slavic inhabitants to the monarchy.

In this speech, "Über die Ergebenheit und Anhänglichkeit der Slawischen Völker an das Erzhaus Österreich," Dobrovský emphasized the numerical predominance of Slavs over all other nationalities in Austria, their greatness as a people (citing the extent of the Russian Empire as evidence of their ability to conquer and administer vast territories), and their contribution to Austria's military power. He had intended to close with a request that Leopold would consent "to protect the Czech nation in this priceless inheritance from their forefathers, in their mother tongue, from all violent measures and hidden coercion."[28] Any use of force to achieve a single state language would be harmful to the true interests of the state. These last thoughts, however, were excised from the speech as read to the monarch, by express order of the Highest Burggrave, Count Rottenhan—a high-handed proceeding that Dobrovský continued to resent years later.[29] Nevertheless, the speech "greatly pleased our Czech Slavic patriots," as Dobrovský commented, and the uncut version was quickly printed in both German and Czech.[30]

Another defense of Czech connected to the enthusiasm generated by Leopold's coronation was Jan Rulík's *Sláva a výbornost jazyka českého*, published in 1792. Just as most of Rulík's historical works were derivative, so his defense of the language borrowed arguments from all his predecessors; but he did gather and effectively restate them in Czech. He stressed the relationship between Czech and the other Slavic languages (or *dialects,* as he called them), he asserted that Czech had no need to borrow words from other languages (citing Balbín's *Dissertatio* for support), and he brought out the now traditional utilitarian arguments for a knowledge of Czech among landowners, military officers, and bureaucrats.[31] Throughout, he modeled his language on the Balbín tradition of baroque rhetoric and patriotic pathos, and in his concern for Czech's purity from foreign borrowings he also echoed the concerns of his baroque forerunners.

With Joseph II dead and gone, and Leopold and his successor Franz slowing down or reversing some of his policies, Rulík did not express the same sort of attitudes as Hanke or Thám to some of the defenders' themes. He was adamant in his lack of sympathy for the Czech Hussites or the Bohemian Estates in 1618, though he did condemn the burning of Czech books during the seventeenth century. He also condemned the school policies of the 1770s, and by implication the 1780s, for forcing Czechs to go to German schools to learn German. Rulík insisted that "the mother tongue is the priceless inheritance of each and every nation, passed down from fathers to sons."[32] The Hungarians set a great example, according to Rulík, for not only the common folk, but also the highest nobles in Hungary supported the Magyar language. In addition to this indirect appeal for the upper classes to support Czech, Rulík called on his colleagues to look at the language with other than an antiquarian interest: it was not enough just to read and appreciate old Czech books; patriots should actively support Czech writing and publishing. "The glory, learning, and improvement of Czech does not only consist in using Czech at home, in meetings, in the market, or society," he reminded his readers. "It is rather through learned and elevated works and through reading books that are now being published once more in pure, unadulterated Czech, that Czech learning improves and perfects itself."[33]

With this last admonition, Rulík in fact claimed for Czech all the functional roles of a developed, literary language. One step on the way to making that goal possible, a move that was widely canvassed at the time of Leopold's coronation, was the establishment of a chair of Czech language and literature at the university in Prague. F. M. Pelcl was eventually chosen to fill this chair in 1793,[34] and as was the custom, he delivered an inaugural address in which he, too, defended the study of Czech. This *Akademische Antrittsrede über den Nutzen und Wichtigkeit der Böhmischen Sprache* strongly reflected the utilitarian arguments that had been important in winning government approval for establishing the chair. It also reflected the extent to which Pelcl had changed his attitude to Joseph II and at least some of his policies. To prove how important it was to know Czech, even for the ruler, Pelcl claimed that Joseph had been unintentionally responsible for the great Bohemian peasant uprising of 1775. When a delegation of peasants presented the co-regent with their complaints, he intended to tell them to take the matter up with their lords— but instead of saying "Jděte k pánům" (go to your lords), he replied, "Jděte na pány" (attack your lords).[35] The Joseph II presented in this far-fetched story is a long way removed from the enlightened "father of his people" from whom the patriotic intellectuals expected so much for the Czech language and culture.[36]

Pelcl also criticized the school policies connected with the last reign, making the novel observation that forcing Czech-speaking students to learn German was only giving them an unfair advantage over monolingual German students, since the bilingual student could take a government post in either German or Slavic-speaking areas of the kingdom. Thus Pelcl became one of the first to draw attention to an area of conflict that would dominate so much of the nationalist struggle of the nineteenth century: competition for places in the state bureaucracy and quarrels over the language it used. In the military and seigneurial jurisdictions, too, Pelcl saw Czech as necessary (quoting directly from Kinský's *Erinnerung*); and like Kinský, Pelcl also stressed the musicality of Czech. Here, however, he cited his own experience, having heard with his own ears how much better suited Czech was to the stage than German, especially in opera.[37] With this final comment Pelcl epitomized the claims of Czech to equal consideration with German for high cultural expression, which suggests that conditions had begun to change from the time when the death of Czech had seemed imminent. In fact, an underlying theme of Pelcl's speech was a more confident view of the continued existence of the Czechs, for "those who predicted under Joseph II that the Czech language would be buried within fifty years were atrociously out in their reckoning."[38]

If Pelcl's inaugural address reflected at least some of the changes that had taken place in the position of Czech since the 1770s—changes to which he had himself contributed—this was equally true of the lecture that his student and successor, Jan Nejedlý, gave in 1801. Rather than merely rehearsing the familiar utilitarian arguments going back to Kinský and appealing to the rationalistic, practical attitudes of Josephinism that had affected Pelcl's generation deeply, Nejedlý concentrated on the aesthetic qualities of Czech that made it worthy of renewal and support. He stressed its richness, energy and clarity; its similarity to Greek, that highly respected classical language; its syntactical flexibility (in contrast to German); and finally its musicality and euphony.[39] These qualities all involved aesthetic taste and could not be empirically proven, only stated. They resembled more nearly the emotional note introduced into Thám's *Obrana* than the reasoned arguments of other defenders of the language. Nejedlý, even more clearly than Pelcl, identified the language issue as a source of tension within the Kingdom of Bohemia and argued that teaching Czech to all Bohemians would be a way to defuse this tension, for "then the hate, the contempt, and bitterness between Czech and German . . . would end; a bond of fraternal friendship would encircle them, the more the German communicated with the Czech, orally or in writing, in the Czech language."[40]

Nejedlý also began to make explicit some changes in the attitude of the patriotic intellectuals to the concept of nation and its relation to the language. It was the language and customs of a nation that differentiated it from every other nation, and if it changed these two essential characteristics, it ceased to be what it was and became something else. A Czech could best serve the state by being a Czech, not by becoming a German. Pride itself demanded that the Czechs support their mother tongue, for otherwise, he asked, "Would we not expose ourselves to contempt and ridicule because we despise the language of *that nation* of which we are *a part?*"[41]

This identification of language with nation was also expressed in K. H. Thám's *Über den Karakter der Slawen,* which was the text of an address he gave when he took up the position of Czech instructor at the Staré Město (Old Town) academic gymnasium. In a pastiche taken from his predecessors' works, Thám recapitulated the developments of the years since the 1770s, quoting (frequently without references) from his own *Obrana jazyka českého,* Josef Dobrovský's *Geschichte der Böhmischen Sprache,* Karel Raphael Ungar's *Böhmische Bibliothek,* Nejedlý's inaugural lecture, Kinský's *Erinnerung,* and Dobrovský's speech for Leopold II. Thám also quoted J. G. Herder's famous passage about the Slavs from his *Ideen zur Philosophie der Geschichte der Menschheit,* as well as this extract from his *Briefe zur Beförderung der Humanität*:

> And does any people (*Volk*), even an uncultivated one, have anything more dear than the language of its fathers? Its entire intellectual wealth of tradition, history, religion, and principles of life lives in it, its entire heart and soul. To degrade or take away the language of such a people means to take away its sole undying possession, which passes on from parents to children. . . . In truth, just as God tolerates all the languages of the world, so a ruler should not only tolerate, but also honor, the different languages of his people.[42]

These ideas of Herder's fell upon fertile soil in Bohemia, as in the rest of Central Europe. His elaboration of a linguistic concept of nationhood fitted in with the ideas and attitudes the patriotic intellectuals such as Thám had been developing. But they did not owe the concept to him; rather, he gave them important support and reinforcement of their views.

These views were expressed most clearly in 1806 in a series of articles published in *Hlasatel český,* a periodical edited by Jan Nejedlý. *Hlasatel český* set itself the task of proving by example that Czech could be used for the highest cultural functions and gathered around it many of the younger patriots who participated in the second generation of the renascence. Nejedlý led off the first volume with an article entitled "O lásce k vlasti," in which he discussed the concept of love of one's country. He went beyond the idea of *vlast* as the region in which one is born and lives and expanded it into a broader concept linked with the language, which one was obliged to love as he loved his own mother. In fact, Nejedlý personified *vlast* as a mother "who has lovingly and carefully raised us, and up to this moment continues to preserve us."[43] The concept of homeland, he wrote, was as old as human society, important to the Greeks and Romans (who knew no more terrible crime than treason to the fatherland) and common to every nation on earth. Nejedlý linked this concept indissolubly with language. He asked whether Jan Žižka could have inspired his soldiers to such acts of bravery if he had not addressed them in Czech. Language was the element distinguishing one nation from another, what determined national identity:

> Every nation is separated from every other nation by its mother tongue and customs, and only according to these two traits is it possible to differentiate it from all other nations; thus if it changes these two basic characteristics it ceases to be the nation that it was, and, transformed into another nation, it joins onto whichever nation it was whose language and customs it has accepted.[44]

But since Nejedlý identified *vlast* with the language and customs of the nation, anyone who harmed "his *vlast*, that is, his *customs and mother tongue*," was no better than a traitor.[45]

The meanings of nation, language, and *vlast* were further developed in the same volume of *Hlasatel český* by Josef Jungmann in two "conversations about the Czech language." In the first one, Jungmann lamented the condition of contemporary Czech. Daniel Adam z Veleslavína, who represented for this generation of Czechs the golden age of the humanist sixteenth century, meets with the shade of an eighteenth-century compatriot in the Elysian Fields.[46] In the course of their conversation, Veleslavín learns, to his shock and horror, the extent to which the language has decayed. The eighteenth-century Czech refers to German as "his language," since to anyone who understands honor or owns a decent coat, "to speak Czech is shameful." The passing shade of a German Bohemian acts as an impartial observer, noting that the Czechs had not followed the German example in developing their language, but reassuring Veleslavín: "that nation is still living, whose language has not completely died."[47]

In his second conversation, Jungmann turned from the state of the Czech language in his own day to prospects for its future development. Slavomil and Protiva (whose names could be loosely rendered as "Pro-Slav" and "Anti-Slav") are discussing the patriotic efforts of the Czech intellectuals to revive their nation and its language. Protiva enters as a defender of the cosmopolitan point of view, claiming that a true cosmopolitan could not love any single part of the world better than another. Slavomil counters that one who loves mankind has a special place in his heart for his own family; and similarly a cosmopolitan has a special regard for his own homeland. Slavomil laments the decline of Czech, and when Protiva argues that the issue is love of the fatherland and not love of language, the other replies that the two are inseparably linked. If the numbers of French in Vienna grew, there would eventually be French and German Austrians, just as there are Czech and German Bohemians, and there would be a French-Austrian homeland where they lived and spoke French. "So there are as many nations as there are languages, and as many fatherlands as nations?" Protiva asks. Slavomil responds:

> We are not quibbling over labels, but arguing about essences; and I believe that if the Czech nation became Germanized, or died out in any other way, . . . then the name Čechy [the Czech term for Bohemia] would properly belong to this land as little as does the name Bohemia, since there have been no more Boii here for ages. . . . For if it is impossible to conceive of a homeland without a nation and a nation without its own language, then I maintain once again that no one who does not love the language of his nation can pride himself on true love for his country.[48]

Here Protiva changes tack, and asks if it would not be better for the Czechs to learn German, since it is an advanced, cultivated language, and a knowledge of it would open up so much in the sciences and the arts. Would it not be better to continue advancing learning in German, rather than go back now and attempt to write learned works in Czech? Slavomil's response assumes that the nation includes all Czech speakers, the bulk of whom will go on speaking Czech, and that if they are to benefit from the progress of learning, that learning will have to be made available to them in Czech. But since Czech is a debased peasants' jargon, Protiva objects, how can this revival take place? Has not Germanization progressed so far that it cannot be turned back? Slavomil points to the example of the Hungarians and reminds his opponent that the entire history of the Czechs has been one of struggle with foreigners. Even if Czech survives only among the lower classes, the nation will not die out:

> The people are Czech; let the nobles speak French or Chaldean (the more rational of them will love the language of their people), what of it? The people will accept them for what they proclaim themselves to be—foreigners—and will love them the less, the less they are loved.[49]

Jungmann closed his conversation with an appeal to the self-interest of the government in supporting better opportunities for Czech in the schools and official life, a call for the organization of a Slavic learned society, and an appeal for more understanding and support for Czech from the Germans.

Jungmann and Nejedlý expressed some significant shifts in the understanding of the words *vlast, nation,* and *patriotism,* and their relationship to the language. Nation in the eighteenth century was primarily understood in a political sense, that is, the *natio* consisted of those with political rights, usually only the nobility. Their patriotism consisted of loyalty to their sovereign, the king, and to the territorial entity of which they were citizens. The other elements in society owed loyalty to those with jurisdiction over them (for the peasants this meant their landlords) and ultimately to the monarch. Patriotism in such a context could have quite slippery meanings: loyalty to the king, to the entire realm the king ruled over, to the historical entity to which the nobility traditionally belonged, to one's region, district, or home village. Language did not have a primary function in defining nation, patriotism, or fatherland. Historical developments had left Bohemia with a heritage of Czech, preserved in the formulae used in the opening and closing of the Bohemian Diet, and in the vernacular dialects used by the country folk of certain regions;

but one could be a Bohemian, even a patriotic Bohemian, without speaking Czech.

The defenders of the language seem to have started out with an almost antiquarian desire to preserve this historical heritage from total annihilation. The great monuments of Czech literature from the golden age of Czech humanism could be valued as part of the Bohemian cultural heritage, but it was pathetically clear when one compared eighteenth-century Czech with these monuments that a drastic decline had set in. This painful comparison provided part of the stimulus for the defensive efforts of the intellectuals. Additional impetus was given to them by the fact that the desire (typical of the Enlightenment) to work for the good of the state, to improve the lot of the citizens, and ensure that each of them made his contribution to the whole, meant that for practical reasons of communication with the people, Czech had to be used once more. Yet as long as *nation* remained a primarily political concept, Czech would not be a national language unless the foremost members of society, those with political rights, used it—hence the concern of the defenders of the language for the social status of Czech and their efforts to encourage especially the nobility to use it. And, indeed, under the pressure of the centralizing tendencies of Vienna (which did not significantly change from the time of Maria Theresa through Joseph and Leopold to Franz), the nobility did become interested in Czech, at least as a symbol of the traditional, historic individuality of the Kingdom of Bohemia.[50] But the likelihood of the nobility's readopting Czech as their primary language was never very great, and the patriotic intelligentsia had to learn to do without the nobles.

In their gradual realization that the Czech language could revive, and the Czech nation survive, even if the nobility never really adopted it, these intellectuals were aided by the implicit extension of the idea of nation in the Enlightenment demand that citizens serve the good of the state. Although political rights were still limited, the idea that everyone contributed to the good of the whole gave even the lowest levels of society a part in its life. As the idea of *vlast* was extended and personified, the object of the citizen's duty shifted from the state as a political-historical-territorial concept to the nation as an ethnic-historical-linguistic concept. The impact of revolutionary France's example affected the Czechs as it had the Germans, as a new kind of nation replaced the old political *natio.* When patriots like Jan Nejedlý personified *vlast* as a mother, the mother tongue assumed primary importance in defining one's relationship to the *vlast.* If its essence was nothing other than the mother tongue and the nation's customs, as Nejedlý asserted, then patriotism meant a love of them and efforts to serve their good. If these were the hallmarks of a true patriot, then the idea of nation itself needed rethinking, since the old *natio* so clearly did not, in general, meet the criteria of patriotism. By the time Jungmann expressed it in his conversations, the nation was coming to mean those people who spoke the mother tongue, of whatever social class or whatever their political rights. The nation would not die as long as someone continued to speak Czech, even if the nobility did not. The heritage of the great Czechs of the past was for all Czech speakers, who were the "descendants" of these patriots, whatever their family tree from generation to generation. But if the Czech nation were to take its rightful place among the nations of the world, then, given the new attitudes toward the key concepts, patriotism demanded that the Czech language take over all the functions of a modern, national language. Thus Jungmann demanded that Czechs write in Czech for Czechs, whatever their subject.

Gradually, then, the aim of the defenders of the language had broadened from a primarily preservative one to the much more ambitious one of making Czech the language of an entire national culture. In this task, the patriotic intellectuals came face to face with the realities of the last century and a half of Czech history. In order to realize their new goal, they had to stabilize and redevelop the language itself, eventually creating entirely new vocabularies to deal with subjects unknown to the Czech authors of the golden age. The Czech defenders of the language had asserted its right to existence, insisting that it was the equal of German or any other language and just as worthy of cultivation; and they had gradually developed and expressed the idea of an emotional, spiritual relationship between a nation and its language. They thus provided the ideological justification for the renewal of the language and also encouraged those already working toward that end.

Whither Czech?

If the Czech language were to have any chance of achieving the status of a literary language capable of all forms of cultural expression, then its greatest need in the latter part of the eighteenth century was for a generally accepted codification of its grammar and stabilization of its lexical base. During its period of decline in the seventeenth and early eighteenth centuries, the writers who used Czech (translators of official proclamations and legal texts, or authors of popular religious manuals) were too frequently ignorant of the rules of Czech usage as they had developed up to the end of the sixteenth century, when the Czech humanist writers had created a golden age for the language. The official Czech used in government publications or in religious works tended to be conservative grammatically, but was frequently marred by borrowings from German or arbitrarily formed neologisms for those expressions for which the author or translator did not know a Czech equivalent. The Czech in the popular-didactic material and the fledgling works of higher literature, on the other hand, was strongly influenced by popular spoken and dialect forms.[51] This situation suggested two possible paths for Czech's future development: either it could cleave to the standards of the humanist era at the risk of being archaic, or it could follow the current spoken usage at the risk of losing contact with its past heritage. One important means of bringing some order into this chaos would naturally be the establishing of some sort of institutional cultivation of the language.

The school system in Bohemia at this time had been stabilized by the great educational reforms of Maria Theresa, which had been further built upon under Joseph II. The Allgemeine Schulordnung, which went into effect in 1775, had established three levels of state schools and made them uniform for the whole monarchy. To further the aim of uniformity, and for purely practical reasons, the system encouraged the spread of German as a subject and language of instruction (which Pelcl's gloomy pronouncement, cited at the outset of this chapter, reflects). But this did not mean that Czech had entirely vanished from the schools, nor indeed that this was the aim of the authorities.[52] It did tend to be limited to the lowest level, the *Trivialschule*, however, and even there teachers were encouraged to introduce German as soon as possible. The teaching of the Czech language was basically limited to imparting mere literacy; instructional materials were scarce and frequently of poor quality. The need for cultivation of Czech at a higher, more scientifically exacting level was evident.[53]

Thus the call for introducing Czech as a subject of instruction in higher educational institutions not only reflected a desire for prestige or recognition of Czech's utilitarian value; it also reflected this need for an authoritative codification of Czech's grammatical and lexical bases. This helps explain the great importance the Czech patriots placed on establishing a chair of Czech language and literature at the Prague university. Another factor adding to the value of the Prague chair of Czech was that it would show that Prague was the equal of Vienna in this respect, for the institutional cultivation of Czech in the eighteenth century did not begin in Bohemia or Moravia at all, but in Lower Austria. The earliest foundation that gave instruction in Czech was the military academy for the sons of noblemen set up in Wiener Neustadt in 1752. Czech was one of the languages taught there from its beginnings, for the very practical reason that the pupils at the academy were destined for careers in the imperial and royal army, and would thus find the knowledge of a Slavic language useful. If this reasoning has a familiar ring to it, it could be because one of the directors of the Wiener Neustadt military academy was none other than Count Franz Joseph Kinský, author of the *Erinnerung über einen wichtigen Gegenstand*. At Wiener Neustadt, Kinský put some of his pedagogical ideas into practice, notably by introducing the so-called colloquia in every class on Sundays. At these gatherings, all the cadets from Bohemia would be required to converse in Czech, those from Hungary in Magyar, and similarly with those from other provinces of the Habsburg monarchy.[54]

Other institutions that included Czech among their subjects of instruction were later established in or around Vienna, including the school for military engineers (established in 1754) and the Theresianische Ritterakademie (1784). The first tertiary-level chair of Czech was set up at the university in Vienna in 1775. Little is known about the earliest Czech instructors at the Wiener Neustadt academy beyond their names, but their later successors, Josef Valentin Zlobický (1743–1810) and Maximilian Šimek (1748–1798), were active participants in the struggle for the codification of Czech. When the university chair of Czech was set up in Vienna, Zlobický became its first incumbent and was replaced at Wiener Neustadt by Šimek. A third Czech instructor who also took an active part in the linguistic revival was the teacher at the Theresianische Ritterakademie, Jan Václav Pohl (1720–1790).[55]

Pohl, the eldest of the three, had entered imperial service to be the Czech tutor to the heir to the throne, Archduke Joseph (later Joseph II), so he wielded great influence in language matters, especially under Maria Theresa.[56] Pohl's outlook was heavily influenced by the puristic tendencies of the baroque, which rejected all borrowed foreign words in Czech. This attitude led him to create neologisms with a verve and abandon equaled only by his lack of a thorough understanding of the rules of word formation in Czech, so that today he is most infamous as representing the apogee of purism in modern Czech.[57] This reputation has tended to obscure the remainder of Pohl's grammatical teaching, which did not in the main deviate very much from traditional Czech grammars. Pohl retained the conservative ending *-ti* in the infinitive (*učiti, mluviti,* etc.), and the form *jest* in the third person singular of the verb *to be.* Where he did depart from the classical orthography, Pohl has usually received the endorsement of modern Czech, such as in his use of *ř* for the older form *rz,* or his replacing of the diphthong *ua* with *v* (today, *u*), although some of these changes were not accepted until fifty years after his death.[58] At the time he wrote, Pohl's suggestions met with hostility and rejection from other philologists.

Josef Dobrovský and a circle of his friends and colleagues were the leaders of the resistance to Pohl.[59] In his negative review of the sixth edition of Pohl's grammar, *Neuverbesserte Böhmische Grammatik* (1783), Dobrovský wrote that anyone coming to Bohemia from Vienna "must discover to his annoyance that no one in Bohemia knows or understands the terms that he has so laboriously learned from Pohl's grammar."[60] He recommended instead Tomsa's *Böhmische Sprachlehre* (1782), which had made the works of Pohl "completely dispensable."[61] Pohl found a supporter, however, in the person of Šimek—who also received short shrift from Dobrovský's circle. Dobrovský attacked the orthography used in Šimek's *Krátký výtah všeobecné historie přirozených věci,* published in 1778, pointing out that those authors outside of Bohemia who adopted the new, "hateful" orthography, recommended by Pohl and used by Šimek, would have to resign themselves to the fact that their works would not be read in Bohemia.[62]

The third of these leading Viennese Czech philologists, Zlobický, was much closer in his views to Dobrovský, with whom he carried on a long and usually friendly correspondence. In fact, before Dobrovský's rise to prominence on the linguistic scene, Zlobický had hopes of becoming the established authority on his native tongue. The *Österreichischer Biedermannschronik* said of him in 1784 (in an article he probably wrote himself) that he was generally known as the

"Czech patriarch."[63] Zlobický was stimulated by the German scholars Schlözer, Gatterer, and Meusel to plan a general Slavic grammar, a classification of all the Slavic *dialects* (as most contemporaries referred to the different Slavic languages), and a history of the language. This scheme counted on the collaboration of scholars in Russia, the Austrian monarchy, and Germany.[64] Unfortunately this ambitious project was never realized, and the only work by Zlobický on these themes that saw the light was the *Handbuch für einen Lehrer der böhmischen Literatur.* Even this was not published by Zlobický himself—Šimek pirated it after the two men had a falling out and published it under his own name in 1785.[65] From this handbook and his comments in correspondence with Dobrovský, however, it can be gathered that Zlobický generally stood close to the conservative Prague philologists, represented by Pelcl and Dobrovský; but he did show himself more open to neologism as a means of enriching the lexicon, as his championship of Thám's dictionary suggests. (This will be discussed later.) In this opinion he was probably influenced by his own experience as an official translator.

Pelcl, whose influence as a historian has already been discussed, was also one of the earliest representatives of the Prague philological school to publish a work on the Czech language. His 1775 *Handbuch zum Gebrauche der Jugend bei Erlernung der deutschen, französischen, und böhmischen Sprache* was based on the language courses he had developed as tutor to the sons of Count Nostitz. For the next several years, however, Pelcl seems to have allowed his historical and literary-historical interests to predominate, and it was not until his appointment as first holder of the chair of Czech at the Prague university that he published a comprehensive grammar. This had been one of the conditions for the successful applicant for the post, and accordingly Pelcl published his *Grundsätze der böhmischen Grammatik* in 1795, accompanied by an article on Czech prosody from Josef Dobrovský.[66]

In his foreword, Pelcl clearly expressed his classical concept of Czech. He wrote of the concern for their language shown by the Czechs, as evidenced by the many grammars they had published in the past. Their efforts were crowned with success, and "in the second half of the sixteenth century [Czech] was just as regular, just as defined and solid, as Greek or Latin. It reached the highest peak of its culture during the reign of Rudolph II, who held court in Prague. . . . The Czech works published then are classics to us and are regarded as models of the language.[67] It was an easy task for grammarians of that time (and since) to abstract rules of grammar from these examples, and Pelcl claimed that he had done the same. His reverence for the golden age of Czech led Pelcl to adopt a very conservative approach to any modifications of the linguistic heritage. At times, he even wrote of Czech as though it were a dead language: "There is nothing more to be improved upon in the Czech language; we must only strive to maintain it in the same condition it was in during its golden age. It is now in the same situation as Latin or Greek."[68]

Pelcl's classicist attitude naturally meant that his grammar, too, was conservative in outlook. It maintained the norms of the sixteenth century in conjugation (for example the form *jest* in the third person singular of the verb *to be*) and in declension (for example insisting on the ending *-y* as the only acceptable form of masculine and neuter nouns in the instrumental plural). Pelcl also kept his orthography very close to that of the Bohemian Brethren as codified in the Kralice Bible, recommending the use of both *l* and *ł* and retaining the *-ti* infinitive ending. He also used other forms, however, which by the eighteenth century had become colloquial only, such as *vo-* at the beginning of words where the modern written form is *o* (*vokno, voráč*), or allowing the spelling *-ej-* for *-ý-* in the interior of words (*vejstraha, vejnos*).[69]

A corollary of Pelcl's conservative, classicist approach was that it made good Czech the exclusive preserve of those with a high enough level of education to appreciate it and looked down on the language of the common people. In a review of a popular-didactic work, Pelcl wrote that "it is simply for the country folk . . . and therefore the translator chose the lowest language of the mob (*Pöbelsprache*), to make it easily understandable. But those Czechs who are accustomed to the language of the Bible do not like such a style of writing."[70] Such an attitude is understandable when the social status of Czech is brought into consideration. By the eighteenth century, Czech was generally considered a vernacular dialect of the lower orders, which might have made those concerned for its revival oversensitive to any suggestion that the spoken dialect should, in fact, be made acceptable for literary usage.

Pelcl's abortive plan for a Czech society, or *Hromada*, was also an expression of his classicist attitude. The purpose of this society, Pelcl wrote in 1794, was to have been the production of a comprehensive dictionary of the Czech of the golden age. Each member, among whom were the leading representatives of the patriotic intelligentsia, was to select a work from the golden age and collect all the words and expressions in it that could not be found in existing dictionaries. The individual contributions would then be pooled, and a new, comprehensive dictionary of classical Czech would be created. One basic rule of the *Hromada* was that its members could converse among themselves only in Czech. "Nothing ever came of the idea, however," Pelcl later admitted, "due to conditions at that time."[71] Several years later, Dobrovský wrote that the blame for the demise of Pelcl's scheme rested with Hofrat J. A. von Riegger, whom he described as an "anti-Slav (*Slawenfeinde*)" for convincing Pelcl that "the Court in Vienna would object to it."[72]

Unlike Pelcl, another Czech grammarian, František Jan Tomsa (1751–1814), showed a much more open attitude toward the developments in Czech since the sixteenth century. He believed that the spoken language could be an especially important source for Czech philologists, reflecting a greater influence on him from the grammars of the seventeenth and eighteenth centuries, especially that of Pavel Doležál (1746). For example, Tomsa accepted both -*y* and -*ami* as endings in the masculine instrumental plural (*s duby, s holuby*, but also *s dubami, s holubami*), he gave the endings -*i* and -*ejí* without distinction in the third-person plural of verbs in *-í* (such as *učí* and *leží*) and he recommended both -t and -ti as spellings for the infinitive ending.[73] In most other important respects, however, Tomsa's earliest grammar, the *Sprachlehre* of 1782, which Dobrovský praised so highly, harmonized with the latter's teachings.[74] The energetic newspaper editor, V. M. Kramerius, who also supported the standard of the golden age for Czech, recommended Tomsa's grammar as the best available and a standard that should be followed by anyone setting out to write Czech, since Tomsa had "collected only those rules which have a solid basis in the works of our classical Czechs."[75]

In his later grammatical works, Tomsa developed his ideas on the importance of the spoken usage for Czech grammar, the possibilities of using other Slavic languages as sources and models, and the need for an orthographic reform of Czech that was more radical than most contemporaries could accept. Tomsa, an avid observer of the living language, frequently accompanied the examples he used in his works with a note of the place, date, and situation in which he heard them.[76] He defended this practice strongly, writing in one passage: "I hope no one will abuse me for supposedly learning Czech only from old wives. A true Czech must not be ashamed to learn from all Czechs, in order to comprehend the entire linguistic usage; but he must test what he hears, in order to be able to teach genuine Czech."[77] He followed his own precept carefully, corresponding with his father, "a Czech peasant," on questions of usage or vocabulary that had to do with cultivation and animal husbandry, and including some of the data thus collected in his *Über die Veränderungen der čechischen Sprache* (1805). In his defense of the language, *Von den Vorzügen der čechischen Sprache,* Tomsa also defended his approach to the common spoken language. After quoting Friedrich Gedike to the effect that "the language of a people can rightly be seen as a mirror of its national character," Tomsa continued:

> The language of a nation always grows, even if the nation teaches itself, by itself, through natural philosophy without

the help of scholars. One should himself, therefore, study not only from good written works, but also from the common speech, if he wants to preserve a more exact knowledge of the living language. Not everything in the common speech is coarse; there is much in it that is fine.[78]

Tomsa also stressed in his works the importance of a knowledge of the other Slavic languages to anyone working on Czech grammar. Already in the outline of a course of Czech that he wrote at the end of 1791 as part of his application for the post at the Prague university (which went to Pelcl), Tomsa included instruction in "the other main dialects of the Slavic nation," especially Russian and Polish.[79] When the Russian armies marched through Prague in 1799 and 1800, Tomsa listened to their speech and later used some of his notes in his books.[80] He considered Czech a "key to the other Slavic languages, although the Czech can also learn quite a lot from the other Slavs," and he hoped that his suggestions for orthographic reform would help bring all the Slavic languages closer together.[81]

It was in these proposed orthographic reforms that Tomsa departed most drastically from the heritage of the sixteenth century. Accordingly, it was this aspect of his grammatical teachings that excited the most opposition from the more classicist philologists. In his earliest work on Czech orthography, *Uvedení k české dobropísemnosti*, published in 1782, Tomsa did not yet suggest any deviations from the accepted orthography based on that of the golden age. A few years later, however, in his popular-didactic monthly paper, *Měsíční spis k poučení a obveselení obecného lidu* (1787), he was already introducing some changes in practice, notably the use of *j* in place of *g* (*já* instead of *gá* for *I, jest* in place of *gest* for *is*).[82] He continued to introduce changes in his later works, earning Pelcl's condemnation of his reprint of the *Život Karla IV*, which appeared in 1791. Tomsa eventually presented a theoretical defense of his new orthography in several of his later linguistic works, especially in *Über die čechische Rechtschreibung* (1802), *Über die Veränderungen der čechischen*

Sprache (1805), and *Grössere čechische Orthographie* (1812). The changes Tomsa introduced were basically the introduction of Latin letters in place of the "Schwabach" or "Gothic" type then in use (which Tomsa castigated as "that monks' script")[83] and the adoption of consistent diacritical marks in order to represent all the sounds of Czech with a single letter each. He replaced the former *ss* with *š*, *cz* with *č*, *rz* with *ř*, and *j* with *í*, while using *j* to replace *g*. In short, the orthography that Tomsa advocated corresponds in almost every way with modern Czech usage. Other reforms he taught included the rejection of the spelling *vo-* at the beginnings of words, an end to the capitalization of all nouns (an unnecessary imitation of the German), and the dropping of the *-i* from the infinitive ending.[84] He even presumed to criticize Veleslavín, blaming the symbolic representative of golden age Czech for introducing the letter *g* for *j*.[85]

Tomsa's orthographic changes met with criticism from almost every quarter. As early as 1790, Zlobický objected to the orthography used in *Mesíční spis* and urged Dobrovský to use his influence to get Tomsa to return to the old forms.[86] Pelcl objected especially to the spelling of the infinitive without the *i*. Tomsa had argued that in the common speech it was hardly ever pronounced, appearing only as a softened final *t* in spoken Czech, while the Poles, Russians, and Lusatian Slavs even left it out of their written languages.[87] Pelcl's response to this reasoning reflects his classicist position: "One writes the infinitive *amare, docere* because that is how Cicero wrote it; therefore also *milovati, učiti* because that is how Veleslavín wrote."[88] Dobrovský also attacked the "singular orthography, contrary to the general national usage of the Czechs," which Tomsa was dictatorially trying to force on the nation.[89] Somehow this question of how to spell the infinitive came to symbolize far more than its actual importance, and it was the focal point of the attacks on Tomsa, many of them ad hominem. Thus Puchmajer wrote to Dobrovský in 1813:

> Tomsa is to be pitied, or rather not to be pitied, since he could live respectably if he would only arrange it so. It is

a shame about him; he is after all the best of Czechs; and if only he would decide to allow the *-ti* its rightful honor I would take up a collection for this physical and mental cripple.[90]

With time Dobrovský arrived at a more tolerant view, which he expressed in his Slavistic collection *Slovanka* (1815), suggesting that each person look to his own sense of taste, and then write *-ti* or not, with sensible moderation. This was a solution Tomsa also suggested.[91]

Another recipient of the ire of the classicist philologists was K. H. Thám, whose *Obrana jazyka českého* figured in the previous section. In addition to being one of Czech's most fervent defenders, Thám was a prolific author of textbooks and dictionaries for it.[92] The more conservative grammarians in Prague, led by Pelcl and his pupil and successor, Jan Nejedlý, objected to what they called Thám's arbitrary approach to the rules of Czech grammar. Pelcl accused Thám of trying to force a set of rules onto an already flourishing language, but his alternative was to take them from the best works of the golden age.[93] Because this was not Thám's method he became, at least in their eyes, tainted with the puristic tendencies of Pohl and the seventeenth- and early eighteenth-century grammarians. Since the classicist philologists had spent much time and energy criticizing Pohl and Šimek, the appearance of Thám's grammatical and lexical works provoked some of them to exasperation, such as Jan Nejedlý, who wrote:

> The Czech language had scarcely begun to recover, to come nearer to the standard of the period of Emperor Rudolph II . . . and then a bungler appeared with a grammatical monstrosity, who wanted to introduce all this barbarity again. Is this what it means to be inspired by true love for the fatherland?[94]

Dobrovský also warned prospective students of Czech, especially Germans, against Thám's promise that by his meth-

ods they could learn Czech "thoroughly, easily, and quickly"
as the title of the later editions of Thám's grammar had it.
"How can something that is by its nature difficult be made
easier?" asked Dobrovský. "All-too-easy methods are usually
shallow, and certainly do not lead to a profound and complete
knowledge of a language as surely as the natural method."[95]

Pelcl and Nejedlý also took Thám to task for introducing
forms from the spoken language, such as *krasnej* instead of
krasný, or the ending *-emi* for the instrumental plural of masculine and neuter nouns.[96] Thám's spirited self-defense suggested ironically that the conservatives were out of touch with
reality. As far as the inclusion of spoken forms in his grammar
was concerned, Thám argued that he wanted "to make the
student, who lives among people and not books, aware of
[spoken forms] as well, which [are] in practically universal
use, and not merely among the mob, but even the educated,
refined classes."[97] The frowns of such as Pelcl and Nejedlý
did not prevent Thám's grammar from going through five editions in his lifetime; but the prestige of the conservative
school, especially its leader, Dobrovský, was so high that in
future years Thám's works were relegated to a subordinate
position in the revival of Czech, just as he himself had to be
content with a post in a gymnasium while his rivals occupied
the university chair of Czech.[98]

In the arguments over the direction Czech should take,
toward the spoken language or back to the classical sixteenth
century, Josef Dobrovský occupied an important position. He
was generally less conservative than Pelcl and was able to remain on friendly terms with the more radical philologists such
as Tomsa, who frequently borrowed grammatical and other
materials from Dobrovský.[99] At the same time, his close
friendship with Pelcl, and his approval of the greater part of
the latter's position, are testified to by the inclusion of Dobrovský's article on Czech prosody in both editions of Pelcl's
grammar.

Dobrovský surpassed both Pelcl and Tomsa in the clarity
of his systematization and in his wide-ranging and detailed

knowledge of Czech philology. Dobrovský's acquaintance with and understanding of the works of the great German philologists was also better than his colleagues'. Adelung and Friedrich Karl Fulda were especially important for Dobrovský's Czech grammar. Fulda's theory of lexical roots, which also influenced Adelung, was the foundation of Dobrovský's teaching on lexicography.[100] Adelung's concept of analogy also played an important role in the development of Dobrovský's ideas on orthography, especially the question of whether to use *i* or *y* after certain consonants such as *z, s,* or *c*.[101] Dobrovský emphasized analogy to such an extent that the few minor changes that he made in the orthography of the Bohemian Brethren came to be known as the analogical orthography.[102]

The foundation of Dobrovský's grammar was still the language of the classical period. In his orthography he showed himself to be less conservative than Pelcl, using only one form of *l*, for instance, or limiting the form *vo-* to dialectisms only. In conjugation and declension, on the other hand, he was more conservative than Tomsa. He held fast to the *-ti* in the infinitive, differentiated between third person plural verb endings in *-í* or *-ejí*, and recognized only the ending *-y* or *-i* in the instrumental plural of masculine and neuter nouns.[103] In general, Dobrovský's deviations from the classical Czech of the sixteenth century were outweighed by his basic adherence to its norms. Such was his personal prestige and the influence of his works that even though succeeding generations have modified his teachings in certain areas, modern-day literary Czech still bears the imprint of his ideas.[104]

The Problem of Neologisms in Czech

One of the questions that was closely tied up with the other problems occupying the Czech philologists was word formation. We have seen how many scholars, such as Pohl and Šimek, advocated purifying the Czech vocabulary of all foreign borrowings; and even the classicist philologists realized that some development of the Czech lexicon would be necessary to deal with topics unknown to the sixteenth century. The issue of foreign influence on the Czech language was not something new—efforts to replace foreign borrowings with Czech equivalents can be traced back as far as the reign of Charles IV or the time of Hus.[105] There was another peak in puristic tendencies during the baroque period, when some patriotic authors became ashamed of the number of Latin and German words they found in Czech and attempted to coin new Czech words to replace them. Men such as Pohl and Šimek were the spiritual heirs of this baroque purism.

Pohl's credentials as a sincere patriot could not be challenged,[106] but he was not, perhaps, best suited to undertake a reform of the Czech vocabulary. He lacked the knowledge of the language of the golden age that was so important to Dobrovský and his group, and he also lacked their grasp of the structure of the language and the rules of word formation. Beginning with the third (1773) edition of his grammar, Pohl included a dictionary, listing in part those words in general use, and in part neologisms of the baroque purists or his own creation. Pohl's neologisms were mainly calques of German or Latin models, though he also included Moravianisms and words from the Viennese dialect of Czech. These neologisms were generally formed without any regard for the characteristics of the language, or even for comprehensibility.[107]

Those Czech philologists who knew and appreciated the great works of Czech humanist literature were quick to see the danger to Czech from such efforts to "purify" it. Tomsa warned that "even if the common folk do not accept such marvelous words and expressions very easily, . . . still those who do not know any better words will adopt them," with evil consequences for the language.[108] Dobrovský also attacked neologisms formed contrary to the "spirit of the language." He continued: "The saddest thing is that such bunglers present themselves as authorities in grammar, such as the recently deceased Wenzel Pohl . . . who wanted to teach us Czechs an entirely new Czech language, invented by himself."[109] Dobrovský similarly criticized neologisms by Šimek, which, he said, were formed "partly without need, partly contrary to the rules of grammar," and in any case, "no one can understand them."[110] In spite of this theoretical resistance to the neologisms of Pohl's school, however, many of the words coined by the purists have survived to enter into present-day literary Czech.[111]

Yet even if they could not successfully resist all of the puristic neologisms, the need to counter what they saw as a harmful development led the conservative philologists to clarify their own views on word formation in Czech. Dobrovský and his friends were aware that Czech could not continue to exist exclusively on the word stock of the sixteenth century. They insisted, however, that "whoever wants to form new words, where it is necessary, must first make himself well acquainted with the rules of derivation."[112] Dobrovský's criticisms of Šimek's neologisms as quoted above summarized three of the guiding principles of the conservatives: newly formed words must be necessary, they must follow the rules of grammar, and they must be comprehensible. Dobrovský's theoretical works on word formation, especially his introduction to Tomsa's 1791 dictionary, "Über die Ursprung und die Bildung der slawischen und insbesondere der böhmischen Sprache," with his *Die Bildsamkeit der Slawischen Sprache* (1799), gave future philologists a firm basis for their work in this field. His more precise definitions of the concepts of root words, prefixes, suffixes, and endings were a necessary first step to the formation of new words that would not be contrary to the "spirit" of the language.[113]

The philologists grouped around Dobrovský warned against too great haste in deciding that a new Czech word was needed for a given concept. First, they believed, a linguist should search through books dealing with the subject, check old dictionaries, and finally ask the people who were actively engaged with the topic in question.[114] Pelcl, who toward the beginning of his career had shown himself relatively open to neologisms, became later more strict, and held that even if a word had once come from another language, the principle of usage could give it Czech citizenship. "A word that is thus accepted and understood by the entire Czech nation is Czech," he insisted.[115] If the need for a new Czech word could finally be established beyond doubt, the conservatives felt that there were better ways of filling this need than by calquing a new word on a German model. One way was to seek out an older word no longer in use and revive it, or, following the example of Adelung, to take over a word from another Slavic "dialect." Puchmajer urged Dobrovský to follow this method in his dictionary, since it would be "a thousand times more reasonable than forging new monstrosities after the German."[116]

Dobrovský questioned the suitability of the grammarian for the task of coining new words, suggesting instead that this be left to the "aesthetic" writer, since the grammarian tended to produce too literal a translation of the foreign model.[117] This was especially dangerous when the model language differed in essence from Czech, in which case a too-literal translation violated the spirit of Czech. Dobrovský's circle recognized the essential difference between Czech and German, the most popular model language—a language through which, as Tomsa warned, "many an enthusiastic Czech has been led astray."[118] Maladroit neologisms from the German, such as Thám's rendering of *horseradish* (German, *Meerrettich*) as *mořská řetkev*, received the full force of Dobrovský's talent for sarcasm:

> The reader must think, according to the Czech meaning, of some wondrously rare, exotic plant, and would hardly anticipate that the Czech *kren*, *křen*, or formerly *chřen*, as it still is among the other Slavs, should be understood here.[119]

Dobrovský insisted that each language had something that was unique to it, and thus Czech could not always express ideas the same way as German. Even Latin could not render German compounds with one word, and frequently had to resort to a phrase or other circumlocution. If Czech philologists ignored this fact as they worked, then "we will no longer write Czech, but German with Czech words."[120]

In practice, however, it was frequently very difficult to find or create appropriate Czech words for German or other expressions. This problem was particularly vital for translators, and it is noteworthy that active translators, especially Zlobický, were more willing to accept neologisms. As the leading authority on Czech in Vienna, Zlobický was entrusted with the official duties of translator and, from 1781, censor of Czech books. He was particularly active as a translator of legal codes and other government texts, and published eight such works between 1781 and 1804. In his translations, Zlobický was plagued by the lack of a developed legal terminology in Czech, and had perforce to try to create one, using German as a model.[121]

Since he had to grapple with these problems at first hand, Zlobický was impatient with some of the criticisms that Dobrovský leveled at him in *Litterarisches Magazin von Böhmen und Mähren* in 1786. Dobrovský had written that no Czech reader could understand the translation of the legal code unless he also knew Latin or German and kept both versions in front of him as he read. Dobrovský blamed both the reader and the translator: the one for not knowing the literary language, and the other for coining new words against the natural trends of Czech.[122] Zlobický argued that it was not for Dobrovský, who did not write in Czech himself and thus did not know the problem of translation from his own experience, to judge. In a rather bitter comment to Ungar (who had had his own quarrels with Dobrovský), Zlobický wrote:

> Dobrovský should only publish something in Czech himself; then we will also poke holes in him, and I will prove in my contributions, just as dictatorially and as unfeelingly as he . . . that he is also human like I am, and has seriously erred in the rules of Czech grammar and his critical notes and interpretations.[123]

Even ten years later Zlobický continued to defend his work against Dobrovský's criticisms, arguing that they were unfounded since he lacked experience in translation, especially of legal texts, "where one is constrained to translate everything as accurately and slavishly as possible."[124] Their differing experience with the problems of translation also led Dobrovský and Zlobický to disagree on the question of the Czech dictionary. The development and publication of a good, norm-giving Czech dictionary was seen as the most effective way to defend the language against further puristic inroads, and Tomsa, Thám and Dobrovský each brought out dictionaries between 1780 and 1815. While none of them totally satisfied the needs of the developing Czech language, and they were all superseded by the great *Slovník česko-německý* (1835–1839) of Josef Jungmann, they did help to further develop the Czech vocabulary and provided Jungmann with valuable sources for his own work.

During the early 1780s, Dobrovský encouraged Tomsa to publish a concise Czech-German dictionary in order to challenge Pohl. The first fruit of this encouragement was Tomsa's *Malý německý a český slovník,* which appeared in 1789.[125] In the meantime, K. H. Thám had published his *Deutsch-böhmisches Nationallexikon* in 1788; but Tomsa continued to enlarge his collections and added Latin explanations, publishing this *Vollständiges Wörterbuch der böhmisch- deutsch- und lateinischen Sprache* in 1791. It was accompanied by a foreword by Dobrovský in which he praised Tomsa's dictionary as the best one currently available and a sure means not only to the "correct judgment of the richness of the language," but also to a better knowledge and understanding of it. Dobrovský denied a place in a good dictionary not only to foreign words (he mentioned specifically *flinta, nudle, litera,* and *breviář*) but also to "the newly formed words, which a few incompetent grammarians have forged in their workshops, but which have never been granted citizenship by the Czech nation."[126]

Dobrovský's praise of Tomsa's dictionary, and his criticisms of Thám's—for precisely this fault of too many neologisms—led to a personal breach between Thám and Dobrovský. Thám had originally expressed himself willing and even eager to submit his work to Dobrovský's criticism, and he had received some assistance from Dobrovský in his lexical work.[127] When he found Dobrovský's comments stronger than he preferred, a sort of contest ensued to determine which dictionary, Thám's or Tomsa's, would become the accepted standard and enshrine this status by reaching a second edition before its rival. While Dobrovský tended to support Tomsa, Zlobický was a champion of Thám.

By 1794, Thám and his publisher were planning a second edition, and Zlobický wrote to Dobrovský urging him to contribute to the project. He was especially excited about the possibility of including not only older forms no longer in daily use, but also dialect words from Moravian and Slovak, and he argued that Adelung had done the same with the German dialects.[128] Dobrovský, in reply, questioned Thám's suitability for the task, saying that he had plans himself to publish the necessary corrections to Tomsa's dictionary and had counted on Zlobický's helping him. On the question of dialectisms, he added, "From the Moravian and the Slovak I believe that only so much as may serve to explain a Czech word should be admitted."[129] Dobrovský was interested in Slavic dialects, but they did not belong in a Czech dictionary. Zlobický questioned this, asking why, since Adelung had included all the German dialects in his work, the Czechs could not do the same. He also expressed his own criticisms of Tomsa's dictionary and announced his decision to support Thám's.[130] In response, Dobrovský asserted that Adelung had not in fact included all dialect words. "He often used dialect words for explanation—and this is the only use that I do not want to exclude in Czech. I would, rather, use Russian, Polish and Illyrian to help. The first aim should nevertheless be *purior bohemismus*."[131]

Dobrovský's more exclusive attitude to dialect words in Czech also carried over into his views on contemporary attempts to raise certain Slavic "dialects" to the level of literary languages. Thus he commented in his correspondence with

Zlobický and Ribay on the efforts made by Antonín Bernolák and others on behalf of Slovak. In one letter to Ribay (who as a Protestant would perhaps also have been unsympathetic to Bernolák's ideas), he wrote:

> It is quite annoying that the Slovaks do not want to stand by us. I have a few songs and prayers in the dialect of Teschen [Těšín]. They are neither Czech nor Polish—but gibberish (*Kauderwelsch*). One should not immediately consider the village dialects to be Doric, Attic or Ionic. The Germans were cleverer in this than we disunited Slavs.[132]

Dobrovský's insistence on the need for keeping the dictionary purely Czech, and his rejection of dialects, strained his friendship with Zlobický, but it survived the test. The latter never gave up his own point of view, however, and he continued to urge on Dobrovský a more open and tolerant attitude to enriching the Czech lexicon.[133]

Yet if the friendship between Zlobický and Dobrovský survived their disagreements over the dictionary and the problem of the Czech lexicon, the same could not be said of Dobrovský's relationship with K. H. Thám. Their disagreements flared into an open polemic when a second edition of Thám's dictionary was announced in 1798. Dobrovský attacked Thám's neologisms, and Thám retorted that he did not understand on what authority Dobrovský had set himself up as "dictator of Czech grammar."[134] Thám accused him of speaking Czech "anxiously, yes, even incorrectly," adding in a footnote that, although Dobrovský had not yet published anything in Czech, the few translations he made at the time of Leopold's coronation showed "how much he is a German-Bohemian, and still a novice in Czech."[135] Allowing of course for rhetorical overstatement, there was a grain of truth in Thám's remarks. Dobrovský's knowledge of Czech was more theoretical than practical: it was precisely this thorough grounding in Czech linguistic theory that gave Dobrovský his concern that any developments taking place in Czech should not run counter to the grammatical rules it had developed over the centuries—what he called the "spirit" of the language. Thám, on the other hand, was more closely concerned with the language in its everyday aspects and was moreover not untouched by the patriotic-puristic zeal of some of his forerunners, as shown especially in his later dictionaries.[136]

The time-consuming polemics and other problems involved in working on his own dictionary, which dragged on for years, did not discourage Dobrovský from carrying on his task.[137] Nor did they keep him from offering advice, criticism, or encouragement to anyone else working on the problem. He wrote to Jungmann in 1813 emphasizing yet again the importance of a knowledge of the language of the countryside to complement the written heritage and the limitations of dialects as aids in explaining word meanings. Again in 1815, he commented on a section of Jungmann's dictionary manuscript, criticizing the number of foreign words in it.[138] Better than most, Dobrovský could advise Jungmann on the problems and frustrations of working on a dictionary, warnings seconded by his longstanding collaborator, Puchmajer:

> Your intention of publishing a Czech dictionary, however praiseworthy it may be, is nevertheless fraught with innumerable difficulties; and if you do not have the patience of Job, when you already complain at the beginning that you are getting stuck in the mud, it will be the worse for you the farther you go, until you end up in the middle of the pool.[139]

Yet these very frustrations, especially the arguments about the nature of the Czech vocabulary and the heritage of the classical period, were important in preparing Czech for its nineteenth-century development.

❋ ❋ ❋

The renewal and revitalization of the Czech language that took place beginning in the last quarter of the eighteenth century was one of the most important developments in the Czech national renascence.[140] It was a precondition for much of the rest of the national revival, especially for the creation of an independent national culture, including literature in Czech at all levels. It also took place at a time when the concept of the nation was changing and the old tradition of territorial loyalty was giving way to ideas of linguistic nationhood. The Czech language was the one characteristic that divided Czechs from German-Bohemians or foreigners in general; as Nejedlý pointed out, it was what made them what they were. Thus the linguistic revival was a necessary starting point for the nineteenth-century national movement. It also gave Czech nationalism one of its most noticeable characteristics, one shared with other nations in East Central Europe. This is its philological bent, dubbed in a recent study its "linguocentrism." Linguistic nationalism became central to the Czech national movement, part of its ideology, expressed in its nationalist slogans.[141]

The process of renewal had two aspects, the defensive justification of renewal efforts and the scholarly work for this renewal by the Czech philologists. The defenders of the language wrote in order to overcome any feeling of inferiority engendered by the loss of Czech political importance and the decline of Czech culture since the Battle of the White Mountain. Defenses of the language written in German were not only directed at the Czechs themselves, but also intended for foreign consumption, to draw attention to the existence of an ancient and highly developed language worthy of further study. Those written in Czech were at one and the same time physical proof that Czech could be used as a literary language and encouragement for other Czech writers to persevere in their efforts.

The resolution of the arguments about the authority of classical sixteenth-century Czech eventually favored, on the strength of Dobrovský's own personal importance, a strong influence of conservative ideas on modern literary Czech. While this division of Czech into literary and colloquial forms may in some ways be a disadvantage, most European languages today distinguish between written and spoken style.

The great service of the conservative philologists was that they kept Czech in touch with its past heritage and avoided a break in the organic linguistic development.

The discussions of lexical enrichment, which became at times so bitter, also influenced the later development of Czech. Even before Jungmann's generation, some philologists clearly recognized that without enriching the lexicon Czech would never be able to fulfill its tasks as a literary and scholarly language. Jungmann's great codification of Czech included many newly formed words, but the complex of discussion, argument, and disagreement over neologisms had served to clarify the issue. Linguists of later generations had the advantage of Dobrovský's clear formulation of the rules of word formation in Czech, as well as, frequently, personal experience of his strict and severe criticism of any attempt at neologizing. Thus when a new word was necessary, it was usually formed not in violation of the spirit of the language but in harmony with it. The polemics of the first generation of awakeners had served as a crucible for the development of Czech into a modern, truly national language.

3

Reclaiming the Czechs' Literary Birthright

*H*istory and language met and flowed together in literary history. What was for the historian an important document was for the philologist frequently a monument of Czech literature as well, and thus a priceless source for the study of the development of the language. And for the patriotic intellectuals whose defenses of the language asserted the right of Czech to equal consideration with other European languages, these monuments of the past were concrete proof that at one time, at least, the Czech language had fulfilled all the functions of a fully developed literary language. Thus, as was happening with Czech history and the Czech language, the cultivation of Czech literature (and eventually the creation of new works) came to be one of the hallmarks of a true patriot. This impulse found expression in two directions: on the one hand it drew scholars' attention to the history of Czech literature, and on the other, it drove some of them to attempt to produce modern literary works in Czech. The first trend, the subject of this chapter, was important in developing Czech literature because it resulted in the reclamation of a part of the Czechs' literary birthright that had been denied them by the events of the seventeenth century.

Scholars studying the history of letters in Bohemia did not at first set out to write a history of *Czech* literature, and they wrote their works in the languages of scholarship, Latin and

German. But gradually, their partial and unsystematic efforts encouraged and were replaced by more coherent and clearly focused studies that eventually concerned themselves with Czech literature *in* Czech. In addition to producing specialized and general studies of Czech literary history, these scholars and their noble patrons embarked on collecting and publishing surviving monuments of the past. Thus they preserved, explained, and transmitted this precious heritage for their contemporaries who were seeking to revitalize Czech literature itself.

Varieties of Literary History in Bohemia

Earlier generations had not, of course, ignored Czech literature. For intellectuals who had applied the critical method to their history, it was natural to do the same for the study of literature. For the first three-quarters of the eighteenth century, practically the only works published in Bohemia that dealt with Czech literary history were those of Antonín Koniáš (1691–1760), a Czech Jesuit and editor of *Clavis haeresim claudens et aperiens* (published in two editions, 1729 and 1749), and *Index Bohemicorum librorum prohibitorum* (1770). These books listed all the Czech works published in the sixteenth, seventeenth, and eighteenth centuries that had been condemned by the church.[1] For critical historians, this approach left something to desired, and many of those who were active in the fields of history and linguistics set themselves the task of providing a more scientific approach to literature.

The Gelehrtengeschichte

One of the earliest and most common type of study was the biographical-bibliographical dictionary, in which scholars were perhaps influenced by the example of German Enlightenment literary history, in which the *Gelehrtengeschichte* was a common phenomenon.[2] There was also a well-known native precedent for this approach to history and literature, namely Balbín's *Bohemia docta*. This work, consisting largely of biographical sketches of Czech men of letters, was extremely influential. (Its reputation among historians was alluded to in chapter 2.) The first such study was Voigt's *Effigies virorum eruditorum atque artificum Bohemiae et Moraviae*, which appeared in two volumes in 1773 and 1775, and in a German version with the collaboration of Pelcl and Born, entitled *Abbildungen Böhmischer und Mährischer Gelehrten und Künstler* (4 vols., 1773–1782).[3]

Voigt accompanied the first volume of his *Effigies-Abbildungen* with a long foreword on the origins and development of the arts and sciences in Bohemia in which he presented an overview of Czech literary history and explained his purpose in writing the work. This purpose was plainly patriotic and defensive. Voigt organized his discussion according to topics, beginning with theology and proceeding through law, medicine, philosophy, mathematics, poetry, rhetoric, history, and languages to fine arts, architecture, painting, sculpture, and music. In each field of activity, he wrote, Bohemia had produced works comparable to those of any other nation. Voigt's defensive patriotism was particularly clear in the section on the language, where he insisted that two hundred years earlier the Czechs had brought their language to such a pitch that "all our scholars, and foreign ones as well, will admit that the Czech language in comparison with other European languages is not inferior to any, whether in richness, refinement, and expressiveness of vocabulary or in appropriate expressions and figures of speech; but rather surpasses many of them." He went on to decry what he called the modern prejudice and debased taste that convinced many of his compatriots to reject Czech, "to prefer foreign things to the native, a foreign language to their own. How much do I wish . . . that we might follow the examples of the Poles and Russians in developing the language!"[4]

Similar themes dominated the closing pages of the introduction to the second volume, which dealt with learning among members of the Bohemian and Moravian nobility.[5] Here Voigt answered some of the criticisms that Wieland's *Der deutsche Merkur* had expressed in a review of the first volume. The reviewer felt that Voigt had been betrayed by his excessive love for his fatherland into exaggerating the achievements of his fellow countrymen. "I will never deny this love for my fatherland," replied Voigt; "but will rather be very proud of it." He insisted that it was historical fact that the Czechs were the first among the Central European nations to cultivate learning. He conceded that he had "in common with many of our greatest and most distinguished patriots the fact that I lament the present-day neglect our Czech mother tongue"; but he denied that he had ever attacked the efforts of those who worked for the further refinement of German—after all, he, too, wrote in German. The *Deutscher Merkur* may claim that the Czechs could have no place on Parnassus unless they first hired a German teacher for tuition in the language; but this was ridiculous. Would the author then deny the English, French, Italians, and other nations a seat among the Muses? "It seems to me," concluded Voigt, "that each nation has its own place on Parnassus; and Apollo and the Muses understand every language."

Voigt's concept of Czech literary history as expressed in these two introductions was quite broad; but his organization of the material by subject, and the necessarily rather superficial treatment of the scholars whose biographies were included, prevented him from creating a truly synthetic study of literary history. Although Voigt's biographies did represent an advance over the works of his predecessors, they tended to be mechanical and stereotyped. First they presented the external facts of the life of their subjects, as far as they could be ascertained, and then a bibliography of their works. In the bibliographies (in an improvement over the practice of Balbín and others) the titles were given exactly and in the original language.[6]

Voigt's approach, influenced by Gelasius Dobner, was also more critical than his predecessors'. In writing of Hájek z Libočan, Voigt took Dobner's position on the veracity of his famous chronicle, and when he granted Bohuslav Balbín the title of the "Czech Pliny" he noted that, like the Roman one, Balbín "allowed himself to be led by an all-too-great gullibility to include matters that, when one tests them according to natural law or the rules of healthy criticism, do not even have the appearance of probability."[7] Unlike Balbín or Koniáš, Voigt did not make religious orthodoxy the most important condition for accepting a writer into Czech literary history. As a Catholic, and in holy orders, he rejected the teachings of the Hussites or other Protestants; but, as he wrote in his biography of Hus: "What right have we to expel from the number of our native scholars a man who truly possessed understanding and learning, only because he misused his capabilities and learning, mixed truth with falsehood, and finally fell completely into error?—an error that he shares with many scholars of every century."[8] Voigt also included several Jewish men of letters among his biographies, noting that "tolerance must be observed in the Republic of Learning even more than in any other public institution."[9]

Shortly after Voigt's *Effigies-Abbildungen* began to appear, two separate editions of his great model, Balbín's *Bohemia docta,* began publication. Thus nearly a century after it was first written, this influential work finally saw the light of day. This is testimony not only to the opinion of contemporaries about the usefulness of the biographical and bibliographical approach to literary history, but also to the respect they had for Balbín as one of their great intellectual ancestors. Both editions, one undertaken by the monk P. Candidus a Sancta Theresia and the other by Karl Raphael Ungar, were carried out in the spirit of critical history. The editors accompanied Balbín's text with extensive footnotes and critical commentary. Ungar published the first part of Balbín's work in 1776; but Candidus did not include this section, beginning his edition with Balbín's section on Czech writers in 1777 and following it in the same year with his section on libraries and archives. Ungar's versions of these two sections were published in 1778 and 1780, respectively. Their application of the critical Maurist methods was clearly an emulation of Dobner's great work, *Wenceslai Hagek a Libočan ... Annales Bohemorum,* and at the same time they made more widely available an important source for Czech literary history, increasing its value to other scholars through their notes and commentary.[10]

The publication of Balbín's *Bohemia docta* was enlivened by a scholarly polemic in which Josef Dobrovský made his first full-fledged appearance on the Prague literary scene. The *Prager Intelligenzblatt* published a laudatory review of Ungar's edition in 1778, and Dobrovský objected to certain slighting comments about Candidus. He sent an anonymous letter to the editors and to Ungar listing some of the mistakes he had found in Ungar's edition. He later identified himself to Ungar as the author of the letter and published his own criticisms in a volume entitled *Corrigenda in Bohemia docta juxta editionem P. Raph. Ungar* (1779). Particularly incensed by these comments, Ungar replied in a vitriolic letter to Dobrovský, and later in the form of a similar critique of one of Dobrovský's publications, the literary periodical *Böhmische Litteratur auf das Jahr 1779* (to be discussed later).[11] Dobrovský was to regret this quarrel, and relations between the two eventually improved to the point that Ungar and Dobrovský even collaborated on later projects.[12]

The historian and philologist, František Martin Pelcl, whom we have seen as a collaborator with Born and Voigt in the *Effigies-Abbildungen,* also published a similar work of his own in 1786, entitled *Böhmische, Mährische, und Schlesische Gelehrte und Schriftsteller aus dem Orden der Jesuiten.* Pelcl set out to write a study of the literary activities of the order, since it had enjoyed a practical monopoly on cultural activities in Bohemia for some time after the White Mountain. In fact, Pelcl called for studies of the activities of other orders, too. Methodologically, his work on the Jesuits did not represent any real advance over Voigt's *Effigies-Abbildungen.* Pelcl organized his biographies chronologically, according to birthdate, but since he included any member of the Jesuits, no matter what his origin, he included much material with little connection to the history of Czech literature. The biographies were similar to those in the *Effigies*; however, Pelcl's approach also reflected his belief in the critical method, in that he did not merely rely for his data on previous authorities, but himself searched the libraries at the Clementinum and at Strahov, where he found much new information that enabled him to correct errors in previous works.[13]

Another scholar who wrote *Gelehrtengeschichte* was Bohumír Jan Dlabač (1758–1830), who gathered material on musicians in Bohemia that later formed the basis of an article in Riegger's *Materialen zur alten und neuen Statistik von Böhmen* (vol. 7, 1788, and vol. 12, 1794), entitled "Versuch eines Verzeichnisses der vorzüglichern Tonkünstler in oder aus Böhmen."[14] These biographies formed a sort of preparatory exercise for Dlabač's great *Allgemeines historisches Künstlerlexikon für Böhmen und zum Theil auch für Mähren und Schlesien* (3 vols., 1815–1818). In these volumes, Dlabač widened his field of study to include artists and musicians as well as purely literary figures, and they represented the fruits of nearly thirty years of work assembling data and editing the biographies.[15] In the foreword to this encyclopedia, Dlabač harked back specifically to Balbín's example in his *Bohemia docta,* saying that he wanted to do for Czech fine artists what Balbín had done for Czech writers. Although his biographies could be faulted for the familiar failings they share with Voigt's and Pelcl's, Dlabač broke new ground by going beyond the written word. Thus he approached a broader understanding of the Czech cultural heritage and presented a model of a functioning "high" culture to the ambitious patriots who were setting out to attempt to create (or re-create) one in Czech.

The Specialized Study

In addition to biographical dictionaries, late eighteenth-century scholars also produced a great number of specialized studies in various forms, among the earliest of which was Voigt's *Acta litteraria Bohemiae et Moraviae* (2 vols., 1774–

1783). Voigt disclaimed any intention of setting this work up as an equal of any of his predecessors' famous efforts; he only wanted to repudiate the unjust reproach of some foreigners that the Czechs were barbaric and ignorant, while at the same time spreading the knowledge of literary matters in his fatherland among his fellow countrymen.[16] To this end, Voigt directed his attention not only to the monuments of Czech literature, but also to the contemporary literary production of Bohemia. *Acta litteraria* also included reviews and descriptions of earlier works (whether in Czech, German, or Latin, as long as they had some connection with Bohemia and Moravia), often reprinting long excerpts. Voigt also published additional biographies as a supplement to his *Effigies,* but the main contribution of the *Acta litteraria* remained its publicity for contemporary literature among the intellectuals.[17]

Following Voigt's example, Dobrovský tried his hand at the form of the literary periodical, though he chose to publish in German.[18] His efforts along these lines were the journals *Böhmische Litteratur auf das Jahr 1779* (1779), continued as *Böhmische und Mährische Litteratur auf das Jahr 1780* (1780–1784), and finally as *Litterarisches Magazin von Böhmen und Mähren* (3 vols., 1785–1787), which covered the state of literature in Bohemia and Moravia from 1781 to 1783. As Voigt had begun, so Dobrovský aimed to go on, devoting attention to contemporary literature so as to present a picture of the state of literature in Bohemia "the way it is."[19] To the supposed objection that this task was already fulfilled by such periodicals as *Das Gelehrte Österreich,* published in Vienna, Dobrovský retorted that "one looks for Czechs [Böhmen] in 'Learned Austria' as little as one would look for Englishmen in 'Learned Hannover.'"[20] The commitment to focus on contemporary literature in Bohemia was not intended to be a limitation, however, and Dobrovský's journals ranged widely over all periods of Czech literary history, frequently discussing questions outside the bounds of a strictly interpreted literary history altogether.

A look at the topics covered in his periodicals shows something of the breadth and depth of Dobrovský's concept of literary history and of his personal literary interests. The universities in Prague and Brno gave him a topic for the opening section of his *Böhmische Litteratur,* and he printed the official programs of lectures, lists of the professors and their works, and eventually even brief histories of both institutions. He continued to follow the fortunes of the universities in his *Litterarisches Magazin* up until 1783, when the university in Brno was moved back to Olomouc as a lyceum.

Although the universities occupied (in theory) the highest position in the world of learning in Bohemia, Dobrovský was perfectly willing to exercise his talent for irony or sarcasm when it came to what he felt were the medieval attitudes surviving in them.[21] Nor did he have any time for vain pedantry or stupidity. In one comment he poured scorn on an unnamed professor who "praised the accuracy of translations to his pupils, in order to demonstrate that Hebrew and Greek could be dispensed with, or more probably to excuse thus his own ignorance of them."[22] This critical and sarcastic approach did not necessarily win him friends; and the particular comment about this professor was to add to his troubles with these journals.

Besides giving information about the universities, Dobrovský discussed the libraries of Bohemia and Moravia, thus deviating somewhat further from the intention of studying only contemporary topics, since he wanted to provide bibliographical information about their holdings of rare and valuable Czech manuscripts and books. He began with the Clementinum and the Metropolitan libraries in Prague, then described the university library in Brno (formed from the former Jesuit library in Olomouc, to which had been added holdings from other Jesuit libraries throughout the province), and concluded with notes on other libraries belonging to religious institutions in Bohemia.

In a separate section Dobrovský brought to his readers' notice particularly rare Czech printed books, mostly from the fifteenth century, in an attempt to correct the mistakes of earlier works on Czech literature that neglected Czech printing in that period. For Dobrovský, the history of book printing was so closely bound up with literary history in general that this bibliophile approach was for him an important and fruitful part of Czech literary history.[23] Indeed, this bibliographical aspect of Dobrovský's work was an important contribution to the study of the Czech literary heritage, and not without its connection to the present. While the supposed reputation of Czech as a language of culture was low, identifying and publicizing surviving examples of early Czech books and manuscripts supported a different interpretation and was an essential prelude to attempts to depict the history of Czech culture in a more synthetic way.

Dobrovský did also fulfill his promise to devote attention to contemporary literature in his journals. Each number was to list all the books published in Bohemia and Moravia in that year, and they also included books published abroad that were either printed in Czech or dealt with topics concerning Bohemia and Moravia. Most of these books were published in German, with Latin second and Czech a distant third. Almost all the Czech books Dobrovský listed were popular religious instruction manuals, in the first issues only Catholic, and then, as the Patent of Toleration (1781) and the new censorship regulations took effect, prevailingly Protestant in orientation. Frequently, these books included reprintings of Protestant works of the sixteenth or seventeenth centuries, so they could also have been of some interest from a literary-historical point of view.

Generally, Dobrovský kept his own opinions to himself, listing merely author, title, publisher, and sometimes a brief summary of the content. When he did discuss a Czech book at greater length, Dobrovský usually focused on the language. As we have seen, he made use of his periodicals to attack the purist approach and unscientific neologisms of Pohl and Ši-mek, and also to criticize Zlobický's translations. In addition to criticism, however, Dobrovský sometimes handed out praise. One modern writer whose work Dobrovský esteemed was Václav Matěj Kramerius, who had "the special merit that he keeps very closely to the Czech literary language as it appears in the best writers of the sixteenth century, the golden age of our mother tongue."[24]

Although he did approve of Kramerius (notably because he kept to the classical standard of Czech humanism), Dobrovský's general opinion of the condition of literature in Bohemia was not high. "When one compares more recent book production, I mean that of the eighteenth century, with that of the fifteenth and sixteenth centuries," he wrote, "it becomes obvious that the art of printing in Moravia as well as Bohemia has not risen at all, but rather noticeably fallen."[25] Thus through his literary-historical periodicals, as well as his more strictly philological works, Dobrovský strove to maintain the authority of the sixteenth century in Czech literature. In this way, he presented his readers with a potent myth of a high culture now in decline, which acted as a powerful motivating force to patriotic efforts of the intelligentsia such as the defenses of the language or the efforts to create modern Czech works of the same level as the classics.

Dobrovský's other journals were occupied with more occasional subjects, as material came his way. These included numismatics, art history (in a contribution by the Prague professor Franz Lothar Ehemant), additions to *Gelehrtengeschichte*, new discoveries, and even a section of books for sale or wanted by buyers. In the later version, the *Litterarisches Magazin*, Dobrovský introduced material on historiography, archaeology, Czech grammar, and Slavic ethnography. He also began a "library" of Czech manuscripts to supplement his information about printed books. Eventually he hoped to publish a complete catalogue of all Czech manuscripts written before the introduction of printing, as well as later ones if they were exceptionally important. This scheme produced only limited fruit, however, in the form of a catalogue of Czech manuscript Bibles published in the *Litterarisches Magazin* in 1786.[26]

As the publishing history of these journals (outlined

earlier) suggests, Dobrovský's efforts to establish literary-historical periodicals did not proceed entirely smoothly. He was first plagued by a bitter polemic with Ungar, sparked off by Dobrovský's criticisms of the edition of *Bohemia docta* and then by problems with the censor. In fact, he noted that a similar fate had overtaken all the previous attempts to create a stable literary periodical, so that such forerunners as *Neue Litteratur, Prager gelehrte Nachrichten,* and Voigt's *Acta litteraria,* as well as his own efforts, had all died after one or at most two years:

> Sometimes it was the poor worth of one or another work itself, sometimes the complacency or lack of talent of the author; sometimes the injured vanity of a professor, a scholar, or even only a printer, who wanted to revenge himself and took refuge in chicanery, sometimes the anxiety of an all-too-strict censor, who had so many reservations about leaving this or that passage in that he must have made the writer tired and despondent of necessity; sometimes also difficulties on the side of the publisher that could not be cleared away immediately; there were many similar causes that hindered and stifled the success of the above undertakings.[27]

In Dobrovský's own case, the difficulties were partly of his own making. When *Böhmische Litteratur auf das Jahr 1779* appeared, Ungar seized the chance to get some of his own back for Dobrovský's *Corrigenda in Bohemia docta.* He published an anonymous pamphlet entitled *Revision der böhmischen Litteratur . . . in Briefen,* which he followed in 1780 with a second installment, and finally with *Beschluss der Revision der böhmischen Litteratur* in the same year. These works were written in the form of letters to the editor of Dobrovský's periodical (that is, Dobrovský himself), and they attacked him for setting himself up as the dictator of Czech literature. The tone of the pamphlets, frequently parodying the style of Dobrovský's own works, was savagely ironic and immoderate, sometimes descending to the level of personal insinuations and insults. Dobrovský replied to Ungar's attacks in his brief *Antwort auf die Revision der böhmischen Litteratur* (1780), this time in a calm, restrained, and polite style. The effect of this moderate response, as well as the success with which Dobrovský countered the material criticisms in Ungar's pamphlet, created such a positive impression that Dobrovský could practically ignore the second and third parts of the *Revision*. He dismissed them briefly in his *Böhmische und Mährische Litteratur* as not worthy of a response, concluding: "I congratulate my reviewer from the heart on his glorious victory."[28] After this the conflict between the two seems to have burned itself out, and Ungar helped Dobrovský in his project to catalogue Czech manuscripts.

The gradual reconciliation with Ungar did not mean the end of Dobrovský's troubles, however. Several other scholars felt themselves affected by the comments in Dobrovský's periodicals, including Dobner, Voigt, and several higher university officials. When he published the second part of *Böhmische Litteratur* for 1779, Dobrovský noted that many people had taken his work "in such aversion that they attempted to defame it and probably even suppress it, in a way not becoming to a true scholar."[29] Although the appearance of the second part proved that these attempt were in vain, further difficulties from a new quarter were to plague Dobrovský's publication.

A certain Ferdinand Voldřich, the professor whose ignorance of Greek and Hebrew had drawn Dobrovský's scorn, complained to the archiepiscopal consistory that he had been wrongfully insulted. Dobrovský was called before the consistory to explain himself in 1780, but no resolution was taken. Some time later, a court decree pointed out that such a case, which involved the honor of the official censor, was not a matter for the consistory, and Dobrovský wrote, "Now, I believe, Professor Voldřich will finally pipe down. If he had held his peace, no one would have known that he was the one who said it."[30]

Whether or not Voldřich gave up at this time we do not know, but the affair was not yet over. According to Pelcl's manuscript chronicle of the 1780s, on 7 February 1781 Dobrovský was called before the censorship and study commission and ordered to make a public apology to Voldřich for his comments. Dobrovský refused, on the technical grounds that the commission was not empowered to dictate punishments and because he could produce witnesses to his version of the offending statements. Nevertheless, on 30 July 1781 a court decree was issued according to which Dobrovský had to retract his comments in the next installment of *Böhmische Litteratur* because "he could not prove it." Thus, Pelcl noted, the chairman of the censorship commission in Prague, Count Věžník, must have sent a false account to Vienna, since Dobrovský had brought forward four reliable witnesses. "I doubt whether Dobrovský will retract," he concluded, "since he would have to declare his witnesses to be false, which he cannot do. Unhappy land, when the highest offices (*praesidia*) are entrusted to such people: vengeful, unjust, vain pedants!"[31]

Dobrovský did not, in fact, retract, and thus the publication of the third installment of *Böhmische und Mährische Litteratur* for 1780 was forbidden by the censor, and it did not appear until after Joseph II's revision of the censorship regulations. At one time, Dobrovský was ready to give up the project of the journals altogether, but the representations of his friends encouraged him to take it up again, with the result not only of the completion of the 1780 volume of *Böhmische und Mährische Litteratur,* but its continuation as *Litterarisches Magazin* for three more years. The third volume of the Magazin was the last, partly because Dobrovský left Prague to take up the duties of vice-rector of the General Seminary at Olomouc, and partly because the journals were losing money.[32]

The demise of his literary-historical periodicals did not, however, mean an end to Dobrovský's interest in Czech literature. Several of the individual studies he published in the *Abhandlungen* of the Society of Sciences were basically additions to or corrections of material first included in his periodicals. Besides this, the *Abhandlungen* published a first version of his monumental *Geschichte der böhmischen Sprache und Litteratur* (discussed more fully later) in 1791, as well as his "Litterarische Nachrichten von einer . . . Reise nach Schweden und Russland" in 1795. Dobrovský's two Slavistic collections, *Slavín* (1806) and *Slovanka* (1814–1815), also contain some material on Czech literature (see chapter 6).

Another scholar who was interested in Czech literary history was František Faustyn Procházka (1749–1809). He began to collect material for a library of Bohemian and Moravian literature in 1771, but for several reasons, notably his involvement with the Czech translation of the Bible together with Václav Fortunat Durych, the project was never realized. He used some of this material, however, when he published *Miscellaneen der Böhmischen und Mährischen Litteratur,* intended as a contribution to filling in the gaps in already published collections on Czech literary history. Procházka's *Miscellaneen* strongly reflected his interest in the works of the sixteenth-century humanists, with whom he shared some of the same concerns and goals. Thus most of the space in the three parts of the *Miscellaneen,* which appeared in 1784 and 1785, was devoted to literary topics from the fifteenth and sixteenth centuries. The nature of these offerings was highly varied, including biographies of literary figures, reports of monuments of literature, published or manuscript, and other material on important intellectual movements and general cultural conditions. Procházka's biographies were more well rounded than those in the *Effigies-Abbildungen,* following the entire development of an author, including influences from family and school, and generally presenting a fuller and more lifelike picture.

The literary production of the eighteenth century also received some attention in the *Miscellaneen,* especially in the long article in part two entitled "Critische Nachrichten von den bisherigen Producten der Pressfreiheit in Böhmen." This article also reflected Procházka's adherence to Enlightenment ideals, though with more restraint than the most enthusiastic Josephinists. Especially in a section dealing with Joseph's reforms of the monasteries, Procházka carefully expressed his reservations and criticisms: "I am no great supporter of the monastic institutions, although I myself committed the youthful folly of becoming a monk. But I am no friend either of those who take pleasure in hurting humanity, even if it might be hidden in a Capuchin's cowl."[33]

Most of the literary production immediately following the relaxation of censorship, Procházka felt, was decidedly poor, a fact that could be partially explained by the sudden widening of the field of possibilities open to a would-be author. He considered with satisfaction, however, that this early period of abuse of the freedom of the press was drawing to a close. Too much of what had been published was written in a tendentious or prejudiced manner, but "we want sources, critical judgments, and impartiality."[34]

Yet whatever reservations Procházka may have had about the effects of freedom of the press in Bohemia in general, in one area at least he welcomed it without question. This was in his work on a new Czech translation of the Bible. Already in 1778 Procházka and his colleague and collaborator, Durych, had published a newly translated Czech New Testament, followed by the complete Bible in 1780. Now, however, Procházka wanted to take advantage of the relaxed censorship restrictions to revise the New Testament portion of their work. If this revised version were to be well received, he wrote, it would be thanks to the fact that his intellect had been freed from its restrictions, "although there are still people . . . who quite dictatorially want to force our reason back into its former dark cell."[35] His involvement with the Czech Bible, however, seriously hampered the publication of the second and third parts of the *Miscellaneen,* as he confessed in their forewords, and eventually Procházka was forced to give it up altogether. Thus his work did not establish itself as a periodical journal either, and remained a collection of individual studies and materials.

Besides his edition of *Bohemia docta,* Ungar published several individual studies on literary-historical themes, often in the *Abhandlungen.* His planned life's work, however, remained only a torso. He intended to produce a systematic bibliography of all books published in the Czech language from the beginning of printing to his own day, under the title *Allgemeine böhmische Bibliothek.* Unfortunately, Ungar was able to publish only the first installment of this bibliography, which covered Czech translations of all or part of the Bible. He accompanied this with a general foreword in which he justified his undertaking and quite bluntly lamented the previous policies of the Counter-Reformation church and state toward Czech culture. "The cause of the extraordinary scarcity of Czech books," he stated, "is the literary tyranny with which the pious literary shock troops (*Bücherstürmer*) burned them or otherwise destroyed them, or at least rendered them practically unusable by stroking through entire passages with Chinese ink." The infamous Index had even included perfectly innocent books by Catholic authors, proscribed only because they were published in Czech.[36] Ungar expressed warm support for the reform policies of Joseph II, and as librarian at the Clementinum benefited from the transfer of books from some of the monastic libraries to the central institution.

Dlabač, another librarian, also produced several shorter studies on aspects of Czech cultural and literary history. In 1792 he published his *Miszellen für Böhmen* in three parts, the first two of which also appeared under the title *Berichtigung einiger historischen Daten für Böhmen.* In the three short studies that made up the *Miszellen,* Dlabač pointed out the value of inscriptions on bells to a history of the written language, investigated whether Albrecht Dürer had ever painted anything for the Czech king Václav IV, and added to the genre of *Gelehrtengeschichte* with a biography of Matthaus Meissner, including a bibliography of his works based on manuscript materials Dlabač had discovered in the Strahov library. An article in the *Abhandlungen* on the arts in Bohemia and an essay on the history of Czech newspapers rounded out his published offerings and underlined his abiding interest in Czech culture in the wider sense.[37]

Synthetic Studies of Czech Literary History

The individual studies discussed above, while they made important contributions to the understanding of Czech literary history, were by their nature isolated and could not give a general picture of the development of Czech literary culture. Even the collections of biographies did not provide a systematic review of the development of Czech literature, though Voigt's introduction to the *Effigies-Abbildungen* was intended to survey the flowering and fate of the arts and sciences in Bohemia. Voigt, like Balbín before him, organized his discussion according to topics, so that within each topic he was able to provide a general summary of developments; but this meant that a complete, coherent picture was lacking.

It was Procházka who first produced a more successful attempt at a synthetic treatment of Czech literary history in his *De saecularibus liberalium artium in Bohemia et Moravia fatis commentarius* (1784). One of its most important innovations was in its strict chronological organization, which Procházka felt would allow his readers to grasp the entire development of Czech literature over time, understanding the causes of the current state of affairs through what had gone before.[38] After an opening section on the ancient Slavs, which was characterized by a more restrained and less idealized picture than that presented by Voigt or Pelcl in their historical works, Procházka discussed the development of Czech literature century by century. His conception of what should be included was broad, and he prefaced each chapter with an introductory study of general cultural trends in the century under discussion, including the influence of outside events on literature. Thus Procházka firmly placed literary affairs into the context of general historical developments.[39]

This broad approach, coupled with the fact that Procházka included all works that appeared in Bohemia or were written by Bohemian authors, whatever their language, forced him to keep to the general and even superficial in his discussions. In his basic attitudes to the various centuries of Czech literary history, Procházka reflected his own reservations about the Czech Reformation and his preference for the humanists of the late fifteenth and sixteenth centuries. In writing of this period, Procházka emphasized that at that time Bohemia did not have to take second place to any country in Europe with regard to its poets and learned men.[40] Although his love for the humanists, especially their elegant Latin poetry, led him to devote much space to aspects of literature that may not have had a great influence on the Czech language or the development of a specifically Czech literature, when it came to other centuries, especially his own eighteenth, Procházka's account was more detailed and important that those of his predecessors or even some of his successors.

Its various drawbacks, and above all the language in which he wrote it, limited the appeal of Procházka's *Commentarius* to the highest levels of educated society; and in many ways it was obsolete even as it was being published. By comparison, the other great synthetic treatment of the history of Czech literature, Josef Dobrovský's *Geschichte der Böhmischen Sprache und Litteratur,* represented in almost every respect a significant advance.[41] The first version of this work appeared in the *Abhandlungen* in 1791 under the title "Geschichte der Böhmischen Sprache." Even this title alone highlighted one of the most important new developments in Dobrovský's conception of his subject, namely that he saw his work as a history of the Czech language. The article was published in an expanded form in 1792 as *Geschichte der Böhmischen Sprache und Litteratur.* In 1818 it appeared yet again in a completely revised and expanded edition entitled *Geschichte der Böhmischen Sprache und ältern Litteratur,* which in spite of its increased length only brought the history of Czech literature down to 1526.

Dobrovský's *Geschichte* was originally intended to be part of his Czech grammar, which he had been preparing for some time. When it became evident, however, that the grammar would not be published in the near future, Dobrovský considered using his historical material as a foreword to Tomsa's trilingual Czech-German-Latin dictionary of 1791.[42] The idea of publishing it in the *Abhandlungen* seems to have come from Pelcl, who wrote to Dobrovský on 1 April 1790: "I have read your history of the Czech language with much enjoyment. It is set up in such a way that, with the exception of the last paragraph, it could be included in our Acta [the *Abhandlungen*] as it stands." Six weeks later, he confirmed to Dobrovský that the article was already in the press.[43] For reasons of space Dobrovský was forced to condense his material for the *Abhandlungen,* mainly by leaving out many of the textual examples that reappeared in the book-length edition of 1792.

In organizing the material for his *Geschichte*, Dobrovský seems to have followed the model of the German philologist Adelung, who had included a concise history of the German language in his grammar. Like Adelung, Dobrovský began his discussion with the prehistory of the nation, placed the development of the different Slavic dialects into the earliest period, as Adelung had done with the German dialects, and followed Adelung's concepts of important influences on the language, such as the acceptance of Christianity, development of urban centers and trading, the importance of the Hussites and the Reformation, and others.[44]

After six sections dealing with the ancient Slavs, their language, dialects, alphabets, and the history of the Slavic liturgy and its fate in Bohemia, Dobrovský then discussed the history of Czech itself, which he divided into six periods. The first period began with the arrival of the Czechs in Bohemia and lasted until the acceptance of Christianity; the second was from the spread of Christianity to the reign of Jan of Luxemburg; the third from thence to Jan Hus or the death of King Václav IV; the fourth, "which can be called the ruling Czech period," from Hus to the spread of printing in Bohemia or to the time of Ferdinand I; the fifth, "the beautiful or golden age," from 1520 to the Battle of the White Mountain

(1620); and the sixth and last, "in which the Czech language goes into a decline," from the expulsion of the Protestants to Dobrovský's own day.[45] Thus unlike Procházka's rather mechanical chronological division of his material century by century, Dobrovský's periodization is based on internal developments in Czech cultural history. He usually began each section with a passage characterizing the general cultural developments of the period, although he devoted less attention to these themes than Procházka did in the *Commentarius*. Then he discussed the linguistic developments of the time, with examples from the most important literary monuments of each period. This was another very significant contribution. Much of the material Dobrovský discussed was presented for the first time in print, with the greatest number of citations falling in the fourth, or "ruling Czech" period, especially in the field of religious writings.[46]

Some modern Czech scholars have interpreted Dobrovský's *Geschichte der Böhmische Sprache und Litteratur* as a conscious act of national patriotism, intended as support for the developing Czech national consciousness by presenting the past glories of the Czech language. Others argue that this is a misinterpretation of the *Geschichte* and Dobrovský's own position in the *obrození*.[47] Certainly Dobrovský did not write for the broader, Czech-speaking masses, who would not have been able to read his history since it was in German. More than that, it was a scholarly work throughout, free from tendentious expressions of patriotism. For example, Dobrovský rejected the idea that the Slavic liturgy and alphabet could ever have been widespread in Bohemia, since the country owed its conversion to German priests of the Latin rite.[48] When discussing the influence of Germans and other foreigners under the last of the Přemyslids and the Luxemburgers, Dobrovský remained the recorder of facts and did not often express any judgments. In fact, he wrote that the example of the Germans' higher culture was important in spurring the Czechs on to emulation.[49] He did not praise the chronicle of the so-called Dalimil, which contained many anti-German passages, writing merely that "it exudes entirely the spirit of the Czechs of that time," and later saying that Dalimil "is not ashamed of many a gross falsehood."[50]

Since his interest was primarily linguistic and historical rather than religious, Dobrovský did not exclude Hus and his followers from their rightful place in the history of Czech literature; but the religious fanaticism of the period was distasteful to him. Of the Taborite song "Kdož jste Boži bojovníci" (All ye warriors of God), he wrote: "It is fully imbued with their enthusiastic, warlike, i.e., cruel spirit: *bíte, zabíte, žádného neživte*" (Strike them, slay them, leave none alive).[51] By the same token, however, Dobrovský the literary historian sharply criticized the book burning carried on by the Jesuits and others after the White Mountain, emphasizing the disastrous consequences for Czech culture of the expulsion of the non-Catholics and the general devastation of the Thirty Years' War. "What would Balbín, whose *Dissertatio apologetica* . . . showed him to be a true Czech patriot who valued his mother tongue, have said of the mischief his brother Jesuits carried out with Czech books soon after his death?" asked Dobrovský.[52]

In the section dealing with the eighteenth century, which he had defined as a period of decline, Dobrovský pointed out the consequences for Czech of the school reforms that favored German and placed the student who knew only Czech at a distinct disadvantage. Even though Dobrovský did not agree with this policy,[53] he nevertheless limited himself to pointing out that with time the numbers of educated bilingual or Czech-speaking candidates for official positions in Czech areas would constantly decline. He was quite pessimistic about the future of Czech, even after chronicling the publications of some of the patriotic enthusiasts: "Whether now through all these new encouragements, efforts, institutions, and expressions of sympathy by a number of patriotically minded Czechs, the Czech language can raise itself to a noticeably higher level of perfection than the one it had in its golden age under Maximilian and Rudolph II, I will leave to the future to decide, since it depends on so many circumstances over which we have no control."[54] A somewhat more defiant and optimistic note was struck in the 1792 version of the *Geschichte* by a final epigraph in the form of a poem by František Knobloch, "Výstraha na hánce jazyka českého." In this word of warning to the slanderers of the language, the poet lamented the condition of Czech, shut out of all learning in favor of German, insisting:

> Teuton! Dear is your tongue to me,
> but never more so than my own Czech;
> in its homeland, come what may,
> it should still have its rightful place.[55]

A concluding verse stressed again the familiar assertion that Czech was as capable of use for all literary genres as any other language.

Perhaps Dobrovský included this poem as a sort of final motto, to give a more clearly patriotic tone to a work that was essentially scholarly. Certainly the attitudes expressed in Knobloch's poem were in keeping with the general revival of interest in Czech at the time, which also led to the establishment of a chair of Czech at the Prague university in 1793. Yet such a tone was generally foreign to Dobrovský's concept of scientific scholarly work, which should be concerned only with the facts. "My main aim," he wrote on another occasion, "is to speak the truth fearlessly, the simple, naked, unadorned truth."[56] To say that Dobrovský did not intend his *Geschichte der Böhmischen Sprache und Litteratur* to be a patriotic tract appealing to a wide audience is not, however, to detract from its importance to the *obrození* or to deny Dobrovský's own patriotism. An excellent characterization of both comes from Benjamin Jedlička:

> This purely scholarly character of Dobrovský's *Geschichte*
> ... does not place Dobrovský in any sort of *isolated* position in the national revival. ... The revival period had a relative sufficiency of Tháms, Melezíneks, Věks, Krameriuses, and even Voigts, but only one Dobrovský. Do-

brovský ... could not waste himself on minor awakening
works, especially when others, lesser perhaps in talent and
importance, carried out this task well and actively; in the
same way he could not take into his works expressions of
patriotic propaganda, if he wanted to maintain and preserve their scientific line pure and undisturbed. In this recognition of where his proper place in the revival efforts lay,
and in the energy with which he drew the consequences
from it, lies the most admirable trait of Dobrovský's work.
Dobrovský's importance to the awakening is in his service
to pure science, which revived the present and gave a foundation and model to the distant future. . . . Dobrovský
served his fatherland through science.[57]

The Preservation of Czech's Literary Monuments

The scholarly studies of Czech literary history just discussed
were still written in Latin or German, and thus remained
without any greater influence among the broad, Czech-
speaking masses, however much they may have encouraged
the educated Czech patriots.[58] More important was another
aspect of the interest in the Czech literary past, namely collecting, editing, and reprinting the monuments of classical
Czech literature. In a way, this was part of the generally increased interest in the publication of original sources that
stemmed from the newer historical methods, and it offered
bibliophiles a logical next step from their passion for collecting old manuscripts and books. These collectors aided scholars
working on Czech literary history by organizing, concentrating, and even rescuing from oblivion many important works.
Among the leading collectors of the early revival period were
Dobrovský's friends Zlobický, Ribay, J. P. Cerroni, and above
all Johann Franz Ritter von Neuberg.[59]

    Neuberg was not only a leading collector, but also the
center of a circle of scholars and patriots who shared his interest in Czech literature, and he thus provided a place where
mutual encouragement and the exchange of ideas could oc-
cur. Pelcl, Dobrovský, Procházka, Tomsa, and Kramerius frequently took part in these informal gatherings, and it was

surely no accident that these men were later so active in working for the revival of Czech literature. Neuberg avidly collected old coins, paintings, engravings, and especially manuscripts and books; and, in an effort to ensure that both of his sons could inherit copies of his treasures, he tirelessly copied manuscripts and had old books reprinted on his own private press. His special interest was Czech grammar, and he had several early grammars reprinted at his expense for distribution among his friends. Among these were the anonymous *Prima principia linguae bohemicae,* published in Prague before 1679, Jakub Tinčín's *Principia linguae Venedicae* (1679), and Veleslavín's 1614 edition of *Pauli Czernoviceni Vocabularium Rythmo bohemicum.* Neuberg was preparing an edition of Masnicia's *Zprávy písma slovenského* (1609), but this was unfinished at the time of his death in 1784.[60] He was deeply mourned by those scholars whose interests he had supported. Dobrovský noted in an obituary in *Litterarisches Magazin* that the passing of Neuberg meant a great loss to Czech literature and other such subjects, and to Dobrovský personally, who had spent "many fruitful and pleasant hours at his bedside" and been "heartened and encouraged" by his support.[61] "I miss him greatly," wrote Dobrovský to his friend Ribay in 1785; "I do not now know any other nobleman so favorably inclined to the Czech language."[62]

Perhaps it was in Neuberg's salon that Pelcl arrived at the idea of publishing a series of older Czech works in order to preserve the high standards of written Czech and protect it from the neologisms of Pohl and his ilk. In 1777 he published the *Příhody Václava Vratislava z Mitrovic,* an account, dating from 1599, of a Czech nobleman's experiences in the Ottoman Empire's capital and its dungeons. Pelcl accompanied the *Příhody* with a defensive foreword in which he praised earlier Czech writers and attacked the Jesuits for their destructive zeal—such that "it is a wonder that here and there a Czech book still turns up!"[63] Writing and publishing in Czech had not altogether died out, he noted ironically, since the surrounding territories where Protestant literature in

Czech was produced brought out more Czech books in a year than were published within Bohemia over many years. Pelcl's enthusiasm for the classical literature of the Czech humanists, and perhaps his aversion to the prevailing Counter-Reformation culture, led him here to a rhetorical exaggeration sometimes echoed by others. The Protestant "literature" to which he refers was almost exclusively religious pamphlets and tracts produced in Protestant Germany and smuggled into Bohemia until Joseph II's Toleration Patent (1781) made it again legal for Protestant devotional material to enter the kingdom. As literature, however, these works were hardly different from the Catholic devotional books that continued to be printed in Bohemia. In any case, much of what was now being produced, whether Protestant or Catholic, was marked by degenerate language, so it seemed to Pelcl that "it would be better to publish the works of our ancestors, rather than to print new ones (for we truly do not know how to write like they did) . . . in the hope that thus our language will regain its glory."

Another step to regained glory for Czech would be for the highest levels of society to use it among themselves, so Pelcl also directed his foreword to encouraging the Bohemian nobility to take up Czech. He referred to the patronage given the language by such exalted figures as Charles IV, Jiří z Poděbrad's son Hynek, Lev z Rožmítalu, or Bohuslav Hasištejnský z Lobkovic, and claimed that in his own day there was "a great number of Czech lords and nobles who are lovers and protectors of their language." This last assertion may well have reflected wishful thinking; at any rate, the *Příhody Václava Vratislava z Mitrovic* remained Pelcl's only foray into the field of reprinting old Czech masterpieces.

Nearly ten years after Pelcl's isolated effort, Procházka announced an ambitious program of publications from among the monuments of Czech literature that took up where Pelcl had left off. The broadsheet announcing the series gave the reasons behind it:

The great lack of Czech books among the people; the love of reading which is practically general among them, and inherited as it were from our ancestors of bygone days, who were almost all of them men of learning; sympathy with the excellent Czech authors who, robbed by lack of readers from a return on their strenuous labors and the enjoyment of fame, flounder in the dust of libraries and bookshops; these and other reasons led me to collect the best Czech books of our learned ancestors, whether published or in manuscript, and thus repair the damage caused in part by the ravages of time, in part by the ignorant zeal of the former missionaries in Bohemia and Moravia.[64]

These works were to appear in four simultaneously appearing series, the first devoted to Czech chronicles and histories, from Dalimil to Beckovský; the second to histories and other works about foreign countries; the third to philosophy and other secular arts; and the fourth to religion, except for those works that harmed Christian love and brotherhood more than they helped it, and except for the Czech Bible, since it had already appeared separately.

During 1786 and 1787 some thirteen titles appeared. Included in the first series were the *Kronika Boleslavská* (Dalimil's chronicle) and the Czech chronicle of Přibik Pulkava z Tradenína. The second series included excerpts from a sixteenth-century version of the Nestorian chronicles and an account of a journey to Palestine. The third series was largely made up of works by Erasmus of Rotterdam, in Czech translations by the humanists Procházka so admired, and the fourth included similar translations of some of the works of Saint Augustine.[65]

Two main trends emerged from Procházka's selections for his library of Czech literature. The first, and the clearest trend in the first two series, was the patriotic tendency; while the dominating theme of the third and fourth series was the need for enlightened religious tolerance. The very choice of Dalimil's chronicle, important as it was from a historical and linguistic standpoint, carried with it patriotic overtones. "It cannot be concealed from the judicious reader, who carefully examines the whole work, what the intention of its writer was . . . namely that he was not concerned nearly so much with writing about Czech history correctly, in detail, and in an orderly manner, as he was with using such a narrative to write a sort of praise and defense of the Czech name and language," Procházka admitted.[66] Dalimil not only used every available opportunity to praise Czech and attack the Germans who were entering Bohemia at that time, but also consciously created such opportunities. That was once understandable, Procházka wrote, but he would not recommend following Dalimil's example in his own day. Nevertheless, "there is no reason why we should not be allowed to publish and read such an upstanding man and worthy Czech."

Procházka had another end in mind as well when he published the *Kronika Boleslavská*. "I know in advance that I am serving investigators of our mother tongue much more than lovers of Czech history in publishing this Czech chronicle," he wrote. As a historical source, the chronicle was plagued by errors and falsehoods, but if these objections were applied to every early chronicle, none would be acceptable. Procházka valued Dalimil's chronicle as a source for the history of Czech and attempted in his edition to keep to the original text as closely as possible. In fact, he compared the version edited and printed by Pavel Ješín (1620) with four unpublished manuscripts. Too many of his readers, however, found the Old Czech difficult to understand, and in response to their demands, Procházka modernized the Czech in his version beginning with the fifteenth chapter.[67] Gaining from this experience the knowledge that "the ancient language of our ancestors already sounds unpleasant in the ears of today's Czechs," Procházka also modernized the language in his other old Czech chronicle, that of Přibik Pulkava.[68]

In the second of Procházka's series, the *Výtah z kroniky Moskevské* is of interest, especially for the extensive quotation from its original foreword written by Daniel Adam z Veleslavína in 1590. In his foreword Veleslavín stressed the ethnic relationship linking Russians with other Slavs like Czechs, Poles, Croats, Serbs, Slovaks, and others, adding that it would be "useful for the Czechs to realize just how widespread their nation is."[69] Practically the same themes were emphasized by patriots of Procházka's own day who wrote of the interrelationship of the Slavic peoples (see chapter 6).

In the third series, Procházka gave rein to his preference for the Czech humanists and their contemporaries, concentrating especially on Erasmus. Since the Czech translations of Erasmus had been burned by the missionaries along with other "heretical" works, Procházka felt impelled to defend him against attack. In an afterword to his edition of *Kniha Erasma Roterodámského jakby se k smrti hotoviti měl*, Procházka admitted that there might be passages in his works which could be given incorrect interpretations, but the same could be said for works by the church fathers as well. "This much more will I say," he continued, "that Erasmus, as is well known, lived and died in the true Christian faith just as well as the most enthusiastic missionary, and possibly even better."[70]

Procházka's defense of Erasmus and his harsh words about the activities of the missionaries prompted an attack on him from a former Jesuit who wrote to his publisher to complain. He responded to this letter and other criticisms in the foreword to a second book by Erasmus, the *Ruční knížka o rytíři křesťanském*, which appeared in 1787. He pointed out that Erasmus had never been judged a heretic by the church and criticized his opponents for the ease with which they bandied the word "heretic" about as an accusation. To him this seemed a pity, since the Catholics claimed to be the truest Christians. If the Protestants were in error according to the Catholics, so to the Protestants the Catholics were mistaken. Procházka pleaded for toleration, that there "may be among us all the peace of Christ."[71] To the objection that the missionaries had never harmed him personally, Procházka was stern: "How did the missionaries harm me?" he repeated.

"They harmed me in nothing, but the fatherland; or rather they also harmed me, because they harmed the fatherland."[72]

In his fourth series, Procházka continued to make a gentle mockery of the attitude of the Counter-Reformation to Czech books. One work in this series was a collection of sayings of the classical philosophers, and Procházka had taken the liberty of providing a gloss on those passages that contradicted the teachings of the church in order to prevent these pagan philosophers from being placed on the Index, should it ever be revived. "Even without that, if they could rise from their graves, they would be unable to find any other reason for [their being banned] than that in the natural order of things they were unable to enjoy the privilege of learning secular philosophy in Jesuit schools, and they would be unable to contain their laughter."[73]

In spite of its sweeping scope, high scholarly standard, and excellent organization, which included a series of distribution centers in bookstores not only in Prague, but also Brno, Opava, Bratislava, Lwów, and Vienna, Procházka's series of old Czech masterpieces ceased publication in 1787 for lack of subscribers, remaining only a fragment of the original concept.[74] Procházka's increasingly important official duties may have contributed to this, for in addition to his work on the Czech Bible he was, from 1786, censor and the director of the three Prague gymnasia. Eventually he succeeded Ungar as university librarian, but although his surviving papers suggest that he kept up his interest in Czech literature, he published nothing more of note.[75]

Other patriots were ready, however, to attempt to carry on in Procházka's footsteps. One of them, František Jan Tomsa, collaborated with Procházka in preparing an edition of the autobiography of Charles IV that was published in 1791. In his foreword, Tomsa thanked Procházka for his linguistic assistance and also held up Charles IV as an example to today's Czechs, who should "remain Czechs and not degrade their nation, but always improve it."[76] Tomsa also brought out a didactic work by the humanist Šimon Lomnický z Budče, *Tobolka zlata,* which warned against the sin of covetousness. Publishing older Czech works, he asserted in the foreword, would remind the Czechs of their inheritance, especially the language, for which their ancestors "shed their blood; and which they had perfected two hundred years ago to such an extent that the Germans had nothing to compare with it."[77] If the Czechs had such good examples before them, the corruption of the language taking place today, "when many write, without having learned to speak," would be prevented.[78]

Tomsa also promised to continue with the preservation of monuments of Czech literature. At one stage he contemplated beginning a periodical, as he explained to Dobrovský in 1793. "I am intending to publish a Czech quarterly (although people will be pleased to call me an idiot in reviews)," he wrote, "for the last rubric I have chosen old Czech manuscripts that have never yet been published, especially poems; may I also count on some pieces from the manuscript that you obtained from Canon Klier?"[79] This proposal for a Czech quarterly never materialized, although Dobrovský did lend Tomsa the manuscript he requested.[80] Tomsa's interest in early monuments of written Czech did continue, however, as the *Čechische Chrestomathie seit dem dreizehnten Jahrhunderts bis jetzt* that he included in his 1805 linguistic work *Über die Veränderungen der Čechischen Sprache* suggests. The fact that this *Chrestomathie* appeared in a technical work written in German already placed it more in the line of Dobrovský's *Geschichte* rather than Procházka's series of old Czech works. Tomsa's main interest here was linguistic, and the examples in his work served primarily to illustrate the history of Czech and Czech orthography rather than to provide literature for the Czech reading public.

Another patriot who devoted at least some of his energies to restoring old monuments of Czech literature was the popular awakener and journalist, Václav Matěj Kramerius (1753–1809). Kramerius had gained his knowledge of the book trade and early Czech literature in Neuberg's service, where from shortly after the time he left university (1778) until Neuberg's death he worked as librarian and director of his employer's printing establishment.[81] This experience stood him in good stead, both in his career as a journalist and as a publisher of books in Czech, mostly aimed at the common people.[82] Kramerius's publishing activities gathered momentum with the establishment in 1790 of the Česká expedice, devoted solely to publishing Czech books in an effort to give Czech readers higher quality reading material than what was generally available at that time. It was quite natural, then, that Kramerius would turn to the earlier periods of Czech literature for some of the titles that he published.

The first old Czech book Kramerius brought out was the *Letopisové Trojánští,* a work that had been very popular with earlier generations. Kramerius's edition of 1790 was the fourth printed version of this tale of the Trojan War, a fact Kramerius cited to support his boast that while the Germans only cultivated their language in the eighteenth century, "the dear language of our fathers had already reached such perfection three hundred years ago that it could not only compare with Greek and Latin in every respect, but surpassed every other language in its vigor, fullness, and the richness of its vocabulary."[83] He urged his readers to support Czech, by supporting those who wrote and (especially) published Czech books.

Most of the reading material produced by the Česká expedice was designed to amuse, or to instruct while amusing.[84] In keeping with this aim, the second earlier Czech work Kramerius published was a Czech translation of Aesop's fables, *Ezopovy básně.* This was one of the earliest printed books in Czech, dating from 1480, and Kramerius had compiled his version after comparing all the previous editions, especially the fifth (Olomouc, ca. 1600), which he had borrowed from Dobrovský. The Czech style in both these publications had been modernized by the editor, for the same reasons that Procházka had eventually recognized. Similarly, he had "here and there slightly amended" the text of Šimon

Lomnický z Budče's *Kratké naučení mladému hospodáři,* a didactic work in verse. In the foreword, Kramerius not only pointed out that it might give an example to those attempting to write Czech poetry in his own day, but also gave what amounted to a programmatic statement on the value of monuments of Czech literature to the movement for the revival of the language. Other nations, he wrote, scorned everything written much more than fifty years ago unless they were interested in the oldest examples of their languages.

> With us Czechs it is the other way around. All old Czech books are highly prized, yes, the older they are the more we value them, and many lovers of literature would pay their weight in gold, if they could discover where they are. This shows clearly to us Czechs how our dear ancestors, diligently cultivating their language, had already brought it to great perfection when other nations had not even called the development of their tongues to mind. For this reason, then, it seemed to several lovers and defenders of our mother tongue that it would be a very useful thing if they republished above all old works, written in excellent and vigorous Czech; so that contemporary lovers and diligent cultivators of the language of their fathers could have them as a model and example, and learn from them the best form of their language.[85]

He gave especial credit to Procházka for his efforts to this end, and also mentioned Tomsa and his own attempts in the Česká expedice. Clearly emerging from this passage is the view that the old monuments of Czech literature provided an indispensable tool for modern writers of Czech, allowing them to measure their efforts against the yardstick of the past and giving them a model to follow in their own works. Until his death in 1809, Kramerius continued to do his best to follow his own exhortations.[86]

❖   ❖   ❖

The researches into literary history carried on by these patriotic scholars helped create a firm foundation for serious study and appreciation of the heritage of Czech literature, often even rescuing from oblivion monuments of the past. In their approach, these scholars eventually went beyond the rather sterile collection of bibliographical data, finally reaching a coherent interpretation of the development of Czech literature that is relevant even today. Their classicist approach led them to include almost all forms of writing in their field of interest, and although it colored their view of medieval and popular folk literature,[87] they were able to dispose of some of the obstacles in the way of a fuller, more objective treatment of Czech literature. While unable to accept the religious fervor of the Hussite period, they insisted on the place of non-Catholic writers and recognized the importance of Hussitism to the history of Czech literature. As Dobrovský observed to Zlobický when talking about the translation of the Bible into Czech, "without the Hussites we would not have had such early Bibles either, no edition of 1475, etcetera. Yet these Hussites were not such evil people as the Jesuits imagined. We no longer care anything about their heresy."[88] A second service to Czech literature was the general rejection, shown clearly in the comments of Procházka, Dobrovský, Ungar and others, of the destruction of Czech books during the seventeenth and eighteenth centuries, and their recognition of the harm this had done to Czech culture and the language. Finally, in their preference for the works of the Czech humanists, they strengthened the authority of the sixteenth century as the golden age of Czech literature, which should establish a norm for modern authors.

Publishing works of early Czech literature helped to make important sources for the study of the language more easily available to linguists and literary historians, but it did more than this. It also provided Czech authors who were starting out to create modern Czech literature with a model from which to learn good Czech usage, and helped fill the pressing need for Czech reading material of a high standard. Such activity was also seen as part of the patriotic effort to prevent the further decline of Czech culture in the countryside by awakening a demand for Czech books among the people (discussed further in chapter 5). This might halt the creeping Germanization promoted by the school reforms. "One reads from childhood on in German, and believes that the workaday Czech is not as good as the elegant German," wrote Dobrovský. "If special arrangements are not made, or some good genius does not arise to help matters along, I have serious doubts, since already in the normal school one is only concerned about German. . . . However, the desire for reading seems to be awakened and maintained by the publication of good books."[89]

Most of all, the research into Czech literary history and the publication of its monuments provided tangible evidence to the entire world that Czech had once been an important literary language, the tool of men as learned as any the other nations around could boast. The activities of these scholars, then, supported the frequently repeated assertions about Czech found in the defenses of the language. Nor should the contribution these works of literary history and the restoration of Czech literary monuments made to the development of modern Czech literature and literary Czech be ignored, especially in their strengthening of the authority of the golden age of Czech—traces of which literary Czech still bears today.

4

Toward a National Cultural Life

*I*f the budding patriots who asserted so boldly and so frequently that Czech was not the debased peasants' jargon that its detractors claimed it to be were not to be merely whistling in the dark, some tangible proof of their assertions was needed. History could show that in the past a Czech culture and independent state organization had flourished in Bohemia; the golden age of the sixteenth century might bear comparison with the literary and linguistic accomplishments of other nations at that time—but what about now? Unless Czech culture could be seen to be growing and developing, some of the ringing phrases about the high standard of the Czech language might sound rather hollow, and the patriots would be left with not much more than a nostalgic appreciation for the good old days similar to some of Dobrovský's more pessimistic pronouncements on the future of Czech language and literature. Such considerations prompted some of the patriots whose activities we have been following to go beyond historical and linguistic studies to promote contemporary cultural activity in Czech. This was essential if they were to prove that, in Voigt's words, their nation did have its own place on Parnassus.

Fortunately for them, the reform program of Joseph II, particularly his loosening of censorship regulations and support for a freer press, helped to create better conditions for such an enterprise than had existed in Bohemia for some time. In several areas, notably the theater, the publication of newspapers and periodicals, and finer works of literature, especially poetry, the final quarter of the eighteenth century marks a watershed. Although they were plagued by all the starts and stops common to every difficult beginning, these patriots laid the foundations for later Czech cultural developments. Their efforts also had a cumulative effect, encouraging others to emulate them while providing the tangible evidence needed to support their claims for their nation and its language.

Enter the Czech Theater

The laying of the foundation stone in 1781 of the new theater established by Count Franz Anton Nostitz-Rieneck, a leading Bohemian nobleman, symbolized the beginning of a new epoch in the history of theatrical life in Bohemia. It was also to symbolize a new beginning for the life of the specifically Czech theater. Nostitz's enterprise was part of a tendency that had spread to the Habsburg monarchy from Germany in preceding decades, as the enlightened concept of regular recited drama in the national language struggled to replace on the one hand the aristocratic theater with its non-national character, where French dramas alternated with Italian opera, and on the other the debased, improvised burlesque comedies that dominated the alternative forms of urban theater at the time.[1] It was not the first attempt to establish a higher level of dramatic production in Prague; but the earlier efforts of J. J. Brunián, director of the theater in the former commercial building known as Kotce from 1769 until 1778, to introduce serious German dramas and comedies met with little success.[2]

The outlook for the new theater, backed as it was by one of the most powerful members of the Bohemian aristocracy, was more hopeful. Its full name, the Count Nostitz National Theater, clearly announced its adherence to the ideas of Gottsched and Lessing, the prophets of enlightened German drama, and mirrors similar attitudes toward the theater in

Vienna and elsewhere. The "national" element in Nostitz's theater was not clearly defined, since there was a distinctly Bohemian patriotic element in his motivation. Yet he clearly envisaged German as the language of the dramas to be performed and saw Bohemia as belonging to a German-speaking cultural sphere, as his public proclamation of 1782 makes clear. In it, he enthusiastically praised the Viennese National Theater, which was being emulated in all the German hereditary lands, and asked: "Shall we Bohemians alone form an exception, and feel less German blood in our veins? To avoid this reproach, I myself will strive above all so that we may have a national theater in our mother tongue [German]."[3] While he preferred German dramas, Nostitz did not rule out any other approved type of play, or any specific language— and this was to provide an opening for Czech performances at his theater, even though Nostitz was himself almost certainly thinking of Italian opera rather than Czech plays.

Even prior to the appearance of Czech on the stage at the Nostitz Theater there had been isolated performances of Czech plays in Prague. One was produced by Brunián in 1771 under the title of *Kníže Honzík*.[4] It was a translation of a popular German comedy called *Herzog Michal,* and although it was published anonymously, the translator was known to be one Jan Zeberer, chancellor of the Nové Město (New Town) of Prague. It attracted favorable attention, including a review in the enlightened journal *Prager gelehrte Nachrichten,* probably from the pen of F. M. Pelcl.[5] The reviewer defended the Czech language and praised Zeberer for his part in attempts to arrest its decline, including some words of approval for the translator's neologisms. He then went on to suggest that Zeberer's next effort be a work by such an author as Gellert or Gessner, instead of a burlesque. This would be good publicity for German culture among the Czechs, and "perhaps many would even forget their Hussite books, which they usually read from boredom, and because they are written in their mother tongue."[6] It was certainly a novel approach to Germanization to encourage the production of works in Czech, and one wonders whether the reviewer's tongue was not in his cheek. In any case, no further works by Zeberer were published or performed.

There were a handful of other Czech performances during the 1760s and 1770s, including one in the Moravian capital of Brno, but these were generally isolated occurrences.[7] Not until a new generation of patriotic actors, producers, translators, and authors came upon the scene, enthusiastically espousing Joseph II's ideas for a reform of the theater, did sustained and more successful efforts to introduce Czech on the Prague stage begin. One of the prime movers in this generation was the young Václav Thám, rightly considered the founder of Czech theater in the period of the revival.

Born and educated in Prague, Thám developed an interest in Czech literature and the ideas of the Enlightenment while rejecting the prevailing Counter-Reformation culture when he was still a student.[8] In 1785 he published the first modern Czech anthology of poetry, the *Básně v řeči vázané*, and in the foreword to the first volume, dated 10 August 1784, he also announced his intention of working for the development of Czech drama. He was interested, he said, in the history of the Czech theater, and if his poems were well received he planned to continue his efforts to translate and publish a series of plays and operas. "And when several volumes of these plays have appeared," he confidently predicted, "there will not be any great difficulty with their public performance."[9] Bringing Czech drama onto the stage in Prague was not, however, to be quite as easy as Thám thought.

Anyone interested in seeing Czech plays on the stage could either try to convince one of the existing Prague theater impresarios that it would be to his advantage to produce them, or apply for permission from the authorities to set up a company of one's own. František Jiřík, a burger of Prague, tried the latter when he requested permission to establish a theater company for Czech and German plays. His petition, coincidentally dated also 10 August 1784, stated clearly his patriotic motive: "His Majesty the Emperor himself shows his support for the Czech language by the professorship that he established in Vienna, and the petitioner believes that the performance of regular Czech plays is the best means of supporting this our mother tongue, which already in the time of Charles IV had received citizenship in the Republic of Learning, and of improving it and implanting love for it."[10] The strong patriotic tone of this petition, as well as its excellent official form, suggest that Václav Thám could have had a hand in its drafting (Thám was then employed in the Prague police administration). The patriotic tone may also, however, have influenced the authorities to reject it. Yet Jiřík's failure to set up an independent Czech theater did not mean the immediate end of hope for Czech drama, since the manager of the Nostitz theater, Pasquale Bondini, established a company of actors at precisely this time—a company that included several actors of Czech origin. Its director was a native of Prague, František Jindřich Bulla, and he soon proved himself open to the idea of Czech performances.[11]

The first Czech performance in the Nostitz Theater took place on 20 January 1785, with the play *Odběhlec z lásky synovské*, a translation of the German comedy *Der Deserteur aus Kindesliebe* by Gottlieb Stephanie. It was enthusiastically received, Pelcl noting in his chronicle of the 1780s that "the attendance was such that the theater could not hold all the spectators."[12] On 25 January it was repeated, and at that performance a poem in honor of the occasion, "Svátek českého jazyka," was distributed among the audience. The poets, Václav Thám, his brother Karel Hynek Thám, and Václav Stach, well expressed the feelings of the Czech patriots on this auspicious occasion:

> Rejoice, oh Prague! at the celebration
> Which love has consecrated.
> Rejoice! For on this day
> It has wakened
> Your own true son,
> to enter for the first time
> Into the Temple of the Arts.[13]

Odběhlec z lásky synovské appeared in print shortly thereafter, anonymously. The foreword was signed simply B ° °, but in a review published in *Das Pragerblättchen,* the translator was identified as the director's brother, Karel Bulla.[14] This identification is also supported by the "Svátek českého jazyka" in a passage describing how "Bulla, enflamed by Czech ardor / Burst with his brother's help / Through the fastened door / Scattering a thousand lowered barriers."[15]

The foreword to *Odběhlec* stressed the advantages to the Czech language of an established Czech theater, since the "special comeliness and beauty which the language gains through the writing of dramas . . . can be comprehended not just by an enlightened, but even by a half-opened mind."[16] Thus the Czech theater was seen as contributing in an important way to the development of the language, a belief that long characterized the patriots' attitudes.

Three other plays made their appearance during this short first "season" for Czech drama at the Nostitz Theater. Next to be performed was a translation of the two-act comedy by Weidmann, *Der Bettelstudent.* This was given the rather baroque Czech title of *Neslychaná náhoda strašlivého hromobiti aneb Žebravý student* by its translator, a doctor named Mertlík. Though not the translator, Václav Thám may have revised and corrected the text.[17] He was definitely responsible for the third Czech play of 1785, *Štěpán Fedynger, aneb Sedlská vojna,* again based on a play by Weidmann. Yet a fourth Czech work, the one-act comic interlude *Vděčný syn,* was also a translation by Václav Thám. Its only performance, on 24 July 1785, marked the end of Czech productions for that year.[18]

The three longer plays, *Odběhlec, Žebravý student,* and *Štěpán Fedynger,* all appeared in print in 1785. Interestingly, they are all filled with the spirit of Josephinism and the Enlightenment, and all revolve around the life of the peasantry. *Odběhlec* concerns a young soldier who deserts his regiment when he learns that his father is being evicted from his home because of unpaid debts and the unfairness of the administrator of the estate to which he is subject. The young man presents his father's case to the emperor in person, who of course resolves the matter in favor of the old peasant. Passages in *Žebravý student* attack the abuses of the landowners and depict the harmful effects of religious superstition and ignorance in the countryside. The material of *Štěpán Fedynger* is more volatile, since it is based on an actual revolt by Austrian peasants in 1626. Such a subject must have reminded people in Prague of the peasants' revolt that took place in Bohemia in 1775, a mere decade before the publication of the play. Yet even in *Štěpán Fedynger* the attacks on the landlords are couched in terms of loyalty to the emperor, and at the end of the play, when the peasants have been defeated, he voluntarily meets their basic demands.

The topicality of these plays, their enlightened outlook, and the fact that the translators strove to cast them into a contemporary, popular form of Czech, contributed to their success. The future of Czech drama in the Nostitz Theater seemed to be bright. Certain elements in Prague society, however, seem to have objected to hearing Czech on the stage of their "national" theater (one wonders whether the objection might have been based on social snobbery as much as on national antagonism) and so effectively pressured the impresario, Bondini, that he gave his Czech actors their three months' notice on 1 December 1785.[19] But before the end of Czech performances in the Nostitz Theater for the time being, there was one last production, Václav Thám's *Břetislav a Jitka, aneb Únos z kláštera.*

With *Břetislav a Jitka*, Czech dramaturgy in the *obrození* reached a new stage in its development, for Thám's play was the first original Czech play performed. The subject is taken from early Czech history, and although the text has not been preserved, we know from contemporary newspaper accounts that it was performed on 10 and 26 January 1786, and that it was very popular. Kramerius, writing in the *Schönfeldské c. k. pražské poštovské noviny*, noted,

This play finds all the more appreciation among the people, since it deals with an especially heroic act of our early prince, Břetislav. . . . The joy of our Czech nation at hearing on the public stage in their mother tongue so much that serves for the enlightening of their minds cannot be described; and it is true that whatever play has been produced in Czech, it has always found a remarkable number of enthusiasts. This is surely a great support for the assertion that there are still very many people who are not allowing that former respect for our language to die out.[20]

Antonín J. Zima, a Prague printer and rhymster, composed a special ode in honor of the event, in which he was particularly enthusiastic about the actress who portrayed Jitka and the author, Václav Thám:

> For you are the one who, through his works
> Conducts the Czech language out of the darkness
> Who brings forth from it fruit
> As from a well-tended orchard.
> May you never scorn this language,
> Be always its faithful defender,
> So that one day the Czechs may call you
> The father of their fatherland.[21]

In the meantime, the Czech actors who had been dismissed by the Nostitz Theater had decided to petition the authorities on their own for permission to form a new company to perform plays in Czech. After their first two attempts failed, they finally decided to stake everything on one more throw of the dice and present their petition in person in Vienna. Once there, they were able to secure the support of Zlobický, and eventually they were granted permission to perform Czech dramas and German operettas and ballets, though the government drew the line at granting them a special *privilegium*.[22] On 12 June 1786 they announced to the citizens of Prague the inauguration of Czech performances in a temporary wooden structure on the Horse Market (today's Václavské náměstí). This structure, dubbed by the Czech public the "Bouda," was to be the main Czech theater in Prague until 1789.

The news that the actors' group had finally been successful was greeted with pleasure in patriotic circles in Prague. Kramerius wrote with admiration about the actors' efforts in the cause of drama, which would support the language, helping it to develop and regain its former glory and "provide many talented Czechs the opportunity either to write original plays, or to translate them from other languages."[23] He called on every "sincere patriot," as well as the "higher circles," to support this venture.

The Bouda opened its doors for the first time on 8 July 1786, with a performance of *Láska a vděčnost k vlasti*, a translation by Maximilian Štván of a play by August Wilhelm Iffland. As with the premiere of Czech plays at the Nostitz Theater, opening night at the Bouda was treated as an event by the Prague populace. A typical account of the scene comes from Kramerius's *Schönfeldské noviny*:

> We would never have said that patriotic love for our Czech nation could have revived all at once like this. For the premiere of the Czech theater . . . such a large crowd gathered, that this room, usually spacious enough, could in no way contain it all. Guests from all walks of life, even the highest, were found here; and, gripped by a kind of patriotic eagerness, they waited to hear in their mother tongue . . . *Láska a vděčnost k vlasti*.[24]

The industrious Zima composed another ode to honor this occasion, "Znamení vlastenské vděčnosti," in which he extravagantly praised Joseph II for his support of Czech and hardly mentioned the performance at all.[25] The fortunes of the Czech theater seemed for the moment to be on the rise, at least while this beginning enthusiasm lasted, and already by 29 July 1786 the company was considering "a larger and more comfortable site" for its performances.[26]

The popularity of the Bouda reached new heights when

Emperor Joseph II attended a performance on 19 September 1786. The play chosen for His Majesty was Václav Thám's translation of Schikaneder's comic operetta *Die Lyranten*, in the Czech version called *Loutníci, aneb Veselá bída*. This was one of Thám's earliest works, dating from 1784, and had already been given one amateur performance in 1785.[27] Apparently the emperor enjoyed himself, for he stayed in his place through the entire performance and gave the theater a gift of twenty-five ducats as a token of his regard. *Loutníci* was quickly to become one of the most popular plays in the Czech repertory, and by the end of 1787 it had been performed no fewer than forty-five times.[28] Joseph II's presence at this performance was not unnaturally hailed as evidence of his support for the Czech language and his approval of these patriotic actors' efforts to create a Czech theater.

Shortly after the emperor's visit, another significant play had its first performance at the Bouda. This was Matěj Stuna's original two-act drama, *Sedlské buřičství v Čechách*, which dealt with the 1775 uprising among the peasants of northern Bohemia. At its first performance on 23 September 1786, the crowd was so large it could not get into the theater, so the play was repeated the following day and was still being performed in 1787.[29] As far as can be gathered, this play, like the other two Czech plays with similar content, treated the peasants' grievances with some sympathy, but without condoning rebellion or voicing criticism of the emperor himself.

Two translations for the stage by Václav Thám's brother, Karel Hynek, were also published in this memorable year of 1786, and it seems reasonable to suppose that they were performed. Thám chose to translate two rather more demanding dramatic works, Shakespeare's *Macbeth* and Schiller's *Die Räuber*, rather than the popular but lightweight comedies more frequently performed at the Bouda. This was a conscious statement on Thám's part, reflecting his twin aims of showing that Czech was capable of rendering the greatest works of past and contemporary dramatists and of improving the cultural and moral standards of the audience. The fore-word to *Macbeth* provides his arguments for the beneficial effects of the theater:

> That the advantages of reading dramas are many-sided is something that no one can deny. For not only is it intel-lectual recreation pure and simple, but it also enlightens the reason, cultivates and improves the heart and mor-als. . . . [Dramas] endeavor always to promote virtue, and to bring vice into ridicule and degradation, painting both of them with their consequences and in all their forms in living colors, presenting them before our very eyes. When such plays are performed in theaters by actors, then all the more . . . do they reach and penetrate our hearts, awak-ening all the emotions in them with positive effects.[30]

Unfortunately, such plays also made great demands on their audiences, greater perhaps than they were yet prepared for. They also made great demands on their translators, and Thám's translations show the common failings of written Czech in his day, Germanisms or unsuccessfully coined neologisms. Nevertheless, Thám's efforts were at least an at-tempt to bring drama of a truly world standard to the Czech stage.

In general the audience at the Bouda had to content themselves—and they were perfectly contented—with dra-mas of a much lower standard. When the first Czech plays began to be produced, there existed hardly any store of Czech works to draw upon, and the producers at the Bouda had to rely on the efforts of such young enthusiasts as Václav Thám and his friends, who literally created a Czech repertory for the first time. This group of young contemporaries (mostly born around 1765),[31] followed German models almost exclu-sively and concentrated for the most part on translations or adaptations from these models. The Viennese stage set the standard for them, to such an extent that one critic (possibly Bohumír Jan Dlabač) sourly remarked that "the Viennese comic authors will get swollen heads if all their works are translated, one after the other."[32] Among the plays performed in Prague in 1785, *Žebravý student, Odběhlec,* and *Vděčný syn* had all appeared on the stages of Vienna in 1781.

Thanks to the efforts of these young enthusiasts, the number of Czech plays gradually grew. By the end of 1787, when Václav Thám sent a list of the Czech plays, printed and in manuscript, that had been performed at the Bouda to Zlobický, it included sixty-five titles. There were twenty-two by Thám himself, four original, five adaptations of foreign models, and thirteen translations.[33] Josef Dobrovský, writing in the 1792 version of his *Geschichte der Böhmischen Sprache und Litteratur,* remarked that since 1786 more than 300 plays had been "well and poorly translated, also some newly written," but lamented that only a very few had been published.[34] The number of Czech plays continued to grow apace, until in 1805 K. H. Thám estimated that at least 1,000 plays had been written since 1786.[35]

Yet even at this stage, Dobrovský's complaint that few of the plays were published remained all too true. Of the Czech repertory of the period, only twenty-one plays appeared in print, including seven by Prokop Šedivý, three each by the brothers Thám, and two by A. J. Zima. Their other works, and those of the rest of the approximately thirty-five authors or translators of Czech dramas, are known only from contemporary references or the handful of surviving copies in manuscript.[36] Václav Thám's ambition to publish a library of all the Czech plays produced in his day was never realized. He expressed one reason in his letter to Zlobický in 1787, when he admitted, "Although the publication of all these Czech manuscripts would be desirable, and would find many supporters, it would still be irresponsible to rob the producers of their capital, for this capital consists of manuscripts. In time, when the works have been performed often enough, it could happen."[37]

Even if his publishing ambitions could not be achieved, Václav Thám and his brother Karel Hynek were recognized by contemporaries as occupying a special place among the

patriotic supporters of the Czech theater. Typical of these
feelings is this excerpt from a lengthy New Year's ode by the
Prague poetaster, Václav Melezínek:

> Rejoice, my fellow patriots,
> Sing again new songs of praise,
> For who does not know that the Czech language
> Had once been totally rejected.
> But now, thanks to the work of many,
> Especially to the brothers Thám
> It achieves renewed promotion
> And resurrection as from the dead.[38]

The Tháms' contribution, the poet continued, was especially their work in writing and translating for the Czech theater. Pelcl referred again to their services, and thus the Czech
language, in a speech delivered in 1793 at his installation as
the first professor of Czech at the Prague university. "The two
brothers Thám," he said, "proved that it is also possible to
move the hearts of the listeners and to bring tears to the
watchers' eyes with [Czech]."[39] The Thám brothers were almost always mentioned in the same breath, but Václav was by
far the more prolific writer for the theater. Karel's position
was rather that of ideologue for the group, as his translations
of Shakespeare and Schiller, especially their introductions,
suggest. Václav's fate was more closely bound up with that of
the Czech theater.

For the moment, that fate seemed fairly secure. The emperor had publicly shown his support during his visit to the
Bouda, and the company of actors was quick to take advantage
of the moment to request confirmation of their permission to
stage plays. The *Schönfeldské noviny* gladly reported that they
were successful, obtaining the long desired *privilegium* on 1
March 1787, which confirmed that "they might, as before,
produce plays in our capital, Prague, for as long as they like
without let or hindrance."[40]

There is very little detailed information about the 1787
season at the Bouda, but we do know that two more works in

the genre of patriotic-historical plays, both by Josef Jakub Tandler, were produced. Tandler translated K. G. Steinsberg's drama based on the legend of Libuše, taken from the earliest myths about the foundation of the Czech kingdom, and this *Libuše, první kněžna a rekyně v Čechách* was performed in the spring with great popular success. An anonymous correspondent to the *Schönfeldské noviny* wrote that "everyone, great or small, wants to show that he has a thorough knowledge of Czech, as though for a competition," adding, "even if this play were performed several times, it would find just as large a number of admirers each time."[41] The success of Tandler's other play, an original work entitled *Jan Žižka z Trocnova*, was even more sensational. This may have been due to its theme, dealing with the career of the great Hussite leader and military hero; in any case, it was repeated several times after a successful premiere on 24 August 1787, each time to a full house.[42]

The other two plays of 1787 about which we know anything were not of such dramatic, historical interest. One was another translation from Wiedmann by Vincenc Haffner, returning to the theme of country life and the value of the peasant to society, called *Vděčná dcera*. In this translation, Haffner attempted to use a form of Czech close to the popular idiom but free from its worst features, while also eschewing the neologisms so frequent in other forms of written Czech. This he did with some success, according to Kramerius, who wrote: "This translation is not crammed full of newly hatched words, but is pure, understandable, and simply corresponds to our contemporary Czech way of speech."[43] Toward the end of the year, the Bouda was visited by another royal personage, the Archduke Franz, later Emperor Franz I of Austria. For his enjoyment, the actors performed a one-act farce with songs adapted by Václav Thám, *Zámek podvadí místra, aneb Ptáček není v kleci*. This second royal visit was interpreted, as was that of Joseph II earlier, as a sign of special favor and success for the Bouda.[44]

This seeming success, however, did not prevent a growing

financial crisis in the spring of 1788. The precise reasons are unclear, but several factors contributed to the situation. The principals in the company had established the Bouda on borrowed money, and the demands of running the theater swallowed up most of the box-office proceeds, so that the Bouda never emerged from the cloud of debt that overshadowed its beginnings. Even though it was popular, so much so that the company could consider extending it, its audience was composed largely of the lower strata of Prague society, and therefore admission could not be very costly. In addition, Austria went to war with the Ottoman Empire in February 1788, and the strains of the wartime economy, as well as the demands of war upon the population, combined to make the climate very poor indeed for the theater.

Finally, in the spring of 1789, the original founders of the Bouda were forced to give up the enterprise. This left the acting company to its own devices, and at first one of its members, Josef Seidl, took over the direction of the Bouda.[45] Kramerius reported his promise to go on producing "the most popular comedies, the greater part of them in Czech, . . . so that among our Czechs the love for their native language can grow all the more"—a promise suggesting that economic need was already pushing "serious" drama, such as that advocated by K. H. Thám, off the stage.[46] Seidl's effort proved to be only a temporary respite at best, and the company of patriotic actors at the Bouda fell apart definitively after the last performance on 21 June 1789. The wooden structure on the Horse Market was dismantled in October of that year.[47]

With the demise of the Bouda, an important chapter in the history of Czech drama in the earliest stages of the *obrození* came to an end, but this did not immediately mean an end to the efforts to establish Czech drama in Prague. Even while the Bouda was still at the height of its success, a rival theater had been established at which Czech plays were also produced. This theater was located in the pleasure gardens, the Rosenthal or Rozentál, owned by the Prague publisher, J. F. von Schönfeld. They were laid out in the shape of the Kingdom of Bohemia, with trees for the cities, paths for roads and highways, and ornamental canals for rivers. In a former inn on the grounds, Schönfeld set up a pavilion that included a ballroom, restaurant, coffee house, and theater.[48] Kramerius first mentioned the Theater in the Rosenthal on 16 September 1786, and two years later he wrote:

> For the encouragement of our Czechs who place some importance on their mother tongue, we would like to point out that, besides the theater on the Horse Market, where already for nearly two years Czech plays have often been performed, a company of true patriots under the direction of Mr. Jiřík, citizen of Prague, has formed, and will also perform plays in our mother tongue in the theater in the so-called Rozentál. . . . This company of patriotic actors deserves the support and assistance of each sincere compatriot, the more so as in this way our precious language may develop and spread considerably.[49]

A few weeks later he noted again with pride, "Here in Prague Czech plays are now being performed in two locations for the improvement and spread of our heroic Czech language."[50] When the Bouda definitively closed in June 1789, one of its actors, Matěj Majober, transferred the remnants of his company to the Theater in the Rosenthal, where Czech plays continued to be produced until 4 October 1789. Thereafter the Theater in the Rosenthal disappears from the sources.[51]

A more permanent location for the survivors from the Czech theater company was found in the former Franciscan monastery (today still standing opposite Prašná Brana and Obecní Dům) known as the Hibernian monastery after its Irish founders. After the dissolution of the monasteries under Joseph II, the buildings were used for secular purposes, and the former library was rented by the Czech actors for their theater. The first production in the new theater, now known as the Patriotic Theater (Vlastenské Divadlo) in the Hibernian Buildings, took place on 12 December 1789, with a curtain-raiser by Václav Thám entitled *Šťastný den* "in which the author himself appeared for the first time in the role of the guardian spirit of Prague."[52] This is the first record of Václav Thám, who had already distinguished himself as an author and translator for the stage, actually stepping on the boards as a professional actor, and it marks his full commitment to the theater as a profession.

The Patriotic Theater continued in its new location, with varying fortunes, for roughly the next ten years. During the first few years it enjoyed a certain measure of success, assisted by yet another royal visit, this time by the newly crowned Leopold II. On 16 September 1791, the Patriotic Theater presented *Žebravý student* as part of the coronation festivities, and the entire royal family was present. "Their Imperial and Royal Highnesses listened throughout the entire play," wrote Kramerius in his *Vlastenské noviny,* "and showed . . . that they also have a special regard for our mother tongue."[53] In an attempt to exploit this success, the director of the Patriotic Theater, one Václav Mihule, negotiated an arrangement with the impresario at the Nostitz Theater to take over responsibility for the German dramas there, leaving the Italian operas to the latter. Now the direction of both the Nostitz and the Patriotic theaters was united in one person, and Mihule took advantage of this opportunity to bring Czech productions back onto the larger stage. This return of Czech to the most prestigious Prague theater did not last, however, because Mihule proved unable to repeat his successful coronation performance for Leopold's son and successor, Franz. The new Czech king left his place in the middle of a German production produced in his honor, and Mihule's contract with the Nostitz Theater was not renewed. Once more Czech left the stage of the Nostitz Theater, and Mihule left Prague in May 1793.[54]

After 1793, the Czech theater never really recovered either the popular and financial success, or the patriotic and artistic importance, that it had enjoyed at the Bouda. The increasingly nervous government of Franz II (Franz I of Austria after 1806), involved in the long, drawn-out wars with France, and suspicious of any liberal activity at home, was very different from the regime of the enlightened despot Joseph II. Censorship was tightened once more, and generally cultural conditions worsened. At the same time, the war produced hardship for the people at large, and especially for the likeliest audiences for Czech productions, the lower urban strata and visitors from the countryside. The result was a continual struggle with the Patriotic Theater's old nemesis, financial difficulties.

In an effort to better the financial situation, one of Mihule's successors, Antonín Grams, decided to compete with the Nostitz Theater directly by producing German drama instead of restricting himself to ballets and operettas in German. This provoked his opposite number at the Nostitz Theater, an Italian named Guardasoni, to stage some Czech translations of Italian *opera buffa*. Two popular comic operas by Paisiello, *La serva padrona* and *Giacomo e Ninetta* were among these translations.[55] Josef Dobrovský wrote to his friend Zlobický that he had heard *Děvka paní (La serva padrona)* on 6 April 1795, and that he and several friends "were especially attentive to the prosody. . . . Everything sounded well and went well with the music, when [three-syllable] words were pronounced according to my rules."[56] Dobrovský was obviously more interested in gaining confirmation of the correctness of his views on Czech prosody, first published in that year, than he was in returning Czech to the Nostitz Theater.

This reappearance of Czech was an isolated phenomenon, but even if Guardasoni did not continue to compete with the Patriotic Theater, the fact remains that neither Grams nor any of his successors was able to keep it afloat. Finally, at the beginning of 1799, an order of sequestration was issued against the theater, meaning that there was official supervision of the box office, with all proceeds going to creditors. By 20 January

1799, the acting company had once more dissolved, and several of the actors, including Václav Thám, left Prague to attempt to earn a living as itinerant players.[57]

The exact date of the end of the Patriotic Theater in the Hibernian Buildings is unknown; there was still a performance there as late as 19 December 1802, but by the end of the year the building had been sold out from under the theater by the heirs of the former owner.[58] The Patriotic Theater found a final home in the Malá Strana quarter of Prague, in the former Dominican monastery, where it remained until its demise in 1811—at which time it was performing only in German.[59] But there was still one more brief flare-up of Czech activity in the former Nostitz Theater, purchased in 1798 by the Bohemian Estates and renamed the Royal Estates Theater. When the Estates also purchased the *privilegium* of the Patriotic Theater in 1803, they once more united the direction of both theaters, and Guardasoni again brought Czech plays onto the larger stage from 1804 until his death in 1806.[60] Attempts made by Guardasoni's successor to gain permission for continued afternoon performances in Czech failed, however, and by 1809 this first period of Czech theatrical activity had definitely come to an end.

Czech theater in the post-Bouda era underwent several significant changes. For one thing, the Patriotic Theater no longer produced Czech plays during the week, and Czech performances were from then on limited to Sundays and holiday matinees, when most of the Czech-speaking populace would be free to attend.[61] The repertory, too, showed some interesting developments during the two decades following the closing of the Bouda. Comedies, especially comic operettas or plays with songs, had always been popular with the Czech audience, and they continued to be the most successful type of production. The other sorts of plays frequently performed at the Bouda, with patriotic-historical subjects or topical themes taken from the countryside, were replaced by musical comedies modeled after the Viennese *Singspiel*, with fairytale plots full of supernatural events and unlikely coincidences.[62] Czech audiences were able to hear one of the greatest works rooted in this tradition, Mozart's *The Magic Flute*, in a translation by Václav Thám that was first staged sometime in 1794. Thereafter it remained extremely popular.[63] Prokop Šedivý created a popular, localized subgenre of the comedy with songs in his Prague farces taken from lower-class daily life, such as *Masné krámy, aneb Sazení do loterie* or *Pražští sládci*.[64] Patriotic-historical plays were still being written or adapted in this later period, but they show some differences in emphasis. The subjects were carefully chosen from moments in the Czech past that demonstrated loyalty to the imperial house, and it was this Austrian loyalty, rather than a purely Czech patriotism, that predominates. Subjects like Žižka and Libuše were replaced with plays about the elevation of Bohemia to a kingdom, or the resistance of Prague citizens and students to the besieging Swedes during the last stages of the Thirty Years' War.[65] Naturally the influence of the political ups and downs of the wars with France, as well as the more restrictive cultural atmosphere, could be seen in this change.

The first period of Czech drama in the revival from 1786 to 1809 displays certain general characteristics that were to remain a part of its traditions in later periods as well.[66] One of these was its orientation, by force of circumstance, toward the people. Since the audience for Czech plays was drawn from lower-level urban dwellers and country folk, Czech drama had to remain in close touch with the tastes and ways of life of the common people. Another trait of Czech theater was its connection with the developing national consciousness and patriotic activity. However much some supporters of Czech theater were merely interested in tapping the market for Czech performances among the lower classes, there was always a group of patriots who viewed the theater as a tool for awakening patriotism and love of the Czech language among the people—in short, as a medium for patriotic propaganda. These patriots also thought that Czech drama had a part to play in raising the cultural level of the masses and thereby helping the nation, as exemplified by K. H. Thám's comments in his foreword to *Makbeth* and echoed by Kramerius when he wrote that a twofold benefit could be expected from Czech plays, "both the refinement of our beloved language, and the enlightenment of the people, which every community these days must regard as very important."[67] Václav Thám echoed these thoughts in his fable, "Kníže a divadlo," which he published during his tenure as editor of *Schönfeldské noviny*. He closed with these words: "Woe to those enemies of the theater, who can never discover its uses! . . . Who is so blind that he cannot recognize the beneficial results that a good theater can have, by reaching princes, nobles, priests, burghers and commoners?"[68]

One of the most programmatic statements of this point of view came from Prokop Šedivý in a free adaptation of Schiller's Mannheim lecture, "Was kann eine gute stehende Schaubühne eigentlich wirken?" In his *Krátké pojednání o užitky, kterýž ustavičně stojící, a dobře spořádané divadlo způsobiti můze*, Šedivý emphasized the enlightening aspects of the theater. He called it a school in which the people learned good morals and renounced superstition and darkness, but he did not ignore the national aspect either. "If we ever see the day when we have a permanent Czech theater, then we will be truly one nation. What else bound the Greeks so firmly together? What else drew the crowds so strongly into the theaters, but that the plays had their patriotic content?"[69] This appreciation of the uses of the theater, and the call for the establishment of a permanent, Czech theater, were to be the driving forces behind the Czech theater movement in the nineteenth century.[70]

Czech Newspapers and the Periodical Press

The reign of Joseph II saw the opening of a new stage in the development of Czech journalism, just as it did in the development of Czech theater.[71] This was not so much a beginning as it was a revitalizing, for the roots of Czech journalism stretch back at least to the beginning of the sixteenth century, when "the Czechs began to instruct their countrymen about various world events through news sheets written in their mother tongue."[72] The first Czech newspaper in the modern sense, however, was established in 1719 by the Prague publisher Rosenmüller, who also published the official German *Prager Postzeitung*. Rosenmüller's *Pražské poštovské noviny* appeared regularly (except during the French occupation of Prague from 1742 to 1744) until 1772, when Sophie Klauser, the widow and heir of the younger Rosenmüller, petitioned the Gubernium for permission to cease publication. She could not find enough subscribers to make the undertaking profitable, with only two in Prague and another two in Vienna. Accordingly, and acting on the recommendation of the Gubernium, Maria Theresa granted Sophie Klauser permission to cease publication of the Czech newspaper with the issue of 4 February 1772.

One year later, an attempt was made to revive the *Poštovské noviny* when a priest named J. A. Schneider wrote to the Highest Burggrave, then Prince Karl Egon Fürstenberg, urging him to get the paper started again. The censorship commission approached Sophie Klauser to ascertain her conditions, and she agreed to begin again if fifty subscribers could be found—and to lower the price, in the bargain. Only nine prospective subscribers came forward, however, so the *Poštovské noviny* remained dormant for the next ten years.[73]

In 1782, the heirs of Rosenmüller's widow decided that the time was ripe to try again. The first issue of the revived *Pražské poštovské noviny* appeared on 5 January 1782, under the editorship of František Kozury (or Kosorius), who had also been the final editor of the paper in 1772. In an introductory verse, Kozury hailed the reappearance of a Czech newspaper, promising to endeavor to ensure "that our St. Václav's language, which was nearing its fall / Once more begin to flourish and renew itself / And that our patriots can read the news in it."[74] Kozury also promised to hold fast to the Czech of the golden age and eschew Germanized expressions.

In spite of this promise, however, Kozury's writing was

not of a very high level, nor was the newspaper successful under his stewardship, and no issues after 1784 are known to exist. In 1786, the right to publish both the German and Czech newspapers was purchased by the publishing magnate Johann Ferdinand von Schönfeld, and he hired Václav Matěj Kramerius to edit the Czech version. Thus Kramerius embarked upon a career that was to contribute much to Czech journalism and to the activities of the patriotic intellectuals in the early stage of the *obrození*.

Kramerius's contacts with like-minded members of the intelligentsia date back to his days at the Prague university after 1773 and his time in the employment of J. F. von Neuberg. He was able to develop an interest in the Czech language as well as a good grounding in its greatest period, the humanist sixteenth century, and he put it to good use in his journalistic and publishing career. Although he had no previous experience, Kramerius soon proved himself a success. The *Schönfeldské císařské královské pražské noviny,* as the paper was now called, reached new heights under his direction, both in popularity and in linguistic level. He used the newspaper not only to report on foreign political developments, but also to raise the cultural and physical standards of the people. He introduced a new section devoted to home economics and, starting in 1787, added another dealing with new crafts and manufacturing techniques. He called on the Czechs to "place more importance on the development of manufacturing . . . for it is impossible to expect that true Czechs could help themselves in any other way" than the economic development of their country.[75]

Connected with this aim was his effort to use the pages of the *Schönfeldské noviny* to combat superstition and ignorance in the countryside. He addressed himself especially to the village clergy (whether Protestant or Catholic) and school-teachers, since they, as influential figures, were best able to encourage the people to read Czech books and newspapers. This effort to develop a Czech readership in order to spread knowledge and combat harmful superstition would also have the effect, as an anonymous correspondent wrote to the *Schönfeldské noviny*, of improving the condition and prestige of the language: "The greater the number of lovers of books written in our dear language, the more the true patriots will strive to provide them with such books, and thus all the hindrances in the way of the improvement of our Czech name, however great they may seem, can be gradually set aside."[76] Dobrovský concurred in the belief that Czech newspapers and good books in Czech would help stimulate a desire for reading among the people.[77]

Another way in which the Czech newspapers could work toward the development of the nation was through publicizing all forms of Czech cultural activity, calling on others to follow their example. The newspapers' interest in the Czech theater, for instance, was illustrated in the preceding section. In fact, the urge to support and encourage patriotic efforts quickly outweighed the tendency to consider any Czech cultural effort critically, at least for the most part. The maxim *český je hezký* (Czech is beautiful) dominated theatrical reporting, at least, until well into the nineteenth century. Where his beloved Czech language was concerned, however, Kramerius was ready to be more critical. "Pay more attention to the particular characteristics of Czech rather than German," he warned one hapless translator, "for a work in which we follow the original too slavishly does not achieve its aim."[78]

Under Kramerius the *Schönfeldské noviny* flourished, gaining subscribers not only in Bohemia and Moravia, but also in other parts of the Habsburg monarchy, especially among the Slovaks of upper Hungary.[79] Yet continuing disagreements with Schönfeld eventually led Kramerius to leave and set up his own newspaper, in competition with his former employer. He announced the new undertaking in a special broadsheet addressed to the "Czech, Moravian and Slavic nation," in which he outlined the format of his paper and referred to the popularity of the *Schönfeldské noviny* during his term at its head. It had spread itself beyond belief, not only in Bohemia, Moravia, and Hungary, but also in Poland and along the Turkish frontier—"wherever our Slavic mother tongue gloriously flourishes. Just see what the hands of one single, private individual can accomplish!"[80]

Schönfeld tried without success to prevent Kramerius from gaining permission to set up his own newspaper and, failing that, resolved to continue publishing with a different editor. Expectations of Kramerius's newspaper were high among the patriotic intellectuals who knew him:

> I believe that Kramerius's will be better [wrote Pelcl to Dobrovský]. . . . Kramerius also plans to publish literary news that concerns the Czechs, and his written style is also better. He had 900 subscribers at Schönfeld's and now hopes to gain a good proportion of them for himself. Recommend the poor devil, he could no longer stand it with that crude and unpleasant Schönfeld.[81]

In fact, Kramerius was able to take more than half of the subscribers of the *Schönfeldské noviny* with him right from his first issue, and by 1793 total subscribers again approached 1,000.[82]

The first issue of *Krameriusovy c. k. pražské poštovské noviny* appeared on 4 July 1789, with an editor's introduction comparing current newspapers with the chronicles of an earlier day. Since so few histories and chronicles were then published in Czech, he felt the need for a Czech newspaper was even more pressing. Again, he linked its fortunes with the language itself. "Read [the newspaper] diligently, my fellow patriots," he urged, "and be kind to your native language; and I will do all I can to give you satisfaction and enjoyment."

Under his own administration, Kramerius continued the course he had laid down while still with the *Schönfeldské noviny*, supporting Czech cultural activity wherever possible and also publishing popular-didactic material. To a greater extent than before, he made use of a network of private correspondents, especially during 1790 and 1791, when the Hungarian Diet was meeting and presenting its national demands to the new monarch, Leopold II. A "good friend from Hungary," probably one of Kramerius's Slovak correspondents, sent him accounts of the popularity of the national language and costume in Hungary, with details of the demands of the Diet. To make sure the message hit home, Kramerius accompanied these accounts with explicit calls on the members of the Bohemian Estates to follow the example of their Hungarian counterparts and add their support to the national desires of the Czech patriots.[83]

In general, Kramerius paid more attention to national themes during the early 1790s than to the enlightening tendency visible in the *Schönfeldské noviny*. Even the new name of his paper, the *Vlastenské noviny* (Patriotic News), which Kramerius adopted after Schönfeld successfully complained that he had no right to use the adjective *poštovské*, reflected this change.[84] Kramerius devoted his attention to current events that gave him the opportunity to write about the Czech nation and its past glories, such as the coronation festivities for Leopold II and his successor Franz II, or the installation of Pelcl at the Prague university. Even the government's efforts to stir up popular support for the wars with France allowed him to stress the military prowess and bravery of the Czechs and also (not coincidentally) their loyalty to the Habsburgs. National cultural efforts, especially new books, were reported on in special sections.[85]

Kramerius did carry on with some popular-didactic work, however, especially in a series of supplements to his *Vlastenské noviny* that were later published as separate books. This aspect of Kramerius's work regained the ascendancy in the opening years of the nineteenth century, as open displays of national feeling were discouraged. Certainly the government viewed Kramerius's newspaper with some suspicion because of its orientation toward the common people. As events in France awakened fears of revolution in the Habsburg dominions, in 1789 the united Bohemian-Austrian Chancellery requested detailed information from the Prague Gubernium about the spread of news from France and its influence on the people's mood. The censor's copies of the Czech newspapers were sent to Vienna, and each district captain (*Kreis-hauptmann, krajský hejtman*) in Bohemia was required to submit a report on the state of opinion among the common people in his district.[86] In these reports, the Czech newspapers were blamed for spreading unrest among the people, since they were read among the lowest levels of the population, which were too unsophisticated to interpret the news from France correctly.[87] Similar reports again reached the Gubernium in 1793, with the result that the censor, at that time F. M. Pelcl, was ordered to control more closely the articles on events in France and elsewhere and to forbid anything that might even unintentionally contribute to a revolutionary mood among the people.[88]

Government suspicion of Kramerius's Czech newspaper was genuinely unnecessary, for Kramerius was no Jacobin. Though he believed in the ideas of the Enlightenment, the excesses of the French Revolution were abhorrent to him, and he always wrote against them in his *Vlastenské noviny*. In 1793, he even published two separate pamphlets based on the reports in his newspaper about the execution of Louis XVI and Marie Antoinette. That same year, Kramerius devoted space to a lengthy article entitled "The Genuine Reasons Why the French are Rebelling." The underlying cause, according to Kramerius, was the uncontrolled growth of the population, which brought with it hunger and poverty. The king was kept in darkness by his flatterers until it was too late, although he tried to do what he could. Then the leaders of the people looked at their neighbors' lands and decided to take them over. To gain the support of the citizens of these countries, they proclaimed that they were bringing them freedom, while all along they intended to exploit them for their own purposes. Thus they involved all of Europe in war. The end result, Kramerius predicted, would be unrest and lawlessness at home in France, the death of thousands of Frenchmen in war, and general famine and disease. Then perhaps the French would be ready to accept "a proper government and the Christian religion again, and afterwards perhaps they will again be as well-off as any other nation."[89]

It would be difficult even for the most suspicious government to find anything subversive in this account of the revolution. And however simplistic and even self-serving it might be, Kramerius's prediction of the future was also not far from the mark in some ways. Certainly those pressures he foresaw for the French also affected his own country, and the fortunes of his newspaper, badly. The pressures of censorship and economic difficulty increased, and at the same time news of the war tended to crowd other subjects out of the *Vlastenské noviny*. In spite of the worsening economic situation, Kramerius was able to keep his paper above the waters without a break until his death; but after 1803 each issue was only four pages of small quarto, usually given over completely to news from the various battlefields. Kramerius's health began to fail and he became bedridden in 1807. He dictated the final issues from his bed, where he died on 22 March 1808.[90]

The *Vlastenské noviny* continued for a time without its founder, edited at first by Kramerius's friend Tomsa, from 26 March 1808 to 14 January 1809. Then Jan Nejedlý edited a single issue, and from 28 January 1809 the task was finally entrusted to Jan Rulík.[91] Unfortunately none of the three had Kramerius's talent as a journalist and were unable to revive the newspaper. The patriots felt Kramerius's loss deeply. Ribay lamented to Dobrovský shortly after news of Kramerius's death, asking: "Is there then no one in Bohemia so well educated that he could be Kramerius's successor?"[92] Josef Jungmann's view was even pithier: "The Austrian newspapers have nothing on Slavic subjects. . . . It is a shame about Kramerius! Tomsa wrote the newspaper badly, and Rulík does not do it any better."[93]

The story of Schönfeld's Czech newspaper after the departure of Kramerius is also one of decline. Václav Thám succeeded Kramerius as editor, and he followed the newspaper's tradition of a popular-didactic interest coupled with a concern for national issues. Thám also followed his own bent by including a special section for theater news. If anything, Thám was an even more enthusiastic supporter of Joseph II than Kramerius had been and, following the death of the emperor in February 1790, filled the pages of the *Schönfeldské noviny* with articles and verses devoted to him.[94] The choice of Thám did not, however, prove to be a happy one. For one thing, his involvement with the theater did not leave him with much time for the newspaper, to its detriment. Pelcl remarked to Dobrovský that it seemed the *Schönfeldské noviny* was written "by the two Tháms, and sometimes someone from the printing shop, whoever has the time."[95] This division of interest, coupled with Thám's increasingly serious drinking problem, led him to neglect his tasks, to the point where he simply pirated an entire issue of Kramerius's newspaper to meet his deadline. After this episode, he was replaced as of 24 April 1790 by another patriot from theatrical circles, Josef Jakub Tandler (1765–1826).[96]

Tandler represented a further decline in quality when compared with Kramerius or Thám at his best. Schönfeld attempted to offset this by issuing a new supplement called *Nové venkovské hospodářské noviny*, which was nothing more than a translation of its German counterpart in the Schönfeld stable, the *Neue Landwirtschaftszeitung*. Eventually he closed down the Czech newspaper and attempted to establish the economic supplement independently, but it folded after a few numbers in 1792. Schönfeld revived his Czech newspaper in 1796, and after 1800 it was renamed the *C. k. privilegírované pražské poštovské noviny*. It had a whole series of editors, but none succeeded in raising it to the level it had enjoyed under Kramerius.

A Czech newspaper established in Vienna in 1813, the *C. k. povolené vídeňské noviny*, showed some promise of advancing beyond the point reached by Kramerius. It was edited by Jan Nepomuk Norbert Hromádko (1783–1850), Zlobický's successor as professor of Czech at the university in Vienna. One of its most important advances was its literary supplement, *Prvotiny pěkných umění,* in which some of the earliest works of the younger generation of patriots, including Jungmann, Marek, and Václav Hanka, first appeared in print.[97] From the outset, however, Hromádko was plagued by financial difficulties, the linguistic level of his work was uneven, and he had unrealistic ambitions, undertaking more than he could possibly fulfill.[98] The economic troubles of wartime restricted Hromádko's prospects, as Dobrovský noted: "[Hromádko] also wants to write a newspaper for the peasants. The taxes can only be squeezed out of them by force, and they should also lay out money for a newspaper? How foolish!"[99] The *Vídenské noviny* finally folded in 1817.

In other kinds of periodical publications during this period, there were only a few more or less isolated attempts, most of which failed to establish themselves. The rapid development of a Czech periodical press began in the second decade of the nineteenth century, but its roots can be found earlier in such popular-didactic monthlies as *Učitel lidu* and Tomsa's *Měsíční spis k poučení a obveselení obecného lidu.* These journals, which appeared briefly in the 1780s, followed naturally from Bohemia's educational reforms, as efforts were made to reach not only children of primary school age, but also working adults. Since so many Bohemians were Czech speakers, enlightening and entertaining material had to be written for them in Czech if they were to be a part of this development. Much of the material in such journals was simply translated from German publications with similar intentions, and none lasted for more than a few years. Other such undertakings included *Český poutník,* published by Johann Georg Meinert, which was a translation of his *Der böhmische Wandersmann.* The Czech version was the work of Jan Nejedlý, but *Český poutník* died in its first year of publication, 1801. A similar fate overtook *Český lidomil, aneb nejnovější pražský vlastenský časopis,* a translation by Jan Hybl of the journal *Der Volksfreund,* published by Franz Anton Pabst. It appeared in 1810, but lasted only fourteen issues.[100]

The first really successful Czech literary periodical was

Jan Nejedlý's *Hlasatel český*, which began to appear quarterly in 1806. Gathered around *Hlasatel český* was a group of contributors that included not only representatives of the older generation of awakeners such as Tomsa, Kramerius, and Dlabač, but also some of the younger patriots, including Jungmann, Josef Liboslav Ziegler, Václav Alois Svoboda, and Antonín Marek. Nejedlý published both poetry and prose on various subjects, much of it intended to educate and enlighten his readers. He also promised to include material on the natural sciences and on advances in art and learning, excerpts from Greek and Latin classics in Czech translation, as well as translations from other modern languages, along with excerpts from rare or unpublished old Czech works. Finally, Nejedlý promised to include reports about new Czech books appearing in Bohemia, Moravia, or Hungary—"in a word, this *Hlasatel* will include everything that cultivates reason, ennobles the heart, serves our common good, and *spreads and improves the Czech language and literature.*"[101]

Nejedlý's final goal suggests that the *Hlasatel český* was self-consciously intended to further the aims of the Czech patriots. The language was one focus, and through the example of the poetry and prose within its covers, *Hlasatel český* could prove that the phrases of the defenders of Czech, asserted now for some thirty years, were true. Nejedlý also managed to strike a more self-confident, almost pugnacious tone, as in his introduction to the first number:

> Go forth, my dear herald! from Prague to your countrymen, Czechs, Moravians, and all the Slavs far and wide, linked by language! Boldly enter the glittering and wonderful houses of the greatest lords and the huts of the common people; proclaim to them their sacred duty to the fatherland. . . . Arise! Hurry to them with flying steps, do not waver in your noble endeavor. True and faithful patriots will receive you with joy and pleasure; and if you come across any foreigner, or any renegade Slav dressed up in foreign clothing, who might disparage you and deride you because you are a Slav, or laugh scornfully at your native

costume, then resist them, rebuke them, for you are sprung from a famous, valiant nation that is the most widespread in the world, and you must not allow any impolite or slanderous aspersions to be cast on your brothers.[102]

In the *Hlasatel český*, Nejedlý and Jungmann clearly formulated a linguistic concept of what the nation was; here also they propounded the idea of the country, the *vlast*, not seen as a political territory, but personified as a mother and identified with the language and customs of the nation. And, according to Nejedlý, he who harms his *vlast*, "that is, his *customs and mother tongue*," is no better than a criminal and traitor.[103]

Hlasatel český appeared from 1806 to 1808, but the fourth and last volume did not appear until 1818, after much delay and difficulty.[104] Czech patriots greeted *Hlasatel český's* return with rejoicing, but a younger generation was now in the forefront of the patriotic activities, and Czech literature no longer automatically followed where Jan Nejedlý led.[105] Before its demise, however, *Hlasatel český* played an important part, together with Kramerius's newspapers, in the course of the Czech revival. The fact that there was a Czech newspaper, or a fairly serious Czech literary journal, at all was seen by the patriots as a positive achievement. Moreover, the content of these two publications was important. In addition to bringing a knowledge of world events to the Czech reader, the *Vlastenské noviny* gave Kramerius a forum for strengthening Czech national consciousness, and especially a love for the language, among his readers. Although aimed at a different audience, Nejedlý's *Hlasatel* was concerned with many of the same issues, and in addition it served as living proof that Czech was capable of filling the roles of a modern literary language, not only in poetry, but also serious prose. It was a heritage that would be built upon in the following decades.

The Revival of Czech Poetry

As vernacular languages claimed the roles previously filled by Latin or other languages of "high" culture, defenders of

Czech as the mother tongue found it very important that poetry be produced in the vernacular. This development affected most European languages at some stage in their history, including German, where the example of French and the supranational baroque culture acted as spurs.[106] The German example in turn provided an impetus to similar efforts in Bohemia, first in the German cultural sphere, and then in Czech. Karl Heinrich Seibt (1735–1806), the first lay professor at the Prague university, appointed in 1763, held an important position in this development in Bohemia. A pupil of Gottsched and Gellert, Seibt began to lecture in German in place of Latin and worked to develop enthusiasm for German literature among his students.[107] The sensation caused by Seibt's teaching affected students from German or Czech-speaking backgrounds equally: the simple idea that any vernacular was a legitimate vehicle for literary expression was heady stuff. The result, as one student of Seibt's later noted, was an explosion of interest in German literature, amid efforts to improve the standard of German in daily use. "To speak good German is to speak like Seibt," he wrote; and similar evaluations of Seibt's impact came from others, such as F. M. Pelcl.[108]

Seibt's colleagues, August Gottlieb Meissner (1753–1807), professor of aesthetics from 1785, and the first Protestant at the university for nearly a century and a half, and Ignac Cornova, whose work as professor of history has already been discussed, also cultivated German literature, especially poetry. Meissner published his own and his students' efforts in a series of almanacs, *Die Erstlinge unserer einsamen Stunden* (1791–1792), while Cornova also produced some German poetry and plays.[109] Apart from a few isolated forerunners, the first real effort to apply these new ideas to Czech poetry was Václav Thám's *Básně v řeči vázané*, which appeared in two volumes in 1785. Thám's almanacs stood at the threshold of modern Czech poetry, but as transitional works they also displayed characteristics typical of the past. Thám's motivation was largely defensive and historical, as he explained in the foreword to the first volume. What were his reasons for publishing it?

> In the first place, so that I may make known the surviving fragments of our Czech poets; secondly so that I may prove that songs and verses may be written in our mother tongue on any topic, just as in other languages; and finally that I may make known to my readers the many people who are working both for the spread of our Czech language and for the cultivation of more elegant poetry in it.[110]

The scheme of the *Básně* reflected Thám's desire to show not only that Czech could compare with other modern European languages, but also that the level of the sixteenth century could be achieved in his own day. He divided each volume into three sections, the first containing examples of Czech poetry from the past, the second, translations from other languages, and the third, original works by contemporary Czech authors. Thus, the fact that only one-third of the poems in Thám's almanacs was original and the remainder either reprinted or translations does not reflect merely the poor state of contemporary Czech literature, but also the historical and defensive point of view of Thám's circle. German poetry in particular was the yardstick by which Thám measured the Czech works, and this demand that Czech prove its ability to compete with modern German literature led in the first instance to its using the same means of expression as German poets.[111]

It is not surprising, therefore, that the general literary genre represented in the poetry of Thám's almanacs should be the anacreontic, since this style also dominated German poetry to a great extent. Following the examples of the German anacreontic poets, Johann Wilhelm Ludwig Gleim, Christian Felix Weisse, Gottfried August Bürger, and Ewald Christian Kleim, the Czech poets in Thám's almanacs occupied themselves with stylized expressions of conventional emotions limited almost exclusively to the topics of wine, women, and song.[112] The first volume Thám published contained fifteen translations of works by Gleim and six by Weisse, while the second added translations of poems by Bürger, Kleist, and Hagedorn. There were also translations directly from Anacreon and Catullus, while the original Czech contributions, by Dlabač, Stach, Thám, František Knobloch, Jan Hynek Kavka, Kramerius, and Štván were simply imitations of this sort of work.

A similar pattern is clear in a separate collection of Czech poems published three years later by Kramerius. His *Noví čeští zpěvové pro krásné pohlaví ženské*, which appeared in 1788, contained translations from Bürger and other German anacreontic poets.[113] These verses were conventional and derivative, and the young poets of Thám's circle were not really blessed with any genuine poetic talent, yet their works were nevertheless important. For the first time in a long while, Czech writers were searching for a language of poetic expression in their mother tongue. More important at this moment, perhaps, was the propaganda effect of the almanacs. They were valued by contemporary patriots as an expression of a desire to defend the status of Czech and encourage its development, and they attracted a list of subscribers including such names as Dobrovský, Durych, Ungar, Dlabač, Pelcl, Procházka, Zlobický and Kramerius, as well as the theatrical figures Majober, Stuna, Zima, and Bulla.[114] Thám's other commitments and problems (already mentioned) interfered with his intention of continuing with his collections of poetry, and further developments had to wait for a decade.[115]

A new stage in the development of Czech poetry was reached in 1795, when Antonín Jaroslav Puchmajer published the first of several volumes of poetry, *Sebrání básně a zpěvů*. The contributors to Puchmajer's almanacs, which appeared in five volumes between 1795 and 1814, were mainly younger patriots who had attended Prague university at about the same time. There they had been introduced to the world of German classicism by Seibt, Meissner, and Cornova.[116] Their interests were not limited to German literature, however: Puchmajer translated or adapted poems by Rousseau, Grenet, and Florian; Kheraskov, Karpiński, Kniażnin, and Krasicki; as well as Bürger and Schiller. While they remained deeply indebted to German anacreontic and idyllic poetry, as were the poets of Thám's circle, the poets of the Puchmajer school showed greater independence in following these models and introduced other influences from German and wider European literatures. These included Bürger's popular ballad form, Klopstock's religious epic, and the elegiac romanticism of such English poets as Thomas Gray.[117]

Puchmajer's translations from Polish and Russian point out another novel element in his almanacs, namely the way they directed the attention of Czech literature to Slavic models. This trend would be continued by Jungmann and other nineteenth-century figures. In contrast to the poetry in Thám's almanacs, the works in Puchmajer's treated openly patriotic themes more frequently. Many of the poets in the circle around Puchmajer addressed works to leading patriotic figures or to heroes of the Czech past. The graduates of the university in Prague remembered some of their teachers most warmly; and accordingly there were odes to Antonín Strnad and Stanislav Vydra, professors of astronomy and mathematics, respectively, in the almanacs. Both men were praised for their example, which influenced their students to believe that "to be a Czech is glorious."[118] Jan Nejedlý called Vydra the "Czech father" of thousands of his students, whom he had taught, echoing Balbín:

Slavnější což může byti,
Nežli čest svým předkům vzdát,
Je i vlast, i jazyk ctíti,
O jich zvelebení dbát?

What can be more glorious,
Than to revere one's ancestors,
To honor them, and the fatherland, and the language,
To strive for their improvement?[119]

Vojtěch Nejedlý struck a sadder note with two odes on the death of F. M. Pelcl and F. F. Procházka, but although they were gone, at least the younger generation of patriots could pay them their respects in this way.[120] Puchmajer turned to Jan Žižka, and in a surprisingly sympathetic tone praised him as a Czech hero (although he deplored the waste of Czech lives in the Hussite wars).[121] But perhaps most typical of the directly patriotic poems in the almanacs was Jan Nejedlý's ode, "Na Čechy," which appeared in the third volume in 1798. Here the tone of darkness and pessimism, which he struck in the opening stanza, gave way to one of light and optimism, forecasting a brighter future for the nation and its language:

> Což má noc navěky, navěky býti?
> Nikdy-li nepočne v Čechách se dníti?
> Dlouho-li český lev ještě chceš spát?
> Slunce již vzešlo, což nemůžes vstát?
>
> . . . .
>
> Plesejmež Čechové! plesejmež bratři!
> Světla že jazyk náš český zas spatří;
> Písně že české zas budou nám znít,
> V slávě že Čechové budou se stkvít.

> Must the night everlasting, everlasting be?
> Will it never begin to lighten over Bohemia?
> Do you still wish, Czech lion, longer to sleep?
> The sun has arisen, what, can you not wake?
>
> . . . .
>
> Let us rejoice, ye Czechs, rejoice my brothers!
> That our Czech language can again see the light;
> That we can once more hear Czech songs in the air,
> That the Czechs will now flourish in glory.[122]

One final, and most significant, difference between Thám's almanacs and the Puchmajer school, however, lies in their differing metrical foundation. It was the declaration of allegiance to the principles of the "accent" theory of Czech prosody by the Puchmajer school, instead of the older tradition of quantitative verse (based on the length of syllables regardless of natural accent), that created the base for the development of modern Czech poetry.

Though he was not a poet himself, let alone a poet writing in Czech, it was Josef Dobrovský who established the principles of the new Czech prosody in his foreword to Pelcl's *Grundsätze der Böhmischen Grammatik.* The problem of Czech prosody had interested him for many years,[123] and some of his earlier thoughts had appeared in the *Litterarisches Magazin* in 1786. Here he questioned whether Czech could make use of the hexameter form, since when following the rules of Václav Rosa (1621–1681), whose work on Czech grammar set out the rules for imitating classical verse forms, the normal Czech pronunciation had to be ignored. "Is it the fault of the language," he asked, "that we have no good Czech poems? Nudožerin said in 1603 'carmina bohemica nulla adhuc gratiam habent,' and in 1782 one can add: since then they have not become any better."[124] The fruit of his years of thought on the subject was Dobrovský's deceptively simple principle that Czech poetry should be governed metrically by accent rather than syllable length, with accented syllables considered metrically long and unaccented ones, short. Linked with this rule was the insistence that in Czech the accent must always be on the first syllable of the word.

Although he had begun his poetical works in the older, quantitative style, Puchmajer eagerly accepted Dobrovský's ideas, revised his earlier efforts, and dedicated his first *Sebrání básně a zpěvů* to Dobrovský, "the originator of the new Czech prosody." He claimed that Dobrovský's rules were "the only correct ones," according to which Czech poets could write "much better than ever any Czech poet did before," and he and his friends adhered strictly to the accent rule in the first two almanacs.[125] Gradually, however, the members of the Puchmajer school realized that theory did not always satisfy every demand of poetic practice. Dobrovský's study of the particular characteristics of Czech had led him regretfully to conclude that "the perfect harmony of the Greek and Latin hexameter is unattainable for us."[126] This conclusion was unacceptable to young poets, fired with a desire to prove Czech capable of any poetic form used in other literatures, especially the classical Latin and Greek. Thus they set out to attempt some form of synthesis of the old rules with the principles of accent. Šebastián Hněvkovský (1770–1847) was one of the poets of the Puchmajer school who devoted some time to this problem. He explained some of his ideas in a letter to Jan Nejedlý, insisting, "I do not want to write any apology for Dobrovský's system, but . . . seek a system that would also compare with the general rules." Puchmajer was no help in this matter, since "he wants to have Dobrovský's rules in rhymes and Rosa's in hexameters. . . . But in my opinion only one single prosody can be correct, and it must serve both for rhyme and rhythm."[127]

However much they may have desired a single, unifying theory, the young poets of the Puchmajer school had to reconcile any theoretical system with the demands of practice. Here, the acid test would be in attempts to translate the classical works of world literature. In his first almanac, Puchmajer published some early attempts at Czech hexameters in a translation from Virgil, and Homer's *Iliad* challenged several poets, including Puchmajer himself, Jan Nejedlý, and the Slovak Jiří (Juraj) Palkovič, who had connections with the Puchmajer school. Nejedlý published his *Homerova Iliada* first, in 1802. He had attempted, he wrote, "to translate everything as it sounds in the Greek, in the truest, most exact, most understandable and most melodious way, into Czech."[128] No less stern a critic than Dobrovský called Nejedlý's hexameters among the best he knew, with only Puchmajer's in the fourth almanac surpassing them. Nevertheless, he continued, "it is obvious that the Czech translator must struggle with very many practically insurmountable problems if he wants to reach, to some extent, Homeric hexameters in his language. The blame lies with the language itself."[129]

The hexameters by Puchmajer came from his translation of Montesquieu's *Le Temple de Gnide*, excerpts of which had appeared in the fourth almanac as "Svatyně Venusina v

Kníde." Puchmajer had been working on this translation since 1798, and it eventually appeared separately in 1804 under the title *Chrám Gnidský*.[130] In the fourth volume of his *Básně*, Puchmajer included an article in which he laid out the system he had used in his translation of Montesquieu. His motive for attempting what Dobrovský had said was impossible emerged clearly when he asked: "If poets can use practically all the verse forms of Latin in German, how much more could they be used in Czech, in this our own language, which has stood firm for three hundred years, and need not give way to any other modern language, even Italian . . . in variety and euphony?"[131] Even Dobrovský admitted that Puchmajer had done well, but he continued to insist that Czech hexameters were hedged about with all sorts of difficulties. "No Czech poet has written better hexameters than these," he wrote in his review of *Chrám Gnidský*, "but they are by far not as flowing as the Latin ones, nor do they have even the variety of the German ones, and they *cannot* have it."[132] This was a verdict the younger poets simply were not prepared to accept.

The Puchmajer school continued to strive for metrical variety, frequently harking back to earlier metrical styles depending on the verse form they were using; but in general its poets remained true to Dobrovský's principle of accent.[133] Others, however, rejected Dobrovský's reforms altogether. In 1805, Václav Stach (with the collaboration of K. H. Thám), published a volume of poems in defense of the old tradition. Stach, who had earlier contributed to Václav Thám's almanacs and translated Klopstock's *Messiah*, launched into a fierce attack on Dobrovský and the new prosody, accusing them both of being unpatriotic, since they rejected the older Czech heritage and mindlessly imitated foreign models.[134] Stach's work was without any great influence, but the prosodic controversy was by no means finished. It broke out anew in the first third of the nineteenth century, and was still a subject for discussion in the twentieth.[135]

There was more to the poets gathered around Puchmajer than the new prosody, however. As we have seen, they were also (Stach's accusations notwithstanding) active patriots who intended by their works not only to show that Czech did indeed deserve a place on Parnassus, but also to awaken love for the language and pride in its achievements among their readers. Puchmajer's patriotic foreword to the second almanac (1797), which he likened to "a voice crying in the wilderness," lamented the decline of Czech in the past and heaped scorn upon those whose uncritical admiration for foreign things led them to neglect their own mother tongue. In a reference to the wars with France, he expressed the hope that the sacrifices of the Czechs would be rewarded by the government with more support for the language:

> We, we Czechs, unrenegate descendants of our glorious ancestors, who during those dangerous and horrible days when our savage, furious foes threatened us with shame and destruction, enthusiastically proved our love for our dear fatherland . . . have we Czechs, then, not deserved that for our remarkable love and loyalty to our country and the king, our ruler, so clearly and obviously demonstrated, our Czech language should be powerfully supported and defended?[136]

The Czech poets felt that part of their duty to their fatherland was to encourage others to work in similar ways for the development of literature and the spread of the Czech language. Puchmajer apologized to Jungmann for not choosing more of the latter's works for his fifth almanac (1814), but "it was necessary to have a care for others, and give them, especially the younger poets, a greater taste for writing."[137] It was important to find a natural poetic language for Czech, one that would truly be capable of the tasks that patriotic zeal set it. Vojtěch Nejedlý, in a programmatic verse from the third almanac (1798), argued that Czech poetry had to be sincere, understandable, and thus had to avoid a rigid reliance on the language of the past. He also called on the patriotic poets to write verses that were Czech in spirit as well as language. This would mean leaving the sterile imitations of classical models behind: "Čechu! chceš-li zpívat hezky, / Mysli, mluv a nos se česky."[138] Other poets echoed this call to try to contribute something to Czech literature. Jan Nejedlý reminded the readers of his translation of Gessner's religious epic, *Smrt Abelova* (1800), that the improvement of the nation could only come through reading and writing serious works in Czech, closing with a short verse:

> Kdož jest Čechem, prosím za to,
> Předků slovutných hlas slyš:
> Český jazyk cti co zlato
> Česky mluv a česky piš.

> Whoever is a true Czech, him I beg,
> Harken to the voice of your renowned ancestors
> Value the Czech language higher than gold
> Speak Czech, and write Czech.[139]

In the first decades of the nineteenth century, this patriotic duty led to an obligation on the part of each patriot to write some Czech verse, talent or no talent. But the more chaff there was, the greater the chance of finding some grain among it.

❊ ❊ ❊

Three broad areas of cultural activity all reflect the same concerns. First, the mere fact of activity in the Czech language in these areas was seen as a patriotic deed by contemporaries. There were still pessimistic voices, such as Dobrovský's, when he wrote of the Czech theater that he "doubted very much whether the Czech language will gain anything on the whole through [the new plays], however sincere the joy with which the Czech rhymster, Václav Melezínek, and other enthusiastic patriots write about them in each New Year's Wish."[140] Yet comments like these tended to serve as a gauntlet thrown down to those patriots influenced by the developments in history and language to which even Dobrovský had contributed so much. The Czech language had been provided with a clear system of grammar, freed from the wilder aberrations of such as Pohl and Simek; and through the researches of Durych, Procházka, Voigt, and others, the literary heritage and some of its monuments had been reclaimed.

Now the patriotic intellectuals were prepared to attempt a task that had seemed impossible to an earlier generation: to create a modern literary and cultural life in Czech. Concern for the Czech language, and through it the entire Czech nation and the *vlast,* was the overriding motive for their activities. It was the basis of attempts to create a Czech theater, it was expressed in the pages of the *Vlastenské noviny,* and it breathed through the almanacs of Thám and Puchmajer. This, they felt, was their duty to their people and their land:

> Who nursed us with her sweet milk, and raised us with anxious care? Who provided us with everything needed for life from our childhood, and generously gave us all good things from her bosom; who has defended us at every opportunity? You, beloved Czech homeland, our mother!!!— And should you then receive nothing in return?[141]

The answer of a true patriot lay in his work for the development of the Czech nation, its language, and its literature.

5

Národ a Lid—
Nation and People

One result of the developments outlined in previous chapters was that gradually, the primary meaning assigned to the concept of nation changed in an interesting way. During most of the eighteenth century it was basically political, denoting the group that enjoyed political rights, however circumscribed: namely, the nobility. This meaning originally chimed well with the scholarly, historical, almost backward-looking concerns of the patriotic intelligentsia; yet the historical, philological, and literary researches of these scholars helped stimulate and complemented other activities, leading to attempts to claim equal status for Czech with German, and to create a modern cultural life in Czech. Most Czech patriots at this time would have welcomed the participation of the nobility in their activities; indeed, they did welcome it where it existed.[1] But as the Czech language came increasingly to dominate the intelligentsia's interests, to the point where use of Czech became the touchstone of belonging to the nation, the nobility began to fade out of their concerns. The nobles, in whose eyes Czech was a low-status language that they knew badly or not at all, were simply not going to begin suddenly to use it in their daily life. This would make them unlikely consumers for a Czech culture, and perforce directed the attention of the patriots to the existing group of Czech speakers, the common people. Some of the intellectuals, characterized as "popular awakeners" (*lidoví buditelé*), already expressed an interest in the common people, and through them the ideas and attitudes of the *obrození* were transmitted to wider levels of society.

Various motives lay behind this interest. The Enlightenment had encouraged the attitude that all the subjects of the monarch were citizens, each with his own contribution to make to the good of the whole. Coupled with physiocratic ideas about the wealth of a country consisting in a healthy and prosperous population, this made the common people and their physical, educational and cultural standards the objects of a concern that was frequently officially encouraged. But the concerns of the patriotic intellectuals who addressed the common people went beyond the aims of an enlightening officialdom. While on the one hand these popular awakeners worked to spread useful knowledge among the people and to raise their standards of hygiene and living, on the other hand they also worked to spread the patriotic attitudes they were developing among the broader masses.[2]

The aims of the patriots tended to reinforce each other. They were increasingly making the Czech language the main element in their idea of the Czech nation, but in general the old political nation declined to use Czech to any great extent (see chapter 2). Like it or not, the common people made up the largest group of Czech speakers. Yet the patriots wanted to claim equal status with other languages for Czech, which meant that they had to translate their historical image of a high Czech culture into a contemporary reality. If the upper classes in the cities would not become consumers of Czech culture, then the patriots would have to turn to the masses. Thus the efforts to improve the level of knowledge and culture in the countryside would also help to increase the number of consumers of Czech culture. In the end, the nation would come to mean the people who used Czech, whatever their social class, and Czech culture would increasingly become their culture.

Enlightening the Common People

The original aims of the enlightened absolutist regime had been much more circumscribed. At a time when it was difficult to get permission from the government to publish textbooks or other works in Czech, Maria Theresa's regime supported the translation of the Bible into Czech and the publication of catechisms and other devotional manuals. The new Czech Bible was the work of F. F. Procházka and Václav Fortunat Durych (1735–1802), both Paulist monks and members of the patriotic intelligentsia. Though the basis for this translation was the Jesuit Bible of 1771, Durych and Procházka had critically compared that version with the Latin Vulgate, Hebrew and Greek texts, and even the Bible of the Czech Brethren of the sixteenth century, the Kralice Bible.[3] The translators made an effort to present the truths of the faith in such a way that they did not support the crudest of popular superstitions and practices of folk piety, but Procházka at least remained unsatisfied. Under the changed censorship conditions following the accession of Joseph II to sole rule in 1780, he worked on a revision of the New Testament section of the Bible of 1778–1780. Once more Procházka applied the method of critical history, and he purposely used such language that the new version (published in 1786) could be used by both Catholics and Protestants in Bohemia. He stressed the importance of the secularization and loosening of the censorship to his endeavor.[4] The Czech Bible was quickly sold out, and Procházka was called upon to direct yet another edition, based on the Latin text approved by the Council of Trent, but as "reviewed, revised, [and] annotated" by himself.[5]

There was a need for more than Bibles, however, especially as Joseph II's reforms in church practices and its relations with the state began to take effect.[6] Prayer books, catechisms and devotional manuals in the vernacular that conformed to the new ideals of reformed Catholicism, as espoused by the Febronians or Muratori, were also necessary. Tomsa and Kramerius were among those who helped fill this need. It is indicative of the state's support for religious material in Czech that the second work Tomsa translated after joining the press of the Prague Normal School in 1777 was a catechism.[7] Under Joseph II, Tomsa continued this activity, publishing translations of two German prayer books by K. H. Seibt, *Kniha katolická, obsahující v sobě naučení a modlitby* (1780), and *Vyučující a modlicí kniha pro mládež* (1784). Seibt, who lectured in such subjects as aesthetics, ethics, and practical philosophy at the university, composed his prayer books fully in the sense of Josephine reformed Catholicism.[8] Kramerius also contributed a translation of a religious manual, *Křesťanská katolická užitečná domovní postilla* (1785), based on a work by the Viennese Josephinist, J. V. Eybel. It was very popular and, in spite of its title, was also used by the newly tolerated Protestants in Bohemia.[9] Stach was another who joined Kramerius and Tomsa, though his translations were either Protestant or neutral in orientation.[10]

Other works by the popular awakeners were directed at the people through the intermediary of their pastors. Since the village priests occupied an important place in the life of their communities, if they could be won over to the new ideas, they could use their influence among the masses.[11] Jiljí Chládek (1743–1806), professor of pastoral theology at the university, published a very influential textbook, *Počátkové opatrnost pastýřské* (1780–1781), for his students. Its message was so in harmony with Joseph II's program that it was officially adopted for use both in Prague and Brno. Chládek stirred up a whiff of controversy by championing the use of the Czech language not only for preaching, but also for the general administrative duties of the parish priest. In his dedication to the third volume, Chládek praised the abbot of the Praemonstratensian monastery at Strahov, who was a supporter of Czech and a collector of manuscripts and books. His example should shame and inspire those Czechs "who, as soon as they reach a position of greater dignity, immediately want neither to read Czech nor to have Czech books in their libraries, and thus contribute to the fact that this, our Slavic language, has few admirers."[12] This was as nothing compared to the reaction provoked by Stach's handbook for the parish priest, *Příručka učitele lidu* (2 vols., 1787). This handbook contained exegeses of biblical texts in a Josephinist sense, moral anecdotes, excerpts from modern philosophers, and pedagogical hints, all intended to be of use to the priests in their tasks.[13] But Stach was a radical and seemed to take delight in provoking the conservative clergy, whom he attacked in the foreword to the second volume. A hint of his radical language and hatred of intolerance comes through in the following passage:

> If only that Spanish voice, so far removed from the meaning of Christ, had never been heard among us, [that voice] with which certain people denounce everything that does not correspond to their power, avarice, and ignorance as heretical, and with which they long for the Spanish Inquisition . . . in that Church clique in which priestly despotism lords it inhumanely over the wiser clergy and is capable of reversing everything that is good, nay, even of inciting the commoners. . . . Such a priest belongs to that corrupt and depraved generation, for whom neither the law of God, nor the law of the land is holy, but only the law of their greed and stupidity.
>
> But why present these diverse opinions? So that the people's teacher can know them, and ponder them, inquiring into what the human reason is doing. A priest should know everything. To the pure, nothing is impure.[14]

Stach also translated a pastoral theology text by Franz Giftschütz, in which he further demonstrated his radical Josephinist stance. It replaced Chládek's *Počátkové* as the textbook at the General Seminary at Olomouc in 1789.[15]

Stach's was not the only voice raised in support of more religious toleration. The Patent of Toleration of 1781, which had recognized the Lutheran and Calvinist confessions, was welcomed by many intellectuals, but there were still people at all levels to whom the idea was anathema. When Johann Leopold von Hay, bishop of Hradec Králové and a leading Josephinist churchman, published a pastoral letter to the clergy of his diocese explaining the new regulations and demanding obedience, Kramerius quickly translated it into Czech. *Církulární spis pána z Háje, biskupa královéhradeckého, na duchovenstvo osady jeho strany tolerancí* (1782) proved to be very popular and quickly sold out. Another work by Kramerius, his *Patentní ruční knížka pro měšťana i sedláka* (1781), publicized the patents of the first two years of Joseph II's reign in Czech translations. It was reprinted in 1787, at which time Kramerius noted that it was extremely useful and important for the people because "in this book [they] will find all the patents and decrees [explained] in their mother-tongue . . . with such clarity that everyone can understand them right away."[16] Placing the texts directly into the hands of the people was a means of preventing obstruction at the periphery from frustrating the intentions of the center.[17]

An even more remarkable piece of propaganda for Josephinism was Kramerius's *Kniha Josefova*, which appeared in 1784. *Kniha Josefova* and its German model were attempts to present the Josephine reform program to the people in a style familiar to them. The language was patterned after the Bible, in the hope of reaching the masses directly, over the heads of the usual intermediaries, the parish priests and landlords' officials. Joseph was presented as the archetypal Old Testament king, a new Solomon, sent by God to bring "enlightenment" to his people. Much of the text was given over to explaining Joseph's religious reforms, and "prophesying" about the future policies toward the church.[18] By May 1784 the book had gone through four editions, and Kramerius noted later (with some pride) that "it burn[ed] no less than salt in the eyes" of its opponents, who banned its circulation since it brought the simple Catholics out of the darkness of ignorance in which many priests would prefer they remain.[19]

Kramerius also put toleration into practice personally, helping to teach Czech to the newly arrived Protestant pastors (who were mostly Calvinist or Lutheran pastors from Hungary) in Prague, and he later kept the idea alive in his *Nový kalendář tolerancí,* which he published yearly from 1787 to 1798. He listed Catholic and Protestant feast days side by side, gave summaries of decrees affecting religion, and also provided much other useful and entertaining material for his readers.[20] Stach also supported the newly arrived Protestants. When a certain Václav Rokos published a work purporting to prove that Lutheran and Calvinist ministers could not claim to be priests "secundum ordinem Melchizedec," Stach published a pseudonymous work refuting Rokos's claims.[21]

A more reserved attitude to the Josephine church reforms characterized the position of Jan Rulík, another of the popular awakeners. He claimed to wish along with the emperor (citing the court decree of 17 April 1783) that "all his subjects would hold to the only saving Catholic faith from their own conviction"; but his comments in his *Kalendář historický* about Joseph's reforms such as the dissolution of the monasteries and the forbidding of certain forms of popular piety suggest a more critical attitude to reform Catholicism.[22] In his own religious publications, Rulík remained true to the traditional piety of the Catholic baroque, albeit in its patriotic form as Balbín expressed it. He was just as well aware as the others, however, of the need for religious material written in good Czech for circulation among the people.[23]

It is worth noting that in their activities as direct publicists for Joseph II, the popular awakeners limited themselves almost exclusively to his religious policies. Kramerius's *Kniha Josefova* did, it is true, mention the Leibeigenschaft Patent of 1781, which abolished hereditary subjection, as well as the school reforms and the loosening of censorship; but the main emphasis and the language of the book were religious. Yet the religious issue was not the only concern of the popular awakeners. They also contributed to the education of adults in Czech, an activity that followed naturally from many of Joseph's reforms. Some improvement in the cultural and economic level of the masses was necessary, and in Bohemia much of this work had to be done in Czech. Thus the state found itself in the curious position of Germanizing with one hand while encouraging Czech education with the other.[24] For the state encouraged and even sponsored such efforts. The Highest Burggrave, Prince Karl Egon Fürstenberg, published a popular educational periodical, *Der Volkslehrer*, from 1786 to 1788. He asked Tomsa to translate it into Czech as *Učitel lidu*, one of the earliest such periodicals to appear in Czech.[25] Tomsa must have found the work challenging, for he left *Učitel lidu* after one year to establish his own monthly, *Měsíční spis k poučení a obveselení obecného lidu* (1787). In this work Tomsa aimed especially at spreading basic knowledge of the physical and natural sciences, so that rational, scientific explanations for natural phenomena could replace harmful superstitions. Each issue also contained an illustration, fables, and moralistic tales.

Měsíční spis was hailed by like-minded patriots, such as Kramerius, who publicized it in his newspaper:

> Mr. Tomsa's friends may clearly see from the contents that their wishes, when they wrote that Mr. Tomsa in his future issues of *Měsíční spis* should explain especially physical matters, of which up to now the common people have had no understanding, are being completely and fully satisfied. . . . Oh! what an early enlightening of the mind can we expect among our Czech people, when they are made acquainted with such knowledge, which had previously never occurred to them![26]

Kramerius also had kind words for Tomsa's use of Czech, saying that he explained the most difficult topics in such clear language that "even the simplest person can understand them."[27] The pressures of other work, however, forced Tomsa to stop producing *Měsíční spis* with the December 1787 issue; but he said, "[I promise] to go on enlightening my fellow countrymen, if I am only given a bit of free time for it."[28]

True to this promise, Tomsa continued to publish enlightened didactic material, though never again in the periodical form. Besides his translations of textbooks for the Normal School, he produced Czech versions of several popular German works dealing with various aspects of life, such as health, proper diet, animal and general husbandry, and especially the proper rearing and behavior of children, usually in the form of fables or short tales. Tomsa also continued in his belief that the Czech readers could benefit from learning about the physical and natural sciences. He left behind him in manuscript a translation of Funk's *Naturgeschichte für Kinder,* parts of which appeared posthumously in Jan Nejedlý's *Hlasatel český.*[29]

A later attempt at a didactic Czech-language periodical, this time in the spirit of Bohemian territorial patriotism, was *Český poutník,* a translation by Jan Nejedlý of J. G. Meinert's *Der böhmische Wandersmann.* This journal, published in 1801, contained information on current affairs, moral teachings, and also information about "those days made especially important by the heroic deeds of our ancestors."[30] *Český poutník* displayed less of that concern for the Czech language and nation characteristic of the patriotic intelligentsia, though some passages remarked on the condition of the language. Like Tomsa's *Měsíční spis,* the *Český poutník* did not wander for long through Bohemia. It ceased publication in Czech at the end of the first volume, because there were only fifty subscribers for the Czech version, and the German version died in 1802.[31]

Kramerius was also an active, and more successful, publisher in the field of popular didactic literature. Typical of his work is *Večerní shromáždění dobrovické obce* (1801), which described a series of evening discussions between a group of villagers and their schoolmaster. The lessons stressed the need for hard work, sobriety, and loyalty, while decrying drunkenness and ignorance. They also expressed patriotic sentiments, however. In one such passage the schoolmaster exclaimed: "Oh, if only you all would feel the same joy I do, when I hear or read something about our dear Czech fatherland!" After detailing what the ancient Czechs did for the language, he wondered "if it is still possible that the present-day Czechs—or at least their descendants—will one day awaken from their deep dream, and, remembering who they are, value their country and mother-tongue above all else, like all the other nations?"[32]

Kramerius published other works with similar themes, sometimes as a supplement to his newspaper prior to independent book publication. One of the best known of these works was his *Přítel lidu*, a popular "encyclopedia" that appeared during 1806 and 1807. He still held true to the popular and didactic goals he had set at the beginning of his career, writing in *Přítel lidu*, "My main intention is, insofar as it is within the power of my intellect, to enlighten and amuse the common people."[33] As before, however, he did not miss the opportunity to encourage patriotic feelings among his readers. *Přítel lidu* included a poem by a Slovak, J. Tkadlic, in praise of the "Slavic" language, and, in a more scholarly vein, translations from German articles comparing the Slavs with the Germans and pointing out that the Slavs taken together outweighed the German element in the Habsburg monarchy.[34]

Kramerius did not address himself only to adult readers. Like Tomsa, he also published didactic works for children. One of these, his *Zrcadlo šlechetnosti pro mládež českou,* he had originally written for his four sons.[35] His most successful venture in this field was a free translation of a work by the German pedagogue, Joachim Heinrich Campe. *Mladší Robinzon,* which was loosely based on the famous story by Daniel Defoe, was finally published after a long delay in 1808. The literary device of the adventures of the castaway sailor provided many opportunities to drive home useful lessons to the young people who were the target of the book.

Campe was also translated into Czech by Jan Rulík, who published one of his works on the rearing of children in 1792.[36] He followed this translation in 1794 with another work on the same theme, *Kastonova užitečná naučení o dobrém zvedení mládeže,* which had a sequel the following year. One theme Rulík included in his works was that of loyalty to the authorities in both Church and state: "Be obedient to authority (*vrchnost*), and perform and render unto it what belongs to it. For there is no power, but from God."[37] Similar works were translated into Czech by authors such as Antonín Borový, whose *Zrcadlo pošetilosti* was published by Kramerius in 1792, and Vavřinec Amort.[38]

These works were addressed mainly to problems of personal or family health and moral well-being, or were simply harmless entertainment. The popular awakeners also worked to raise the standard of living and level of economic modernization in the countryside. Already under Maria Theresa, the Habsburg government had concerned itself with the problem of improving the peasants' condition, and it supported the establishment of the Society for Agriculture and the Free Arts in Bohemia, transformed in 1778 into the Imperial and Royal Patriotic-Economic Society (K. und k. Patriotisch-Ökonomische Gesellschaft, C. k. vlastenecko-hospodářská společnost).[39] The society was organized in order to spread new agricultural methods, to make Bohemian farming more efficient, and to popularize new crops or improved varieties of traditional ones. Many books and pamhlets were published with these aims in mind, but nearly always in German.[40] Since the majority of the peasantry on the fertile Bohemian plain spoke only Czech, it was necessary to publicize these same discoveries and techniques in Czech—a task the popular awakeners took to with alacrity. As editor of the *Schönfeldské noviny* from 1786 to 1789, Kramerius devoted a special section of the paper to encouraging the use of new crops or methods; and later in his own *Krameriusovy c. k. vlastenské noviny* he continued with this practice. In addition, an important section of his *Nový kalendář tolerancí* was devoted to such topics. Tomsa, Amort, and Rulík also contributed to this effort by translations of works in German.[41] They concentrated on areas that could be improved relatively easily, with advice on raising livestock, especially sheep; on how to grow fodder even on poor fields unsuitable for other crops; and on the techniques of veterinary medicine.

One other concern that can be seen in the popular awakeners' work is to change the popular idea of the status of the peasantry. They praised the peasants as a necessary part of society, arguing that they should not be objects of scorn. Kramerius publicized such ideas in his *Noviny*, stressing that "the deeds of the peasants' estate are dignified and, like those of any other, important."[42] Rulík also maintained that "nobility and honor can dwell even in the village," and in 1798 wrote a discussion of the peasant's estate, *Krátký spísek o stavu sedlském, aneb voráčském.*[43] Here he idealized the status of the country dweller, and his value to society:

> I do not know why so many people are so retarded in understanding, that they consider the peasants' or ploughmans' estate, which puts bread practically into the mouths of all the other estates, to be coarse and worthy of scorn. Of course only senseless people think this way. . . . This estate is the oldest in the world, the oldest form of work, practically as old as the human race. You therefore, oh farmers, when you cultivate your fields, remember this also, that you are called to work and produce bread not only for yourselves, but for the common good.[44]

Certainly such sentiments could be interpreted as a cynical effort to keep the peasants happy in their miserable lot. Yet it could also be argued that the popular awakeners believed in the value of the peasant, not only to the state, but also to the nation. After all, he had kept the Czech language alive through the centuries.[45] In his *Krátký spísek,* Rulík did emphasize the agricultural society of the early Slavs, and he linked the peasantry with the legendary Czech past through the popular figure of Přemysl, founder of the first native Czech dynasty.[46]

The Cultivation of National Consciousness

The popular awakeners' activities in didactic publishing suggest that the popular press could be useful in reaching the countryside. But publicity for government policies and in the interests of the state was not the only kind of information the popular awakeners spread. They were also active in disseminating news of current events, local or international, through newspapers, almanacs, and calendars. Kramerius's *Nový kalendář toleranci,* priced so low that it was well circulated, was only one example of such works. Perhaps the crowning achievement of his life, however, was his twenty-two years as a newspaper editor, first for the Prague publisher J. F. von Schönfeld, and on his own account from 1789 until his death in 1808. After this, his friends Tomsa and Rulík attempted to continue his newspaper, but without noticeable success. Kramerius has an important place in the development of journalism in Czech (as described in chapter 4). In one sense, Kramerius saw his newspapers as "nothing other than chronicles and tales of years, which are written for posterity to eternal memory."[47] Yet they were also useful to the present generation, to awaken patriotism and national consciousness among their readers. These aims were most evident during the earlier years of his career, before the worsening economic situation and the wars with France had taken their toll, but even in later issues Kramerius did not ignore them. This application of journalism to agitation for the national cause was one of the activities that won him a place among the awakeners.

Kramerius exploited every possible opportunity in Prague to deliver his national message, paying particular attention to literary efforts of other patriots (as well as his own), plays, new books, and also political events that evoked the honor and glory of the Czech kingdom. In the 1780s especially, Kramerius followed in detail the fortunes of the Czech theater, which he saw as possibly turning the people away from frivolous and superstitious fairy tales to more useful reading.[48] He announced forthcoming performances and reviewed plays. The establishment of companies of actors to perform Czech plays was welcome, "all the more," he said, "since in this way our dear language can improve and extend itself a great deal."[49] When the Czech acting company included German plays in its repertory as well as Czech, out of fear that they would not be able to attract an audience for Czech plays alone, Kramerius published some critical comments. Taking his remarks from an anonymous pamphlet in German that he translated into his newspaper, Kramerius wrote:

> The members of this patriotic theater company called themselves a patriotic society, and actually, if they would stick to the native plays, they would deserve all encouragement. But they should leave out the German plays which they mix in. . . . One can tell that they are more competent in their native tongue, and that every action suits them better in it.[50]

Of course, there was a shortage of Czech plays to perform, and Kramerius himself tried his hand at translating for the theater in 1788 with a comedy, *Albert a Lotte*. Though it was performed, it enjoyed little success.[51] The *Vlastenské noviny* also mentioned two plays by Jan Rulík in 1795, *Paní podle mody* and *Strašidlo s bubnem*.[52] Notices of Czech plays gradually decreased in number, partly because of the increase in war news, and partly because of the decline in the fortunes of the Czech theater itself. Literary comments did not, however, disappear entirely from Kramerius's newspaper. When new Czech books were published, the *Vlastenské noviny* publicized them, and Kramerius frequently gave space to an entire section for news of books for sale or wanted.

Current political events, too, gave Kramerius the chance to emphasize patriotic themes. When Joseph II died, the political situation was grave, with Hungary on the verge of revolt and the Estates in the Bohemian and Austrian lands simmering. The new monarch, Leopold II, called the Estates together to hear their grievances, and Kramerius reported these developments. Especially through his correspondents in Hungary, he kept his readers informed of the demands of the Hungarian Diet, the most outspoken of the Estates, and called upon their Bohemian counterparts to request similar concessions for themselves. What the patriots wanted for Bohemia might even be presented as moderate in comparison with Hungarian demands. When the Hungarians added to their other demands that at his coronation Leopold should be dressed in Hungarian national costume, Kramerius reported it, and then commented:

> As far as we Czechs, ever loyal to the House of Austria, are concerned, we would have no other or more humble request for His Royal Highness . . . than that he reintroduce into all our schools and government offices our mother tongue, for thus alone will our glorious nation again recover, and never demur at giving its life for our monarch. Oh that this wish of thousands upon thousands of true patriots would be graciously fulfilled![53]

He printed glowing accounts, sent to him by his Budapest correspondent, of the popularity of Magyar among all walks of life there, followed by the question, "What are the Bohemian Estates intending to do at present in the cause of the Czech language?"[54] This sort of reporting served as a clarion call to action. "What are we," demanded Kramerius. "Are we not Czechs? What is our kingdom? Is it not Czech? And is it then fitting that we should unlearn our language?"[55]

The Czech language received particular attention. In 1791 Kramerius wrote with joy that all paths were opening up for the language again, because the emperor had granted permission for a chair of Czech at the university in Prague.[56] It was not until 1793, as we have seen, that Pelcl was finally appointed first holder of this chair. Kramerius reported the installation ceremony at length, welcoming this long-awaited sign that "the Czechs can be of good hope that their language, which in this century practically sank into oblivion, is slowly beginning to reach a higher level, and greater perfection and glory."[57]

The coronations of Leopold and Franz provided Kramerius with further opportunities to recall the bygone glories of the Czech kingdom. Leopold's coronation involved the return of the Crown of Saint Václav from the Viennese exile where Joseph II had taken it, and Kramerius presented this as a sign that perhaps the golden age was returning.[58] The speech Josef Dobrovský read in the presence of the emperor also appeared in Kramerius's newspaper, in a translation by K. H. Thám (see chapter 2).[59] The coronation of Franz II also received extensive coverage in the *Vlastenské noviny*, especially the "country celebration" put on by the Estates in the emperor's honor. At this festival, representatives of each district of the kingdom appeared in their native costumes, and the fact that royalty was graciously pleased was hailed as a great honor for the Czech nation.[60]

The example Kramerius set in using political and other current events as opportunities to deliver a national message inspired Jan Rulík, too. In his *Kalendář historický* he gave some attention to cultural events, for example noting that in 1786, "to the great delight of the Czech nation," Czech newspapers began to appear again, and Czech was heard on the stage.[61] He wrote enthusiastically of the return of the Bohemian crown and the coronation of Leopold II:

> This is a memorable century, especially for the Czech nation and kingdom, in which our renowned Czech kingdom and nation enjoyed great fame, when they not only received back their priceless Crown of St. Václav from foreign lands, but also crowned their King. . . . It is fitting that we Czechs, together with our descendants, hold it in glorious memory forever.[62]

Other patriots and their activities also provided an opportunity for national publicity. The appearance of a new book, the appointment of a patriot to an official position, the granting of a government honor, all this created a chance to praise the living patriot and stress the glorious past. A sort of cult of the sincere patriot and the glorious ancestors grew up, and the litany of honored names was recounted at each appropriate moment. Tomsa, the brothers Thám, Rulík, Pelcl, Procházka, Dobrovský, and others were celebrated in the pages of Kramerius's *Vlastenské noviny*, while Rulík dedicated volumes of his *Kalendář historický* to Antonín Strnad, Pelcl, Kramerius, and Jan Nejedlý. Rulík also wrote occasional poems in honor of Pelcl and Nejedlý.[63] It was these men, and others like them, "who day by day [took] more pains and effort, that their language through their untiring work could achieve again the perfection that flourished during its golden age two hundred years ago."[64]

Rulík devoted several independent works to the celebration of past and present patriots. His *Velmi užitečná historie o slovutném národu českém*, published in 1793, was a popularized summary of the development and character of the Czech nation from the earliest Slavic tribes to the present. Rulík stressed the fact that the Czechs were Slavic and accused the Germans of folly when, because of this, they "turned their sharpened pens against us, ascribing to us excesses, unkindliness, insatiable robber's greed."[65] The Czechs had never been like that; on the contrary, they were honorable, loyal, and brave in battle. They were also talented in the arts, and intelligent—though this was often wasted, Rulík said, because Czech was not cultivated in the schools any longer. The Czechs' beautiful and richly endowed homeland had given birth to many learned and holy men who should act as examples to the present generation: "Therefore, my Czechs, true patriots," concluded Rulík, "let us also act the same; let us care about that name, Czech, the nation, and the language," so that "our descendants will also bless us for this zeal . . . as we now bless our dear ancestors of glorious memory."[66]

The continuity between ancestors and posterity was especially important for Rulík. To preserve the memory of his contemporaries fittingly, he dedicated a literary laurel wreath to them in his *Věnec pocty k poctivosti učených, výborných a statečných Čechů* (1795). This work was basically a catalogue of the patriotic efforts of his colleagues, praising them by name, and including as a sort of proof of their success a list of all Czech books published between 1782 and 1795. In a later work he extended this bibliography down to 1805.[67]

Two other works of Rulík's took a more historical point of view. *Učená Čechia* was basically a translation and paraphrase of M. A. Voigt's introductions to the volumes of his *Effigies virorum eruditorum atque artificum Bohemiae et Moraviae*, originally published in 1773–1774. Rulík's choice of title harked back consciously to Balbín's *Bohemia docta* and had a similar defensive and patriotic aim, if a more limited conception. After presenting the examples of a gloriously learned past that Voigt's work gave him, Rulík called on his readers to take to heart the fact that they came from a nation that was once the most renowned in Europe, both for its scholarship and its valor. He urged them to follow in the footsteps of their ancestors, of whom they should certainly not be ashamed. "Would that our descendants also will not be ashamed of us, when, remembering us, they say: we are their ancestors, and Czechs!"[68] The second work was also a historically conceived collection of biographical sketches, *Galerie, aneb vyobrazenost nejslovutnějších a nejvyznamnějších osob země české*, based on a German work by Josef Schiffner, beginning with the fabulous traditions of Krok and Libuše and continuing down to the eighteenth century.

The example of the ancient Czechs was of use to the government during the Napoleonic wars, when appeals were made to the martial traditions of the past in order to stir up the fighting spirit of the people, especially in 1796, 1800, and 1809, when local militia units were organized to protect Bohemia from invasion.[69] Kramerius and Rulík devoted space in their works to the proclamations of the Archduke Karl as commander-in-chief, and other official proclamations. They also reported a great patriotic response from the people.[70]

The awakeners contributed occasional verses or songs

harking back to the military traditions of the Czechs, and even sometimes mentioning the exploits of the Hussites, as in these stanzas from a song by Pelcl:

> Let us also remember our ancestors,
> Let us stand in battle as they did,
> Victory will surely be ours.
> Thus have the Czechs always fought
> They swept the enemy from the field
> And preserved the fatherland for us.
>
> We must not pass over the Táborites
> Nor may we forget
> What heroes they were.
> Blind Jan Žižka led them
> They always overthrew the foe,
> They were all Czechs![71]

František Vavák, Stach, and others produced many similar patriotic poems.[72] Prose works also attempted to spread the government's view of events during the war years, such as Dlabač's *Rozmlouvání o nynější vojně mezi farářem a sedlákem českým* (1809), in which a priest and a Czech peasant discuss the course of the war. Dlabač also appealed to tradition with a summary of the examples of martial valor from the Czech past, also published in 1809.[73] In 1814, he returned to his role as purveyor of the official viewpoint on the military conflict with a series of letters on current events, *Listy českým krajanům v nynějších přihodách psaní.*

Rulík also contributed to the efforts to stir up support for the war effort, with a play published in 1808, *Vlastenský mladý rekruta.* The action was set in the time of the eleventh-century Czech prince, Oldřich, when the Czechs were fighting the Poles; but the relevance of the message to the Napoleonic wars was obvious. The hero, a young boy originally refused by the recruiting sergeant because of his age, eventually prevails upon the prince himself to accept him as a drummer boy. The Czech characters, not surprisingly, were depicted as loyal and ready to sacrifice their lives for their ruler. "Let others set a value on their blood if they wish, sell it for what they wish," exclaimed one recruit as he refused the bonus for signing on, "I come out of the simple love that I bear for my lord."[74]

The appeals to the glories of the Czech past were, from the government's point of view, intended only to serve its needs for manpower and to help the population bear with the inevitable sacrifices of wartime. Such propaganda, however, could have results beyond the intentions of the government that encouraged or sponsored it. Certainly the free rein given to the patriotic intellectuals to evoke images from the past, even from the Hussite past, also allowed them to introduce elements of the patriotic themes with which they were concerned. Although the popular awakeners were in the main just as loyal as any other subjects, they were also not unaware of the fact that in this case their interests coincided with the government's.

The Popular Awakeners and the Czech Language

The unifying thread through practically all of the popular awakeners' work is concern for the Czech language. They agitated for its spread, attempted to improve its condition, and used it in their own works. The awakeners also worked to create a desire for Czech reading material in the countryside and to make available worthwhile books to read. Beyond the fact that they used Czech themselves in the works they aimed at the common people, the popular awakeners joined others in defending the language, stressing its historical excellence, and publishing again some of the monuments of its golden age. While the attitudes of the intellectuals to the language, their efforts to assert its social and cultural value, and their struggle to develop and stabilize its grammatical and lexical base are discussed in chapter 2, it would be worthwhile to consider for a moment how the popular awakeners used the language in their work to reach the common people.

Rulík and Tomsa contributed directly to the "defenses of

the language," and Kramerius frequently included defensive passages in his newspapers and other works. In 1792, Rulík published his *Sláva a výbornost jazyka českého*, which, though it did not present any new arguments, was filled with a burning sense of love for the language. Rulík likened it to "a gift from God and the priceless inheritance of each and every nation."[75] It was one of the five main branches of the Slavic language, and thus widespread, it had a rich vocabulary, and borrowed words from foreign languages only because it was copying the German example. Rulík described the decline of Czech following the Battle of the White Mountain in 1620, and although he did not condone the rebellion, he also condemned the burning of Czech books. Every nation should strive to cultivate its mother tongue, Rulík insisted, and held up the example of Hungary, where even the highest magnates in the land supported Magyar.[76] Tomsa's *Von den Vorzügen der čechischen Sprache* was, as we have seen, rather more like the earliest defenses, a throwback to an already outdated approach. He repeated the arguments about Czech's long history as a language of high culture, its simplicity, pithiness of expression, and rich vocabulary. "And should it then not be worthwhile," he demanded, "to maintain and improve a . . . language such as Czech—the native tongue (*Landessprache*) of a not insignificant kingdom?"[77] It may well be that Tomsa's work was not addressed, really, to the common people; but rather to the officials in the school system and elsewhere in the administration, both in Bohemia and Vienna, who were loath to give official support to Czech publishing.

Kramerius's passages about the language, by contrast, were definitely intended to stir up interest in the hearts of the common people. The themes Kramerius stressed included the assertion that it was by language alone that one people was differentiated from another, and that the mother tongue was like a rare jewel that even barbaric and ignorant nations knew how to value. "Russians speak Russian, the French, French, Italians, Italian, and thus in the whole world each nation has its own language; why then should the Czechs alone have to betray and disown their mother tongue?" he asked.[78]

The fact that Czech was related to the other Slavic languages was often given as a reason for its importance. Like others among the patriotic intelligentsia, the popular awakeners frequently identified Czech as a dialect of a single Slavic language and the Czechs as only a branch of the Slavic nation. Rulík emphasized the Slavic ancestors of the Czechs in his *Velmi užitečná historie* and in *Sláva a výbornost jazyka českého*, and Kramerius dedicated his newspaper to the "Czech, Moravian, and glorious, widespread Slavic nation."[79] He begged his fellow countrymen to get rid of their obsolete antipathy for their language, promising that they would then realize "that Russians, Poles, Pomeranians, Silesians, Moravians, Slovaks, Dalmatians, Bosnians, Moldavians, Serbs, Wends, Croats, and many other famous nations spread to all corners of the world are [their] brothers, and use the glorious Slavic language, with only slight differences."[80]

Whenever the opportunity arose, the popular awakeners urged their readers to learn and use Czech. In 1792, for example, Vavřinec Amort announced that he would offer free Czech lessons to anyone who was interested. Kramerius publicized the offer in his *Vlastenské noviny*, pointing out that "since now the Czech language is beginning to flourish in our kingdom, everyone will gradually but unavoidably need to know it."[81] Unfortunately, the response to this call for students was not terribly enthusiastic; but this did not diminish the frequency of appeals to the Czechs to raise their opinion of their language and begin to use it once more.[82] Other patriots published works aimed at helping the Czechs to do precisely that. Chládek, whose views on the importance of Czech to the clergy in Bohemia have been mentioned, published a short handbook on how to speak and write Czech in 1795. He intended it especially for those who, "although they speak Czech from childhood, still make countless errors and are ignorant of the rules of grammar."[83] As correct models to emulate, Chládek recommended especially the works of Procházka, Tomsa, and Kramerius. Tomsa published a similar work directed at the lower grades of the public schools and those who would work in them.[84]

However much the popular awakeners insisted that Czechs need not be ashamed of their language, however much they stressed its relationship with the other Slavic tongues, however enthusiastically they urged their countrymen to use it, they were all well aware of the sorry state of Czech in their own day, and the serious decline it had suffered since its golden age in the sixteenth century. They knew all too well that many of its most precious monuments "were in part damaged and destroyed by coarse ignorance, in part given up to the flames by senseless zeal."[85] One way to improve the quality of the language and to make good at least part of the losses it had suffered was to put back into the hands of the Czech reader decent books written in Czech.

It was natural, then, that the popular awakeners would be involved in the attempts (discussed in chapter 3) to reclaim the existing monuments of earlier Czech literature. Tomsa published the autobiography of Charles IV and a moralistic tract by Šimon Lomnický z Budče in 1791. Kramerius published another work by Lomnický in 1794, with the additional aim of helping budding Czech poets, since *Krátké naučení mladému hospodáři* was written in verse.[86] Other Czech works from the humanist period that Kramerius published included the chronicles of the Trojan War (1790), Aesop's fables (1791), and the travels of the mythical Sir John Mandeville (1795). He continued this activity into the new century, adding Josephus's history of the Jewish wars in 1806, reissuing Václav Vratislav z Mitrovic's adventures (already published by Pelcl in 1777) in 1807, and publishing Xenophon's biography of Cyrus the Elder in 1809.[87] Although it was a modern Czech version of a Latin original, Jiří z Drachova's *Cesta z Moskvy do Číny*, which Rulík translated and published in 1800, fits in well with the subjects of these other republications, and it also fed the popular interest in Russia during the wars with France.[88]

The popular awakeners published and edited these books to spread good written Czech and to promote Czech literature among the people. They proved, as Kramerius proudly noted, that the Czech language had reached such a peak of development two centuries earlier, that it equaled Latin or Greek.[89] Through reading these books, the patriots hoped, their audience would be reminded of who they were and from whom they were descended, and that they would also remember their language and not harm it further.[90] For, as Rulík vividly expressed it,

> experience shows that there is no other way to the hope of preserving the purity of a language, and also that it cannot be better spread than by reading excellent books. Otherwise it would become plucked and bare, like Aesop's magpie, from which all the other birds (Oh! would that our native ones did not act that way!) pulled the feathers.[91]

Although they held the Czech of the golden age in veneration, the popular awakeners were more aware than their contemporaries that the language could not be forced into a sixteenth-century mold of perfection. Their activities as translators and popularizers brought home to them the difficulties of finding suitable Czech words for all topics, in spite of their repeated assertions that Czech was lexically rich.[92] If the language was to be a meaningful tool in spreading knowledge and national consciousness, it would have to remain in contact with the people who spoke it daily. Tomsa, who was also an active philologist and lexicographer, emphasized in his professional works the need to stay close to Czech as it was spoken (see chapter 2). Especially in technical fields, the translator or lexicographer should learn from the person who does the work, and if he is too proud to learn Czech from a laborer, peasant, or servant, he should give up writing rather than become a corrupter of the language.[93] Tomsa did not, however, recommend the uncritical acceptance of everything in the spoken language. "A true Czech must not be ashamed to learn from all Czechs in order to comprehend the complete linguistic usage," he wrote; "but he must test what he hears, in order to be able to teach correct Czech."[94]

In the interests of making their works understandable to the average Czech, the popular awakeners did not hesitate to modify even the language of the golden age. Kramerius, for example, edited the Czech in his Aesop's fables so that it conformed with contemporary spoken usage, which had been done (he argued) in each of its six previous editions.[95] Rulík's major concern in his translation of *Cesta z Moskvy do Číny* was to ensure that everyone who read it would understand everything in "their natural language," and Tomsa and Procházka modernized the Czech in their version of the autobiography of Charles IV.[96] More traditionally minded patriots criticized this attitude to the language, and Tomsa especially was the target for their attacks; but the popular awakeners persevered in their efforts.[97]

The popular awakeners did not limit their efforts on behalf of Czech literature to the publication of monuments of the past. In any case, the supply of available works was limited, and the taste of the Czech reader was often not ready to appreciate them. Probably the most common type of Czech reading material available to the common people was religious in content, consisting of pamphlets, saints' lives and "keys to heaven" (*nebeklíče*, collections of devotional prayers, songs, and meditations). Aside from these religious works, the most popular form of reading among the people was the so-called knightly romance (*rytířský roman*), usually badly modeled after German tales, or fairy stories filled with witches, magic, enchanted princesses, and the like.[98] Both the content and the language of these stories were not at a very high level. In an effort to wean the Czech reader away from such tales, the popular awakeners worked to replace them with reading material along similar lines, but written in good Czech and with a slightly more useful content.

During the last quarter of the eighteenth century, more and more Czech books were published in Bohemia. In addition to the press of the Normal School, the Prague publishers von Schönfeld, Diesbach, Herrl, and others all carried Czech books on their lists at one time or another. But for most of these publishers Czech books were a sideline at best, since they also published in German or other languages. Not until Kramerius organized his Czech Expedition (*Česká expedice*) in 1790 did a publishing house devoted exclusively to Czech literature came into existence.[99] At first, Kramerius was forced to publish works that were basically the same as those he hoped to replace, but gradually he was able to attempt to ensure that "the country people would get rid of many of that sort of tale, which indeed for its contemptibility deserves to be expunged completely from our Czech nation."[100] The books that the Czech Expedition published were usually travelogues or historical tales set in faraway places—a trend also visible in the publications of monuments from the past. They were frequently in the dialogue form and acquainted their readers with foreign countries and customs. But they were more than lessons in elementary geography, since they covered economics, culture, and religion also. Kramerius continued to praise reason and tolerance, as for example in his *Historické vypsání, kterak . . . Amerika od Kolumbusa vynálezená byla* (1803). The Spaniards' greed for gold and their behavior toward the natives were both criticized by Kramerius, who reminded his readers that "many Christians are much worse than people who know nothing about our holy religion."[101] The Czech Expedition also published works by other writers, among them Prokop Šedivý, whose tale *České amazonky*, published in 1792, had a laudatory foreword by Kramerius. He stressed that it was an original Czech story (taken from Hájek's chronicle), and boasted that for a change it was being translated from Czech into German.[102] Rulík also tried his hand at providing entertaining, but enlightening material for the Czech readership.[103]

As literature, the works published by the Czech Expedition were not particularly valuable. Yet they did begin the process of raising the taste of the common people, however little, and they did spread a much higher standard of Czech into the countryside. Through works such as Kramerius's travelogues and didactic encyclopedias like *Přítel lidu*, the general level of knowledge among the common people began to rise. The Czech Expedition, as an organization dedicated solely to publishing in Czech for Czechs, also played an important role as a center of patriotic activity. The depiction in Alois Jirásek's novel about the *obrození, F. L. Věk* (1887–1905), is probably not entirely a nationalistic exaggeration.

☼   ☼   ☼

Only Jan Rulík ever addressed himself specifically to defining what *enlightenment* meant, and he attempted it only in 1804, long after the heyday of enlightened absolutism was over. In a didactic work in the form of a priest's conversations with his village parishioners, he defined enlightenment as nothing more than making known something that had previously been unknown. From this it followed that there could be good and bad enlightenment; it was good when the new knowledge helped the community, and bad when it harmed it. According to Rulík, the man who truly had the good of the people at heart "gives the rules, according to which [they] should maintain their health, . . . he teaches how children should be reared, and . . . he sincerely places in the hands of the husbandman what he should do to improve his husbandry."[104] Though Rulík was probably the most conservative of the patriots who were concerned with the common people, his account hits the main points of all their activities.

The work of the popular awakeners went farther than this, however. Tomsa, Kramerius, and others tried to spread an enlightened religious outlook freed from the superstition and intolerance of the preceding centuries. Thus they began at least to prepare the common people for the changes that were to take place in succeeding years. In this, they were motivated by a desire to serve, not so much the state, as the *vlast* and nation. They believed that "the first and foremost duty of wise and truth-loving men in this century is to enlighten the human understanding more and more each day; and the nation that gains the light of reason from their praiseworthy, resolute efforts cannot but be considered happy and truly blessed."[105] To raise the level of understanding and living standards in the countryside was thus a part of their concept of their patriotic duty. By helping enlighten the Czech people, the popular awakeners sought to enable their nation proudly to take its rightful place among the other enlightened nations of Europe.[106]

As we have seen, the popular awakeners also worked to spread patriotism and Czech national consciousness among the people. They repeatedly held up the example of the early Czechs for their learning, bravery, and love of their language. It was the duty of every true Czech to strive to be a worthy descendant of such ancestors, and the publicity they gave to contemporary patriots was designed to inspire others to copy them. Above all, the popular awakeners worked for the Czech language, encouraged its use in all areas of life, and stressed again and again that a true patriot should love it and try to improve and spread it. As Kramerius warned, "If we someday allow our language to be wiped out through our negligence, it will not be otherwise, than that we will cease to be that which we are, *the Czech nation,* and with time change into a completely different and foreign nation."[107]

Finally, the popular awakeners contributed in an important way to solving the problem posed by the shift in meaning of the concept of nation. Their work in raising the standard of Czech reading material in the countryside, of propagandizing for Czech culture in a fuller sense, and of proving in practice that Czech could be used for a variety of functions, began the process of changing the patriots' attitudes to the nobles and the common people. At this time, the process was far from over, and many Czech patriots were still appalled at the relative unconcern of the nobility for the national cause. The Slovak patriot Bohuslav Tablic wrote to Jan Nejedlý about the support given by the Hungarian nobles, not only to Magyar, but also, in notable cases, to the Slovak tongue. "Only the Czech magnates and gentry do not want to write in Czech. How deeply your nation has fallen. Is it not possible to awaken it from this slumber?"[108] Josef Rautenkranc echoed this lament that the scholars and nobility did not use Czech, though he predicted that it would still be possible to win over "at least the young nobles—and then, it's won!"[109]

Others, however, were more willing to place their reliance on the simple country folk, giving up any hopes of converting the nobility to the national cause. Šebastián Hněvkovský rejected the idea of dedicating his epic poem, *Děvín,* to anyone (such dedications were the common practice), writing, "I do not request anything from all these noble scoundrels."[110] Rulík warned those who dismissed Czech because it was used only among the common people that "what is among the people should not instantly be considered vulgar; certainly there is no language that would not be in use in the countryside or villages."[111] Josef Jungmann also maintained that "every language in its home is a country language." The peasant is the most important citizen of the land and has the right to demand to be spoken to in his own tongue.[112] Vojtěch Nejedlý eventually gave credit to the common people in the countryside for maintaining the existence of the Czech nation. Putting the words into the mouth of Pelcl, he wrote: "We would already have been buried, had the country dwellers not continued to regard [Žižka's] virtues; it is they who maintain us, and purify our blood."[113] These ideas reflect the beginnings of a new way of looking at the common people, as the core of the nation, the class that kept alive the language and the national existence through dark days in the past and would be its security for the future. The common people were not pariahs, but patriots.[114] The popular awakeners played an important role in the realization of that fact.

6

"The Glorious, Widespread Slavic Nation"

*T*he Czechs were a Slavic people: of that fact the patriotic intellectuals had no doubt, and frequently expressed their consciousness of this Slavic heritage in their works. The precise meaning of this Slavic consciousness to Czech nationalism, however, has long been the subject of discussion, scholarly and otherwise.[1] A tradition of belonging to a larger Slavic whole had existed in various forms in Czech history, stretching back through the "baroque Slavism" of such as Bohuslav Balbín and Tomáš Pešina z Čechorodu, to the Hussite period and even farther. Conditions in the later eighteenth century, however, increasingly favored more contacts among the Slavs, including the Czechs, and this made possible the development of attitudes that differed from the traditional feelings of Slavic reciprocity. Although many of these contacts touched only the educated elite and therefore had a limited, scholarly character, there were also moments when even the wider masses were exposed to other Slavs and thus given the opportunity to confront the question of their relationship with them. This was especially true during the wars with France at the close of the century.[2]

The attitudes to the Slavs of the intelligentsia (and, to a more limited extent, the broader masses), were thus shaped by the same developments that affected their attitudes to their own nation, its past, its language, and its future possibilities. This naturally poses the question of the link between this Slavism and the Czech national consciousness that the patriotic intellectuals were articulating.[3] I will explore this link by examining the contacts between the Czechs and the other Slavs, to discover to what extent coherent attitudes to the Slavs were expressed and the part they played in this phase of the renascence.

Intellectual Contacts between Bohemia and the Slavic World

Before the revolutions in transportation and communication of the industrial era, direct links between the Czech lands and the lands of the other Slavs, especially Russia, were limited.[4] Thus it was largely the scholarly and cultural intelligentsia who could acquire knowledge of and form opinions about the rest of Europe, including the Slavic world. The development of learning in the eighteenth century provided the background for the growth of these contacts, as the world of scholarship became an increasingly international one. The cosmopolitanism of the Enlightenment encouraged the exchange of ideas among the members of the "republic of learning." The establishment of academies of science, which elected honorary and corresponding members from abroad, provided a forum for the creative clash of ideas and their exchange with sister institutions elsewhere.[5] Bohemia was a part of this European development; and by the latter part of the eighteenth century it had produced several scholars of international repute and given birth to a learned society of its own, the Royal Bohemian Society of Sciences.[6]

One Bohemian scholar with a truly European reputation was the historian Gelasius Dobner, and his greatest work also involved him in links of a kind with the Slavic world. This was his famous edition of Hájek z Libočan's chronicle, which earned him the title "father of Czech critical historiography" and provoked heated polemical discussions when it was published in 1761 (see chapter 1).[7] The charge was that Dobner had "thrown out on genuine critical grounds, as a simple fable arising no earlier than the thirteenth century, the national fathers (*Stammväter*) of the Czech and Polish nations, Čech and Lech, who had previously been believed in as an article of faith."[8] This brought down on Dobner's head the opprobrium of his fellow countrymen who "believed that the honor and history of Bohemia had been damaged in the extreme," and also ranged on the side of his opponents a learned society in Leipzig, the Societas Jablonoviana, and its founder, the Polish prince J. A. Jabłonowski.

Jabłonowski's partisanship of Lech and his brother stemmed from family pride as well as conservative "patriotism," since according to Dobner the prince claimed descent in the direct line from Lech himself.[9] The Societas Jablonoviana became a sort of sponsor and center of attacks on Dobner, and efforts to prove the existence of the national fathers filled the pages of its journal, the *Acta Societatis Jablonovianae*. Jabłonowski corresponded with Dobner's Czech opponents, especially Pubička and Duchovský, and he published some of their articles attacking Dobner in the *Acta*. The literary fruits of the collaboration between the Prague "Čechists" and Jabłonowski's society did not amount to more than a few articles, but their contacts were close enough to lead one scholar to speak of a "Prague branch" of the Societas Jablonoviana.[10] In addition to bringing about contacts between Bohemian scholars and Poles, the quarrel over Čech and Lech expanded to include, at least tangentially, the Russians. The antagonists searched for evidence to support them and refute the opposition, and both sides turned to Russian sources, such as Nestor's chronicle or the works of Lomonosov or Schlözer, to buttress their arguments.[11]

Such contacts as were created by the controversy tended to die down as time and the spread of critical historical method gave Dobner the better of the argument, though an attack on his views appeared as late as 1784.[12] Beyond the fact that the principals were mostly Bohemians and Poles, and words like *patriotism* and *unpatriotic* were bandied about in some of the polemics, there was little in the way of Slavic consciousness expressed during this quarrel. The center of gravity of the conflict lay in the political organization of the earliest Slavs, and the clash was largely between two differing concepts of how nations originate: an older, traditional, even feudal one, and a more modern, enlightened one.[13] The traditional view was well suited to the patriotism of the privileged levels of Bohemian society, who were affected by the centralizing reforms of the Habsburg state and whose arguments against its attacks on their position were usually couched in political, legal and historical terms. Even the rather far-fetched genealogical fancies of such as Prince Jabłonowski (which had their counterparts among the Bohemian nobility) served to establish the antiquity and validity of their claims. Yet, as the idea of the nation broadened, these foundations were no longer an adequate basis for resisting the demands of the modern state. Dobner's picture of the origins of the Czech nation was already better suited to the newer cultural and linguistic definition of the nation in whose name centralization should be resisted. In any case, the contacts with the Slavic worlds created by the dispute over Čech and Lech were, for the time being, limited.

Better-organized and longer-lasting relations with the foreign scholarly world, including the Slavic, were made possible by the Royal Bohemian Society of Sciences. This was especially true of contacts between Bohemia and the St. Petersburg Academy of Sciences in Russia. Direct contacts between the two institutions were at first largely concentrated in the natural sciences. Ignac von Born, who had been instrumental in founding the Bohemian society, corresponded with P. S. Pallas in St. Petersburg on geological and mineralogical topics, while other members of the society, such as the astronomer Franz Johann Gerstner, or the brothers Johann and Joseph Mayer, followed with interest the activities of their colleagues in Russia. Articles and notices in the journal of the society, *Abhandlungen einer Privatgesellschaft in Böhmen*, and the exchange of this and other publications with St. Petersburg, testified to the scope and nature of the contacts thus engendered. To crown them, the St. Petersburg Academy elected Born an honorary member at its fiftieth anniversary session in 1776—the only scholar from the Habsburg monarchy to be so honored.[14]

It seems difficult to relate these contacts between Russia and Bohemian natural scientists, many of whom were not of Slavic origin, directly to the development of national consciousness and the Czech national renascence. Certainly there was no expression of Slavic solidarity or Russophilism in them. Admittedly scientific subject matter did not lend itself to such expressions; but it is not necessary to posit the existence of such attitudes in order to account for interest in Russia. For one thing, Russian science enjoyed an international reputation, making it a natural object of interest for any scientist. There was also a general European curiosity about emergent Russia in the age of "enlightened absolutism," as epitomized by Voltaire's correspondence with Catherine II. In addition, many Russian scientists were Germans, either from the Baltic provinces or the states of the empire. In any case, the Bohemian Society of Sciences, like its sister institutions, maintained links with the entire world of European scholarship—and when it elected its first foreign members they all came from the Habsburg lands or the Holy Roman Empire.[15]

The Bohemian Society of Sciences did, however, send two of its leading members to Russia during 1792 and 1793. They were Josef Dobrovský and Count Joachim von Sternberg, the former being sent on a mission to collect literary evidence for the history of Czech, and the latter exploring the state of the natural sciences in Russia. The society had been blessed with a gift of 6,000 guilders by the newly crowned king of Bohemia, Leopold II, and it was decided to use the money to finance journeys by Dobrovský to Sweden and Russia in search of examples of Czech literature that might have been scattered through the region after the Swedes plundered Prague during the Thirty Years' War.[16] Dobrovský had considered a similar journey some years before,[17] but had never progressed beyond the planning stage because of the financial and other logistical problems. Thanks to the Society of Sciences, Dobrovský now had financial support, and had also gained a congenial traveling companion. Both men published works based on their experiences and observations on this journey, works that provided a rather critical insight into Catherine's Russia.[18]

Though Dobrovský was quick to broaden the terms of his mandate to include Slavic literature in general, as well as monuments of Czech in particular,[19] his *Litterarische Nachrichten* that he published upon his return (in the *Abhandlungen* in 1795 and separately in 1796) kept quite closely to his literary subject. Dobrovský's correspondence with friends written on his journey contains a few more revealing remarks about the Slavs outside Bohemia as he saw them. A fairly unflattering description comes from a letter to Jiří Ribay:

> Our dear Slavic brethren are, by the hair color, still the same as Procopius described them. But their morals are no longer so simple and unspoiled. I was very displeased with their talent for stealing, and could have called them with Saint Boniface *foedissimum genus hominum.* The Poles are, however, somewhat better behaved than the Russians, but still *slavicae fidei,* as the German annalists say. Your Slovaks are already very cultivated people, when compared with these.[20]

These comments were probably not intended to apply to the men of learning whom Dobrovský met in Russia, a group that included such figures as P. S. Pallas, Count Musin-Pushkin, and others; but his general opinion of cultural life in Russia and the state of Russian literature did not seem very high. As late as 1813 he remarked of the Russians, "These people are usually lacking in the humanities, and it is difficult to speak with them about fundamental principles."[21] Nevertheless, Dobrovský found the impressions of his experience, and especially the books he brought back with him, very valuable. "I do not like to give away anything of the *Slavicis* I have brought," he wrote to Kopitar, "for they remind me of Russia."[22] In later years, as the diary of Count Eugen Czernin bears witness, Dobrovský greatly enjoyed recalling his journey.[23]

Exchanges between learned societies and fleeting personal contacts were not as important in the scholarly traffic between the Czech lands and the rest of the Slavic world as the flourishing literary correspondence carried on by many people who never met face to face. In this way information was gathered and views exchanged even after political developments made travel difficult and dangerous. Much of the network of mutual encouragement thus created centered on Dobrovský, who came to be called the "patriarch" of Slavic studies, and his own extensive personal correspondence is a good example of the phenomenon.

In matters Slavic, Dobrovský found valuable assistance from his correspondents in Vienna, chiefly Durych and Zlobický, to whom the younger Slovene scholar, Jernej Kopitar was later added. Each of these men not only exchanged ideas and information with him themselves, but also acted as intermediaries for other Slavic scholars. When Dobrovský visited Vienna briefly in 1796, Durych and Zlobický introduced him to several other academics, including a young Polish intellectual, Samuel Bogumil Linde, with whom Dobrovský continued to correspond in later years.[24] Durych was also acquainted with a Croat, Adam Alois Baričević, who assisted him in his magnum opus, the *Bibliotheca slavica* (1795).[25] Baričević also corresponded with Dobrovský's friend Dlabáč, who acted as a go-between for Baričević and the German slavist from Lusatia, Karl Gottlob von Anton.[26] Durych had a lively interest in Russian literature in his field, though he lacked Dobrovský's good fortune in being able to travel to Russia. Nevertheless, his *Bibliotheca slavica* gives eloquent proof of the extent of his acquaintance with early Slavic literary monuments of Russian provenance.[27]

Dobrovský himself had a fairly extensive acquaintance, both personal and through Kopitar, with South Slav scholars.

While he was in Vienna in 1796, he met both Marijan Lano-sović, the grammarian from Slavonia, and Joachim Stulli, a lexicographer from Dubrovnik.[28] He was also acquainted with a leading representative of the Croat intelligentsia, the bishop of Zagreb, Maksimilijan Vrhovac, from whom he requested contributions on the Croats for a journal of Slavic studies he was contemplating.[29] Vrhovac continued to express interest in Dobrovský's Slavic researches, even to the point of offering to help finance a journey to the Slavic monastery on Mount Athos, which was to have similar aims to Dobrovský's Russian travels.[30] Other Croat scholars with whom Dobrovský was in contact included the bishop of Djakovo, Antun Mandić, and Josip Voltić-Voltiggi, whose trilingual Latin-German-Croat dictionary was published in 1803. Dobrovský was also familiar with the work of the Piarist from Dubrovnik, Franjo Marija Appendini, and criticized his views on the relative age of Slavic settlement in Illyria.[31]

Among Slovenes, Dobrovský corresponded with Baron Zois, the patriotic nobleman and Maecenas, the grammarian, Valentin Vodnik, and a less well-known Slavist, Franz Metelko. He was also well acquainted with the Slovene church historian, from 1782 professor of church history at Prague, Kaspar Royko. Royko's major work, a history of the Council of Constance that was very sympathetic to Jan Hus, was favorably reviewed by Dobrovský.[32] His most durable contacts with a Slovene, however, were probably with Baron Zois's young protégé, Jernej Kopitar. Kopitar, who eventually became librarian at the Hofbibliothek in Vienna, corresponded with Dobrovský over a twenty-year period, and his own works, especially the *Grammatik der slavischen Sprache in Krain, Kärnten und Steyermark* (1809), clearly showed his mentor's influence.[33]

Dobrovský's contacts with Serbs were rather fewer. He was acquainted with Dimitrije Davidović, who published a Serbian newspaper in Vienna, and his colleague, Dimitrije Frusić, and he corresponded with the physicist, Atanasij Stojković, from 1803 to 1812.[34] Stojković was employed at the university in Kharkov as a professor of physics, and at his instigation, Dobrovský was elected an honorary member of the university. Dobrovský's own account of this honor, conveyed to Kopitar, suggests that he saw it as a chance to encourage scholarly contacts, but did not find this view shared on the other side:

> Stojković is writing Russian textbooks of physics *et alia* in Kharkov. They made me an honorary member of the university, and ordered Bohemian garnets from me for the Kharkov beauties. Rather than burdening me with such commissions, they should have sent me some Russian books.[35]

Dobrovský followed the works of the great Serb grammarian and lexicographer, Vuk Stefanović Karadžić, with interest, subscribing in advance to six copies of his second collection of Serbian folk songs. But he did not approve of Vuk's efforts to create a literary language out of the dialect spoken by the common people. In keeping with his views on the Czech language (see chapter 2), Dobrovský argued that Vuk's proceedings would create a break between the literature of the past and modern works. Although Dobrovský's authority helped preserve the norm-giving status of the language of the sixteenth century for Czech, in the case of Serbian, Vuk's arguments won the day. Their disagreement did not prevent friendly relations between the two, however, and Vuk left behind an engaging word-portrait of Dobrovský some ten years before the latter's death:

> I first saw this patriarch of Slavonic literature at Davidović's last Saturday . . . great as was my joy at seeing Dobrovský, it was even greater to find in him not some paunchy, dumpy, stooping monk, but a tall, thin old man who really steps out like a young fellow of a third of his years.[36]

Dobrovský gained some knowledge of the state of learning in the Polish lands when his return journey from Russia in 1793 led him through Warsaw, Kraków, and other towns.[37]

Aside from this first-hand experience, however, his direct contacts with Poles were relatively few. Some letters from younger scholars in Dobrovský's archives seem to be only formal rituals of homage to the "patriarch" of Slavic studies, such as those from Jan Paweł Woronicz or Julian Ursyn Niemcewicz. More concrete and fruitful contacts took place in his correspondence with Linde and the librarian at Kraków, Jerzy Samuel Bandtke.

Dobrovský met Linde in Vienna in 1796, as we have seen, but their surviving correspondence dates from 1808. At that time, Linde, a protégé of the Polish patriot, Count J. M. Ossoliński, was already beginning work on his six-volume Polish dictionary (1807–1814).[38] Since Dobrovský was working on his own dictionary of Czech, Linde's undertaking interested him greatly, and much of their correspondence was given over to Dobrovský's comments and criticisms of Linde's work. Dobrovský had some reservations about the result, but both men continued to hold each other in high regard. Linde was elected a member of the Bohemian Society of Sciences upon Dobrovský's nomination, and he returned the favor in 1804, securing Dobrovský's admission to the Society of Friends of Science (Towarzystwa Przyjaciół Nauk) in Warsaw.[39]

Bandtke initiated correspondence with Dobrovský in 1810, and the two men exchanged views on a wide range of subjects, from Slavic history through folklore to mythology. Bandtke contributed to Dobrovský's periodical *Slovanka* (1814–1815), and Dobrovský's influence can be seen in Bandtke's *Polnische Grammatik* (1808) and his articles "Über den reinsten der slawischen Dialekte" (1815) and "Uwagi nad językiem czeskim, polskim i terazniejszym rosyjskim" (1815). Bandtke, like Linde, sealed his scholarly friendship with Dobrovský by sponsoring his election to honorary membership in the Kraków learned society in 1816.[40]

Dobrovský did not limit his contacts and interests only to the major Slavic nations. As a theological student in Prague, he met and befriended some Lusatian students at the Lusatian seminar, and he stayed in contact with some of them to the end of his life.[41] Dobrovský's correspondence with the German Lusatian scholar K. G. von Anton, and with the translator of the Bible, I. F. Fryco, survives today.[42] Throughout his life he was interested in Sorbian, and although he once characterized it as "an awkward and disfigured language, which a Czech or Moravian would be ashamed of," he nevertheless continued work on a grammar of it during his last years.[43]

There was, then, a significant degree of contact between the Czech scholars interested in Slavic topics and others with similar interests, including other Slavs. Through personal contacts, links between learned societies, and correspondence, they exchanged information, compared notes, and criticized each other's works. In the process, they stimulated the growth and development of Slavic studies as a discipline, first as an incidental theme in works devoted to other topics, and eventually as a subject in itself. Since many of the scholars involved in these developments were themselves Slavs, their works and their correspondence make it possible to glean some ideas about their attitudes toward the Slavs and the nature of their own Slavic consciousness.

Slavic Studies and the Works of Czech Scholars

Their interest in Czech history, language, and literature would have made it difficult for the patriotic intellectuals to ignore entirely the early history of the Slavs and their culture. In fact, most of them clearly stressed both the greatness of the Slavs and the part played by the Czechs in the general Slavic cultural heritage. These writers had a strong consciousness of the Slavic origin of the Czechs, and in their minds anything that reflected poorly on the Slavs also reflected poorly on the Czechs. This feeling accounted for the sometimes defensive tone of some of their statements.

Among Bohemian historians in the late eighteenth century, F. M. Pelcl had a special place because of the great popularity of his general history of Bohemia, which saw three editions during his lifetime and a posthumous one in 1817.

In the section about the Slavs at the beginning of his *Kurz-gefasste Geschichte der Böhmen*, Pelcl wrote enthusiastically: "There is no nation on the entire earth that has spread itself, its language, its power, and colonies so astonishingly widely, as the Slavic." Wherever one looked, from the Adriatic to the Kamchatka peninsula, one met Slavic peoples everywhere. "The Russians, a branch of this great nation, send their fleet into the Archipelago on the one side and the Sea of Japan on the other."[44] These thoughts, which became one of the leit-motivs of Czech statements on the Slavs, were repeated in Pelcl's Czech version of this work, which he thoroughly revised and expanded, *Nová kronyka česká* (1791). The picture Pelcl drew of the cultural life of the early Slavs showed them to be at least as cultivated as other pagan nations, and he argued that their religious beliefs were even more rational (there speaks the voice of the Enlightenment!) than the pantheons of the Greeks and Romans, since the Slavs based theirs on observations of nature.[45]

Pelcl's colleague, M. A. Voigt, also presented a positive, not to say idealized, picture of the early Slavs. In his *Über den Geist der Böhmischen Gesetze* (1788), he admitted that there was very little known about the early laws and social organization of the Slavs. But this was because they had no written language before the adoption of Christianity, and it did not mean that they had no organized social life. The very fact that they were able to conquer and spread through such a large part of Europe argued the opposite.[46] Voigt described the early Slavs as pugnacious and warlike, but also hospitable and upright. In addition to hunting for food, they practiced the more peaceful arts of farming and animal husbandry. His attitude toward the Slavs was strongly defensive, directed mainly at the Germans, who "den[ied] the ancient Slavic peoples all cultivation, order, and political organization, and present[ed] them as the most unintelligent and uncivilized barbarians. This is the result of the historically well-known national hatred of the Germans for the Czechs."[47] Voigt's arguments were propagated in Czech by the popular awakener,

Jan Rulík, in *Velmi užitečná historie o slovutném národu českém* (1793). If Rulík was not original in his ideas, he did provide a link between scholars who wrote mostly in German or
Latin and the people who read only Czech. He, too, attacked
the German view of the Slavs as barbarians and the Czechs
as no better than thieves and brigands. Regrettably, this view
had been absorbed even by such Czech chroniclers as Hájek
and Dubravský.[48]

Bohemian writers on the history of Czech and Slavic literature also discussed the early Slavs and their importance,
defending them against outside criticism. Procházka's *De saecularibus liberalium artium* included information on the customs and beliefs of the ancient Slavs and the first Czechs. This
work was also one of Rulík's sources, and he lamented that it
had not been written in Czech.[49] Even more influential,
though also written in Latin, was Durych's *Bibliotheca slavica,* the first volume of which appeared in 1795. Durych's
interest in early Slavic literature had grown out of his research
into the first translations of the Bible by the Slavs, published
in 1777 as *De Slavo-bohemica sacri codicis versione dissertatio.* In addition to providing a history of translations of the
Bible, Durych's *Dissertatio* also contributed to the material
on the Czech language that was to aid in efforts to improve
the condition of contemporary Czech.[50] The scope of his *Bibliotheca slavica* was much wider. The work was planned to fill
seven volumes, which were to cover the earliest Slavs, the
development of Slavic written languages, and other topics.
Before the project could be realized, however, Durych died.
Only the first volume was published, and the manuscript of
the second was apparently lost at the publisher's in Budapest.
Yet even the first volume contained an impressive amount of
material. It dealt with the origins of the different Slavic tribes
and their languages, especially the literary languages; it discussed the morals of the early Slavs, the beginnings of learning in their territories, and the relationship of Czech to the
Slavic literary language during different periods.[51] Durych's

picture of the early Slavs was, in keeping with the views of his colleagues, quite positive.

The Slavs made their appearance in Josef Dobrovský's history of the Czech language in each of its versions, beginning with the first, in the *Abhandlungen* of the Bohemian Society of Sciences for 1791. "Since the sixth century," wrote Dobrovský, "the Slavs have played an important role on the great stage of the world." He, too, rejected the picture of the Slavs as a barbaric people without political organization, writing that "for ages the Serbs, Croats, Poles, Czechs and Russians have appeared in history as great and powerful nations (*Volksstämme*) who founded their own states and to whom the other, weaker nations attached themselves."[52]

The early history of the Czech nation, and the study of the Czech language, reminded these Bohemian scholars of their ties with the other Slavs. Yet their interest and concern were still limited in certain ways. For many of the historians, the Slavs in general, and Russia in particular, represented possible sources of information that could be used to answer questions about the Czech past. The quarrel over Čech and Lech was a quarrel over the origin of the Czech nation, and the Russian historians to whom the Bohemian researchers turned were brought into the argument only for the light they could shed on its earliest history.[53] Bohemian historians tended to focus on the independence and state-forming abilities of the earliest Slavs, including the Czechs, the relationship between the medieval Bohemian kingdom and the Holy Roman Empire, and, by implication at least, the rights of Bohemia in its contemporary relationship with Vienna.[54] The interest in the Slavs expressed by these scholars was still a long way removed from any sort of pan-Slav tendency. Similar limitations apply to the attitudes of the students of Czech literary history. The other Slavs could provide much useful information on the history of the Czech language and the development of its literature, and much of the interest in them was motivated by this consideration. Even Dobrovský's celebrated trip to Russia, already mentioned, was undertaken not to provide the Society of Sciences with information on a contemporary Slavic empire, but to search for ancient Czech literary monuments.

This is not to deny the clear perception of a Slavic ethnic relationship and a concern for the reputation of the Slavs that was expressed in these scholars' works of history and literary history. Such notes were also frequently sounded in their correspondence, stimulating further work, until eventually the study of the Slavs began to be seen as a subject in its own right, and not just as the first chapter of the study of the Czechs. A sense that the world of learning had not given the Slavs their due showed through in Dobrovský's complaint to Ribay that in biblical criticism far more attention was being paid to inferior Persian, Armenian, or other versions of the Bible, while Slavic translations were being ignored: "It is, however, a not inconsiderable honor for us Slavs, that we can contribute something important to the criticism of the New Testament."[55] Again, when he complimented Fryco on his Sorbian translation of the Old Testament, Dobrovský reminded him, "Belonging to one nation, the Slavic, we stand always within the bond of linguistic relationship,"[56] and he reiterated to Kopitar the idea that "we Slavs must stick together."[57] "If Czech and Lech were brothers," he assured Bandtke when the latter first wrote to him, "so we are at least cousins. . . . That we Slavs should concern ourselves so little with our reputation! Foreigners seldom do us justice as it is."[58]

Similar attitudes were echoed by other scholars, but it was one thing to agree that "Slavs should stick together" and another to be able to do anything concrete. Keeping informed on the progress of scholarship in the Slavic world was a problem, and the correspondence carried on by these men contains frequent references to difficulties. "If only there were a closer bond among us Slavs," wrote Dobrovský. "But the Slavic world is too large, literary traffic too small, etc."[59] Later he complained in a similar way to Kopitar, writing, "Unfortunately, we here know practically nothing of what is going on with you, and the Poles . . . also know nothing of our efforts."[60] Mutual ignorance could lead one Slavic nation to belittle the achievements of others in comparison with its own, a circumstance Dobrovský deplored. "We must not ignore each other," he insisted.[61]

At various times, Dobrovský and his correspondents discussed plans to improve cooperation and communication among the Slavs. One such scheme was for a multilingual dictionary of the Slavic languages, a Slavic polyglot, on which scholars from the different lands would cooperate. Zlobický suggested the germ of such an idea as early as 1781, advocating work on a general Slavic grammar, classification of the Slavic dialects, and a history of the Slavic languages.[62] Later Dobrovský discussed a somewhat similar plan with Ribay: "What do you say to my intention of creating a proposal for a Slavic polyglot? When I have organized my scattered ideas on the subject, I am thinking of presenting it to the Empress of Russia, or the Holy Roman Emperor, who rules over practically all the Slavic nations. . . . It would be a pity if all this should remain only a dream!"[63]

Ribay was in favor of the scheme, especially since the Russians were already working on something similar. He felt, however, that it would be better to submit the project to the Russian empress rather than the Austrian ruler, because such things were better supported in Russia.[64] Nothing definite came of the idea at this time, however, and the St. Petersburg Academy of Sciences published its own comparative dictionary, *Glossarium linguarum totius orbis* (1787–1789), by itself. The plan did not die out altogether, especially since the *Glossarium* did not earn an entirely favorable opinion from other Slavic scholars.[65] Much later, Dobrovský and Kopitar agreed that some form of general Slavic reference work based on the materials collected by Durych for his *Bibliotheca slavica* would be worthwhile. There would still be a number of serious problems to overcome, however, and Dobrovský remarked pessimistically, "Who shall help us now? In my case a sickly old age draws near. Others do not have enough leisure. The zeal and enthusiasm of one and another decline, etc."[66] In this case, too, his pessimism was justified.

There were other schemes to rectify the situation of Slavic scholars, and one of the more promising of these was enthusiastically broached to Dobrovský by Kopitar in 1810:

> It would be very desirable if the scattered Slavists, often working *in contrarium sensum,* had a general conductor. . . . And the continuation of *Slavín* [Dobrovský's literary periodical, see below] would be the best means to that end. Thus a Slavic academy . . . would gradually form. . . . The Prague, Warsaw, Petersburg, and the future Illyrian Academies would become so many offshoots of this Slavic Academy![67]

Dobrovský's response was rather cautious: he reminded Kopitar of the fate of Pelcl's *Hromada,* which, according to Dobrovský, came to nothing because of the opposition of Riegger, who feared that the authorities in Vienna would be suspicious of the idea. "Perhaps, however, other Slavs are less suspect than the zealous Czechs, whose language has long been regarded in Austria as the rebel (revolutionary, in the new style) language," he concluded.[68] In any case, he predicted, quarrels over alphabet and orthography would ensure that such an academy would fall apart due to internal dissension. In a letter to Bandtke about the idea, Dobrovský regretfully concluded that without greater religious and political unity among the Slavs, such a central Slavic academy could never come about.[69] One political problem he foresaw was the task of persuading the existing academies, especially the Russian one, to take a subordinate place to Vienna. "An Imperial Russian Academy should degrade itself into an affiliated branch?" he sarcastically demanded.[70] Basically, Dobrovský considered the idea of a central Slavic academy in Vienna as much a pious hope as he did Puchmajer's plans to revive Pelcl's *Hromada.*[71]

Since different orthographies helped keep the Slavs apart, the development of a common orthography for the Slavic languages was another idea the patriotic scholars canvassed in their correspondence. The complexities of differing versions of the Cyrillic alphabet, Latin letters, or the German, "Schwabach" type, made the idea of a single, universally accepted system attractive. "If only all the Slavs had our own, truly good orthography!" wrote Dobrovský to Ribay. "But they write as they please, especially the Dalmatians."[72] He thought it was a shame that peoples so closely related linguistically should thus artificially divide themselves,[73] but, as he reminded Kopitar, the greatest obstacle was the impossibility of reaching a compromise acceptable to all parties. Although he and Kopitar exchanged possible alphabets throughout their correspondence, Dobrovský remained somewhat skeptical of the younger man's enthusiasm. "Kopitar . . . is a young hothead who sees the salvation of the Slavic world in the Latin alphabet," he wrote to Bandtke, who himself had doubts about the possibility of a common orthography.[74]

One member of the intelligentsia who suggested a series of practical reforms, only to have them rejected by Dobrovský and his friends, was F. J. Tomsa, the linguist and popular awakener. His proposals were set out in his *Grössere čechische Orthographie* (1812), and one of his arguments, reflected in the full title of the work, was that the new orthography could be used for all the Slavic languages.[75] Even this failed to win Tomsa any appreciable following at the time, although ironically enough his changes have all been accepted by modern Czech.

More far-fetched than Tomsa's proposals was the suggestion, put forward in Puchmajer's *Pravopis rusko-český* (1805), that Czech should be written with the Russian alphabet. This idea did not meet with approval among Slavic scholars, either. Dobrovský expressed his opposition to it in forceful language: "If the Czechs should ever become Russian subjects, one could well consider how one might read the text of an *ukaz* in Czech and Russian at the same time. At present we want to go on writing Czech, as long as one is able to read it." Bandtke agreed that it was a pity to see a Czech give up his

own heritage for that of Moscow.[76] Not everyone objected to
the idea, however. The proposal that the Slavs should all
adopt the Russian alphabet came up later in a conversation
between Dobrovský and the president of the Russian Academy, Aleksandr Shishkov. Dobrovský's account of their meeting, as he described it to Kopitar, left little doubt about where
his own views lay:

> Shishkov expressed himself on the question thus: Why do
> you need to break your heads over it? Just take our alpha-
> bet. To the exception that even some Russians wanted to
> write with Latin letters, the answer was: Such people
> should have their heads cut off. . . . This results in the de-
> nationalizing of a people. You may negotiate with such
> decapitators; I will let it be, [at the risk of being] de-
> nounced as such a great heretic.[77]

Another more promising idea for encouraging contacts
among Slavic scholars, which contributed much to the emergence of Slavic studies as an independent subject, was the
suggestion of creating a periodical devoted to Slavic topics.
One enthusiastic advocate of this plan was Anton, who in the
latter half of the 1780s urged Dobrovský to add his support,
even suggesting that Dobrovský was best fitted to be the editor of such a journal. At this time, Dobrovský's own views
were less sanguine. He pointed out that his location (at the
time he was vice-rector of the General Seminary near Olomouc in Moravia) and lack of spare time posed certain problems. Vienna would be the only useful place from which to
publish such a periodical.[78] A decade later, however, Dobrovský had returned to Prague, and his opinions had changed.
He expressed himself quite positively to Anton on the subject,
and early in 1797 he told Zlobický that he had in fact decided
to publish a Slavic journal himself.[79]

He began to collect material and appealed to his friends
for contributions, but not until 1806 could he publish the first
of his Slavic collections. *Slawin. Bothschaft aus Böhmen an
alle Slawischen Völker, oder Beiträge zur Kenntniss der Sla-*

wischen Literatur nach allen Mundarten presented a composite picture of the contemporary state of Slavic studies and included material on the characteristics of the ancient Slavs, the Glagolitic alphabet, biographies of Slavic literary figures, reports on the habits, dress, and appearance of various Slavic nations, including the Illyrians, Slovenes, Cossacks, and Russians, and a selection of Russian folk proverbs. Dobrovský presented the Slavs as a peace-loving people, in particular by including the famous section from J. G. Herder's *Ideen zur Philosophie der Geschichte der Menschheit* about the Slavs (with minor omissions due to the censor).[80] He made the same point in his introduction, though less directly, while at the same time contriving to stress once more the geographic range and linguistic ties of the Slavs. He quoted the angels' "Gloria" in Luke 2:14, from the earliest Slavic translation of the Bible, and then continued:

> Go forth from Bohemia to your Slavic brethren, dear Slavín; bring them these joyous tidings. . . . How could many a Slavic people living among Germans in the year 1805 expect that it could still understand completely and easily a verse from the Gospel translated about the year 865? That you should find Slavic-speaking people anywhere who cannot understand a single word of it, is hardly to be believed.[81]

The censor had approved Dobrovský's request to be allowed to publish *Slavín* as a periodical, but this first volume was all that ever appeared (it was reissued in 1808 with a slightly altered title page). Dobrovský made a second attempt, however, to establish a journal of Slavic studies with his *Slovanka. Zur Kentniss der alten und neuen slawischen Literatur, der Sprachkunde nach allen Mundarten, der Geschichte und Alterthümer*, which appeared in two volumes in 1814 and 1815. *Slovanka* could well be seen as a delayed continuation of *Slavín*—certainly they both had a similarly wide scope. *Slovanka* contained material on the Slavic languages, the history of the Slavic Bible, ethnographic material on the Bulgarians,

Poles, Slovenes, and Ruthenians, and reviews of contemporary works on Slavic topics.

In one section of *Slovanka,* Dobrovský showed again how defensive these scholars could become when the Slavs were denigrated. He reprinted a rather negatively colored article by a German author about the Slavs in the sub-Carpathian regions of the Kingdom of Hungary, "Russniaken in der Marmarosch," interpellating defensive footnotes whenever the author made a particularly offensive statement (reproduced in the excerpts below in parentheses). The article began by describing the personal appearance of these Ruthenes: "Their facial features are completely Slavic in both sexes, and yet one can sometimes find among the younger women a few with pleasant, regular features. (What then are completely Slavic features but the opposite of pleasant and regular? Rohrer describes Slavic faces completely differently)." Next the author commented on their general character, noting,

> [It] corresponds fully with that of all Slavs (the author does not appear, however, to be acquainted with the general character of all the Slavs), it is only more strongly expressed by their greater crudeness and negligence than is the case with their other brothers in Europe. . . . In marriage they are frequently untrue to each other, and know no bounds therein, which may be the reason that venereal disease is always so rife among them. (Bonifacius, however, praises the unclean Wends of his time for their marital fidelity).

This running criticism of the lack of knowledge displayed by the author is a good example of Dobrovský's almost personal involvement with his subject.[82]

The tone and language of *Slavín* and *Slovanka* was scholarly, and therefore their impact outside of exclusively academic circles was limited; but within them, they further solidified Dobrovský's reputation as the patriarch of Slavic studies and encouraged younger scholars to enter the field.[83] With these two publications of Dobrovský's, the study of the Slavs among the Czechs went beyond the limits of repeated assertions of the Slavic relationship in language and culture, defenses of the ancient Slavs against their critics, and expressions of admiration for the geographic spread of the Slavic nation. It also went beyond its role as a support for the worth of Czech history, language, and culture, and became, even while it influenced later aspects of the renascence in the works of men like Kollár and Šafařík, a subject of study in its own right.

An interesting feature of the attitudes toward the Slavs expressed by the patriotic intellectuals in their works and their correspondence is that they almost entirely avoided commenting on current political affairs affecting the Slavs. Even such major issues as the partitions of Poland or Russia's fortunes in the Napoleonic wars received scant attention, and there is almost nothing on the future of Slavdom in the Slavophile tone found in some of the private correspondence of the younger Czech patriots such as Josef Jungmann and his friend, Antonín Marek (to be discussed later). The rare moments in which Dobrovský wrote in broad and prophetic terms were usually connected with his periodic attacks of severe depression and mental instability and did not find a response among his correspondents. Usually when they alluded to political events it was only briefly or when they had a direct bearing on topics of more interest to them. For example, Ribay wrote to Dobrovský in 1790 about the national aspirations of the "Illyrians" at the coming Hungarian Diet, reporting plans to demand recognition as a separate community with all the freedoms and privileges of citizenship, and the right to set up their own university and national library. They were going to invite scholars from Russia to aid them, and "that would be a rich source of *Slavicorum!*" Dobrovský's response was that he had always valued the Illyrian nation, especially now, when it was giving thought to its culture.[84] These events, then, interested Dobrovský and Ribay because of the opportunity they offered of opening up new sources of information for Slavic studies.

With Kopitar, too, Dobrovský touched on the position of

the Slavs in Hungary vis-à-vis the Magyars. "It is impossible to discuss anything sensible with the Magyars, when it interferes with their patriotism," he wrote in 1810. "Still they will never bring matters as far as some enthusiasts would like to, since many still champion Latin."[85] He returned to the topic later, alluding to the action of the Bohemian Estates in 1615, when they had made Czech the official language of their kingdom:

> The Hungarian parliamentary resolution of 1805 regarding the state language in Hungary will not, to be sure, be torn up as quickly as the ordinance of our own Estates was. But neither will it have eternal validity. The Slovaks are opposing it bravely enough, and if they ever did have to exchange their language for another, there would at least be a better choice.[86]

The fate of Poland at the end of the Napoleonic wars also caught Dobrovský's attention. In a letter to his friend Bandtke, Dobrovský wrote this advice: "You Poles are indeed very warm patriots; I could only wish you still more endurance and discretion. It would be a pity if the Russians should swallow up not only Polish territory, but also the Polish language. A single stream is not always as beneficial as variety."[87] This sort of comment was rather unusual. Much more typical of Dobrovský was the way in which he made the transition from New Year's greetings for 1810 to Kopitar, with a mention of wartime sufferings, to the statement that "otherwise, that which depends upon political relations should not concern us at all. *Ergo ad slavica.* . . ."[88] Even in 1812, the year of Napoleon's disastrous Russian campaign, Dobrovský was only slightly more expansive: "The Russians may gain glory for themselves with deeds of war, in which even the Germans must wish them luck; we want to busy ourselves in *Grammaticis.*"[89]

Although comments of a broader nature on the fate of the Slavs and their role in history were rare in Dobrovský's letters, and his correspondents seem to have taken their tone from him, at times he departed from his usual pattern. Certain comments in a visionary and prophetic tone about the future of his beloved Slavs can be found in his correspondence, such as the following passage from his letter to Fryco. After lamenting the orthographic disunity of the Slavs, Dobrovský continued: "If the Slavs were united in one state [orthographic union] could happen more easily. In this we should allow Providence to decide over the fate of nations. Perhaps it lies in its plans to unite one day again, after endless deviations and disarray, the peoples of the same origin."[90]

At times Dobrovský seemed to believe that the Slavs had a special part to play in the future development of the world, as when he remarked to Zlobický, "It seems as if the Slavs, the Russians with the Poles and the Czechs, are yet destined before others to accomplish great things. But I may not be, and do not want to be, a prophet."[91] In spite of this disclaimer, however, Dobrovský returned to his prophetic mood several times. In one of the most striking and frequently quoted of these statements, he compared the Slavs to the Germans and French, commenting on the future of the Poles in particular:

> The new enlightenment of the world must arise from the Slavs, even if the Germans may have been the first heralds of the better methods. Slavic *um* is still, if it is purely conceived, the most unspoiled of this most extremely far-strayed humanity. German *Verstand* is not to be despised, but not to be considered the equal of our *um*. French *ésprit* is too volatile, and can hardly be pinned down. . . . The Poles remain dear to me, and I will not desist from working for their national freedom with all my strength, as though it were my own fatherland. The time is not at all far off, when that which all true and brave Poles want and hope for shall be realized (not through insurrection, but by more radical means).[92]

Some questions remain about how these passages should be interpreted. Dobrovský's friends usually passed them over in silence, or reacted with polite disinterest. "I would have preferred . . . to read something about Slavic literature," wrote Ribay in response to one such letter, "rather than about the enlightenment of the Slavic nation and about chiliasm. I must confess to you that I do not know how to go on in these matters."[93] From the age of thirty-four, Dobrovský was subject to intermittent attacks of mental instability of a manic-depressive variety, and most of his mystical and prophetic flights of fancy seem to be connected with these attacks.[94] Certainly their tone is far removed from Dobrovský's usually calm, critical (even hypercritical) outlook and scholarly detachment. But even if Dobrovský would not have expressed himself in precisely this manner but for his illness, the deep and abiding interest in the Slavs, and the belief in their future, which he showed in these passages was genuine and shared by the other scholars with whom he associated. It was a belief and interest, not in politics, but in linguistic and cultural developments.

The Slavs and the Czech Linguistic Revival

Language gave the clearest evidence that the Czechs and the other Slavs were related, as the linguists and grammarians who worked to preserve and defend the Czech language were well aware. Here, too, the other Slavs tended to be viewed primarily as sources to serve Czech concerns. Czech lexicographers, for example, were particularly aware of the value of the other Slavic languages as a source of lexical enrichment for Czech—a value increased by the often heedless and puristic neologisms of such as Václav Pohl.[95] Dobrovský, citing the example of the German philologist, Adelung, was willing to use Russian, Polish, or Serbo-Croatian words to help explain the etymology of the Czech words in his dictionary, but he was generally against direct borrowing. Where there was no suitable Czech word, Dobroský favored forming a new word on the principle of analogy.[96] He maintained this attitude throughout his career, as he showed in 1813 when writing to Josef Jungmann about a proposal for a Czech dictionary by the Slovak Juraj Palkovič:

The reason I wish that the work already begun would be finished by a Czech is this, that the words which still live in the mouths of our Czechs (and do not appear at all in writing) can be known only to Czechs. I do not mean to belittle the Slovak by this; much more, I would take not only Slovak but also Russian roots, if they only explained a *nomen proprium.*[97]

Dobrovský's friend and colleague F. J. Tomsa also believed that "a Czech can learn not a little from the other Slavs," a precept he had the opportunity to put into practice in 1799 when Russian troops marched through Prague.[98]

Dobrovský's resistance to excessive borrowing from other languages was not shared by all his colleagues. His longtime correspondent in Vienna, Zlobický, knew at first hand the problems of adapting Czech to technical topics, since he had been responsible for translating the Austrian legal codes into Czech. He approved of efforts at lexical enrichment, arguing that "one must persevere in them, if he wants to set our word-rich language into motion. The Germans do it, why should we not?"[99] Zlobický preferred calques, or loan translations, as means to the enrichment of Czech, but others widened the field to include the direct transfer of words from other languages. K. H. Thám, who fell out with Dobrovský from the time of his critical review of Thám's Czech dictionary (1788), was another champion of lexical enrichment. He went beyond calques in his attempts, including direct loans from Polish and Russian, such as *bohosloví* (theology, taken from the Russian).[100] Even such a close collaborator and protégé of Dobrovský's as Puchmajer argued, "Since I am convinced that we Czechs . . . lack many appropriate words in the aforementioned subjects, we could do nothing better than to plunder the dialects of the other Slavs and make their words our own. This would be a thousand times more reasonable than forging new monstrosities after the German."[101]

This more tolerant attitude was also shared by Jungmann and others, who realized that without lexical expansion Czech could never take the place of a truly national language in all areas of life. The other Slavic languages offered a pool of root words and raw materials for calquing, as well as a source for direct loans, which could make a practical contribution to the development of Czech.

It was in efforts to create contemporary literature in Czech that this practical contribution was most evident. If Czech were to make good its claim to be a language of high culture, then the literary genres cultivated in other European languages would also have to be produced in Czech. This attitude made translations particularly important, and the Czech intellectuals who worked to create Czech literature, especially poetry, began to turn to Slavic literatures for models and for practical assistance.[102] An early sign of this trend was Puchmajer's attempt in about 1795 to translate an ode by the Russian poet Kheraskov.[103] When Dobrovský informed his friend Durych of this effort, Durych responded, asking for biographical information so that he could include Puchmajer and his collaborator, Antonín Pišelý, in his *Bibliotheca slavica*, and asking Dobrovský to "greet these Slavophiles most courteously in [his] name."[104] Kheraskov's ode "On the Greatness of God" appeared in Puchmajer's first almanac, *Sebrání básně a zpěvů* (1795). This was the only poem in the collection based on a Slavic model; otherwise the first volume was quite similar to Thám's *Básně v řeči vázané* (2 vols., 1785).

With his second almanac, however, Puchmajer began to follow Slavic models more frequently, and this time he turned to Polish poets. He was acquainted with Polish poetry collections in the almanac form, and had at least two of them, Józef Ondrzej Załuski's *Bibliotheca poetarum polonorum* (1752) and *Zebranie rytmów wierszopisów żyjących* (1752–1756), in his personal library.[105] Perhaps it was from these examples that Puchmajer concluded that one of the best ways to write good Czech poetry would be to follow the example of the more highly developed Polish poetry. Certainly by the middle of 1797 he was actively expressing this view to his friends. In July of that year he wrote to his friend Šebastián Hněvkovský about Jan Nejedlý's work on a translation of Homer. He had borrowed the Greek and French versions, but Puchmajer wrote that he would be glad if Nejedlý would use Dmochowski's Polish version, because "it would not be so much work for him . . . [and] he could see how one should translate into Czech according to Polish."[106]

Puchmajer's second almanac (1797) already showed signs of this attitude. It contained paraphrases and translations of poems by F. D. Kniažnin and F. Karpiński, fables by Kniažnin, and others based on French, German, or Latin models. This pattern was reproduced in the three succeeding almanacs, published under the title *Nové básně* in 1798, 1802, and 1814. In addition to works by Karpiński and Kniažnin, these volumes included paraphrases of fables by Ignacy Krasicki, and an excerpt from Montesquieu's "Le temple de Gnide," based on a translation by Józef Szymanowski.[107]

Puchmajer's *Chram Gnidský* was his most ambitious project. Besides the excerpt mentioned above, which appeared in 1802, it was published in book form in 1804. In his foreword to the book version, Puchmajer discussed the translations into Italian and German, but placed the Polish translation above all the others. "The most excellent translator of this poem is, without a doubt, Józef Szymanowski, a Pole, of whom Franciszek Kniažnin says with right, 'It is one of the most beautiful of Szymanowski's poems, and he thus brings honor to Polish literature.'" This translation, Puchmajer acknowledged, was the model for his own version.[108] Later on in the foreword, Puchmajer gave what amounted to a programmatic statement of his views on translation:

> This nation [the Poles], linguistically related to us, can become our inexhaustible source of the most pleasant poems. . . . Two advantages to us will follow from this: first, while translating something from a foreign language into Czech, we will save ourselves half of our work if we have the Polish translation in our hands as well; and second, we will learn better the Slavic ways of expressing ourselves, and thus it will not be necessary to fear that everything will be marred by that awkward, germanized Czech.

Finally, Puchmajer felt that his method of translation, by bringing the Poles and Czechs closer together, might help contribute to the realization of "the pleasant dream" of uniting the Slavs, or at least those Slavs living under Austrian rule and using the Latin alphabet.

Josef Jungmann put similar ideas into practice in his translations of Chateaubriand's *Atala* and Milton's *Paradise Lost*. In these translations, Jungmann did not hesitate to make use of words "better known to the other Slavs than to Czechs," even though he had to include explanatory notes in his text.[109] He did the same thing in his *Jana Miltona Ztracený ráj*, published in 1811. Again he defended his use of words unknown in Czech, advising his readers that, since they were Slavs, it would be best for them to get used to Slavic words, so that the Czechs could gradually enter into a general Slavic literary language. In his work on *Ztracený ráj*, Jungmann made use of the Polish translation published by Jacek Przybylski in 1791, although the references to this translation by name were dropped from subsequent editions of Jungmann's poem.[110] Jungmann also made some translations of Russian works, including some of Novikov's short prose which appeared in Jan Nejedlý's *Hlasatel český*, and a version of the "Lay of the Host of Igor," which was not published until modern times.[111]

Jungmann continued to champion emulating Russian and Polish literature, telling his pupils in Litoměřice in 1810 that without a knowledge of Russian and Polish they could not even become good Czechs.[112] But Puchmajer, toward the end of his life, felt that the younger generation of poets was carrying things too far. He expressed this feeling to Dobrovský, and even more strongly to Jan Nejedlý, when he wrote, "Russian only spoils the young Czechs, because they cram it into Czech without need or understanding. I do not want to have anything to do with that. . . . I have also occupied myself with Russian, and especially with Polish; but I hope that I have nevertheless avoided contamination and remained pure, and true to my Czech."[113]

Puchmajer did not reject his earlier views entirely; but he called for more restraint in following foreign models. To both the linguists and those who were attempting to create Czech literature, the Slavic languages and their literatures were important. Puchmajer and his circle found in Slavic literature the models for their own translations and a storehouse of words and poetic phrases to help them create a modern literature in Czech. Once again, the primary interest driving these patriotic intellectuals to the other Slavs was an interest in Czech and its development, not a concern for the other Slavic languages and literatures in their own right. This interpretation is reinforced by the recognition that Puchmajer and his friends used their Polish and Russian models in a limited way, as means rather than ends. They were to be the roads on which Czech literature reached classical and West European literatures. Montesquieu, Milton, and Homer were filtered through their Polish translations, but a direct Polish influence on Czech literature in style and substance had not yet taken place. Toward the end of our period, some harbingers of a more direct influence of Slavic literature on Czech, and an interest in the other Slavs in their own right, did appear, such as Jungmann's translation of the "Lay of the Host of Igor," or Václav Hanka's translation in 1817 of Vuk Stefanović Karadžić's collection of Serbian folk songs, *Prostonárodní srbská muza do Čech převedená.*[114] This trend was to be fully realized only by later generations.

Only when these patriotic intellectuals turned from studying Czech, or attempting to write in it, to creating works whose primary purpose was to defend it and encourage its use, did the Slavic world became more than a storehouse for historical, literary, philological, or linguistic material. In these "defenses of the language" (to which could be added defensive passages in works whose primary focus was elsewhere), several other attitudes toward the Slavs emerged.[115] For one thing, the ethnic and linguistic relationship between the Czechs and the other Slavs moved into the foreground. Hanke von Hankenstein, in his *Empfehlung der Böhmischen*

Sprache und Litteratur, wrote that one good reason for an acquaintance with Czech literature was that it led naturally to Polish and Russian, and thus to a knowledge of general Slavic literary history.[116] Czech and the other Slavic languages were among the most widespread in the world, an assertion that turned up in Thám's *Obrana* and in the speech Josef Dobrovský gave in the presence of Leopold II in 1791.[117] Jan Rulík made the same point in his *Sláva a výbornost jazyka českého*, cataloguing the countries in which the "Slavic language" was spoken.[118]

Not only did these authors stress the fact that the Slavic languages were widespread; they also claimed that a knowledge of Czech would make a person able to understand the languages of the other Slavs. In fact, they frequently wrote of a single Slavic language, of which Czech was only a major "dialect." The first two holders of the chair of Czech language and literature at the university in Prague, Pelcl and Jan Nejedlý, both considered Czech a useful tool for learning other Slavic languages and being understood by other Slavs.[119] When Puchmajer dedicated his *Pravopis rusko-český* to the bishop of Budějovice, Arnošt Růžička, he wrote that the latter had proved (by speaking with his hosts on a journey to Russia in "Slavic") that "a Czech can traverse, with Czech, that precious treasure of which malevolent people do not scruple to deprive him, a greater and wider portion of the world, and can reach agreement with more nations, than any other nation under heaven can with its language."[120] One of the most enthusiastic patrons of this idea was Václav Matej Kramerius, who dedicated his *Vlastenské noviny* to the "glorious, widespread Slavic nation."[121] He assured his countrymen that if they could overcome their prejudice against their mother tongue, they would realize that "Russians, Poles, Pomeranians, Silesians, Moravians, Slovaks, Dalmatians, Bosnians, Moldavians, Serbs, Wends, Croats and many other famous nations spread to all corners of the world are [their] brothers, and use the same glorious Slavic language, with only slight differences."[122]

Overshadowing this stress on the wide spread of the Slavic language was a sense of admiration and even pride in the vast extent of territory ruled by fellow Slavs, the Russians. The scope of Russia's dominions was cited by Pelcl in his *Kurzgefasste Geschichte,* and it was a point Dobrovský made to the Emperor Leopold II also. After proving that the Slavs constituted a majority of the Austrian monarchy's inhabitants, Dobrovský went on: "Now they rule, in and through the Russian Slavic tribe, from the Black Sea to the Arctic, make treaties on the borders of the Chinese Empire, send *ukazes* in their language far and wide for more than two hundred miles, and make discoveries in the ocean between Asia and America."[123]

In the context of a defense of the Czech language, emphasizing the size and power of Russia made good psychological sense. Here was a Slavic nation, related to the Czechs, that was not only independent (which the Czechs no longer were), but a great power (which the Czechs had never been). Yet even the "moral support" the patriotic intelligentsia could draw from contemplating Russia's greatness did not necessarily amount to the elaboration of a Russian orientation among its members. An alternative did exist: the House of Habsburg already ruled over thousands of Slavic subjects, and prospects of Austrian expansion into the Balkans meant the possible addition of thousands more. The Czechs might, then, look to a Slavic-dominated Austria as a "moral support" in their exposed position, as well as to Russia.[124]

In any case, it was rare for this enthusiasm for the "Slavic language" to reflect an organized interest in the languages of the other Slavs in themselves. The defenders of Czech were above all else concerned with their own language, with arresting its decline and raising it once more to the level of a truly national language. Thus when they wrote of the glorious history and geographic scope of the Slavic language, they were supporting their arguments for Czech, rather than seeking to submerge it in a broader stream.[125] By pointing to the greatness of the Slavs, these awakeners could argue that

Czech was more than an obsolete dialect spoken only by the peasants and lower urban classes, but part of the family of Slavic languages—one of which, Russian, was the state language of a vast empire.

Slavism in the Popular Milieu

They may have argued that Czech was more than a peasants' jargon, but the patriotic scholars never denied that it was at least a language that still lived on in the mouths of the country folk and the lower levels of urban society. And if the obvious relationship between Czech and other Slavic languages spoke of the ethnic ties among the Slavs to the intellectuals, a natural question would be what effect this had on the wider masses. What did they know of the Slavic world, from where did they receive their knowledge, and what sort of attitudes to the Slavs did they express? This issue involves, of course, the problem of whether the attitudes of the nationally conscious intelligentsia were able to penetrate into the popular masses, and it is further complicated by the fragmentary nature of available sources. It is still possible, however, to reach some provisional conclusions about popular attitudes in this period.[126]

Some acquaintance with the attitudes of the intelligentsia was possible through the efforts of certain popular awakeners to address the masses directly. Just as they worked to raise the general level of knowledge, standard of living, and national consciousness in the countryside, the popular awakeners could, through their works, spread the attitudes toward the Slavs they held themselves.[127] The themes of the wide distribution of the Slavic peoples, of the ethnic ties between the Czechs and the other Slavs, and of the greatness of the Slavic nation, especially the Russians, were all expressed in their writings for the common people, as was the moral drawn from them: that the Czechs could be proud of being Slavs.

Some of the works of old Czech literature that the patriotic intelligentsia republished were also sources of information about the other Slavs, such as the *Výtahy z kroniky moskevské,* which Procházka reissued in 1786. This was a sixteenth-century translation of the Russian historical chronicles, with Sigismund von Herberstein's account of his journey to Moscow as ambassador from the Holy Roman Empire added as an appendix. Basic information about the history and condition of Russia, even though now outdated, was thus included in the work. In his foreword, Procházka pointed out that many developments had taken place since the original works were written, so that customs and manners were much improved, especially under Peter the Great and Catherine II.[128] But the main purpose of his republication, implied in Procházka's quotation from the original foreword to the 1590 edition (written by Daniel Adam z Veleslavína) was to encourage the Czechs to value their language: "Since the Muscovites and Russians come from the same nation as we Czechs, and use the same language, which we and other Slavic nations, such as Poles, Croats, Slovaks, Serbs, etc. use . . . it is worthwhile for our Czechs to know and to realize how widespread their nation is."[129]

At a time when the wars with Napoleon were exciting further interest in Russia, both Jan Rulík and Kramerius published works that helped meet this interest. Rulík's *Cesta z Moskvy do Číny* was a seventeenth-century travel account by Jiří z Drachova, which he translated and published in 1800. Kramerius's contribution was an article in his *Vlastenské noviny* giving a brief description of the Russian Empire. In it he placed special emphasis on the size and strength of Russia, noting that it was thirty-three times as big as the German Empire, had a population of at least 36 million, an army of 600,000 men, and a fleet that rivaled Great Britain's.[130]

Other writers also echoed this awareness of the ties among the Slavs, and especially of the greatness and strength of Russia. Take for example a New Year's poem published in Kramerius's newspaper in 1792 (signed J. N———k):

> To you, also, Poles and Moravians,
> You Slavs living here and there,

I wish in all sincerity,
A happy New Year without deceit.
. . . .
To you, however, dear brother Russians,
Or, let me say, victorious heroes,
I wish success, endurance in bravery,
Also everything good in plenty,
As a gift of the New Year.
I know, and believe with certainty,
That you will demonstrate for all time
The courage of the Slavic nation.[131]

Popular awakeners also followed Russian cultural developments. Kramerius reported on a proposal for a Russian circumnavigation of the globe, in which a member of the Bohemian Society of Sciences, Josef Mayer, was to take part.[132] He also wrote of a plan by the Russian scholar Lebedev to translate the classics of Russian, French, and German literature into the "Indian" language, adding that "the Russians are thus the first . . . to earn that great honor, that they are beginning to enlighten even the Indian nations."[133] In the same number, Kramerius pointed with approval to a competition sponsored by the Russian Academy for the best play in Russian on a theme from Russian history. Money for the prize had been donated by an anonymous patriot, prompting Kramerius to exclaim, "That is remarkable love of country, nation, and language!"[134]

The Russians were not the only Slavs whose activities were reported on by the popular awakeners, nor was everything they did automatically approved. Rulík sympathized with the Poles in their struggles with the Russians, although he remained reticent about the Austrian role in the Polish partitions.[135] Writing of the final partition of Poland, Rulík described it as a "horrible event, [which] decided the fate of the Polish nation, so that this kingdom, formerly so glorious, came to partition and dismemberment."[136] Kramerius, too, appeared to have some sympathy for the Poles. In a report from Paris in 1804, he described the celebration of Kościuszko's birthday, referring to the Polish hero as the man "who ten years ago attempted to liberate his homeland."[137]

When the Serbian revolt against the Ottoman Turks began in 1804, Kramerius carried some reports of the fighting in his *Vlastenské noviny*. The information he printed was usually gleaned from reports in other newspapers, and, following his usual practice, he refrained from any extended editorial commentary on the events; but by carrying such news at all, Kramerius provided a source of information about the South Slavs. He published details of the success of the rebels, expressed admiration for the speed with which a Serbian army of 18,000 men was formed, and praised their effective organization under their leader, "Jiří Černý" (Karadjordje).[138] Kramerius did not report the Serbs' struggle in a way that expressed too much support—at the height of the decades of war with revolutionary and Napoleonic France, their activities threatened the principle of legitimacy. He used the word *buřiče* (rebels) to describe the Serbs, but he did attempt to justify them when he emphasized that their struggle was against the abuses of the Janissaries, and not with the Turkish central government.[139]

Serbian cultural developments also received some coverage in Kramerius's newspaper. When the internal administration of Serbia was reorganized after the first revolt, he noted, "that Slavic land will receive a new constitution."[140] He praised the work of Dositej Obradović in educating Serbian youth in Belgrade, and found it noteworthy that when the new, autonomous administration began functioning, all laws and ordinances would be published in "the Illyrian, or Slavic language."[141]

His interest in this last point reflects the overriding concern in Kramerius's work, and the context in which he most frequently wrote about the Slavic world: language. His appeal to his readers to recognize their brotherhood, shared with all the Slavs, was quoted above, and he utilized each opportunity that came his way to continue to stress this relationship. A typical example is his announcement of the publication of a grammar of the Slovene language, which deserved advertisement because it showed that "not only we Slavic Czechs, but also others of our linguistic brethren . . . are working for the improvement and spread of the language of the glorious Slavic nation."[142] In an article devoted to developments in Turkey, Kramerius claimed that the "Illyrian" language, even though it was a Slavic tongue, was spoken by almost all Turks, and even used at court,

> from which we Czechs may flatteringly see, that our Slavic language—for our Czech is a Slavic language—is spread far and wide, and not limited to some minuscule part of the world like, for example, the German Empire. *Nota* for those who are so gullible that they believe that a Czech, having traversed his kingdom and Moravia, already cannot even continue any further with his mother tongue.[143]

Given that this was Kramerius's attitude toward his language, it is not surprising that he gave great publicity to defenses of the language, such as Rulík's *Sláva a výbornost jazyka českého*. He recommended this work to "the entire Slavic nation, whether in Bohemia, Moravia, Silesia, Hungary, Poland, Russia, or also Dalmatia, Bosnia, Serbia and in other Slavic lands," assuring them that from it they would at least learn what they ought to think about their native language.[144]

When Kramerius wrote about practical proposals, however, he lowered his horizons somewhat. He was convinced of the useful part that newspapers could play in revitalizing and spreading the language, holding up the example of the Germans, who published some sixty newspapers that circulated throughout the entire German Empire. He thus welcomed the advent of a Slavic newspaper in Banská Bystrica, remarking that it was time the Slavic nation looked to the spread of its language. As centers in which newspapers should be published, Kramerius suggested (in addition to Prague) five cities: Vienna, Bratislava (Pressburg), Lwów, Brno, and Opava.[145] The fact that all these cities were within the Habsburg monarchy, and that the language used for their newspapers, with the exception of Lwów, would have been Czech (for Czech still dominated as the literary language among the Slovaks), points up once more that Kramerius and the other patriots were primarily interested in their own language, Czech. When they placed such emphasis on the "glorious, widespread Slavic language," it was mainly as a way of supporting their demands and hopes for Czech.

A perusal of Kramerius's newspapers or Rulík's *Kalendář historický* gives some idea of the sort of information about the other Slavs that was available to the common people. Through literate individuals in the countryside, priests, schoolteachers, or self-taught farmers, some of this information could spread farther into the masses than subscription figures or publication runs might suggest.[146] It is difficult to ascertain how clear a picture the common people had of Russia or the world outside their locality in general; but at least one document suggests that they were not only aware of the international situation, but also able to judge the policies of all three major East Central European empires quite critically. This is the celebrated "Selský 'Otče náš'," a parody of the Lord's Prayer, dating from the late eighteenth century:

> Our Father, who art in Vienna, Petersburg and Berlin,
> Hallowed be Thy name in Thy territories.
> Thy kingdom come not into Poland.
> Thy will be done, in Austria and Muscovy
> As it is in Brandenburg.
> Our daily bread Thou takest away,
> Thou dismissest our freedom,
> While we must give food to those who trespass against us.
> Lead us not into greater poverty,
> But deliver us from our feudal dues. Amen.[147]

The Napoleonic Wars, the Slavs, and the Czechs

The thirty years of conflict that engulfed Europe after the French Revolution have long been credited with an important role in the development of the Czech renascence.[148] They not only affected the political, social and economic order, but also enabled people in the Czech lands and elsewhere to gain first-hand experience of the greatest Slavic power, by bringing Russia to the center of the European stage. In 1798–1800, 1805–1806, and 1813–1815, Russian armies were on Czech soil, and Russia's role in the eventual defeat of Napoleon was great. The influence of these events on Czech attitudes toward the Slavs has often been stressed, especially by the post-1948 Czech historians.[149] But the society on which these events worked was by no means uniform, and the responses called forth were not the same at all social levels.

Reactions to the role of the Slavs in the Napoleonic wars could be divided into three groups. Among the intellectuals, one group, which may be called "loyal," viewed Russia chiefly as the main ally in the struggle with Napoleon; and their awareness of the Slavic link they shared with this ally, and their enthusiasm for its successes, never crossed the boundaries of loyalty to the Austrian state. Beside this group, however, was another, younger group of intellectuals who expressed admiration for Russia to the point of genuine Russophilism—including the hope that Russia would help the Czechs achieve a better situation for themselves. The third group of attitudes would be that of the common people, mainly the peasants in the countryside. Their reaction to the Russians was primarily influenced by the effect the Russian presence had on their daily lives. Thus the well-known report that the president of the Czech Gubernium, Count Kolovrat-Liebsteinský, sent to Vienna in February 1813, reporting that the whole nation was rejoicing over the news of Napoleon's defeat in Russia, rather oversimplified the matter, since it left out of consideration the motives for this rejoicing.[150]

The "loyal" attitude to the Slavs was expressed in the newspaper reports of the progress of the fighting, in occasional verses or government-sponsored propaganda, especially when the Austrian authorities were trying to generate enthusiasm for local militias in 1799–1800 and 1808–1809.[151] Efforts to stir up support for these home guards usually harked back to the glorious past of the Slavic Czechs and sometimes widened their appeals to include other Slavic peoples; but they almost always clearly showed their authors' outlook by limiting their appeals to the Austrian Slavs. Thus Václav Stach in his poem "Hlas k Čechům" mentioned only Moravians and Silesians in addition to the Czechs—in other words, peoples who had belonged to the medieval Czech kingdom.[152] Similarly, another song in honor of the Czech militia, published as an appendix to Rulík's *Vlastenský mladý rekruta,* clearly limited its appeal to the Habsburg Slavs:

> Rejoice ye nations
> All the dear Slavs!
> . . . .
> It is happiness to be under the scepter
> Of our most glorious ruler:
> Ours, and the fatherland's, is the wish
> God save the emperor.[153]

František Vavák's battle march for the militia in 1809 saluted the Hungarians, Poles, Moravians, Silesians, Croatians, Slovaks, and Czechs—an impressive list of nations, but once more only those represented within the Habsburg monarchy.[154]

When Russia entered the war on the side of Austria, however, and especially when Suvorov's troops crossed Bohemia and Moravia on their way to the front, interest in the Russians was expressed more frequently. One of these expressions was a spate of *kramařské písně,* cheaply printed ballads set to old Czech popular tunes and peddled in the market towns throughout the countryside. One particular example full of praise for the "heroic Russians" went quickly through three printings.[155] Yet, though the song does make many complimentary remarks about the Russians, the main message of the later stanzas is that the country people should deliver any necessary supplies, even if requisitioned, without resistance. Since this was exactly what the responsible government officials would have desired, these multiple printings seem unconvincing proof of the song's popularity.[156] In fact, another *kramařská píseň*, on the march of the Russians through Moravia to Bohemia, expressed some of the people's complaints about the contributions of food or draft animals the Russians required.[157]

Among the "loyal" intelligentsia, the more commonly expressed attitudes ranged from curiosity to enthusiasm. Rulík called Suvorov "this heroic Slavic general" and printed a brief account of his life and military exploits.[158] Kramerius also included reports about the Russians in his *Vlastenské noviny*, and both he and Rulík devoted special attention to the arrival of the Russian troops in Prague during 1799. "Almost all the inhabitants of Prague turned out to look at these heroic Slavs, who use with us Czechs practically one language," Kramerius reported. Of the Russian soldiers he said that "true Slavic bravery shone forth from the eyes of all this people."[159] The enthusiasm of the Praguers for the Russians was demonstrated again in 1813 at the performance of J. N. Štěpánek's play celebrating the victory of the allies in the Battle of the Nations at Leipzig. The Russian army was sympathetically presented, and when the Cossacks came on stage under their leader, Pavel Kuchov (played by Štěpánek himself), the theater shook to the loud "hurrah" from the audience.[160] This enthusiastic reception of the Russians was firmly connected with the fortunes of war. From being merely Austrian allies, the Russians had progressed to being instrumental in a decisive victory, which clearly brought the end of the war in sight. This in itself was a great cause for rejoicing, so that the response of the Prague crowds to Štěpánek's play was more than an index of the people's opinion of Russia.[161]

One thing that the Czechs did recognize in the Russians was their linguistic relationship. "It was a great pleasure for us," wrote Rulík, "and they also had great joy from the fact that we could speak the Slavic language with them, and they with us."[162] Even Josef Dobrovský, who ordinarily remained aloof from political events, took advantage of the public interest in the Russian language to publish an anonymous booklet entitled *Neues Hülfsmittel die Russische Sprache leichter zu verstehen* in 1799. As its full title makes clear, this small work was intended not only for the Czech-speaking, but also for the German-speaking inhabitants of Bohemia, and even for the Russians who wanted to communicate with the Czechs.[163] Enthusiasm for Russian was so high that this work was quickly plagiarized and published in a pirated edition as *Der russische Dollmetscher*. When the Russian armies returned in 1813, Dobrovský's friend Tomsa published a small Russian dictionary that was basically an expanded version of the vocabulary lists in Dobrovský's *Neues Hülfsmittel*.[164] The sense of kinship which the similarities between the languages fostered spread also into the country through Kramerius's newspaper and songs such as the previously mentioned description of the march of the Russians through Moravia— which, after naming the different nationalities in the Russian army, including Russians, Poles, Circassians, Cossacks, Kalmuks and Tatars—continued:

> And they all had one language,
> They all understood one another,
> And many of us as well.
> And we, when we gave our attention,
> Recognized in them our own nation,
> These ancient Slavs.[165]

Fundamentally, these "loyal" attitudes toward Russia and the Slavs during the wars were similar to those expressed in the defenses of the language. Their message was that the Czechs should be proud of the ethnic heritage they shared with the Russians and should take courage from the fact that this related Slavic state was a great empire. Russian greatness should stir the Czechs to an awareness of their own language and the proud traditions, especially the martial traditions, of their own past. Such attitudes were fairly frequently expressed in the public forum through newspapers, books such as Dobrovský's, or other means. Among some of the younger intellectuals, however (most openly in the circle of friends around Josef Jungmann), attitudes toward the Russians went far beyond admiration for the success of an ally. Their opinions were expressed in private correspondence, with the most Russophile passages frequently written in Cyrillic (perhaps on the assumption that the censor would be unlikely to decipher them).

Jungmann and his friends had a firm belief that the future would bring better conditions for the Czechs, and they hoped that this better future could be brought about with Russian help. In a letter to his friend Antonín Marek, Jungmann wrote of his belief and expectation that, even if they were not there to see it in person, all would be well with their fatherland in the future. "Our affair is drawing to its end," he said, writing in Cyrillic, "Poland is almost entirely conquered by the Warsavians; the Russians are helping them; the Hungarians do little; the Austrians are in the hands of Napoleon . . . Bohemia and Moravia must suffer. But the phoenix will arise from the ashes!"[166] When the opportunity to meet with Russians face-to-face came to Jungmann in Litoměřice in 1813, he grasped it eagerly, as he told Marek:

> The Russians march through here frequently, today we expect 120,000, whose passage will cost the city 9,000 guilders. I diligently *govoriu* with them, and find that there are among them very good-hearted people, and that what is said about their thieving and stealing here, especially by the Germans, must be blamed not on them, but on their poorly organized commissariat. . . . It will not hurt the Czechs to become a little acquainted with the Russians; at least they will realize that there are more Slavs in the world.[167]

At times Jungmann seemed to doubt whether his generation would live to see a better future for Bohemia, but he was certain that it was from Russia that the salvation of future generations of Czechs would come.[168] After Napoleon's Russian disaster in 1812, and with the march of the Russian armies westward, it began to seem as though this salvation might come sooner than expected. Jungmann's correspondent Marek wrote during the first half of 1813, "Our Slavs are now so close . . . [that] it appears as though our sighs have reached to Heaven, and that things will now develop at least somewhat according to our wishes."[169] Just what these wishes were was never openly expressed, but attitudes such as these clearly went beyond the loyal enthusiasm for the Russians typical of other sections of the intelligentsia.

The attitudes of Jungmann's circle regarding other events, particularly the fate of Poland, also showed an interesting contrast to those of the "loyal" patriots. The latter group did not consider that perhaps the Poles preferred the French to the Russians, but only saw that the Russians were Napoleon's enemies. Jan Nejedlý wrote, during the struggle between the French and Poles on one side and the Russians on the other, that "our valiant Slavs the Russians" had thrown the French out of Warsaw and had issued a proclamation to the Poles saying that if they caused trouble, not a child would be left living, nor one stone standing on another. "God grant," continued Nejedlý, "that our courageous Slavs overthrow this bane of the entire world, Napoleon."[170] Jungmann's attitude to the Poles was quite different. "I am glad," he wrote, "that a part of the Slavs is again freed from the German yoke—in Poland—and expect that even more will be."[171] When the Grand Duchy of Warsaw marched into Russia with the French in 1811, Jungmann's view was that at least Slavs would be victorious on one side or the other. "Either the Polish monarchy will flourish in its entirety under King Josef Napoleon [*sic*] . . . or, what would be perhaps even better, the Russians will overrun half of Europe, and merge and unite the greater part of the Slavs."[172] On the other hand, this attitude of Jungmann's, coupled with a basically pro-Russian outlook, enabled him to dismiss the catastrophe of the Poles after Napoleon's downfall with a verbal shrug: "I am sorry for the Poles, that they have bought their subjection so dearly! But what of it?

At least it will be a step to the further unification of the Slavs!"[173] This statement contrasts strongly with Dobrovský's expressions of sympathy to his Polish friend, Bandtke, and his recognition, already noted, that "it would be a pity if the Russians should swallow up not only Polish territory, but also the Polish language."

The "loyal" and "Russophile" attitudes were basically expressed among members of the intelligentsia, or in the literate urban setting in general. The majority of the population, the peasants, also had an opportunity to experience the Russians at first hand during the years of war. Though evidence is fragmentary, it appears that the critical attitude to the consequences of great-power politics found in the "Selský 'Otče náš'" was also expressed by the people during the wars. War meant economic hardship for the peasant, the more so as the Russian army was plagued by the commissariat troubles Jungmann mentioned.[174] Jan Rulík recorded the economic difficulties caused by the armies in his *Kalendář historický,* and the evidence of the family chronicles kept by literate farmers suggests that his perception was an accurate reflection of feeling in the countryside.[175] This resentment was not directed particularly at the Russians, of course: any army, whether their "own" Austrian, allied Russian or Prussian, or enemy French, caused the peasant hardship. Martin Novák of Drinov complained, "Here, whether it was wood for fuel or building, whether it was straw or rye in the barn, whatever it was, as long as it only had a name, everything they took off to the encampment."[176] The length of the war made the difficulties harder to bear, as Petr Martinovský of Slavětín lamented. In 1812, his area suffered from several thousand Russian troops who bivouacked there for two days, and consumed or destroyed everything in the fields.[177] Václav Tachezí of Budyně had the experience of having some 800 allied troops quartered in his area and wrote, "This was always the way of it; we were always having to give them oats, hay and bread."[178] Nor was it only economic hardships that the armies inflicted.

Martin Novák blamed the sick Russian and Prussian troops for the outbreaks of disease that began in the winter of 1813 and killed many people.[179]

Conspicuous by its absence from the comments about the Russians in these chronicles is an interest in the Slavic brotherhood between Czechs and Russians. While there is some evidence of sympathy among the peasants for deserting soldiers,[180] this was more likely to be based on social, rather than ethnic, foundations. General attitudes toward Russia and its role in the wars were more usually cast in religious terms. Napoleon, frequently portrayed as the Antichrist, was punished by God using the instrument of Russia. The chroniclers dwelt on the fate of those who opposed God's will, not on the might and Slavic character of his chosen instrument.[181] The presence of Russian armies in Bohemia, then, could hardly be said to have caused a surge of Russophilism among the people. They were not fascinated by the Slavic link between Czechs and Russians, as the intelligentsia frequently were, and in the area of most concern to them, their economic situation, the Russians made things worse. This was most pungently captured by the well-to-do farmer, František Vavák, in a New Year's carol for 1800:

> Těch Rusů našich hosti
> Již máme všichni dosti.
> Jestli tu dlouho budou,
> Učiní zemi chudou.
> Již prvé malo měla,
> Neb všecka zhuboněla
> Skrz tak dlouhý čas vojny.

> Already we've all had enough
> Of these Russians, our guests.
> If they remain here long,
> They'll impoverish the land.
> It had little enough before,
> For everything has grown thin
> Through such a long time of war.[182]

Sympathy for the individual Russian soldier was the result of fellow feeling for a peasant forced into an army, not of Slavic brotherhood. Czech Slavophilism on a mass level simply did not yet exist.

❋   ❋   ❋

Czech Slavism, then, presented a complex and varied picture during this period. Certain features do stand out, however, and they serve to illuminate its nature and function in the renascence at this time. One factor limiting the influence that Slavism could exert was the extent of knowledge about the Slavs in Bohemian society. Organized and well-founded knowledge about the other Slavs was almost entirely limited to the intelligentsia, embracing their more official contacts with the Slavic world of learning through the Royal Bohemian Society of Sciences and the less formal literary correspondence among scholars. The former contacts were not necessarily motivated by a consciousness of a Slavic ethnic tie, but were part of a general pattern of international scholarly traffic. The latter type of contact did testify to a shared interest in Slavic studies among its participants, but its influence was also limited by its scholarly character.

These Slavic scholars eschewed politics for the most part, concentrating on linguistic and cultural developments and the problems of communication on these issues. In their own disciplines, in history, linguistics, and studies of the literature of the Czech or Slavic past, the intellectuals viewed the Slavic world in general and Russia in particular as a storehouse of source material, as well as a part of the wider subject. Their interest in the Slavs was centered on the ancient past, on their earliest social organizations, on the development of their literature. This focus gave them a certain freedom, based on scarcity of sources, to picture the early Slavs as they wanted; but it also restricted the applicability of their interests to the present. The development of literature was practically the only subject these scholars pursued right up to their own day;

certainly a wider interest in the modern history and political development of the Slavic nations was not yet there. Among the general literate public, knowledge of Slavic matters was more restricted. Some of the ideas of the scholars working in Slavic fields were accepted and transmitted to wider circles by men such as Rulík, who popularized the findings of Voigt and Procházka. Kramerius's *Vlastenské noviny* was another source of information, but items about the Slavs generally appeared only sporadically, even there. Kramerius in his newspaper, Rulík and others in their works, did spread the concept of the linguistic tie between Czechs and other Slavs and of the size and far-flung settlement of the Slavic peoples. But this was only a vague idea, inherited from previous centuries and not really reflecting an organized interest in the Slavs or the Slavic languages. Veleslavín's words, written in 1590 as a foreword to *Výtahy z kroniky moskevské,* could have been taken, without deletion or addition, from the pages of the *Vlastenské noviny* two centuries later.

Slavism at this time played only a supporting role to Czech national consciousness. It grew out of the developing Czech national feeling and served its purposes, rather than vice versa. The defensive stress on the Slavic note and Russia's greatness supported the specifically Czech concern with the mother tongue and its fate. Other Slavs could serve as inspirational examples, and both linguistic and literary works could gain practical assistance from the Slavic languages. Russia's greatness in particular lent status to the Czech language and the Czech nation as fellow Slavs, but beyond that it had very little to do with them. The importance of the Slavic world for this phase of the Czech national renascence, then, was as an instrument and as a symbol to be manipulated in a purely Czech context for ends defined by the Bohemian intellectuals themselves.

Even the appearance of the Russians on the Czech stage during the Napoleonic wars did not have an immediate, far-reaching impact on Czech national consciousness. It did provide occasions for enthusiastic salutation of this brave Slavic land in the spirit of "loyal" patriotism, but this attitude toward the Russians was still basically the same as that of Veleslavín or Balbín. Among the common people, too, the Russian presence did not immediately arouse fervent pan-Slav or Russophile sentiments. Only among a small group of younger patriots did admiration for Russia go beyond the inheritance of the past and the needs of Czech national consciousness. Perhaps in the retrospective view of later nineteenth-century patriots the role of Russia in the Napoleonic wars loomed larger than it did at the time, but it was not until the national renascence had entered its second phase, dominated by the generation of Josef Jungmann, that these possibilities were fully realized.

Conclusion

As the new century neared the end of its first decade, the feeling grew among patriots that a generation was coming to a close. Most of the prominent scholars whose activities we have followed were gone from the scene: Pelcl, Procházka, Tomsa, Kramerius, Durych, Voigt and others were dead. Their loss was keenly felt. To those who survived them, it seemed that "the handful of sincere patriots is disappearing slowly, one by one, and when the Germans have devoured everything, there will not even be anyone left to say a prayer over their ashes."[1] Yet this changing of the guard forced younger patriots to realize that they stood on a threshold and that what happened next depended on them. This awareness could strengthen the self-confidence of the new generation, as well as provoking a mood of elegaic appreciation of its predecessor. Josef Jungmann wrote to his friend Marek in 1809:

> Those sorrowful thoughts which grieve you are also dogging my steps. Durych, Pelcl, Procházka have passed on; only Dobrovský [is] still among us. . . . It is already devolving *upon us* to care for the fatherland. When the old husbandman dies, the young one must see to the household; if he does not have the experience—what of it! He will gain it! It is up to us always to work in every way we can so that (if possible) we will preserve the fatherland for our descendants in better condition than it was when be-

queathed to us by our predecessors. If the fatherland dies, let it be after we are gone; while we are here, so long as we struggle and are equal to our task, it will not die.[2]

In their efforts to "preserve the fatherland" for their descendants, the patriots of the new generation would build on the inheritance they had received from this period of transition between the Enlightenment and romanticism.

What was the nature of this intellectual inheritance? From around the mid-eighteenth century to the end of the Napoleonic wars, the national renascence and the developing Czech national consciousness gradually involved more and more aspects of Bohemia's cultural life. Out of the complex of attitudes developed and articulated during this first phase of the renascence, the next generation would develop a Czech national ideology, as a genuine nationalist movement emerged. The process took shape toward the middle of the eighteenth century with the spread of modern critical methods in science. These ideas, reinforced by the general outlook of the European Enlightenment, most affected the development of Czech national consciousness through their impact on historical work, but they were also applied to the physical and natural sciences. In the study of history, the effect of the new trends was to free Czech history from dependence on established authority. This new critical freedom allowed Czech historians to go beyond the interpretations of the Counter-Reformation in Bohemia, with its negation of the Czech cultural achievements between 1415 and 1618 and its suspicion of the Czech language. The traditional approach to the Hussite period and its aftermath was challenged, but so too were other, older traditions about the founding of the Czech nation and state.

To be sure, the historical writing of the Enlightenment had certain weaknesses. Its emphasis on reason made it difficult to understand certain periods of history, such as the Middle Ages, or the more recent baroque period. Its critical method could sometimes degenerate into hypercriticism, and none of the historians active during this period succeeded in producing the major synthesis of Czech history that Dobner's patron had called for. Even Pelcl's *Kurzgefasste Geschichte* fell short of that ideal, and only later in the nineteenth century could František Palacký produce such a work for Czech history up to 1526. Nevertheless, championing the critical, Maurist historical methods and subjecting historical evidence to the test of reason was an advance in historical method and helped prepare the way for later developments. At the same time, the new ideas carried with them a new, enlightened concept of patriotism, which expressed itself in the desire to remove from the record all the irrational, fabulous accretions of earlier ages. Thus cleansed, Czech history could (so these patriots hoped) stand with the history of other enlightened nations as an equal. As we have seen, even this enlightened criticism was not unmixed with defensive patriotism, aimed at protecting the nation's heroes from the attacks of foreigners.

The consciousness of a shared historical heritage which was expressed in the works of Bohemian historians during this period could still be all-embracing. Czech and German both could accept Charles IV or even Žižka as national heroes, fully within the ideals of Bohemian *Landespatriotismus*. Yet the development of Czech national consciousness did not stop there. Philology, so useful to scholars as a methodological training and auxiliary tool for history, as well as a subject of study in itself, led them to study the Czech language. Here their efforts were strongly influenced by their enlightened classicist outlook, which viewed the usage of the sixteenth-century golden age of Czech as a model. The suspicion of the Counter-Reformation was supplanted by the view that the Czech of the humanists should be the norm for their eighteenth-century followers. Only a few grammarians argued the case for considering contemporary oral practice; and the authority of Dobrovský, who took a generally conservative view, was so great that even Jungmann's generation accepted much of his outlook. Down to the present, literary Czech bears traces of Dobrovský's ideas. Again, the interests of these patriotic scholars were rather one-sided. They did not appreciate the use of the language developed in some of the great preaching and hymn writing of the baroque, just as medieval literature was unattractive to them. They liked the humanists as much because they approved of some of the ideas in their works as because of the supposed classical standard of their language. These attitudes colored their lack of sympathy for the spoken usage. Philological interest in the Czech language also led to more publicist works in defense of Czech. Kinský's *Erinnerung* paved the way for an entire series of defenses of the language, stressing its heritage, suppleness, lexical richness, and euphony. In time, these works came to be written in Czech, a first step toward the urge to develop Czech again as a language of high culture.

The two concerns of Czech linguistic scholars, the defensive and the philological, found reinforcement from research into Czech literary history. Through the studies of scholars like Voigt, Procházka, and Dobrovský, the rich literary heritage of Czech was brought to light. They and others provided concrete evidence to support the assertions of Czech's qualities made in the defenses of the language. Literary history also reinforced the classicist, conservative bent of the philologists. Literary historians added weight to the view that the Czech of the humanists should be the model for all attempts at modern Czech writing. The publication of surviving works from the golden age, an area in which Procházka's contributions were exceptionally great, further strengthened this trend. That these monuments were more than merely interesting documents for literary-historical study can be seen in Kramerius's introduction to his edition of Lomnický's *Kratké naučení mladému hospodáři* and elsewhere.

Yet even this interest in the history of Czech language and culture did not in itself represent a parting of the ways of territorial patriotism and Czech national consciousness. Kinský's support of Czech was coupled with admiration for the flourishing culture of Germany, and he was not alone. The heritage of the Czech language and its literature could still be accepted as part of the common heritage of both Czech- and German-speaking Bohemians. The patronage extended to the native vernacular by the Bohemian aristocracy shows this to be so; the language was also, of course, useful to the nobles as a symbol of the political distinctness of the Kingdom of Bohemia. Nevertheless, the works of literary historians and the republication of great examples of Czech literature helped forge a potent myth of a flourishing Czech golden age that was absorbed into the historical consciousness of Czech patriots.

The linguists' interest in the language and literary historians' study of its monuments created a regard among patriotic intellectuals for the Czech language. But not until some of them attempted to recreate a complete cultural life in Czech did the language and its fate become central to their concerns. This "linguocentrism," as one study dubs it, quite typical of nationalist movements, remained characteristic of Czech renascence culture well into the nineteenth century.[3] As language became central to the patriots' concerns, the process of ethnic separation began. It was one thing to appreciate the glories of sixteenth-century Czech literature, and quite another to use Czech to create a modern high culture. Such efforts were at first either directed consciously to the lower urban classes, as the only audience for works in Czech, or to the peasants. They thus frequently had enlightening, didactic aims in addition to patriotic ones. The role of the theater as a moral educator of the common people was fully accepted by the Czech dramatists, and Kramerius's Czech newspaper and publishing house also had both patriotic and enlightening concerns. Even the early attempts at belles lettres, such as Tham's poetic almanacs, were in large part inspired by the same motives as the defenses of the language. In the works of the Puchmajer school and the literary journals of the first decade of the nineteenth century, especially Jan Nejedlý's *Hlasatel český*, the ideas of *vlast* and mother tongue were further developed until in Nejedlý's and Jungmann's writing we find a formulation of the ethnolinguistic concept of nationhood. From these circles the call began to go up for Czech to be used in all branches of writing, not merely for works aimed at the common people.

> When scholars write and publish their learned works in their mother tongue, even foreign nations, mindful of the learning of all peoples, will be eager to learn our language. When our Czech books are announced in the catalogues of foreign booksellers, reviewed in foreign journals, translated into French, Italian, English and German, then, then our Czech nation (*obec*) will shine more brightly—more brightly than under Charles, Václav, Matthias or Rudolph![4]

With the call for Czech to take over all areas of cultural life, the bounds of territorial patriotism were finally passed. From the time of the next generation down through the nineteenth century, the mark of the patriot was to be one's attitude toward, and use of, the Czech language. These patriots no longer limited themselves to studying the past glories of Czech or writing defensive poems in it. They demanded the reintroduction of Czech into the schools, the administration, and—in short—into every sphere of the daily life of the educated urban classes as well as the country dweller.[5]

The language was perforce a concern of those patriots who worked especially for the common people. Under the influence of Enlightenment ideas on the role of all inhabitants and their value to the state, the popular awakeners worked to fight religious prejudice, intolerance, and ignorance among the common people, while at the same time spreading knowledge designed to raise their economic and cultural standards. Since the great mass of the people spoke only Czech, they had to carry on this work in Czech, to develop it, and to try to raise the standards of Czech in the countryside. The work of these patriots contributed to the reevaluation of the peasant, not only to the state, but also the nation. Thus it prepared the way for the nationalist identification of all the national virtues with the simple, "unspoiled" peasantry.[6] As it became clear that the vast majority of the highest levels of the "political nation" in Bohemia, the nobility, would never adopt the linguocentrism of the Czech patriots, such identification of the nation with the common people was strengthened still further. This may help account for some of the features of nineteenth-century Czech nationalism which distinguish it from the "gentry" nationalism of its neighbors, Hungary and Poland.

With the change in national consciousness from a political-territorial to an ethnolinguistic base, the role of Slavism became more important. During this opening phase of the renascence, Slavism had mainly served the needs of the Czech patriots, providing lexical material, scholarly contacts, and the moral support needed to raise the prestige of the nation. But when the chances of fully winning the nobility over to the national cause faded with the elaboration of an ethnolinguistic concept of nationhood, the Slavic world seemed to offer a new ally. Although the possibility of creating a single, acceptable Slavic literary language (as the Germans had done earlier for themselves) was not very great, the idea of "Slavic reciprocity" as developed in Jan Kollár's work provided a possible substitute. Here, as in other areas we have discussed, the patriots of the second and third phases of the renascence built with the materials inherited from the generation active between the Enlightenment and romanticism. As the Czech national movement developed, certain threads from this inheritance would be absorbed, others discarded, many colored with fresh meanings, and gradually woven into the complex fabric of Czech nationalism.

Abbreviations
Used in Notes

In the notes and bibliography, Czech sources are cited in modern spellings. However, German sources are cited as they were spelled at the time of publication: for example, *th* for modern German *t*; these are often Austrian usages.

Abhandlungen, 1. Folge: *Abhandlungen der Böhmischen Gesellschaft der Wissenschaften zu Prag,* 4 vols., Prague, 1785–1788.

Abhandlungen, 2. Folge: *Neuere Abhandlungen der königlichen Böhmischen Gesellschaft der Wissenschaften,* 3 vols., 1791–1795.

Abhandlungen, 3. Folge: *Abhandlungen der königlichen Böhmischen Gesellschaft der Wissenschaften auf das Jahr . . . ,* 8 vols., Prague, 1804–1824.

Abhandlungen einer Privatgesellschaft: Abhandlungen einger Privatgesellschaft in Böhmen zur Aufnahme der Mathematik, der vaterländische Geschichte und der Naturgeschichte, 6 vols., Prague, 1775–1784.

AUC: Acta Universitatis Carolinae

ČAVU: Česká akademie císaře Františka Josefa pro vědy, slovesnost a umění

ČČH: Český časopis historický

ČNM: *Časopis národního musea,* including earlier titles: 1855–1922, *Časopis Musea království Českého;* 1831–1854, *Časopis českého museum [musea];* 1827–1830, *Časopis společnosti vlasteneckého Museum v Čechách*

ČsČH: Československý časopis historický

ČSAV: Československá akademie věd

DA: *Der Briefwechsel zwischen Josef Dobrovský und Karl Gottlob von An-*

ton. Ed. Miroslav Krbec and Věra Michálková. Veröffentlichungen des Instituts für Slawistik, no. 21. Berlin, 1959.

DB: Korrespondence Josefa Dobrovského. II. Vzájemné dopisy Josefa Dobrovského a Jiřího Samuele Bandtkeho z let 1810–1827. Ed. Adolf Patera. Sbírka pramenův ku poznání literárního života v Čechách, na Moravě a ve Slezsku, Skupina 2, číslo 8. Prague, 1906.

DD: Korrespondence Josefa Dobrovského. I. Vzájemné dopisy Josefa Dobrovského a Fortunata Duricha z let 1778–1899. Ed. Adolf Patera. Sbírka pramenův ku poznání literárního života v Čechách, na Moravě a ve Slezsku, Skupina 2, číslo 2. Prague, 1895.

DK: Der Briefwechsel zwischen Dobrowsky und Kopitar, 1808–1828. Ed. V. Jagič. Berlin, 1885.

DR: Korrespondence Josefa Dobrovského. IV. Vzájemné listy Josefa Dobrovského a Jiřího Ribaye z let 1783–1810. Ed. Adolf Patera. Sbírka pramenův ku poznání literárního života v Čechách, na Moravě a ve Slezsku, Skupina 2, číslo 18. Prague, 1913.

DZ: Korrespondence Josefa Dobrovského. III. Vzájemné listy Josefa Dobrovského a Josefa Valentina Zlobického z let 1781–1807. Ed. Adolf Patera. Sbírka pramenův ku poznání literárního života v Čechách, na Moravě a ve Slezsku, Skupina 2, číslo 9. Prague, 1908.

EEQ: East European Quarterly

LA PNP: Literární archiv Památníku národního písemnictví, Prague.

Neue Briefe: Neue Briefe von Dobrowsky, Kopitar und andere Süd- und Westslawen. Ed. V. Jagič. Berlin, 1897.

SEER: Slavonic and East European Review

Spisy a projevy: Spisy a projevy Josefa Dobrovského, vycházející péčí Komise pro vydávání Spisů Josefa Dobrovského při Královské české společnosti nauk. Since 1953 published by the Československá akademie věd.

Notes

Unless otherwise indicated, all translations are by the author.

Introduction

1. See Petr Čornej, "Minulost plná schémat," in *Tvar. Literární týdeník,* nos. 16–17, 21 and 28 June 1990. Čornej was reacting to a polemic between Eva Kantůrková and Miroslav Truc in *Svobodný zítřek.*

2. Ibid., no. 16, 21 June 1990.

3. Especially in the trilogy "Jan Hus," "Jan Žižka," and "Proti všem." See Jiří Rak, "'Boj o duši národa' ve filmu 50. let," *Dějiny a současnost* 13, no. 2 (1991): 34–40.

4. Especially through a series of works published in the 1890s, including *Česká otázka* (Prague, 1895); *Naše nynější krise* (Prague, 1895); *Jan Hus, naše obrození a naše reformace* (Prague, 1896); *Karel Havlíček. Snahy a tužby politického probuzení* (Prague, 1896); *Otázka sociální* (Prague, 1898); and *Palackého idea českého národa* (Prague, 1898). Significant parts of *Česká otázka* and other essays were published in English as Tomáš Garrigue Masaryk, *The Meaning of Czech History,* ed. and intro. René Wellek, trans. Paul Kussi (Chapel Hill, 1974).

5. Čornej, "Minulost plná schémat," pt. 1. See also Albert Pražák, "Názory na české obrození," *České obrození,* pp. 64–66; and Rossos, "Czech Historiography, Part 2," pp. 360–72.

6. On Goll, see the evaluation by his pupil Josef Šusta, "Jaroslav Goll," *Český časopis historický* 35 (1929): 475–88, and Rossos, "Czech Historiography, Part 2," pp. 369–70.

7. Čornej, "Minulost plná schémat," pt. 2; Rossos, "Czech Historiography, Part 2," pp. 375–76. Especially in his critical biography of Jan Žižka, Pekař stirred up significant public controversy and polemics both

scholarly and popular. Jiří Rak has suggested that if the war and Communist period had not interrupted the natural development of Czech historiography, the traditional nationalist interpretations would have been settled with much sooner (Rak, "'Boj o duši národa,'" pp. 35–36). A selection of Pekař's works on the meaning of Czech history has been published as Josef Pekař, *O smyslu českých dějin* (Prague, 1990).

8. Krofta's *Žižka a husitská revoluce* (Prague, 1936) was an attempt to respond to Pekař's criticisms in his *Žižka a jeho doba*, 4 vols. (Prague, 1927–1933). Krofta also produced a (posthumous) synthetic historical survey, *Dějiny československé* (Prague, 1947). The term *Bohemian Estates* refers to the traditional feudal legislature of the Kingdom of Bohemia. Its name was taken from the fact that it supposedly represented the three "estates" of the kingdom: the clergy, the nobility, and the burghers. In practice it was controlled by the nobility.

9. Pražák, "Názory na české obrození," p. 108. See also Joseph F. Zacek, "Nationalism in Czechoslovakia," in *Nationalism in Eastern Europe*, ed. Sugar and Lederer, pp. 175–77.

10. A typical survey of this sort is Arnošt Klima, *Na prahu nové společnosti* (1781–1848) (Prague, 1979). See also Zacek, "Nationalism in Czechoslovakia," p. 176. For a "Marxist" discussion of previous historiography on the renascence, see Josef Kočí, *České národní obrození* (Prague, 1978), pp. 145–56.

11. Albert Pražák, "Názory na české obrození," pp. 109–10.

12. Pražák's other great work on the history of Czech national identity, *Národ se bránil,* is even more strongly marked by this tone.

13. For a discussion of the different terminology used to describe the renascence, see Pražák, "Názory na české obrození," pp. 63–65. I translate the Czech word *obrození* by the term "renascence" instead of "revival" (which is not uncommon, especially in American works on Czech history), because I think it more accurately reflects the etymological meaning of the Czech. The use of the form "renascence" will, I hope, serve to distinguish it from the general European Renaissance.

14. See Anthony D. Smith, *The Ethnic Origins of Nations* (Oxford, 1987), pp. 7–13. An argument for the first position is Leonard Doob, *Patriotism and Nationalism: Their Psychological Foundations* (New Haven, 1964); a classic among many examples of the other approach is Elie Kedourie, *Nationalism,* rev. ed. (London, 1985).

15. The most recent edition of the *Kronika Boleslavská* is Jiří Daňhelka, Karel Hádek, Bohuslav Havránek and Naděžda Kvítková, eds., *Staročeská kronika tak řečeného Dalimila,* 2 vols. (Prague, 1988). For examples of the attitudes of the chronicler, see p. 105, where the establishment of the Czechs in Bohemia is called "the beginnings of the Czech *language*" (emphasis added), or p. 129, which contains Libuše's famous

prophecy promising weal to the kingdom if it will preserve its language. Other examples abound.

16. Banac, *The National Question in Yugoslavia,* p. 21.

17. Singapore's efforts to create a "national ideology" represent a good example of "nation-building." See the *Economist* 310, no. 7586 (21 January 1989): 38.

18. See John A. Armstrong, *Nations before Nationalism* (Chapel Hill, 1982), most succinctly pp. 283–99.

19. "Ty jsi dědic české země, rozpomeň se na své plémě, nedej zahynouti nám ni budoucím" (Thou art the heir of the Czech land, call to remembrance thy kindred, do not allow us or future generations to die out), runs the ancient Czech hymn to Saint Václav. See also Novák, *Czech Literature,* pp. 26–27.

20. František Graus, *Die Nationenbildung der Westslawen im Mittelalter* (Sigmaringen, 1980), pp. 51–64, 87–113, devotes special attention to Bohemia; see pp. 139–43. See also his "Die Bildung eines Nationalbewusstseins im mittelalterlichen Böhmen (die vorhussitische Zeit)," *Historica* 12 (1966): 73–84. On earlier forms of ethnic Czech self-awareness, see František Šmahel, "The Idea of the Czech Nation in Hussite Bohemia," *Historica* 16 (1969): 143–247; ibid. 17 (1970): 93–197; and Jaroslav Mezník, "Dějiny národu českého v Moravě (Nárys vývoje národního vědomí na Moravě do poloviny 19. století)," *Český časopis historický* 88 (1990): 34–62.

21. Graus, *Die Nationenbildung,* pp. 146–47.

22. See Petr Čornej, *Tajemství českých kronik* (Prague, 1986), p. 304.

23. Kutnar, *Přehledné dějiny českého a slovenského dějepisectví,* pp. 64–73. Important studies of this baroque culture include Vilém Bitnar, *Postavy a problemy českého baroku literárního* (Prague, 1939); the volume *Pragensia Svatojanská: Sborník statí o kultuře českého baroka* (Prague, 1929), ed. Vilém Bitnar and Karel Procházka; and Zdeněk Kalista, *České baroko: studie, texty, poznamky* (Prague, 1941). Kalista was silenced by the Communists and spent more than a decade in prison. He published another work on the baroque culture of Bohemia abroad, *Tvář baroka: poznámky, které zabloudily na okraj života, skicář problemů a odpovědi* (Munich, 1982).

24. For a survey of Czech and Slovak nationalism, see Zacek, "Nationalism in Czechoslovakia," pp. 167–206, and "Czech and Slovak Nationalism," *Canadian Review of Studies in Nationalism,* 17 (1990): 327–31.

25. See Smith, *Ethnic Origins,* pp. 130–34, on which much of this discussion rests. The "triple revolution" and its impact on nationalism is discussed in different ways in Benedict Anderson, *Imagined Communities: Reflections on the Origin and Spread of Nationalism* (London, 1983), and Ernest Gellner, *Nations and Nationalism* (Ithaca and London, 1983). An older, slightly different interpretation, stressing the development of ideas,

is Kohn, *The Idea of Nationalism,* which deals with the Czech renascence on pp. 551–60.

26. Cornelia Navari, "The Origins of the Nation-State," in *The Nation State: The Formation of Modern Politics,* ed. Leonard Tivey (New York, 1981), pp. 13–36. See also Charles Tilly, ed., *The Formation of National States in Western Europe* (Princeton, 1975).

27. See Anderson, *Imagined Communities,* esp. chap. 4. For a slightly different explanation of this cultural revolution, linking it to the demands of modern industrialized society, see Gellner, *Nations and Nationalism,* esp. pp. 19–38.

28. John Breuilly, *Nationalism and the State* (Manchester, 1982) stresses the political nature of modern nationalism. See esp. pp. 1–35, 352–84.

29. Ibid., pp. 334–50.

30. Banac, *The National Question,* p. 27.

31. Hroch, *Die Vorkämpfer der nationalen Bewegung bei den kleinen Völker Europas,* pp. 24–26, recently translated as *Social Preconditions of National Revival in Europe* (Cambridge, 1985).

32. Miroslav Hroch once characterized the "awakeners" of this phase as "patriots without a nation." See "Vlastenci bez národy," in *Naše živá a mrtvá minulost. Osm esejí o českých dějinách* (Prague, 1968).

33. See T.C.W. Blanning, *Joseph II and Enlightened Despotism* (London, 1970). Other works linking the national revivals with "enlightened despotism" include Eduard Winter, *Barock, Absolutismus und Aufklärung in der Donaumonarchie* (Vienna, 1971); and Józef Chlebowczyk, *Procesy narodotwórcze we wschodniej europie środkowej w dobie kapitalizmu* (od schyłku XVIII do początków XX w.) (Warsaw and Cracow, 1975), esp. pp. 77–112. An abridged version of the latter work is in *On Small and Young Nations in Europe* (Wrocław, 1980).

34. For a debate on the place of the intelligentsia in nationalism, see Anthony D. Smith, *Theories of Nationalism* (London, 1971), esp. chaps. 6, 10; Breuilly, *Nationalism and the State,* pp. 327–33; Kedourie, *Nationalism*; and Anderson, *Imagined Communities.*

35. Hugh Seton-Watson, "Nationalismus und Nationalbewusstsein," *Österreichische Osthefte* 8 (1966): 3–4. Conflicting views of the place of the nobility in the national renascence can be found in Josef Pekař's review of Josef Hanuš, *Národní museum a naše obrození,* vol. I (Prague, 1921), in *ČČH* 28 (1922): 469–77; Jan Muk, *Po stopách národního vědomí české šlechty pobělohorské* (Prague, 1931); and Kapras, "Národní vědomí české šlechty."

36. Rogger, *National Consciousness in Eighteenth Century Russia,* p. 3, defines national consciousness primarily in cultural terms. See also Aleksandr Sergeevich Myl'nikov, "Kul'tura i natsional'noe samosoznanie

narodov tsentral'noi i iugovostochnoi evropy v epokhu natsional'nogo vozrozhdeniia," *Sovetskoe slavianovedenie* 4 (1974), pp. 73–84.

37. See Joseph Frederick Zacek, "The Czech Enlightenment and the Czech National Revival," *Canadian Review of Studies in Nationalism* 10 (1983): 17–28; and Mikuláš Teich, "Bohemia: From Darkness into Light," in *The Enlightenment in National Context,* ed. Roy Porter and Mikuláš Teich (Cambridge, 1981), pp. 141–63. See also Myl'nikov, *Vznik národně osvícenské ideologie v českých zemích 18. století. Prameny národního obrození* and *Epocha prosveshcheniia v cheshskikh zemliakh*; and Haubelt, *České osvícenství.*

38. Agnew, "Josephinism and the Patriotic Intelligentsia in Bohemia." See also Pavel Bělina, "Teoretické kořeny a státní praxe osvícenského absolutismu v habsburské monarchii," *ČsČH* 29 (1981): 879–905.

39. Joseph Anton Ritter von Riegger, *Skizze einer statistischen Landeskunde Böhmens* (Leipzig and Prague, 1795), pp. 98–99.

40. The Hungarian reaction to Josephinism is described in Béla K. Király, *Hungary in the Late Eighteenth Century: The Decline of Enlightened Despotism* (New York, 1969). See also Kerner, *Bohemia in the Eighteenth Century.*

41. Zacek, "Nationalism in Czechoslovakia," p. 177.

42. Breuilly, *Nationalism and the State,* p. 113.

43. The Bohemian Germans had few alternatives to becoming German nationalists. Surveys of Czech nationalism in English are scarce. See Zacek, "Nationalism in Czechoslovakia"; Jan Havránek, "The Development of Czech Nationalism," *Austrian History Yearbook* 3, pt. 2 (1967): 223–60; Bruce Garver, *The Young Czech Party, 1874–1901, and the Emergence of a Multi-Party System* (New Haven, 1978); František Červinka, *Český nacionalismus v XIX. století* (Prague, 1965); and Kočí, *České národní obrození.*

44. See Stanley Z. Pech, *The Czech Revolution of 1848* (Chapel Hill, 1969).

Chapter 1. The Presence of the Past

1. When exactly he earned this epithet I have been unable to ascertain, but it was common among his contemporaries and immediate successors. See Palacký, *Dějiny národu českého v Čechách a na Moravě,* p. 13.

2. See Rossos, "Czech Historiography, Part 1," *Canadian Slavonic Papers,* pp. 245–60, and "Czech Historiography, Part 2," pp. 359–85.

3. Kerner, *Bohemia in the Eighteenth Century,* pp. 3–25.

4. Pražák, *České obrození,* p. 120. See also František Kutnar, *Přehledné dějiny českého a slovenského dějepisectví: Od počátků národní kultury až po vyznění obrodného úkolu dějepisectví v druhé polovině 19. století* (Prague, 1973), pp. 64–68.

5. See Kutnar, *Přehledné dějiny . . . dějepisectví*, pp. 70–73.

6. That the place of Balbín and the Czech baroque in the history of Czech culture is still a lively topic is testified to by the fate of Kučera and Rak, *Bohuslav Balbín a jeho místo v české kultuře*: a very small print run rapidly sold out, but the book was not reprinted following unfavorable reviews in the official journals, and the authors lost their jobs. An example of Czechoslovak "Marxist" historiography on the Balbín tradition is Haubelt, "Počátky historiografické práce Gelasia Dobnera." Haubelt was one of the leaders in the attack on Rak and Kučera.

7. Kutnar, *Přehledné dějiny . . . dějepisectví*, pp. 72–73.

8. The publisher was František Martin Pelcl, who gave it this Latin title. The edition was proscribed after original approval was withdrawn by the censor, and all unsold copies were confiscated. See Prokeš, "Osudy prvního vydání Balbínovy 'Obrany jazyka českého,'" pp. 245–59; and chap. 2.

9. Schamschula, *Die Anfänge*, pp. 23–24; Kutnar, *Přehledné dějiny . . . dějepisectví*, pp. 74–75.

10. On Bollandist traditions, see Thompson, *A History of Historical Writing* 2:8–13.

11. See Fueter, *Geschichte der neueren Historiographie*; and Kutnar, *Přehledné dějiny . . . dějepisectví*, pp. 45–51.

12. Thompson, *Historical Writing*, pp. 18–19; Kutnar, *Přehledné dějiny . . . dějepisectví*, pp. 93–101.

13. Fueter, *Historiographie*, pp. 308–09.

14. Thompson, *Historical Writing*, p. 47; Kutnar, *Přehledné dejiny . . . dějepisectví*, pp. 93–101.

15. See Hanuš et al., *Literatura česká devatenáctého století*, 1:66–93.

16. Hanuš, *Národní museum a naše obrození* 1:57–58. See also Schamschula, *Die Anfänge*, p. 319; on Ziegelbauer's career, see ibid., pp. 44–57.

17. Hanuš, *Národní museum*, 1:57–58.

18. Kinský, in other respects a rather typical representative of the *Landespatriotischer* Bohemian nobility, seems to have had a reasonably good knowledge of Czech, which he sometimes used in letters to friends. See Pekař, "Naše šlechta a jazyk český v 18. století."

19. Hanuš, *Národní museum*, 1:60. See also Šimeček, "Počátky osvícenského dějepisectví v českých zemích a studium dějin slovanských národů," pp. 307–08.

20. Ibid., p. 61; Myľnikov, *Vznik národně osvícenské ideologie*, p. 102. In September 1745 Ziegelbauer wrote to his friend Oliver Legipont that the MS had already cost him some 1,200 guilders.

21. Hanuš, *Národní museum*, 1:40; Slavík, *Od Dobnera k Dobrovskému*, pp. 17–29. See also Němec, "The First Austrian Learned Society."

22. Myl'nikov, *Vznik národně osvícenské ideologie*, p. 143. See also Myl'nikov, "Vozniknoveniie ranneprosvetitel'skikh ob"edinenii v cheshskikh zemliakh," in *Razvitie kapitalizma i natsional'nye dvizheniia v slavianskikh stranakh* (Moscow, 1970), p. 39.

23. Hanuš, *Národní museum*, 1:40; Myl'nikov, *Vznik národně osvícenské ideologie*, p. 144. Schamschula discusses the careers of most of the members of the Societas Incognitorum at some length in *Die Anfänge*, pp. 44–78.

24. Hanuš, *Národní museum*, 1:40–44.

25. Summarized in Myl'nikov, *Vznik národně osvícenské ideologie*, p. 145.

26. Hanuš, *Národní museum*, 1:47.

27. Ibid., p. 49; Myl'nikov, *Vznik národně osvícenské ideologie*, pp. 145–46. Cf. Němec, "The First Austrian Learned Society," p. 152, where he states that the journal published only two volumes, 1747 and 1748.

28. Pražák, *České obrození*, pp. 34–35.

29. Ibid., p. 34; Schamschula, *Die Anfänge*, pp. 72–78; Kutnar, *Přehledné dějiny . . . dějepisectví*, pp. 83–84.

30. Lemberg, *Grundlagen der nationalen Erwachens in Böhmen*, p. 34; Prokeš, *Počátky České společnosti nauk do konce XVIII. století*, pp. 147–48. Myl'nikov discounts the importance of this link with the nobility, but not always consistently. Compare his "Ideino-politicheskie predposylki prosveshcheniia v cheshskikh zemliakh i ego rannii period," in *Istoria, kul'tura, folklor i etnografiia slavianskikh narodov* (Moscow, 1968), p. 87, with *Vznik národně osvícenské ideologie*, p. 101.

31. Josef Hanuš, "Boh. Balbína Bohemia docta," *ČČH* 12 (1906): 425.

32. See Hanuš, "Počátky kritického dějezpytu v Čechách," pp. 202–91. See also Slavík, *Od Dobnera k Dobrovskému*, pp. 73–75.

33. See Haubelt, "Počátky historiografické práce Gelasia Dobnera," pp. 714–15.

34. Gelasius Dobner, MS autobiography, LA PNP, Prague, sign. I/4/1, published by Hanuš in *ČČH* 23 (1917): 129–38.

35. Ibid.

36. The critical edition is Václav Hájek z Libočan, *Kronika česká*, ed. Václav Flajšhans, 4 vols. (Prague, 1918–1933), which includes an introductory study by the editor. See also Rossos, "Czech Historiography, Part I," pp. 251–52; and Kutnar, *Přehledné dějiny . . . dějepisectví*, p. 55.

37. Kutnar, *Přehledné dějiny . . . dějepisectví*, pp. 55–57. See also Novák, *Czech Literature*, p. 68; and Jan Jakubec, *Dějiny literatury české*, 2d ed. (Prague, 1929), 1:655–66.

38. See Banac, *The National Question in Yugoslavia*, p. 73.

39. See Krofta, "F. Pubička, předchůdce Palackého v zemském dě-

jepisectví Českém." In fact, Dobner's explanation for the derivation of the name *Czech* has not been given the seal of historical acceptance either. The point here, however, is that he had destroyed the traditional legend as contained in Hájek's chronicle beyond scholarly repair (and, incidentally, completely revised his own attitudes to Hájek of a decade earlier). See Haubelt, "Počátky historiografické práce Gelasia Dobnera," pp. 707–13.

40. Dobner, *Epistola apologetica adversus Luciferem urentem et non lucentem* (1767), cited by Hanuš in "Počátky kritického dějezpytu," p. 451. Dobner discusses his opponents' attacks in his autobiography; see also Kudělka, *Spor Gelasia Dobnera o Hájkovu kroniky.* The international and pan-Slavic repercussions of the Čech-Lech controversy are treated in chap. 6.

41. Palacký, *Dějiny národu českého,* p. 13. Palacký, himself a Protestant, may have been less sympathetic toward Hájek's reputation than other historians.

42. Myl'nikov, *Epokha prosveshcheniia v cheshskikh zemliakh,* pp. 67–97. See also Hanuš et al., *Literatura česká devatenáctého století,* pp. 93–99; and Vlček, *Dějiny české literatury,* 2:153–57.

43. See Born's comment in the foreword to *Abhandlungen einer Privatgesellschaft* 3 (1777): n.p. See also Haubelt, "Ignac Born," and *Studie o Ignaci Bornovi*; and Slavík, *Od Dobnera k Dobrovskému,* pp. 48–60.

44. Myl'nikov, "Vozniknovenie ranneprosvetitel'skikh ob"edinenii v cheshskikh zemliakh," pp. 48–52. On the place of the Prague literary periodicals in the national revival, see Arnošt Kraus, *Pražské časopisy 1770–1774 a české probuzení* (Prague, 1909); and Jan Strakoš, *Počátky obrozenského historizmu v pražských časopisech a Mikuláš Adaukt Voigt. Příspěvek k historii protiosvícenské reakce v národním obrození* (Prague, 1929).

45. Zacek, "The Virtuosi of Bohemia," pp. 152–53; and Teich, "The Royal Bohemian Society of Sciences and the First Phase of Organized Scientific Advance in Bohemia," p. 161.

46. See Hemmerle, "Der Josephinismus und die Gründungsmitglieder der Gelehrten Gesellschaft der Wissenschaften in Prag."

47. Originally entitled *Abhandlungen einer Privatgesellschaft in Böhmen zur Aufnahme der Mathematik, der vaterländischen Geschichte und der Naturgeschichte,* 6 vols. (1775–1784), the journal's name was changed to *Abhandlungen der böhmischen Gesellschaft der Wissenschaften zu Prag,* 4 vols. (1785–1788). Then came three volumes of *Neuere Abhandlungen der königlichen Böhmischen Gesellschaft der Wissenschaften* (1790–1798), and finally it appeared as *Abhandlungen der k. b. Gesellschaft der Wissenschaften vom Jahre . . . ,* 8 vols. (1804–1824).

48. Dobner, "Kritische Untersuchung, wann das Land Mähren ein Markgrafthum geworden . . . sey," p. 183; Dobner, "Historischer Beweis, dass Wladislaw der Zweyte . . . gekront worden," p. 2.

49. Dobner, "Wann das Land Mähren," p. 229.

50. For example, see Dobner, "Historisch-kritische Beobachtungen über den Ursprung," pp. 252–53, or his "Historischer Beweis, dass Wladislaw der Zweyte . . . gekront worden," pp. 1–2, where he takes on his old opponent František Pubička.

51. Dobner, "Abhandlung über das Alter der Böhmischen Bibelübersetzung," p. 284.

52. Dobrovský to J. V. Zlobicky, 15 April 1796; *DZ*, p. 107.

53. Dobner, *Vindiciae Sigillo Confessionis diui Joannis Nepomuceni Protomartyris Poenitentiae assertae.*

54. Dobrovský, *Litterarisches Magazin von Böhmen und Mähren*, 3:121. Dobrovský reviewed an entire series of works on the subject, pp. 101–26.

55. Voigt, "Untersuchung über die Einfuhrung, den Gebrauch, und die Abänderung der Buchstaben und des Schreibens in Böhmen"; "Von dem Alterthume und Gebrauche des Kirchengesanges in Böhmen"; "Versuch einer Geschichte der Universität Prag"; and "Nachricht von merkwürdigen böhmischen Macenaten."

56. Pelcl, "Biographie des Adauct Voigt," p. 17.

57. Voigt, "Nachricht von . . . Macenaten," p. 337.

58. Voigt, *Über den Geist der Böhmischen Gesetze*, pp. 9–10.

59. Ibid., p. 200.

60. See ČSAV, *Dějiny české literatury. II. Literatura národního obrození* (Prague, 1960), p. 36.

61. Ungar, "Versuch einer Geschichte der Bibliotheken in Böhmen," and "Neue Beiträge zur alten Geschichte der Buchdruckerkunst in Böhmen."

62. Ungar, "Žižka's militärische Briefe und Verordnungen."

63. Hanuš, *František Martin Pelcl*, pp. 3–5.

64. Pelcl, "Wann ist Kaiser Karl IV. Markgraf in Mähren geworden."

65. Pelcl, "Das Edikt des Kaisers, Karl des Vierten."

66. Schamschula, *Die Anfänge*, p. 110. See also Hanuš et al., *Česká literatura devatenáctého století*, pp. 157–278.

67. Dobrovský, "Wie man die alten Urkunden," p. 200. Dobner had already begun an attempt at such a collection with his *Monumenta historica Boemia nusquam antehac edita*, and Dobrovský and Pelcl collaborated on another series, *Scriptores rerum bohemicarum*, 2 vols. This collection included some of the important early chronicles, notably that of Cosmas of Prague, but it was not continued beyond the second volume until František Palacký published a third in 1829.

68. It was published in 1929 by V. Flajšhans, *Jos. Dobrovského kritická rozprava o legendě Prokopské* (Prague, 1929).

69. Dobrovský, "Kritische Versuche, die ältere böhmische Geschichte," p. 3.

70. Dobrovský, "Geschichte der Böhmischen Pikarden und Adamiten," p. 308.

71. Dobrovský, "Beyträge zur Geschichte des Kelchs in Böhmen."

72. Dobrovský, *Litterarisches Magazin von Böhmen und Mähren* 1:77.

73. See Peter F. Sugar, "External and Domestic Roots of Eastern European Nationalism," in *Nationalism in Eastern Europe*, ed. Sugar and Lederer, pp. 25–26; and Anderson, *Lineages of the Absolutist State*, pp. 204–06. An interesting comparative perspective is provided in Banac and Bushkovitch, eds., *The Nobility in Russia and Eastern Europe* (New Haven: Yale Concilium on International Studies).

74. Dobner, "Kritische Abhandlung von den Grenzen Altmährens."

75. Dobner, "Kritische Untersuchung . . . das Christenthum in Böhmen," and "Über die Einführung des Christenthums in Böhmen."

76. Pelcl, "Abhandlung über den Samo, König der Slawen," and "Über das Vaterland des Jacobus de Misa, genannt Jacobellus."

77. For an account of Cornova's career, see Kutnar, "Život a dílo Ignace Cornovy."

78. Cornova, "Über das Verhaltniss zwischen König Premisl Ottokar II und den Päbsten."

79. Cornova, "Hat Schirach König Georgen von Böhmen."

80. Cornova, "Über Karl des IV. Betragen gegen das Bayerische Haus," p. 84.

81. Dobrovský's review of Royko in *Litterarisches Magazin von Böhmen und Mähren* 3 (1787): 140. Royko was reported to the Religion Commision in Vienna over certain passages in his work, but his contacts at court seem to have stood him in good stead. See Pelcl to Dobrovský, 9 April 1788, LA PNP, Prague, Dobrovský collection, sign. I/5/6; and Schamschula, "Der slowenische Kirchenhistoriker Kaspar Royko (Rojko) und die tschechische nationale Erneuerung," pp. 105–06, 108.

82. Pelcl, *Lebensgeschichte des Romischen und Böhmischen König Wenceslaus*, 2:635–37.

83. Pelcl, *Kaiser Karl der Vierte, König in Böhmen*, 2:972.

84. Voigt, foreword to *Beschreibung der bisher bekannten Böhmischen Münzen nach chronologischer Ordnung*, vol. 2.

85. Ibid., p. 135.

86. Krofta, "F. Pubička, předchůdce Palackého," p. 12.

87. See Dobrovský's review of vol. 2, pt. 4, *Litterarisches Magazin von Böhmen und Mähren* 1 (1786): 471.

88. Ibid., pp. 47, 65–66.

89. Pelcl, foreword to *Kurzgefasste Geschichte der Böhmen*.

90. Pelcl, ibid., pp. 619–21.

91. Ibid., pp. 18ff.

92. See Frederick G. Heymann, "The Hussite Movement in the Historiography of the Czech Awakening," in *The Czech Renascence of the Nineteenth Century*, ed. Peter Brock and H. Gordon Skilling (Toronto, 1970), pp. 228–29.

93. Pelcl, foreword to *Kurzgefasste Geschichte der Böhmen*.

94. Hanuš, *František Martin Pelcl*, pp. 54–64; Heymann, "The Hussite Movement," pp. 228–29.

95. Pelcl, foreword to *Nová kronyka česká*, vol. 1. It is doubtful whether the countess was particularly fluent in Czech.

96. Kerner, *Bohemia in the Eighteenth Century*, pp. 360–63. Drabek discusses the general ideological position of the Estates in 1791 in "Die Desiderien der böhmischen Stände von 1791," pp. 132–42. See also ČSAV, *Dějiny české literatury*, pp. 36–37.

97. Pelcl's plans for Žižka's biography are mentioned in Ungar, "Žižka's militärische Briefe," pp. 371–72.

98. Pražák, *České obrození*, p. 36.

99. Pařízek was closely involved with the Prague Normal School, set up to serve as the model and training ground for the Bohemian school system. See Berls, "The Elementary School Reforms of Maria Theresa and Joseph II in Bohemia," pp. 177–79. Pařízek's history was criticized by the Gubernium because of its intolerantly Catholic outlook, and eventually not adopted.

100. It is not necessary, however, to see Dobner as expressing a "bourgeois" Czech historical ideology, as does Haubelt in "O Gelasiovi Dobnerovi," pp. 165, 172.

101. Václav Stach [Václav Petryn, pseud.], *Historie velikého sněmu kostnického*.

102. The Czech "popular awakeners" are discussed at greater length in chap. 5. See also Agnew, "Enlightenment and National Consciousness: Three Czech 'Popular Awakeners,'" pp. 201–26.

103. See chap. 3.

104. Rulík, *Velmi užitečná historie o slovutném národu Českém*, p. 11.

105. Rulík, *Gallerie, aneb vyobrazenost nejslovutnějších a nejznamenitějších osob země České*, 1:3–8. The first two volumes covered the famous personalities from ancient and medieval history, the third the Hussite period, and the fourth and fifth the sixteenth to the eighteenth centuries. In Prague I was able to locate only vols. 1 and 2, but Jungmann, in *Historie literatury České*, describes the contents of the other volumes.

106. Rulík, *Památky starožitného a veleslávného kláštěra Sedleckého bliž Hory Kutné v království Českém*, p. 15.

107. Rulík, foreword to *Kalendář historický*.

108. On Vavák, see Kutnar, *František Jan Vavák*; and Luděk Šmid, *Lidoví kronikáři středního Polabí*. Vavák's voluminous *Paměti* were published by J. Skopec, 3 vols. in 8 parts (Prague, 1907–1924).

109. Rulík to Vavák, 28 December 1799, LA PNP, Prague, Vavák collection, sign. I/13/39.

110. From a review by Dobrovský, reprinted in *Literární a prozodická bohemika,* Spisy a projevy (Prague, 1974), 6:127.

111. A Czech work on historical consciousness in nineteenth-century European national movements, including the Czech, is *Úloha historického povědomí v evropském národním hnutí v 19. století,* ed. Miroslav Hroch, AUC, Philosophica et Historica 5, 1976, *Studia Historica* 15 (Prague, 1976). See esp. pp. 7–14.

112. The relationship of Palacký to Dobner is treated, not always convincingly, by Haubelt in "František Palacký a Gelasius Dobner."

113. Schamschula, *Die Anfänge,* pp. 97–114.

114. Dobrovský, "Kritische Versuche," p. 2.

115. Jan Jakubec, writing in Hanuš et al., *Literatura česká devatenáctého století,* emphasises that the historical writing of this period had a distinctly anti-Josephine stance, however much the historians might otherwise have admired Joseph II. See pp. 62–66.

Chapter 2. "Our Natural Language"

1. Pelcl, "Wann ist Karl IV. Markgraf in Mähren geworden."

2. See for example Lemberg, "Der deutsche Anteil am Erwachen des tschechischen Volkes," pp. 311–12. See also Hanuš et al., *Literatura česká devatenáctého století,* pp. 295–361.

3. F. M. Pelcl, "Geschichte der Deutschen und ihrer Sprache in Böhmen," *Abhandlungen* 2 (1791): 301.

4. See Dobrovský's comments years later to Jernej Kopitar and Jerzy Samuel Bandtke, in *DK,* p. 107 (letter of 6 March 1810), and *DB,* p. 48 (undated [1812?]). I believe that parts of Pelcl's "Geschichte," especially where he discusses the sixteenth- and eighteenth-century reprintings of Dalimil's chronicle, with its pronounced anti-German bias, reveal a certain ironic tone behind the apparent despair.

5. Kohn's discussion of the development of German nationalism in *The Idea of Nationalism,* pp. 329–451, has much on this question (see esp. pp. 334–48); and for a lapidary summary of these developments, Gordon A. Craig, *The Germans,* (Harmondsworth, Middlesex, 1984), pp. 312–13.

6. Schamschula, *Die Anfänge,* pp. 123–24, 221–30; Svobodová, *Dobrovský a německá filologie.*

7. See Pražák, *Národ se bránil;* and Krejčí, "Obrana českého jazyka ze stanoviska literárního druhu." Cf. Rogger, *National Consciousness in Eighteenth-Century Russia,* esp. chap. 4.

8. Kinsky, *Erinnerung über einen wichtingen Gegenstand,* p. 57.

9. Ibid.

10. Kinský's arguments summarized in the following discussion may be found in ibid., pp. 57–59.

11. Ibid., pp. 112–13.

12. For example, Arnošt Kraus: "This Austrian General is a Slav, a Czech, and a German at the same time!" (cited in Schamschula, *Die Anfänge*, p. 119). See also Hanuš in *Národní museum* 1:103.

13. Pekař, "Naše šlechta a jazyk český," pp. 80–82.

14. See ČSAV, *Dějiny české literatury*, pp. 37–39.

15. Krejčí, "Obrany jazyka českého," pp. 84–86.

16. Johanides, *František Martin Pelcl*, pp. 107–46.

17. See Dobrovský, *Geschichte der böhmischen Sprache und Litteratur*, p. 196.

18. Hanke von Hankenstein, *Empfehlung der böhmischen Sprache und Litteratur*, pp. 4–6.

19. Ibid., pp. 12, 16–17.

20. Ibid., pp. 43–44.

21. Krejčí, "Obrany českého jazyka," p. 86.

22. K. H. Thám, *Obrana jazyka českého proti zlobivým jeho utrháčům*, p. 19.

23. Ibid., p. 21.

24. Ibid., pp. 24–26.

25. See Thám's closing appeal to the emperor, ibid., pp. 43–44.

26. Josef Dobrovský, review in *Litterarisches Magazin von Böhmen und Mähren* 3 (1787): 143–44. The implication is that the answer would be no.

27. Not only had Joseph refused to be crowned king of Bohemia (or king of Hungary), he had retained the crown of Saint Václav in Vienna for safekeeping—an action viewed as a deliberate slight by patriotic Bohemians. The return of the crown for Leopold's coronation ceremony was hailed as a great omen. See, for example, Rulík, *Kalendář historický*, 1:120, 137; entries for January and 9 August 1791.

28. Dobrovský, *Über die Ergebenheit und Anhänglichkeit der Slawischen Völker an das Erzhaus Österreich*, p. 5. For his earlier intention, see Dobrovský to Ribay, 28 August 1791, *DR*, p. 196.

29. Dobrovský to an unnamed friend in 1795: "My insignificant little work, which I read in the presence of Emperor Leopold, was changed in several places by Count Rottenhan, then Highest Burggrave. They were greatly concerned not to leave anything which would be too free (noble)." Cited in Francev, introduction to *Řeč Josefa Dobrovského, proslovená . . . v České učené společnosti*, p. 20.

30. Dobrovský to Ribay, 9 October 1791, *DR*, p. 204. The Czech version was translated by K. H. Thám and printed by V. M. Kramerius in *Krameriusovy c. k. vlastenské noviny*, 7 January 1792.

31. Rulík, *Sláva a výbornost jazyka českého,* pp. 6–7, 12–13, 17, 23.
32. Ibid., pp. 32–33, 36.
33. Ibid., p. 45.
34. Johanides, *Pelcl,* pp. 210–28. At one time there was talk of more than one chair, with Pelcl to be professor of Czech history and Dobrovský professor of literature and the Czech language. See the letter of Count Friedrich Nostitz to Dobrovský, 12 June 1792, LA PNP, Prague, Dobrovský collection, sign. I/5/6.
35. Pelcl, *Akademische Antrittsrede über den Nutzen und Wichtigkeit der Böhmischen Sprache,* p. 5.
36. I have not been able to corroborate Pelcl's story about Joseph II's slip of the tongue. Josef Petráň, *Nevolnické povstání 1775,* AUC, Philosophica et Historica, Monographia XLII-1972 (Prague, 1973), does not mention it, nor does the edition of documents, Miroslav Toegel, Josef Petráň, and Jindřich Obršlík, eds., *Prameny k nevolnickému povstání v Čechách a na Moravě v roce 1775* (Prague, 1975).
37. Ibid., pp. 9–13, 15–16.
38. Ibid., p. 20. The reference is undoubtedly to Pelcl's own "Geschichte der Deutschen und ihre Sprache in Böhmen."
39. Nejedlý, *Akademische Antrittsrede gehalten den 16. November 1801,* p. 20. These emphases were to become typical of the second renascence generation, while they also harked back to some of the familiar *topoi* of baroque authors. See Macura, *Znamení zrodu,* esp. pp. 155–61.
40. Ibid., p. 21. Notice that Nejedlý, too, assumes that Czechs would automatically learn German and that the Germans would have to be convinced to learn Czech!
41. Ibid., p. 23, emphasis in original.
42. K. H. Thám, *Über den Karakter der Slawen, dann über den Ursprung, die Schicksale, Vollkommenheiten, die Nützlichkeit und Wichtigkeit der böhmischen Sprache* (Prague, 1803), p. 3.
43. Jan Nejedlý, "O lásce k vlasti," in *Hlasatel česky* 1, no. 1 (1806): 3–5.
44. Ibid., p. 15.
45. Ibid., p. 16, emphasis in original.
46. Daniel Adam z Veleslavína (1546–1599) was active as a publisher and translator, making a successful enterprise out of the printing house he inherited from his father-in-law, Jiří Melantrich. Some Czech literary historians challenge the uncritical idealization of Veleslavín as a "classical" figure and the humanist period as a golden age. Thus Arne Novák: "It is only in the deceptive perspective of a subsequent decadence that this period, one without independent ideas and without any appreciation of literary art, can be considered an era of literary flowering. It was called a golden age, but it was only fool's gold that glittered so vaingloriously in letters" (*Czech Literature,* p. 71).

47. Jungmann, "O jazyku českém. Rozmlouvání první."
48. Jungmann, "O jazyku českém. Rozmlouvání druhé," pp. 322–36.
49. Ibid., p. 344.
50. See chap. 1, n. 93.
51. Havránek, "Vývoj spisovného jazyka českého," 2:80. See also Václav Flajšhans, *Náš jazyk mateřský* (Prague, 1924).
52. Hanzal, "Jazyková otázka ve vývoji obrozenského školství." See also Hanuš et al., *Literatura česká devatenáctého století*, pp. 295–315; and Peter Burian, "Joseph II. und die nationale Frage: Die Sprachenpolitik," *Zeitschrift für Ostforschung* 31 (1982): 191–99.
53. On the state of Czech instruction, see Jelínek, *Nástin dějin vyúčování českému jazyku v letech 1774–1918*, pp. 13–93, esp. pp. 91–93. See also Berls, "The Elementary School Reforms of Maria Theresa and Joseph II in Bohemia," pp. 263–91.
54. Eymer, ed., *Pädagogische Schriften des Grafen Franz Joseph Kinsky*, p. 19.
55. Schamschula, *Die Anfänge*, pp. 146–57. The first two Czech teachers at Wiener Neustadt were Wenzel [Václav] Neumann from Plzeň and Anton Globas, or Klobas.
56. Ibid., p. 160. On Pohl's life and career, see A. Lisický, "Jan Václav Pohl v zápase o české slovo."
57. The seventeenth-century grammarian Václav Rosa was an important influence on Pohl, combined with similar purist trends in contemporary German. See Thomas, "The Role of Calques"; and Schamschula, *Die Anfänge*, p. 162.
58. Schamschula, *Die Anfänge*, p. 162.
59. ČSAV, *Dějiny české literatury*, pp. 42–44.
60. *Litterarisches Magazin von Böhmen und Mähren* 3 (1787): 138.
61. Ibid., p. 139.
62. *Böhmische Litteratur auf das Jahr 1779* 1 (1779): 165. Dobrovský contintued to criticize Pohl and Šimek in his *Böhmische und Mährische Litteratur auf das Jahr 1780* 3 (1784).
63. Schamschula, "Der tschechische Anteil an den 'Österreichischer Biedermannschronik,'" p. 275.
64. Zlobický to Dobrovský, 4 June 1781, *DZ*, p. 3.
65. Schamschula, *Die Anfänge*, p. 153.
66. The grammar, including a slightly revised version of Dobrovský's article, was published in a second edition in 1798.
67. Pelcl, foreword to *Grundsätze der böhmischen Grammatik* (Prague, 1793). See also Jaromír Bělič, "František Martin Pelcl a český jazyk," *Slavica Pragensia* 21 (1978): 115–32.
68. In a review in Riegger's *Lieferungen für Böhmen von Böhmen* (1794), as cited in Schamschula, "Dobrovský's und Pelzel's Beiträge zu den

'Lieferungen für Böhmen von Böhmen,'" *Aus der Geisteswelt der Slawen. Dankesgabe an Erwin Koschmieder* (Munich, 1967), p. 157.

69. Havránek, "Vývoj," p. 83.

70. Cited in Schamschula, "Dobrovský's und Pelzel's Beiträge," p. 157.

71. Cited in ibid., pp. 159–60.

72. Dobrovsky to Kopitar, 6 March 1810, *DK*, p. 107; Dobrovský to Bandtke, n.d. (1812?), *DB*, p. 48.

73. Havránek, "Vývoj," p. 83.

74. See for example Dobrovský's comment in *Litterarisches Magazin von Böhmen und Mähren* 3 (1787): 139.

75. See the review in *Krameriusovy vlastenské noviny*, 1 October 1791.

76. See for example Tomsa, *Über die Bedeutung, Abwandlung und Gebrauch der čechischen Zeitwörter* (Prague, 1804), pp. 127, 130.

77. Ibid., p. 103n.

78. Tomsa, *Von den Vorzügen der čechischen Sprache*, pp. 40–42.

79. Cited in Zeil, "Die Bedeutung des tschechischen Josefiners František Jan Tomsa (1751–1814) für die Entwicklung seiner Muttersprache," p. 603.

80. See Tomsa, *Über die Aussprache der čechischen Buchstaben, Sylben und Wörter nebst Leseübungen*, p. 15n.

81. Tomsa, *Über die Bedeutung*, p. 7; foreword to *Über die čechische Rechtschreibung mit einem Anhange, welcher dreizehn čechischen Gedichte enthält*; and *Grössere čechische Orthographie*, p. 3.

82. Tomsa, *Měsíční spis k poučení a obveselení obecného lidu* 9 (September 1787).

83. Tomsa, *Grössere čechische Orthographie*, p. 3. This modification meant significant changes also in the technology of printing Czech books, especially casting new type faces. See Rudolf K. Nesvera, "Zásluha Františka Jana Tomsy o český knihtisk," pp. 72–82.

84. Tomsa, *Grössere čechische Orthographie*, pp. 3–9.

85. Ibid., p. 19. Tomsa was also the first to replace the German terms *Böhmen*, *böhmisch* with *Čechen*, *čechisch*.

86. Zlobický to Dobrovsky, 28 October 1790, *DZ*, p. 75.

87. Tomsa, *Über die Veränderungen*, p. 42; and *Grössere čechische Orthographie*, pp. 8–9.

88. Cited in Schamschula, "Dobrovský's und Pelzel's Beiträge," p. 157.

89. This comment appeared in a review of Tomsa's *Modlitby pro křest'any katolické* (Prague, 1801), reprinted in Dobrovský, *Literární a prozodická bohemika*, p. 123. It seems to contradict Zeil's assertion, "Dobrovsky begrüsste Tomsas initiative sehr; er schrieb seinen Freunden darüber

und förderte sie auf, diesem Beispiel zu folgen" (Dobrovský welcomed Tomsa's initiative warmly; he wrote his friends about it and urged them to follow his example), in "Die Bedeutung des František Jan Tomsa," p. 606.

90. Puchmajer to Dobrovský, 12 March 1813, LA PNP, Prague, Dobrovský collection, sign. I/5/6.

91. Tomsa, *Über die Veränderungen,* p. 44n: "Doch wer keine andre Energie in der čechische Sprache findt, als das i des Infinitivs, der mag es immer behalten" (But he who finds no other energy in the Czech language than the i of the infinitive may continue to retain it).

92. Thám's *Kurzgefasste böhmische Sprachlehre* went through five editions between 1785 and 1804, and he also published a Czech-German dictionary (2 eds., 1798 and 1805), and several other technical dictionaries.

93. Pelcl, foreword to *Grundsätze.*

94. Nejedly, *Kritische Revision der Thamischen Grammatik,* p. 13. This pamphlet and Thám's response are in LA PNP, Prague, K. H. Thám collection, sign. I/12/29.

95. Dobrovský, *Ausführliches Lehrgebäude der Böhmischen Sprache,* p. xv.

96. See Pelcl's note to Thám, 1798, in LA PNP, K. H. Thám collection, sign. I/12/29.

97. K. H. Thám, *Erklärung über die jüngst erschienene falsche Revision meiner Grammatik.*

98. Thám's quarrel with Nejedlý flared up again in 1804 over his teaching activities at the Staroměstské and Malostranské gymnasia. See Hanzal, "Jazyková otázka," pp. 325–27.

99. For example, see Tomsa's letter of thanks to Dobrovský for such a loan, 6 March 1793, LA PNP, Prague, Dobrovský collection, sign. I/5/7. Tomsa called Dobrovský "the greatest Czech philologist" in *Von den Vorzügen,* p. 38. See also Walter Schamschula, "Sprachreform und Sprachpflege bei den Tschechen im Zeitalter des Josephinismus," *Zeitschrift für Ostforschung* 31 (1982): 200–07.

100. Schamschula, *Die Anfänge,* pp. 215–28; Svobodová, *Dobrovský a německá filologie.*

101. Compare the treatments in the 1809 and 1819 editions of Dobrovský's Lehrgebäude, published in parallel form in *Spisy a projevy* vol. 9, esp. pp. 58, 31.

102. Schamschula, *Die Anfänge,* p. 229.

103. Havránek, "Vývoj," p. 84. For an overview of Dobrovský's teaching on declension and conjugation, see his pamphlet *Böhmische Biegungen,* "P. učiteli J. N[ejedlé]mu a jeho učencům obětovano od J. D[obrovské]ho" (Prague, n.d.).

104. Hanuš et al., *Literatura česká devatenáctého století,* pp. 217–32.

105. A. Lisický, "Z dějin zápasu o české slovo," *Osvěta* 49 (1919): 475–78.

106. His grammar, *Grammatica lingua bohemicae, oder die Böhmische Sprach-Kunst* (Vienna, 1756), was accompanied by a patriotic-defensive foreword.

107. See Thomas, "The Role of Calques," p. 485; and Lisický, "Jan Václav Pohl," p. 160.

108. Tomsa, *Böhmische Sprachlehre*, p. 425.

109. Dobrovský, "Über den Ursprung und die Bildung der slawischen und insbesondere der böhmischen Sprache," foreword to Tomsa, *Vollständiges Wörterbuch der böhmisch- deutsch- und lateinischen Sprache* (Prague, 1791), p. 32.

110. Dobrovský, *Böhmische Litteratur*, p. 165.

111. See Thomas, "The Role of Calques," pp. 486–87, for a list of neologisms that have survived into the present, or at least lasted throughout the revival period.

112. Dobrovský, *Die Bildsamkeit der Slawischen Sprache*, p. 9.

113. Dostál, "Práce Josefa Dobrovského o tvoření slov," pp. 130–35; Schamschula, *Die Anfänge*, p. 226.

114. Tomsa, *Böhmische Sprachlehre*, p. 440.

115. Pelcl, *Akademische Antrittsrede*, p. 8. Much earlier he had expressed approval of such neologisms as *veselá činohra* for *Lustspiel*, *zátah* for *Aufzug*, *nástup* for *Auftritt*, and *divadelna* for *Schauplatz*. See the *Prager gelehrte Nachrichten*, 3 March 1772, a review of the play *Kníže Honzík*.

116. Puchmajer to Dobrovský, 23 March 1801, LA PNP, Prague, Dobrovský collection, sign. I/5/6.

117. Dobrovsky, *Böhmische Litteratur* (1779), p. 329. Zlobický also echoed this view; see Schamschula, *Die Anfänge*, p. 155.

118. Tomsa, *Über die Veränderungen*, p. 28.

119. Dobrovský, *Ankündigung eines deutsch-böhmischen Lexicons* (Prague, 1798), n.p. It can be found with the rest of the polemical pamphlets about Thám in the LA PNP, Prague, K. H. Thám collection, sign. I/12/29. Ironically, Thám was led astray by the Viennese dialect Kren, which was a German borrowing from the Czech!

120. Dobrovský, *Böhmische und Mährische Litteratur auf das Jahr 1780* 1 (1780): 100.

121. Schamschula, *Die Anfänge*, pp. 148–49.

122. Dobrovský, *Litterarisches Magazin von Böhmen und Mähren* 1 (1786): 111.

123. Zlobický to Ungar, 24 October 1786, printed as an appendix to *DZ*, p. 172.

124. Zlobický to Dobrovský, 14 February 1795, *DZ*, p. 89.

125. Dobrovský to Ribay, 16 January 1785, *DR*, p. 3.

126. Dobrovský, foreword to Tomsa, *Wörterbuch*, pp. 3–10.

127. For this original attitude, see Thám to Dobrovský, 21 February 1788, LA PNP, Dobrovský collection, sign. I/5/7.

128. Zlobický to Dobrovský, 26 November 1794, *DZ*, pp. 82–83.

129. Dobrovský to Zlobický, 11 December 1794, ibid., p. 84.

130. Zlobický to Dobrovský, 14 February 1795, ibid., pp. 88–90.

131. Dobrovský to Zlobický, 3 March 1795, ibid., p. 95.

132. Dobrovský to Ribay, 10 August 1794, *DR*, pp. 243–44. See also his remarks in the *Lehrgebäude*, p. xi. Bernolák, especially in his *Dissertatio de orthographia slavica*, attempted to create a separate Slovak literary language distinct from the old Czech used by the Slovak Protestants—which, since he and his circle were staunch Catholics, was not a purely academic question. See Brock, *The Slovak National Awakening*.

133. See, for example, Zlobický to Dobrovský, 13 August 1797, *DZ*, p. 114.

134. K. H. Thám, in a brief pamphlet titled *Antikritik, oder Rechtfertigung*, dated 9 April 1798, LA PNP, Prague, K. H. Thám collection, sign. I/12/29.

135. K. H. Thám, *Dritte und Letzte Antikritik*, dated 21 June 1798.

136. Lisický, "Jan Václav Pohl," p. 290.

137. See especially his correspondence with Puchmajer, who became his closest collaborator, LA PNP, Prague, Dobrovský collection, sign. I/5/7. It has been published by Křívský, "Korespondence Antonína Jaroslava Puchmajera s Josefem Dobrovským."

138. Dobrovský to Jungmann, 26 January 1813, 2 April 1815, LA PNP, Prague, Jungmann collection, sign. I/14/1.

139. Puchmajer to Jungmann, 18 June 1814, LA PNP, Prague, Jungmann collection, sign. I/14/2.

140. See A. G. Shirokova and G. P. Neshchimenko, "Vozrozhdenie cheshskogo literaturnogo iazika kak neobkhodimyi komponent formirovaniia cheshskoi natsii"; and Schamschula, *Die Anfänge*, pp. 246–49.

141. Macura, *Znamení zrodu*, pp. 47–68. See also Sussex, "Lingua Nostra: The Nineteenth Century Slavonic Language Revivals."

Chapter 3. Reclaiming the Czechs' Literary Birthright

1. Jedlička, *Dobrovského "Geschichte,"* pp. 23–24.

2. Schamschula, *Die Anfänge*, pp. 260–61.

3. The first two volumes of the German version were merely translations of Voigt's *Effigies*, but the third and fourth volumes were more independent additions to and revisions of Voigt's material, mostly by Pelcl.

4. Voigt, "Von der Aufnahme . . . der Wissenschaften und Kunste in Böhmen."

5. Voigt, "Vorrede von dem Gelehrten Adel in Böhmen und Mähren." The following passages are found on pp. xxiv–xxvi.

6. Jedlička, *Dobrovského "Geschichte,"* p. 171.

7. *Abbildungen* 1:52.

8. Ibid., 1:61.

9. Ibid., 1:118.

10. In places, the critical apparatus outstripped the text, especially in Ungar's second and third parts. He even took over Candidus's commentary for these parts, adding it to his own footnotes. See Ungar, *Bohuslai Balbini . . . Bohemia docta.*

11. Dobrovský's correspondence with Ungar on these matters was published by Fischer, "Z korrespondence Dobrovského."

12. See Dobrovský's letter to Jernej Kopitar [January 1809], in which he warns Kopitar to avoid polemics with Valentin Vodnik, based on his own experience (*DK*, 20–28).

13. Pelcl, *Böhmische, Mährische und Schlesische Gelehrte* pp. ii–vi.

14. Dlabač was not listed as author of the article, but the frequent internal allusions to him—"der geschickte und mit der Musik wohl bekannte Praemonstratener in Strahof Dlabacz" (Dlabač, the clever and musically well-informed Praemonstratensian in Strahov) or "Dlabacz führt in seiner schriftl. Materialien . . . " (Dlabač states in his written material . . .) and so on—suggest that it was his work on which it was based. See *Materialen zur alten und neuen Statistik von Böhmen* (1788), 7:136; and (1794), 12:243, 257, 270, 286.

15. Dlabač, foreword to *Allgemeines historisches Künstlerlexikon fur Böhmen*, 1:x–xi.

16. Voigt, *Acta litteraria Bohemiae et Moraviae*, 1:xii.

17. Jedlička, *Dobrovského "Geschichte,"* pp. 25n, 172.

18. ČSAV, *Dějiny české literatury*, pp. 40–41.

19. Dobrovský, *Böhmische Litteratur auf das Jahr 1779*, p. 5.

20. Ibid., p. 9.

21. Hanuš, "Dobrovského časopisy," p. 380.

22. Dobrovský, foreword to *Böhmische und Mährische Litteratur auf das Jahr 1780.*

23. He commented in *Böhmische Litteratur* (1779), p. 139, that literary history was so closely bound up with the introduction and spread of printing that the knowledge of one was necessary for the study of the other: "Die meisten Fehler, die man in beiden Ausgaben Bohemiae doctae des Balbíns häufig antrifft, sind aus Mangel der Bücherkunde . . . entstanden," (most of the mistakes that one encounters so frequently in both editions of Balbín's *Bohemia docta* arise out of lack of knowledge of books).

24. A review of Kramerius's *Cirkulární spis pána z Haye*, in *Litterarisches Magazin* 2 (1786): 143.

25. *Böhmische und Mährische Litteratur*, 1790, p. 36.

26. He gained the help of his former polemical opponent, Ungar, on

this project. See *Litterarisches Magazin* 2 (1786): 30–50; and Hanuš, "Dobrovského časopisy," pp. 388–89.

27. Dobrovský, foreword to *Litterarisches Magazin* 1 (1786).

28. *Böhmische und Mährische Litteratur*, 1780, p. 56.

29. *Böhmische Litteratur*, 1779, p. 85.

30. In a letter to an unknown addressee dated 8 September 1780, cited in Hanuš, "Dobrovského časopisy," pp. 490–91.

31. Pelcl, *Paměti*, pp. 38–39, 43; entries for 7 February and 30 July 1781.

32. Hanuš, "Dobrovského časopisy," pp. 492–93.

33. Procházka, *Miscellaneen*, pt. 2, p. 248.

34. Ibid., p. 240.

35. Ibid. p. 253.

36. Ungar, *Allgemeine böhmische Bibliothek*, pp. 6–8.

37. See Dlabač, *Berichtigung einiger historischen Daten fur Böhmen, Miszellen fur Böhmen*, "Von den Schicksalen der Kunste in Böhmen," and *Nachricht von den . . . Zeitungen.*

38. Procházka, foreword to *De saecularibus liberalium artium in Bohemia et Moravia.*

39. For a further discussion of Procházka's literary history method, see Hanuš, *František Faustyn Procházka*, pp. 89–92.

40. Procházka, *Commentarius*, pp. 333–34.

41. ČSAV, *Dějiny české literatury*, pp. 41–42.

42. Hanuš, "Josefa Dobrovského Geschichte der Böhmischen Sprache," p. 499.

43. Pelcl to Dobrovský, 1 April and 15 May 1790; LA PNP, Prague, Dobrovský collection, sign. I/5/7.

44. See Schamschula, *Die Anfänge*, pp. 258–59; and Hanuš, "Dobrovského Geschichte," p. 498n. Adelung wrote a history of the Czech language for the foreword to K. H. Thám's *Deutsch-böhmisches National-lexikon*, but this work was a derivative compilation (Adelung did not himself know Czech) and appears not to have influenced Dobrovský greatly.

45. The three versions of Dobrovský's *Geschichte* were published in a single volume (ed. Benjamin Jedlička) entitled *Dejiny české řeči a literatury, Spisy a projevy*, vol. 7 (Prague, 1936). The citations in the following discussion are from the 1792 version in Jedlička's edition, with original pagination in parentheses. The periodization is found at p. 86 (52).

46. See the comparative tables compiled by Jedlička in *Dobrovského "Geschichte,"* pp. 32–71, esp. "Nova Dobrovského 'Geschichte,'" pp. 70–71.

47. Compare, for example, Hanuš, "Dobrovského Geschichte," pp. 570–74, with Jedlička, *Dobrovského "Geschichte,"* pp. 142–49.

48. Dobrovský, *Dějiny*, pp. 79–80 (38–39).

49. Ibid., p. 95 (69–71).

50. Ibid., pp. 107 (94–95), 110 (101).

51. Ibid., p. 128 (134).

52. Ibid., p. 161 (196).

53. See Dobrovský, *Über die Ergebenheit und Anhänglichkeit der Slavischen Völker*, p. 8.

54. Dobrovský, *Dějiny*, p. 171 (216–17).

55. Ibid., pp. 172–73 (218–19).

56. Dobrovský, *Böhmische und Mährische Litteratur auf das Jahr 1780*, p. 5.

57. Jedlička, *Dobrovského "Geschichte,"* p. 148n.

58. The popular awakener Jan Rulík did attempt to transmit to the Czech-speaking public some of the work of Procházka, Voigt and others in *Velmi užitečná historie o slovutném národu českém* and *Učená Cechia*. His works are discussed more fully in chap. 5. Dlabač began, but never completed, a Czech translation of Dobrovský's *Geschichte*; the manuscript was published as an appendix to Dobrovský, *Dějiny*, pp. 435–50.

59. Schamschula, *Die Anfänge*, pp. 253–54. Dobrovský's correspondence with Cerroni, published as *Dopisy Josefa Dobrovského s Janem Petrem Cerronim*, consists largely of bibliographical information.

60. Hanuš, *Národní museum*, 1:155–56.

61. *Litterarisches Magazin* 3 (1787): 179.

62. Dobrovský to Ribay, 23 March 1785, *DR*, p. 12.

63. Pelcl, foreword to *Příhody Václava Vratislava . . . z Mitrovic* . Further citations are from this source.

64. The text of this announcement, entitled simply *Zpráva*, was published by Vodička in "Neznámé svědectví o vydavatelské činnosti Fr. F. Procházky." The cited passage is on p. 691.

65. Hanuš, *František Faustyn Procházka*, lists all the titles on pp. 107–08.

66. Procházka, foreword to *Kronika Boleslavská*. Further citations are from this source.

67. Vodička, "Neznámé svědectví," p. 690.

68. Procházka, foreword to *Kronika česká, od Přibíka Pulkavy z Tradenína*.

69. Procházka, foreword to *Výtahy z kroniky Moskevské*.

70. Procházka, *Kniha Erasma Roterodámského . . . jakby se k smrti hotoviti měl*, p. 198.

71. Procházka, *Erasma Roterodámského ruční knížka o rytíři křesťanském*, pp. ix–x.

72. Ibid.

73. Procházka, foreword to *Příkladné řeči*.

74. Vodička, "Neznámé svědectví," p. 694. See also Hanuš et al., *Literatura česká devatenáctého století*, pp. 383–407.

75. Hanuš, *Procházka*, pp. 122–23.

76. Tomsa, foreword to *Život Karla IV.*

77. Tomsa, foreword to *Šimon Lomnický z Budče, Tobolka zlata.*

78. Ibid.

79. Tomsa to Dobrovský, 6 March 1793, LA PNP, Prague, Dobrovský collection, sign. I/5/7. The manuscript referred to is the fourteenth-century *Rukopis Hradecký*, containing a series of religious and moralistic poems. See Dobrovský, *Dějiny*, p. 105 (91).

80. See Dobrovský to Ribay, 28 June 1793, *DR*, p. 233: Dobrovský lists the people Ribay should visit in Prague, including "Herrn Tomsa, bey welchem Sie mein alter Mst. auf Pergamen in Böhmischen Reimen sehen werden."

81. Novotný, *Matěj Václav Kramerius*, p. 20; Rybička, *Přední křísitelé národu českého*, 1:20.

82. For more on these aspects of Kramerius's career, see chaps. 4 and 5.

83. Kramerius, foreword to *Letopísové Trójanští.* This argument says more for Kramerius's feelings about Czech than for his knowledge of German literature.

84. See Hanuš, *Literatura česká devatenáctého století*, pp. 388–99.

85. Kramerius, foreword to *Šimona Lomnického z Budče, Kratké naučení mladému hospodáři.*

86. His later editions of early Czech works include a Czech version of the travels of Sir John Mandeville (1795); *Krátká historie o válce židovské* (1806), a humanist translation of Josephus; another editon of *Příhody Václava Vratislava z Mitrovic* (1807); and a posthumous version of Xenophon's biography of Cyrus the Elder (1809).

87. Schamschula, *Die Anfänge*, pp. 256–57.

88. Dobrovský to Zlobický, 15 April 1796; *DZ*, p. 107. For the last two sentences, Dobrovský changed from German to Czech, which, according to him, denoted a "special sincerity." See his letter to Zlobický of 8 April 1785, *DZ*, p. l00.

89. Dobrovský to Ribay, 16 February 1791, *DR*, pp. 185–86.

Chapter 4. Toward a National Cultural Life

1. Kačer, *Václav Thám*, pp. 16–17.

2. Vondráček, *Dějiny českého divadla. Doba obrozenská, 1771–1824*, pp. 33–34. On Czech drama in this period, see Jan Máchal in Hanuš et al., *Literatura česká devatenáctého století*, pp. 429–85; and ČSAV, *Dějiny českého divadla. II. Národní obrození.*

3. Cited in ČSAV, *Dějiny českého divadla. II. Národní obrození*, p. 59.

4. Ibid., p. 21.

5. See Hanuš, *Pelcl*, p. 18.

6. *Prager gelehrte Nachrichten,* 3 March 1772.

7. Kačer, *Václav Thám,* p. 22.

8. Baťha, "Václav Thám," pp. 128–29. From the period of Thám's studies, his MS copies of two letters of Jan Žižka and some poems of the sixteenth-century humanist, Bohuslav Hasištejnský, have survived.

9. V. Thám, foreword to *Básně v řeči vázané, první sebrání,* pp. 7, 11–12.

10. Jiřík's petition is printed in Baťha, "Dva dokumenty k historii počátků českého divadla v Praze," p. 751.

11. Vondráček, *Dějiny českého divadla,* pp. 68–69.

12. Pelcl, *Paměti,* p. 62.

13. Stach, V. Thám, and K. H. Thám, "Svátek českého jazyka."

14. See Kačer, *Václav Thám,* p. 29.

15. Stach, V. Thám, and H. K. Thám, "Svátek českého jazyka."

16. Foreword to Bulla, *Odběhlec z lásky synovské,* p. iv.

17. Kačer, *Václav Thám,* p. 34.

18. Vondráček, *Dějiny,* p. 71.

19. Ibid., p. 95. See also Kočí, *České národní obrození,* pp. 168–69.

20. Kramerius, in *Schönfeldské c. k. pražské poštovské noviny,* 14 January 1786.

21. Zima, "Na den provozovaní české původní hry Břetislava a Jitky."

22. Vondráček, *Dějiny,* pp. 105–07. Zlobický remained interested in the development of the Czech theater, as his surviving correspondence with Václav Thám shows. It is in LA PNP, Prague, Zlobický collection, sign. I/32/74.

23. Kramerius, in *Schönfeldské noviny,* 14 June 1786.

24. Ibid., 15 July 1786.

25. Zima, "Znamení vlastenské vděčnosti."

26. Zima, in *Schönfeldské noviny,* 29 July 1786.

27. Baťha, "Nejstarší obrozenecký divadelní překlad," p. 54.

28. V. Thám to Zlobický, 20 December 1787, LA PNP, Prague, Zlobický collection, sign. I/32/74.

29. Vondráček, *Dějiny,* p. 128.

30. K. H. Thám, *Makbeth,* pp. iii–iv.

31. Kačer, *Václav Thám,* p. 49.

32. From a review in *Das Pragerblättchen* signed "B-h-m," cited in Vondráček, *Dějiny,* p. 121.

33. Thám to Zlobický, 20 December 1787.

34. Dobrovský, *Geschichte der Böhmischen Sprache und Litteratur,* p. 215.

35. Vondráček, *Dějiny,* p. 122.

36. Ibid., pp. 121–22.

37. Thám to Zlobický, 20 December 1787.

38. Václav Melezínek, "Dar nového léta 1787."
39. Pelcl, *Akademische Antrittsrede*, p. 22.
40. Schönfeldské noviny, 10 March 1787.
41. Ibid., 2 June 1787.
42. Ibid., 1 September 1787.
43. Ibid., 10 March 1787.
44. Vondráček, *Dějiny*, pp. 147–48.
45. Ibid., p. 160.
46. Kramerius, in *Schönfeldské noviny*, 11 April 1789.
47. Vondráček, *Dějiny*, pp. 162–65.
48. Ibid., pp. 140–41.
49. Kramerius, in *Schönfeldské noviny*, 12 April 1788.
50. Ibid., 3 May 1788.
51. See Vondráček, *Dějiny*, pp. 163–65.
52. Ibid., pp. 177–78.
53. *Krameriusovy c. k. vlastenské noviny*, 24 September 1791.
54. Kačer, *Václav Thám*, pp. 69–72.
55. Ibid., pp. 82–83.
56. Dobrovský to Zlobický, 8 April 1795, *DZ*, p. 101.
57. Kačer, *Václav Thám*, p. 88.
58. A theater poster from the Patriotic Theater announcing a performance of this date is reproduced in Novotný, *Matěj Václav Kramerius*, between pp. 80–81. Cf. Vondráček, *Dějiny*, p. 271.
59. Vondráček, *Dějiny*, p. 339.
60. Ibid., p. 292.
61. See Dobrovský, *Geschichte der Böhmische Sprache und Litteratur*, p. 215.
62. Kačer, *Václav Thám*, pp. 78–79.
63. The autograph MS of Thám's translation, *Kouzedlná píšťala*, is in LA PNP, Prague, V. Thám collection, sign. I/12/30. It is dated 7 June 1794, but the exact date of its performance is unknown.
64. The former was published in 1796, and the latter, though not printed until 1819, was definitely performed much earlier.
65. Václav Thám produced *Povýšení českého knížetství na království, Fridrich Rakouský neb Věrnost českého národu*, and *Švedská vojna v Čechách neb udatnost pražských měšťanů a studentů*. See Kačer, *Václav Thám*, p. 69.
66. ČSAV, *Dějiny české literatury*, pp. 92–94.
67. Kramerius, in *Schönfeldské noviny*, 29 July 1786.
68. V. Thám, in *Schönfeldské noviny*, 2 January 1790.
69. Šedivý, *Krátké pojednání*, p. 20. Schiller's original lecture was given in 1784 and published in 1787. See ČSAV, *Dějiny českého divadla*, vol. 2, *Národní obrození*, p. 65.

70. See Kimball, *Czech Nationalism.*

71. ČSAV, *Dějiny české literatury,* pp. 49–51.

72. Dlabač, *Nachricht von den . . . Zeitungen,* p. 3. Modern studies of Czech journalism include Volf, *Dějiny novin v Čechách;* and Vladimír Klimeš, *Počátky českého a slovenského novinářství.* Przedak, in *Geschichte des deutschen Zeitschriftenwesens in Böhmen,* covers German-language journalism in Bohemia.

73. Klimeš, *Počátky,* pp. 58–59.

74. "Předchůzné řádky českých novin," in *Pražské poštovské noviny,* 5 January 1782, cited in Volf, *Dějiny novin v Čechách,* p. 131.

75. Kramerius, *Schönfeldské noviny,* 3 March 1787.

76. Ibid., 21 July 1787. The efforts of Kramerius and others to enlighten the common people are treated at greater length in chap. 5.

77. Dobrovský to Ribay, 16 February 1791, *DR,* 186: "Indessen scheint doch die Leselust erwecket und erhalten zu werden bey Herausgabe mancher guten Schriften. . . . Ein gutes Vehiculum dazu sind die Böhm. Zeitungen" (However, a taste for reading seems to be awakened and sustained by the publication of good works. . . . The Czech newspapers are a good vehicle for this).

78. *Krameriusovy vlastenské noviny,* 28 April 1792.

79. Dlabač, *Nachricht von den Zeitungen,* p. 27.

80. Kramerius, *Obzvláštní zprava,* 6 June 1789.

81. Pelcl to Dobrovský, 24 June 1789, LA PNP, Prague, Dobrovský collection, sign. I/5/7.

82. According to the official reports of stamp tax paid by both Kramerius and Schönfeld between 1 July and 24 August 1789, printed in Volf, "Vyšetřování vlivu novinářských zpráv," p. 568. Cf. Roubík, "Ohlas francouzské revoluce na českém venkově," p. 181n., where according to a report by the post office, Kramerius posted 641 copies of his paper to addresses within Bohemia, 19 to Vienna, 55 to Hungary, and 187 to Moravia.

83. *Vlastenské noviny,* 7 May 1791.

84. Schönfeld had complained to the authorities that he had an exclusive right to the adjective *poštovské,* so Kramerius was forced to change the name of his paper to *Vlastenské noviny* effective from the issue for 29 January 1791. See Klimeš, *Počátky,* p. 72.

85. Usually these supplements were simply called "Závěsek" (Supplement) or sometimes "Literální zpráva" (Literary report). The national aspect of Kramerius's newspapers as it affected the common people is discussed further in chap. 5.

86. Volf, "Vyšetřování vlivu," p. 568.

87. See, for example, ibid., p. 579n, the report of the Tábor district captain Streeruwitz.

88. Roubík, "Ohlas francouzské revoluce," p. 177.

89. *Krameriusovy vlastenské noviny*, 2 March 1793. The two pamphlets on the death of the king and queen of France were *Přežalostné zprávy o nešťastném Ludvíkovi XVI, králi francouzském, a o jeho katovýma rukama odpravení* and *Náležité vypsaní ukrutné smrti, kterouž Marie Antonia, králonva francouzska, od nešlechetné buřičské roty odsouzená byvší . . . na gilotině postoupiti musila*, both published in Prague in 1793.

90. Osvald, *Vychovatel lidu M. V. Kramerius*, p. 37.

91. See the MS notes in Dlabač's hand in the bound copies of the *Vlastenské noviny* for 1808 and 1809, Strahovská knihovna, Prague, sign. AA XIII 34–35.

92. Ribay to Dobrovský, 28 March 1808, *DR*, p. 282.

93. Jungmann to Antonín Marek, 29 March 1809, "Listy Josefa Jungmanna k Antonínu Markovi," p. 504.

94. See the *Schönfeldské noviny*, 20 and 27 March, and 3 April 1790.

95. Pelcl to Dobrovský, 24 June 1789, LA PNP, Prague, Dobrovský collection, sign. I/5/7.

96. Klimeš, *Počátky*, p. 91.

97. Ibid., 92. Jan Jakubec gives a more detailed discussion in Hanuš et al., *Literatura česká devatenáctého století*, pp. 591–609.

98. See Hromádko's letter to an unknown addressee, 19 March 1813, recounting some of his difficulties, and the overambitious announcement of his newspaper dated 10 December 1816, both in LA PNP, Prague, Hromádko collection.

99. Dobrovský to Kopitar, 19 February 1813, *DK*, p. 327.

100. See Klimeš, *Počátky*, pp. 108, 117; and Lemberg, *Grundlagen der nationalen Erwachens in Böhmen*, pp. 108–10.

101. Jan Nejedlý, "Zpráva o tomto spisu čtvrtletním," *Hlasatel český* 1 (1806): 482–83, emphasis in original.

102. Jan Nejedlý, "Promluvení k Hlasateli," *Hlasatel český* 1 (1806): 3–4.

103. Jan Nejedlý, "O lásce k vlasti," *Hlasatel český* 1 (1806): 16, emphasis in original. See also chap. 2.

104. See Jan Nejedlý's letter to his brother Vojtěch, 7 December 1809, LA PNP, Prague, Vojtěch Nejedlý collection, sign. I/3/60: "A nyní papír a tisk tak přenáramně jest drahy, že ani doposavad Hlasatele nemohu dati tisknout, ač pořád pro ni zbírám" (And now paper and printing are so incredibly expensive, that up to now I haven't even been able to have Hlasatel printed, though I'm still collecting for it).

105. Puchmajer to Jan Nejedlý, 13 August 1818, LA PNP, Prague, Jan Nejedlý collection, sign. I/3/59.

106. Lemberg, *Wege und Wandlungen des Nationalbewusstseins*, pp. 142–44.

107. See Slavík, *Od Dobnera k Dobrovskému*, pp. 43–47.
108. Lemberg, "Der deutsche Anteil am Erwachen des tschechischen Volkes," pp. 311–12; Pelcl, "Geschichte der Deutschen und ihrer Sprache in Böhmen," pp. 300–01.
109. Schamschula, *Die Anfänge*, p. 274; Kutnar, "Život a dílo Ignace Cornovy," pp. 334–39.
110. V. Thám, foreword to *Básně v řeči vázané*. *První sebrání*, p. 8.
111. See Schamschula, *Die Anfänge*, pp. 270–71; Vlček, in Hanuš et al., *Literatura česká devatenáctého století*, pp. 519–41; and ČSAV, *Dějiny české literatury*, vol. 2, *Literatura národního obrození*, pp. 51–53.
112. ČSAV, *Dějiny české literatury*, 2:68.
113. J. Šťastný, in "Krameriovi 'Noví čeští zpěvové,'" pp. 23–30, compares Kramerius's poems with their German models.
114. The list of subscribers was published at the end of the second volume.
115. *Krameriusovy vlastenské noviny*, 30 June 1792, refers to Thám's intentions and the difficulties in the way.
116. The semester reports for Vojtěch Nejedlý, for instance, show that in 1790 and 1791 he heard Seibt's lectures in logic, metaphysics, and morals; Cornova's in history; and Meissner's in classics and aesthetics (LA PNP, Prague, Vojtěch Nejedlý collection, sign. I/3/60).
117. Šebastián Hněvkovský's comic-heroic epic *Děvín* (1805) and other balladlike works in the almanacs owed much to Bürger's influence; while V. Nejedlý's *Poslední soud* (1804) was influenced by Klopstock, as were the works of Václav Stach. See Hýsek, "Bürgerovy ohlasy v české literatuře," pp. 106–21.
118. From A. Pavlovský's ode to Antonín Strnad, in *Nové básně vydané od Antonína Puchmajera* (1798), p. 146.
119. Jan Nejedlý, "Oda na důstojného Pána, Pana Stanislava Vydru. Roku 1798," *Nové básně* (1802): 57, 59.
120. The ode to Pelcl appeared in *Nové básně, svazek čtvrtý* (1802), and the one to Procházka in vol. 5 (1814).
121. Puchmajer, "Oda na Jana Žižku z Trocnova," in *Nové básně, svazek čtvrtý* (1802), p. 63.
122. Jan Nejedlý, "Na Čechy," in *Nové básně, vydané od Antonína Puchmajera* (1798), 136–40.
123. See Dobrovský, "Prosodie," in Pelcl, *Grundsätze der Böhmischen Grammatik*, p. 234, where he said had had been trying to "uncover the secret of Czech prosody" since 1788.
124. Dobrovský, *Litterarisches Magazin von Böhmen und Mähren* 2 (1786): 131–34, 137.
125. Puchmajer, *Sebrání básně a zpěvů* 1:ii.
126. Dobrovský, "Prosodie," p. 236.

127. Šebastián Hněvkovský to Jan Nejedlý, n.d. [1802?], LA PNP, Prague, J. Nejedlý collection, sign. I/3/59.

128. Nejedlý, *Homerova Iliada*, p. iv.

129. Dobrovský, review of ibid., originally published in the *Annalen der Literatur und Kunst* (1803), rpt. in *Literární a prozodická bohemika*, pp. 115–21.

130. Szyjkowski, *Polská účast v českém národním obrození*, 1:94–95.

131. Puchmajer, "Přidávek k prozodii české," *Nové básně* (1802), 4:1–2.

132. Dobrovský, review of *Chrám Gnidský*, in *Annalen der Literatur und Kunst* (1805), rpt. in *Literární a prozodická bohemika*, p. 132.

133. See Horálek, "K poetice A. Puchmajera," pp. 160–69.

134. ČSAV, *Dějiny české literatury*, p. 74. K. H. Thám had already conducted a polemic with Dobrovský over his dictionary. See chap. 2.

135. Mukařovský, "Dobrovského 'České prosodie,'" pp. 1–29.

136. Puchmajer, "Hlas volající na poušti," *Sebrání básně a zpěvů*, 2:6.

137. Puchmajer to Jungmann, 18 June 1814, LA PNP, Prague, Jungmann collection, sign. I/14/2.

138. "Czech! if you wish to sing beautifully, / Think, and speak, and bear yourself like a Czech." V. Nejedlý, "Psaní na Jaroslava Puchmíra," *Nové básně, vydané od Antonína Puchmajera* (1798), pp. 53–59.

139. J. Nejedlý, *Smrt Abelova*, p. 5. See also Jakubec, in Hanuš et al., *Literatura česká devatenáctého století*, pp. 555–64.

140. Dobrovský, *Geschichte der Böhmischen Sprache und Litteratur*, p. 215.

141. J. Nejedlý, foreword to *Homerova Iliada*, pp. iii–iv.

Chapter 5. Národ a Lid—Nation and People

1. Hanus, *Národní museum a naše obrození*, 2 vols., details the contribution of the Czech nobility to the foundation of the Bohemian National Museum, for example.

2. See J. Novotný, "Příspěvek k otázce úlohy některých lidových buditelů," pp. 600–32; and Vlček, *Dějiny české literatury*, 2:147–52.

3. See Slavík, *Od Dobnera k Dobrovskému*, p. 219. The New Testament appeared in 1778 and the entire Bible in 1780.

4. See Procházka, foreword to *Pismo svaté nového zakona*.

5. Procházka, *Biblí česká*.

6. Joseph's government urged the religious authorities to ensure that the people could have the sacraments, especially the Eucharist and baptism, in their mother tongue, to strengthen their effect and the teaching to be derived from them. See instruction to the Prague Gubernium dated 21 February 1786, in the Archiv Národního muzea, Prague, Fond Staré sbírky, ser. D, carton 23, 1786–1790.

7. Tomsa, "Kurze Lebensbeschreibung des Franz Tomsa," LA PNP, Prague, Dobrovský collection, sign. I/5/7; see also Pelcl, *Paměti*, p. 27.

8. The publication of these works was part of Seibt's defense against attempts by opponents in Prague and Vienna to have him removed from the university for unorthodox religious teachings. See Slavík, *Od Dobnera k Dobrovskému*, p. 46.

9. Novotný, *Kramerius*, pp. 38–39. On Eybel's career, see Bernard, *Jesuits and Jacobins*, pp. 58–59, 67–68, 72–73.

10. Stach, *Rozmlouvání mezi otcem a dítětem*, from the German of the Lutheran J. F. Seiler; *Kniha mravů křesťanských pro měšťana a sedláka*, from the German of Jakob Federsen.

11. Josephine church authorities attached much importance to pastoral ministry and education in the local language; this is revealed by the record of an episcopal visitation by Bishop J. L. von Hay to the parishes of the Chrudim Kreis in 1782. Bishop Hay recommends the exchange of one village priest with another who had a "well-grounded understanding of the Czech language, [whereas] the former does not have the gift of communicating with his parish children." Archiv Národního muzea v Praze, Fond Staré sbírky, ser. D, carton 22, 1782–1785.

12. Chládek, dedication to *Počátkové opatrnosti pastýřské*, vol. 3.

13. Stach, *Příručka učitele lidu*, 1:4.

14. Foreword to ibid., vol. 2.

15. Stach, *Počátkové k veřejnému v c. k. zemích předepsanému výkladání pastýřské theologie*.

16. Kramerius, in *Schönfeldské noviny*, 11 August 1787.

17. Bishop Hay's letter provoked complaints from elements in the clergy, but he was fully supported by Joseph's government. See the copies of the original letter in Latin, and petitions complaining about it, in the Archiv Národního muzea, Prague, Fond Staré sbírky, ser. D, carton 22, 1782–1785.

18. Kramerius, *Kniha Josefova*, was based on a German model, *Das Buch Joseph* (Prague, 1783), published by F. A. Zieger. See Hanuš et al., *Literatura česká devatenáctého století*, p. 389. The unabridged text of Kramerius's version was printed as an appendix to Novotný, *Kramerius*, pp. 265–301.

19. Kramerius, foreword to *Křesťanská katolická užitečná domovní postilla* (Prague, 1785).

20. On his activities with the Protestant pastors, see Dobrovský's letter to Ribay, 11 May 1786, *DR*, p. 42.

21. Rokos, *Důkaz, že kazatele Augspurského a Helvetského vyznání nejsou*; Stach, *Psaní školního místra Petra Záchodského z Slevízu k obraně evangelických ucitelů*.

22. See Rulík, *Kalendář historický*, 1:41.

23. See Rulík's comments in his announcement of *Krátké katechetické kázání na neděle přes celý rok*, in *Krameriusovy vlastenské noviny*, 13 October 1799.

24. See Hanuš et al., *Literatura česká devatenáctého století*, pp. 295–315.

25. See Laiske, *Časopisectví v Čechách, 1650–1847* (Prague, 1959), pp. 126, 133.

26. Kramerius, in *Schönfeldské noviny*, 24 February 1787.

27. Ibid., 7 April 1787.

28. Tomsa, *Měsíční spis*.

29. Tomsa's didactic works included *Pomoc v potřebě* (1791), *Nešťastné příhody k straze nezkušené mládeže* (1794), *Katechismus o zdraví pro chrámy a školy* (1794), and *Knížka mravná, s 60 historiemi a povídáčkami pro dítky* (1810). Excerpts from his translations of Funk appeared in *Hlasatel český* 4 (1818).

30. Meinert, *Český poutník*, pp. 3–4.

31. Ibid., p. 422; Lemberg, *Grundlagen der nationalen Erwachens in Böhmen*, pp. 108–10.

32. Kramerius, *Večerní shromáždění dobrovické obce*, pp. 143–44.

33. Kramerius, *Přítel lidu*, 1:4.

34. Ibid., 1:5–6, 54–55.

35. Kramerius, *Zrcadlo šlechetnosti pro mládež českou*, pp. 3–4.

36. Rulík, *Cvíčení dítek jednohokaždého stavu*.

37. Rulík, *Kastonova užitečná naučení o dobrém zvedení mládeže*, p. 76.

38. Amort published *Pravidla zdvořilosti, opatrnosti a zachování zdraví*, while Borový translated, and Kramerius published, *Zrcadlo pošetilosti* and *Zrcadlo příkladů k naučení a obveselení*.

39. The archives of the society are housed in Státní ústřední archiv, Prague, Fond Vlastenecko-hopodářská společnost. From the minutes of meetings held during the first decades of the society's existence it is clear that its activities were limited in large part to landowners and government officials and that its direct contacts with the Czech-speaking people were limited. Not until the 1830s was a periodical in Czech established to support the goals of the society. See, for example, SÚA, Prague, VHS, Protokolle, vol. 10, pp. 98–99 (22 August 1832), when the issue was discussed at length.

40. Hanuš, *Národní museum*, 1:307; Teich, "The Royal Bohemian Society of Sciences and the First Phase of Scientific Advance in Bohemia," p. 161.

41. These included Tomsa's *Tejné rady Šubarta dobře miněné volání na všecky sedláky* (1785), *Laciný prostředek, jak i ze špatných a suchopárných polí živá a dobytku příjemná píce v hojnosti dostat se může* (1787), and *Způsob, jakby se vyplemenil všechen hmyz bez jedu* (1810); Amort's

Uvedení jak snadným a sprostým spůsobem se hedbavní dílo konati má (1783); and Rulík's *Krátce obsahnutá pravidla k správě hospodářů* (1801) and *Laciné, a vpravdě hojící dobytka lekářství* (1810).

42. Kramerius, referring to *Chvalořeč při pohřby jistého sedláka* in *Schönfeldské noviny*, 25 August 1787.

43. Rulík to Vavák, n.d. [1798?], LA PNP, Prague, Vavák collection, sign. I/13/39.

44. Rulík, *Krátký spísek o stavu sedlském*, pp. 7–8.

45. Cf. Novotný, "Příspěvek"; and Albert Pražák, *České obrození*, pp. 20–22.

46. Rulík, *Krátký spísek*, p. 9.

47. *Krameriusovy poštovské noviny*, 1 July 1789.

48. Kramerius, in *Schönfeldské noviny*, 28 April 1787.

49. Ibid., 12 April 1788.

50. Ibid., 5 May 1787.

51. Ibid., 3 May 1788.

52. *Krameriusovy vlastenské noviny*, 18 April 1795. *Strašidlo s bubnem* was an adaptation of the popular *Singspiel* by Karl Ditters von Dittersdorf, *Das Gespenst mit der Trommel*. See Vondráček, *Dějiny*, p. 607.

53. *Krameriusovy poštovské noviny*, 10 April 1790.

54. *Krameriusovy vlastenské noviny*, 7 May 1791.

55. *Krameriusovy poštovské noviny*, 17 March 1790.

56. *Krameriusovy vlastenské noviny*, 3 December 1791.

57. Ibid., 26 January 1793.

58. Ibid., 10 September 1791.

59. Ibid., 7 January 1792.

60. Ibid., 18 August 1792.

61. Rulík, *Kalendář historický*, 1:41.

62. Ibid., 130.

63. Rulík, "Vlastenské plesání a díků činění nad slavném uvedení cís. král. profesora jazyka českého na učitelskou stolice v slavné pražské universí" (1793), and "Na den uvedení král. Profesora české literatury p. Jana Nejedlého na učitelskou stolici v slavné učené pražské universí léta 1801" (1801).

64. *Krameriusovy vlastenské noviny*, 4 April 1795.

65. Rulík, *Velmi užitečná historie o slovutném národu českém*, p. 6.

66. Ibid., pp. 79.

67. Rulík, *Věnec pocty, passim*, and *Vesnického faráře rozmlouvání se svými osadníky*, pp. 40–47.

68. Rulík, *Učená Čechia*, 2:18.

69. See Kollman, "Obrana Čech v letech 1796 a 1800"; and Ernstberger, *Böhmens freiwilliger Kriegseinsatz gegen Napoleon 1809*.

70. See, for example, Rulík, *Kalendář historický* 4:105, or *Krameriusovy vlastenské noviny*, 1 November 1800.

71. Pelcl, "Píseň pro český vojensky výbor," printed as an appendix to Tomsa, ed. *Naučení, jak se ma dobře česky psat.*
72. See LA PNP, Prague, Vavák collection, sign. I/13/39 to I/13/42; and the Stach collection in the same archive, sign. I/12/24, which includes, among other works, his MS *Vlastenské písně,* dated from 1801 and dedicated to the Bohemian Estates.
73. Dlabač, *Udatnost slavného českého národu.*
74. Rulík, *Vlastenský mladý rekruta,* p. 3.
75. Rulík, *Sláva a výbornost jazyka českého,* p. 35. On defenses of the language, see Albert Pražák, *Národ se bránil,* and other sources cited in chap. 2.
76. Ibid., arguments summarized from pp. 7, 12, 32–33.
77. Tomsa, *Von den Vorzügen der čechischen Sprache,* p. 38.
78. Kramerius, *Zrcadlo šlechetnosti,* pp. 33, 78.
79. Kramerius, in a broadsheet announcing the establishment of his newspaper, *Obzvláštní zpráva veškerému národu českému, moravskému a slovanskému,* 6 June 1789.
80. *Krameriusovy poštovské noviny,* 2 January 1790.
81. *Krameriusovy vlastenské noviny,* 18 February 1792.
82. Ibid., 12 May 1792.
83. Chládek, *Naučení, kterakby se mělo dobře mluviti česky, a psáti,* p. 4.
84. Tomsa, *Naučení, jak se má dobře česky psát.*
85. Kramerius, *Večerní shromáždění,* p. 153.
86. Kramerius, foreword to *Šimona Lomnického z Budče, Krátké naučení mladému hospodáři.*
87. These works were *Letopisové trojanští, Ezopovy básně, Jana Mandivilly . . . Cesta po svetě, Krátká historie o válce židovské, Příhody Václava Vratislava . . . z Mitrovic,* and *Xenofonta . . . život a skutkové Cyra staršího.*
88. Rulík, foreword to *Cesta z Moskvy do Číny.*
89. Kramerius, foreword to *Letopisové trojanští.*
90. Tomsa, foreword to *Tobolka zlatá.*
91. Rulík, foreword to *Cesta z Moskvy do Číny.*
92. See Thomas, "The Role of Calques," pp. 481–504.
93. Tomsa, *Böhmische Sprachlehre,* p. 440.
94. Tomsa, *Über die Bedeutung, Abwandlung, und Gebrauch der čechischen Zeitwörter,* p. 103n.
95. Kramerius, foreword to *Ezopovy básně.*
96. Rulík, foreword to *Cesta z Moskvy do Číny;* and Tomsa, foreword to *Život Karla IV.*
97. See Schamschula, *Die Anfänge,* p. 240.
98. See ČSAV, *Dějiny české literatury, II. Literatura národního obrození,* pp. 88–90; and Teplý, "Z lidové četby konce XVIII. a první polovice XIX. stol.," pp. 232–46.

99. Thón, "Vydavání českých knih v době Krameriusové," pp. 132–37.
100. *Krameriusovy vlastenské noviny*, 31 December 1791, announcing the publication of *Maran a Onýra. Americký příběh.*
101. Kramerius, *Historické vypsání, kterak . . . Amerika . . . vynálezená byla*, p. 40.
102. *Krameriusovy vlastenské noviny*, 13 October 1792.
103. Esp. in his *Veselý Kubíček* and its sequel, *Boženka, veselého Kubíčka manželka.*
104. Rulík, *Vesnického faráře rozmlouvání*, pp. 13–14.
105. Kramerius, foreword to *Křesťanská katolická užitečná domovní postilla.*
106. See Schamschula, *Die Anfänge*, pp. 114–16, where he discusses the historians. I believe his point could be made more generally about all the patriots.
107. Kramerius, foreword to *Večerní shromáždění*, p. 4, emphasis in original.
108. Bohuslav Tablic to Jan Nejedlý, n.d. [1801?], LA PNP, Prague, J. Nejedlý collection, sign. I/3/59.
109. J. R. [Josef Rautenkranc], letter to *Hlasatel český* 1 (1806): 316–17.
110. Hněvkovský to J. Nejedlý, 7 November 1804, in Jaroslav Šťastný, ed., "Korrespondence Seb. Hněvkovského, II."
111. Rulík, *Kalendář historický*, vol. 2.
112. Jungmann, "O jazyku českém. Rozmlouvání druhé," *Hlasatel český* 1 (1806): 344.
113. Vojtěch Nejedlý, "Rozmlouvání mezi mrtvými. I. Žižka a Pelcl," *Hlasatel český* 4 (1818): 302.
114. An interesting discussion of parallel trends among German patriots is Gagliardo, *From Pariah to Patriot.*

Chapter 6. "The Glorious, Widespread Slavic Nation"

1. A well-balanaced study of Slavism and its impact on the Czech renascence is *Slovanství v národním životě Čechů a Slováků*, ed. Šťastný et al., which complements Frank Wollman, *Slovanství v jazykově literárním obrození u Slovanů* (Brno, 1958). Other works concentrate on Czech relations with individual Slavic nations: the landmark study of Czech-Russian relations is Florovskii, *Chekhi i vostochnye slaviane*; see also ČSAV, *Dějiny česko-ruských vztahů, 1770–1917.* The ČSAV was also responsible for the two-volume *Češi a Poláci v minulosti*, and *Češi a Jihoslované v minulosti*, ed. Žáček et al. See also Szyjkowski, *Polská účast v českém národním obrození.*
2. See Kohn, *The Idea of Nationalism*, pp. 557–58.

3. See Jan Jakubec, in Hanuš et al., *Literatura česká devatenáctého století*, pp. 117–57. Hans Kohn touches on this problem in *Pan-Slavism: Its History and Ideology*, 2d rev. ed. (New York, 1960), esp. pp. 3–26. Kohn focuses on the later period, however.

4. See, for example, Florovskii, *Česko-ruské obchodní styky v minulosti (X.-XVIII. století)* (Prague, 1954); Vávra, "Podstata a problemy česko-ruských kulturních vztahů"; and Vávra, "Böhmen und Russland im 18. Jahrhundert," pp. 510–16.

5. Vávra, "Podstata a problemy česko-ruských kulturních vztahů," pp. 259–61.

6. See chap. 1; and Zacek, "The Virtuosi of Bohemia," pp. 147–59; for a history of the society, see Josef Kalousek, *Děje král. české společnosti nauk*, 2 vols. (Prague, 1884–85).

7. The earliest review, basically positive, appeared in the *Neue Zeitungen von Gelehrten Sachen auf das Jahr 1762* (Leipzig), but it was quickly followed by attacks on Dobner, first in a history of the liturgy in Bohemia by Karel Kříž (1764), and then in Vaclav Duchovský's *Lucifer lucens non urens*, and a work by an Augustinian monk, P. Athanasius, *Dissertatio historico-chronologico-critica*, both published in 1765.

8. Dobner, MS autobiography, LA PNP, Prague, sign. I/4/1, n.p.

9. Ibid.

10. With some exaggeration. See Myl'nikov, *Vznik národně osvícenské ideologie*, pp. 160–64.

11. Vávra, "Tschechisch-russisches Zusammentreffen auf dem Gebiet der Aufklärungsgeschichtsschreibung," pp. 173–75.

12. Kudělka, *Spor Gelasia Dobnera o Hájkovu kroniku*, p. 32.

13. Ibid., pp. 50–55, 65–66; Hanuš, "Počátky kritického dějezpytu v Čechách," p. 450.

14. Vávra, *Osvícenská era v česko-ruských vědeckych stycích*, pp. 10–15; *Dějiny česko-ruských vztahů*, p. 21.

15. Kalousek, *Děje král. české společnosti nauk*, pp. 42–43.

16. Dobrovský, *Litterarische Nachrichten von einer . . . Reise*, pp. 1–5; Kubka, *Dobrovský a Rusko*, p. 58.

17. See Dobrovský to Zlobický, 25 January 1788: "Ich entschloß mich sogar auf 3 oder mehr Jahre nach Russland zu reisen" (I made up my mind to go to Russia for 3 or even more years), *DZ*, p. 17.

18. Sternberg, *Reise von Moskau über Sofia nach Königsberg* (1793) and *Bemerkungen über Russland auf einer Reise gemacht im Jahre 1792 u. 93* (1794), esp. the final sections. Cf. the rather more rare comments scattered through Dobrovský's *Litterarische Nachrichten*; and Zeil, "Das Russlandbild der böhmischen Aufklärung im letzten Drittel des 18. Jh.," pp. 109–15.

19. Dobrovský's letter to K. G. von Anton, 6 May 1792: "In Russland mache ich mir die slaw. Litteratur zum Zweck." *DA*, p. 46.

20. Dobrovský to Ribay, 8 February 1793, *DR*, p. 223.
21. Dobrovský to Kopitar, 22 June 1818, *DK*, p. 353. See also Kubka, *Dobrovský a Rusko*, pp. 61–64.
22. Dobrovský to Kopitar, 30 January 1811, *DK*, p. 188.
23. See esp. the entry for 30 July 1810. Portions of the diary were published by Ondřej Franta, "Po stopách Dobrovského v deníku hraběte Eugena Černína z Chudenic," in *Bratislava* 3 (1929): 868–91.
24. Szyjkowski, *Polská účast v českém národním obrození*, 1:17; ČSAV, *Češi a Poláci v minulosti*, 2:102. Dobrovský's letters to Linde were published as an appendix to *DK*, and Linde's to Dobrovský in V. A. Francev, *Pol'skoe slavianovedenie kontsa XVIII i pervoi chetverti XIX st.* (Prague, 1906).
25. See Pribić, *Adam Aloisius Baričević*, p. 111.
26. Bechyňová, "Adam Alois Baričević a Václav Fortunat Durych," pp. 131–32.
27. Bechyňová, "Ruská literatura v díle V. F. Durych," pp. 258–68, and "Václav Fortunat Durych a jeho Bibliotheca slavica," pp. 145–84.
28. Dukat, "Dobrovský i Hrvati," p. 44.
29. Dobrovský to Zlobický, 15 February 1798, and Zlobický's reply, 30 November 1798, *DZ*, pp. 122, 148. Dobrovský's Slavic journals, *Slavín* and *Slovanka*, are discussed below.
30. Žáček et al., eds., *Češi a Jihoslované*, p. 241.
31. Dukat, "Dobrovský a Hrvati," pp. 51–53.
32. In Dobrovský's *Litterarisches Magazin von Böhmen und Mähren* 3 (1787): 140.
33. Žáček et al., eds., *Češi a Jihoslované*, p. 244.
34. ČSAV, *Dějiny česko-ruských vztahů*, p. 58.
35. Dobrovský to Kopitar, 3 May 1812, *DK*, p. 262.
36. Vuk to Frusić, 1819; cited in Duncan Wilson, *The Life and Times of Vuk Stefanović Karadžić, 1787–1864. Literacy, Literature, and National Independence in Serbia* (Oxford, 1970), p. 151n.
37. See Dobrovský to Ribay, 8 February 1793, *DR*, p. 224.
38. Szyjkowski, *Polská účast*, 1:17.
39. Ibid.; ČSAV, *Češi a Poláci*, 2:106.
40. ČSAV, *Češi a Poláci*, 2:106–08.
41. Pata, "Dobrovský a Lužice," p. 260.
42. See *DA*; and, for the correspondence with Fryco, *Neue Briefe von Dobrowský, Kopitar und andere Süd- und Westslawen*, ed. V. Jagič (Berlin, 1897).
43. Dobrovský to Zlobický, 15 February 1798, *DZ*, p. 122. He destroyed the MS of his grammar of Sorbian during one of his attacks of mental illness in 1828. See Mysliveček, "Duševní choroba Josefa Dobrovského," p. 829.

44. Pelcl, *Kurzgefasste Geschichte der Böhmen*, 1:18.
45. Pelcl, *Nová kronyka česká*, 1:47–56.
46. Voigt, *Über den Geist der Böhmischen Gesetze*, p. 10.
47. Ibid., p. 9.
48. Rulík, *Velmi užitečná historie*, pp. 6–7.
49. Ibid., p. 11.
50. Slavík, *Od Dobnera k Dobrovskému*, pp. 231–33.
51. Durych, *Bibliotheca Slavica*, esp. pp. xxxxv–xxxxviii, a summary of the projected contents of all seven volumes.
52. Dobrovský, "Geschichte der böhmischen Sprache," pp. 311–15.
53. Vávra, "Tschechisch-russisches Zusammentreffen," pp. 187–88.
54. See chap. 1.
55. Dobrovský to Ribay, 22 May 1787, *DR*, p. 77.
56. Dobrovský to Fryco, 14 August 1797, *Neue Briefe*, p. 624.
57. Dobrovský to Kopitar, 13 March 1809, *DK*, pp. 43, 45.
58. Dobrovský to Bandtke, 5 June 1810, *DB*, pp. 7–8.
59. Dobrovský to Bandtke, 27–31 January 1811, *DB*, p. 24.
60. Dobrovský to Kopitar, 22 July 1811, *DK* p. 212.
61. Szyjkowski, *Polská účast*, 1:27–28.
62. Zlobický to Dobrovský, 4 June 1781, *DZ*, pp. 3–4.
63. Dobrovský to Ribay, 2 March 1789, *DR*, p. 119.
64. Ribay to Dobrovský, 16 May 1788, *DR*, p. 97.
65. See, for example, Dobrovský's comments to Zlobický, 11 January 1789, *DZ*, p. 36; and to Anton, 15 April 1796, *DA*, pp. 50–51; and Ribay to Dobrovský, 19 January 1791, *DR*, p. 154.
66. Dobrovský to Kopitar, 6 March 1810, *DK*, p. 126.
67. Kopitar to Dobrovský, 1–5 February 1810, *DK*, p. 91.
68. Dobrovský to Kopitar, 6 March 1810, ibid.
69. Dobrovský to Bandtke, 5 June 1810, *DB*, p. 7.
70. Dobrovský to Kopitar, 7 August 1810, *DK*, p. 157.
71. Dobrovský to Kopitar, 30 January 1811, *DK*, p. 188.
72. Dobrovský to Ribay, 6 December 1789, *DR*, p. 150.
73. Dobrovský to Fryco, 14 August 1797, *Neue Briefe*, p. 624.
74. Dobrovský to Bandtke, 5 June 1810, and Bandtke's reply, 15 June 1810, *DB*, pp. 7, 13.
75. See chap. 2.
76. Dobrovský to Bandtke, 17–31 January 1811, and Bandtke's reply, 2–15 July 1811, *DB* pp. 22–23, 29.
77. Dobrovský to Kopitar, 17 October 1813, *DK*, pp. 360–61.
78. Dobrovský to Ribay, 27 September 1789, *DR*, p. 142.
79. Dobrovský to Anton, 15 April 1796, *DA*, pp. 50–51; Dobrovský to Zlobický, 2 February 1797, *DZ*, p. 108.
80. Dobrovský, *Slavín*, pp. 9–13. The censor required Dobrovský to

drop the phrases "gegen ihre christlichen Herren und Räuber" (against your Christian lords and robbers), and "von eueren Sklavenketten befreyt" (freed from your slave's fetters), without showing in any way that anything had been deleted. See the letter to Dobrovský from the K. auch K. und k. Bücherrevisionsamt, dated 15 May 1806, LA PNP, Prague, Dobrovský collection, sign. I/5/8.

81. Dobrovský, *Slavín*, pp. 1–2.

82. Dobrovský, *Slovanka*, 1:104–06. The original article had appeared in the *Vaterländischen Blätter* of July, 1812.

83. See, for example, Kopitar to Dobrovský, 30 March 1808, *DK*, pp. 1–5.

84. Ribay to Dobrovský, 4 July 1790, and Dobrovský's reply, 30 August 1790, *DR*, pp. 169, 171.

85. Dobrovský to Kopitar, 1 January 1810, *DK*, p. 76.

86. Dobovský to Kopitar, 22 July 1811, *DK*, p. 212. The "better choice" would apparently be literary Czech.

87. Dobrovský to Bandtke, 11 September 1815, *DB*, p. 91.

88. Dobrovský to Kopitar, 1 January 1810, *DK*, p. 73.

89. Dobrovský to Kopitar, 25 December 1813, *DK*, pp. 309–10.

90. Dobrovský to Fryco, 14 August 1797, *Neue Briefe*, p. 625.

91. Dobrovský to Zlobický, 15 February 1798, *DZ*, p. 122.

92. Dobrovský to Kopitar, 7 May 1815, *DK*, p. 404.

93. Ribay to Dobrovský, 21 January 1796, *DR*, pp. 262–63.

94. Mysliveček, "Duševní choroba Josefa Dobrovského," p. 830.

95. See chap. 2.

96. Dobrovský to Zlobický, 3 March 1795, *DZ*, p. 95; Thomas, "The Role of Calques," pp. 491–98.

97. Dobrovský to Jungmann, 26 January 1813, LA PNP, Prague, Jungmann collection, sign I/14/1.

98. See Tomsa, *Über die Bedeutung, Abwandlung, und Gebrauch der čechischen Zeitwörter*, p. 7, and *Über die Aussprache der čechischen Buchstabe, Sylben, und Wörter nebst Leseubungen*, p. 15n: "Die alten Čechen sagten stoi und die Russen sagen es noch, wovon sich jeder aufmerksame Čeche, als die Russen im Jahre 1799 und 1800 durch Prag marschirten, uberzeugen könnte, da sie das teutsche Kommandowort halt durch *stoi* und Marsch! durch *stupai* ausdrükten" (The old Czechs said *stoi* and the Russian still do, which any attentive Czech could have ascertained when the Russians marched through Prague in 1799 and 1800, for they expressed the German word of command "halt" by *stoi* and "march" by *stupai*).

99. Zlobický to Dobrovský, 13 August 1797, *DZ*, p. 114.

100. Thomas, "The Role of Calques," p. 500.

101. Puchmajer to Dobrovský, 23 March 1801, LA PNP, Prague, Dobrovský collection, sign. I/5/6.

102. Macura, *Znamení zrodu,* pp. 69–89, discusses the "překlado-vost" of renascence culture, which suggests that this was a long-lived attitude, since Macura's focus is on the 1830s and 1840s.

103. "There are two theological alumni in Prague, who love things Slavic, especially Russian; they are now translating one of Kheraskov's odes in *Opyt trudov* most elegantly into Czech" (Dobrovský to Durych, 14 January 1795, *DD,* 327).

104. Durych to Dobrovský, 24 January 1795, *DD,* p. 331.

105. Szyjkowski, *Polská účast,* p. 63.

106. Puchmajer to Hněvkovský, 1 July 1797, cited in ibid., p. 80.

107. See the bibliography of Puchmajer's Polish sources in ibid., p. 489.

108. Puchmajer, foreword to *Chram Gnidský. Báseň.* Further citations are to this source.

109. Szyjkowski, *Polská účast,* p. 187. Jungmann's *Atala, aneb Láska dvou divochů v poušti* was published in 1805. See also Hanuš et al., *Literatura česká devatenáctého století,* pp. 633–655.

110. Ibid., pp. 187–93.

111. See, for example, Jungmann, "Příběh satirický (z Ruského)," *Hlasatel český* 2 (1807): 144–52. See also ČSAV, *Dějiny česko-ruských vztahů,* p. 57.

112. ČSAV, *Dějiny česko-ruských vztahů,* p. 60.

113. Puchmajer to J. Nejedlý, 10 May 1820, LA PNP, Prague, Jan Nejedlý collection, sign. I/3/59; see also Puchmajer to Dobrovský, 7 June 1820, LA PNP, Prague, Dobrovský collection, sign. I/5/6.

114. Žáček et al., eds., *Češi a Jihoslované,* p. 233.

115. See chap. 2.

116. Hanke, *Empfehlung,* p. 42.

117. K. H. Thám, *Obrana jazyka českého;* Dobrovský, *Über die Ergebenheit,* p. 5.

118. Rulík, *Sláva a výbornost jazyka českého,* p. 7.

119. See Pelcl, *Akademische Antrittsrede,* p. 4; and J. Nejedlý, *Akademische Antrittsrede,* p. 22.

120. Puchmajer, foreword to *Pravopis rusko-český.*

121. Kramerius, *Obzvláštní zpráva,* 6 June 1789, n.p.

122. *Krameriusovy poštovské noviny,* 2 January 1790.

123. Dobrovský, *Über die Ergebenheit,* p. 5.

124. This was Dobrovský's main burden in ibid., pp. 7–8. See also Šimeček, "Studium českých dějin, slavistika a austroslavismus," pp. 115–42.

125. See Milan Kudělka, "Počátky obrozenského slovanství v českých zemích," in *Slovanství v národním životě Čechů a Slováků,* p. 98.

126. Antonín Robek devoted many works to this problem, which, in

spite of their tendentious conclusions, bring much interesting material to the discussion: *Lidové zdroje národního obrození*, "Názory vesnické společnosti na úloha Ruská při porážce Napoleona v roce 1812," "K otázkám lidových zdrojů národního obrození," and *Městské lidové zdroje národního obrození*. Robek sought to prove that intellectuals had little to do with the renascence (which had much more to do with 1968 and aftermath than with the late eighteenth century).

127. See chap. 5.

128. Procházka, foreword to *Výtahy z kroniky moskevské*.

129. Ibid.

130. Kramerius, "Krátké popsaní ruského císařství," *Krameriusovy vlastenské noviny*, 15 March 1800.

131. J. N——k, "Dar nového roku veškerému slavnému slovanskému národu," *Krameriusovy vlastenské noviny*, 7 January 1792.

132. *Schönfeldské noviny*, 22 September 1787.

133. *Krameriusovy vlastenské noviny*, 1 September 1804.

134. Ibid.

135. Rulík, *Kalendář historický*, 2:101. Rulík refers to the Poles as "that famous nation" and says that it was a pity that Catherine proceeded with the second partition.

136. Rulík, *Kalendář historický*, 1:227.

137. *Krameriusovy vlastenské noviny*, 1 December 1804.

138. Ibid., 21 April 1804.

139. Ibid., 31 August 1805.

140. Ibid., 19 December 1807.

141. Ibid., 30 January 1808.

142. Ibid., 8 February 1791. The author was Georg Selenko.

143. Ibid., 24 December 1791. The belittling in passing of the German Empire highlights the sort of psychological support the Czech patriots could get in their exposed position from contemplating the size of the "Slavic nation."

144. Ibid., 5 May 1792.

145. Ibid., 21 January 1792.

146. See Volf, "Vyšetřování vlivu," pp. 565–83.

147. Original in Hudební archiv městského musea v Hradci Kralové, cited in Švankmajer, "Počátky českého rusofilství," p. 191.

148. The theme is surveyed in Zacek, "The French Revolution, Napoleon and the Czechs." See also Novák, "Války osvobozovaci a naše obrození"; Kutnar, "Veliká revoluce francouzská v naši soudobé critice" and "Reakce státu v Čechách na Velkou revoluci francouzskou." For a "Marxist" approach, still emphasizing the important role of the revolution, see Mejdřička, *Listy ze stromu svobody*.

149. A typical example is Kočí, *České národní obrození*, pp. 230–31, 250–51. See also Amort, *Ruská vojska u nás*.

150. Švankmajer, "Počátky českého rusofilství," p. 184.

151. See Kollmann, "Obrana Čech v letech 1796 a 1800"; and Ernstberger, *Böhmens freiwilliger Kriegseinsatz gegen Napoleon, 1809.*

152. See Stach's MS "Vlastenské písně od Václava Stacha," dedicated to the Bohemian Estates and dated 1801, LA PNP, Prague, Stach collection, sign. I/12/24.

153. Jan Kruchina z Švanberga, "České zemské obrany píseň," in Rulík, *Vlastenský mladý rekruta*, p. 20.

154. Vavák, "Marš dobrých Čechů k boji," LA PNP, Prague, Vavák collection, sign. I/13/21.

155. Kočí, *České národní obrození*, p. 231.

156. The complete text appears as an appendix to Amort, *Ruská vojska u nás*, pp. 313–16.

157. Ibid., pp. 321–29.

158. Rulík, *Kalendář historický*, 1:130, 156–61.

159. *Krameriusovy vlastenské noviny*, 13 and 20 July 1799.

160. Vondráček, *Dějiny českého divadla*, pp. 371–72.

161. One could just as well call the English crowds who came out in droves to gawk at the tsar and other notables in post-victory London Russophiles.

162. Rulík, *Kalendář historický*, 3:201.

163. [Dobrovský], *Neues Hülfsmittel die Russische Sprache leichter zu verstehen.*

164. [Tomsa], *Verzeichniss der russischen Wörter und Redensarten.* See Dobrovský's own account in his autobiography, published in *Bratislava* 3 (1929): 365–66. Also Vávra, "K počátkům rusko-českého slovníkařství."

165. Amort, *Ruská vojska u nás*, p. 324.

166. Jungmann to Marek, 20 June 1809, *ČNM* 55 (1881): 504.

167. Jungmann to Marek, 24 September 1813, *ČNM* 56 (1882): 37–38.

168. Jungmann to Marek, undated [1810?], *ČNM* 55 (1881): 514.

169. Marek to Jungmann, 2 April 1813, in "Ze vzájemné korespondence Josefa Jungmanna a Antonína Marka," ed. Havel, p. 23.

170. J. Nejedlý to Hněvkovský, 27 November 1806, cited in *Dějiny česko-ruských vztahů*, p. 54.

171. Jungmann to Marek, 5 December 1809, *ČNM* 55 (1881): 505.

172. Jungmann to Marek, 10 August 1811, *ČNM* 55 (1881): 521.

173. Jungmann to Marek, 2 January 1813, *ČNM* 56 (1882): 30.

174. Florovskii, *Chekhi i vostochnye slaviane*, 2:466.

175. Rulík, *Kalendář historický*, 4:41: "Přezimující v Čechách Rusové mnohému hospodáři dosti těžkých a nesnesitedlných dní způsobili," (The Russians wintering over in Bohemia caused many a head of household quite difficult and unbearable days).

176. Some family chronicles are quoted extensively in Robek, *Lidové zdroje národního obrození*, with this passage cited on p. 106.
177. Ibid., p. 107.
178. Ibid.
179. Ibid., pp. 108–09.
180. The Russian representative in Prague, Baron Bühler, complained that deserters were hiding in Czech villages "with the knowledge and consent of the peasants." Cited in *Dějiny česko-ruských vztahů*, p. 71.
181. Robek, "Názory vesnické společnosti," pp. 32–34.
182. LA PNP, Vavák collection, sign. I/13/40. There are at least three different copies of this verse among Vavák's papers.

Conclusion

1. Puchmajer to Dobrovský, 13 April 1806, LA PNP, Prague, Dobrovský collection, sign. I/5/6.
2. Jungmann to Marek, 30 December 1809, *ČNM* 55 (1881): 506.
3. See Macura, *Znamení zrodu*, pp. 47–68.
4. Letter from J. R. [Josef Rautenkranc?] to Jan Nejedlý, published in *Hlasatel český* 1 (1806): 317.
5. The excitement with which they welcomed the new regulations of 1816, making certain concessions to Czech in school and administration, can be seen in Puchmajer's ode "Na jazyk český," the uncensored MS of which is in LA PNP, Prague, Puchmajer collection, sign. I/4/13; cf. Puchmajer's letter to Jungmann, 25 February 1816, LA PNP, Jungmann collection, sign. I/14/2.
6. Kutnar, "Povaha obrozeneckého vlastenectví," p. 13.

Bibliography

Primary Sources

Archival Material

Archiv Národního muzea, Prague, Fond Staré Sbírky, documents of varied provenance gathered by the archivists of the National Museum and organized chronologically from the fifteenth to the nineteenth centuries. Řada D covers 1781–1800.

Literární archiv, Památník národního písemnictví, Prague. Correspondence and other personal papers of Czech literary figures, and related material. Collections consulted for this study include:

Dobner, Gelasius, (1719–1790), sign. I/4/1.

Dobrovský, Josef (1753–1829), sign. I/5/2/–I/5/9

Jungmann, Josef (1773–1847), sign. I/14/1–I/14/2.

Kopitar, Bartoloměj [Jernej] (1780–1844), sign. I/K/30.

Kramerius, Václav Matěj (1753–1808), sign. I/11/1.

Nejedlý, Vojtěch (1772–1844), sign. I/3/60.

Nejedlý, Jan (1776–1834), sign. I/3/59.

Puchmajer, Antonín Jaroslav (1769–1820), sign. I/4/13.

Ryba, Jakub Jan (1765–1815), sign. I/4/17.

Sedláček, Vojtěch Jan (1785–1836), sign. II/A/35.

Stach, Václav (1755–1831), sign. I/12/24–I/12/25.

Thám, Karel Hynek (1763–1816), sign. I/12/29.

Thám, Václav (1765–1816), sign. I/12/30.

Vavák, František (1741–1816), sign. I/12/39–I/12/42.

Ziegler, Josef Liboslav (1782–1846), sign. I/4/81–I/4/82.

Zlobický, Josef Valentin (1743–1810), sign. I/32/47.

Státní ústřední archiv, Prague, Fond Vlastenecko-hospodářská společnost. Includes indexes and protocols of meetings of the society from the 1770s to the dissolution of the society in 1872.

Edited Sources and Correspondence

Dobner, Gelasius. "Autobiographie." Ed. Josef Hanuš. *Český časopis historický* 23 (1917): 129–38.

Dobrovský, Josef. *Dějiny české řeči a literatury*. Ed. Benjamin Jedlička. Spisy a projevy Josefa Dobrovského, 8. Prague, 1926.

———. *Literární a prozodická bohemika*. Ed. Miroslav Heřman. Spisy a projevy Josefa Dobrovského, 6. Prague, 1958.

———. *O zavedení a rozšíření knihtisku v Čechách*. Ed. Mirjam Daňková. Spisy a projevy Josefa Dobrovského, 19. Prague, 1974.

Emler, Josef, ed. "Listy Josefa Jungmanna k Antonínu Markovi." *Časopis Musea Království českého* 55 (1881): 491–530; ibid., 56 (1882): 26–44, 161–84, 445–76.

Fischer, Josef L., ed., with notes by F. Bartoš. "Z korrespondence Dobrovského." *Časopis národního musea* 103 (1929): 145–63.

Flajšhans, Václav. *Jos. Dobrovského kritická rozprava o legendě Prokopské*. Prague, 1929.

Francev, V. A. *Řeč Josefa Dobrovského proslovená dne 25. září v České učené společnosti*. Prague, 1921.

Havel, Rudolf, ed. "Ze vzájemné korespondence Josefa Jungmanna a Antonína Marka." *Literární archiv* 8-9 (1974): 5–51.

Jagič, V., ed. *Der Briefwechsel zwischen Dobrowsky und Kopitar, (1808–1828)*. Berlin, 1885.

Jagič, V., ed. *Neue Briefe von Dobrowsky, Kopitar und andere Süd- und Westslaven*. Berlin, 1897.

Křívský, Pavel, ed. "Korespondence Antonín Jaroslava Puchmajera s Josefem Dobrovským." *Literární archiv* 8-9 (1973–74): 199–256.

Krbec, Miroslav, and Věra Michálková, eds. *Der Briefwechsel zwischen Josef Dobrovký und Karl Gottlob von Anton*. Veröffentlichungen des Instituts für Slawistik, 21. Berlin, 1959.

Patera, Adolf, ed. *Korrespondence Josefa Dobrovského*. Vol 1: *Vzájemné dopisy Josefa Dobrovského a Fortunata Duricha z let 1778–1800*. Sbírka pramenův ku poznání literárního života v Čechách, na Moravě, a ve Slezsku, Skupina 2, číslo 2. Prague, 1895.

———. Vol. 2: *Vzájemné dopisy Josefa Dobrovského a Jiřího Samuele Bandtkeho z let 1810–1827, číslo 8*. Prague, 1906.

———. Vol. 3: *Vzájemné listy Josefa Dobrovského a Josefa Valentina Zlobického z let 1781–1807, číslo 9*. Prague, 1908.

———. Vol. 4: *Vzájemné listy Josefa Dobrovského a Jiřího Ribaye z let 1783–1810, číslo 18*. Prague, 1913.

Pelcl, František. *Paměti*. Trans. Jan Pán; foreword by Jiří Černý. Prague, 1956.

Riegger, Josef Anton Ritter von, ed. "Ein Paar merkwürdige Briefe, des um die Böhmische Geschichte so verdienten Piaristen, Adauct Voigt."

Archiv der Geschichte und Statistik, insbesondere von Böhmen. Vol. 1. Dresden, 1792.

Schamschula, Walter. "Drei unveröffentliche Briefe von Michael Denis an Josef Dobrovský." *Zeitschrift für Slavische Philologie* 33 (1967): 321–31.

Šťastný, Jaroslav, ed. "Korrespondence Šeb. Hněvkovského, II." *Výroční zpráva cís. král. vyššího gymnasia českého na Novém městě v Praze v Truhlářské ulici za školní rok 1909–1910.* Prague, 1910.

Contemporary Published Sources

Abhandlungen der böhmischen Gesellschaft der Wissenschaften zu Prag. 4 vols. Prague, 1785–88.

Abhandlungen der königlichen böhmischen Gesellschaft der Wissenschaften vom Jahre . . . 8 vols. Prague, 1804–24.

Abhandlungen einer Privatgesellschaft in Böhmen zur Aufnahme der Mathematik, der vaterländischen Geschichte und der Naturgeschichte. 6 vols. Prague, 1775–84.

Amort, Vavřinec. *Pravidla zdvořilosti, opatrnosti a zachování zdraví.* Prague, 1794.

———. *Uvedení jak snadným a sprostým spůsobem se hedvabní dílo konati má.* Prague, 1783.

Borový, Antonín. *Zrcadlo příkladů k naučení a obveselení.* Prague, 1794.

———. *Zrcadlo pošetilosti, aneb nové a staré, pěkné i daremné, pravdivé i nepravdivé povídáčky neb historie jichž to jest asi čtyři sta.* Prague, 1792.

Bulla, Karel. *Odběhlec z lásky synovské. Veselohra v třech jednáních, v němčině sepsaná od Stephanie mladšího.* Prague, 1785.

Chládek, Jiljí Bartoleměj. *Naučení, kterakby se mělo dobře mluviti česky, a psáti. Sepsané nejvíce pro ty, kteříž slyší pastorální teologii v jazyku českém, aneb již skutečně týmž jazykem úřad pastýřský konají.* Prague, 1795.

———. *Počátkové opatrnosti pastýřské, neb krátká naučení, jak by se pastýřové duchovní v povolání svém chovati měli.* 3 vols. Prague, 1781.

Cornova, Ignac. "Hat Schirach König Georgen von Böhmen . . . Religion überhaupt, mit grund abgesprochen?" *Neuere Abhandlungen der königlichen böhmischen Gesellschaft der Wissenschaften* 3 (1798): 161–72.

———. "Über das Verhaltniss zwischen König Premisl Ottokar II. und den Päbsten seiner Zeit." *Neuere Abhandlungen der königlichen böhmischen Gesellschaft der Wissenschaften* 1 (1790): 75–96.

———. "Über Karl des IV. Betragen gegen das Bayerische Haus." *Neuere Abhandlungen der königlichen böhmischen Gesellschaft der Wissenschaften* 2 (1795): 82–111.

306   **Bibliography**

Der Volkslehrer. Prague, 1786–88.

Dlabač, Bohumír Jan. *Allgemeines historisches Künstlerlexikon für Böhmen und zum Theil auch für Mähren und Schlesien.* 3 vols. Prague, 1815.

———. *Berichtigung einiger historischen Daten für Böhmen.* Görlitz, 1792.

———. *Listy českým krajanům v nynějších příhodách psaní.* Prague, 1814.

———. *Miszellen für Böhmen.* Görlitz, 1792.

———. *Nachricht von den in Böhmischer Sprache verfassten und herausgegebenen Zeitungen.* Prague, 1803.

———. *Rozmlouvání o nynější vojně mezi farářem a sedlákem českým.* Prague, 1809.

———. *Udatnost slavného českého národu podle vlastenské historie . . . představená.* Prague, 1809.

———. "Von den Schicksalen der Künste in Böhmen." *Neuere Abhandlungen der königlichen Böhmischen Gesellschaft der Wissenschaften* 3 (1798): 107–39.

Dobner, Gelasius. "Abhandlung über das Alter der Böhmischen Bibelübersetzung." *Abhandlungen der böhmischen Gesellschaft der Wissenschaften zu Prag* 4 (1788): 283–99.

———. "Historischer Beweis, dass Wladislaw der Zweyte Herzog in Böhmen zu Anfang des 1158sten Jahr zu Regensburg gekront worden, und dass der goldene Reif (Circulus) so ihme und seiner Thronfolgern Kaiser Friederich der Erste ertheilet hat, eine wahre königliche Krone gewesen sey." *Abhandlungen einer Privatgesellschaft in Böhmen* 5 (1782): 1–54.

———. "Historisch-kritische Beobachtungen über den Ursprung, Abänderung und Verdoppelung des böhmischen Wappenschildes." *Abhandlungen einer Privatgesellschaft in Böhmen* 4 (1779): 185–253.

———. "Kritische Abhandlung von den Grenzen Altmährens, oder des grossen mährischen Reichs im neunten Jahrhundert." *Abhandlungen einer Privatgesellschaft in Böhmen* 6 (1784): 1–45.

———. "Kritische Untersuchung, wann das Land Mähren ein Markgrafthum geworden, und wer dessen erster Markgraf gewesen sey." *Abhandlungen einer Privatgesellschaft in Böhmen* 2 (1776): 183–229.

———. "Kritische Untersuchung: Ob das Christenthum in Böhmen . . . nach den Grundsätzen, Lehre und Gebrauchen der römische-lateinische oder der griechischen Kirche eingeführet worden?" *Abhandlungen der böhmischen Gesellschaft der Wissenschaften zu Prag* 1 (1785): 140–77.

———. *Monumenta historica Boemia nusquam antehac edita.* 6 vols. Prague, 1764–85.

———. "Über die Einführung des Christenthums in Böhmen." *Abhandlungen der böhmischen Gesellschaft der Wissenschaften zu Prag* 1 (1785): 101–39.

————. *Vindiciae Sigillo Confessionis diui Joannis Nepomuceni Protomartyris Poenitentiae assertae.* Prague and Vienna, 1784.

————. *Wenceslai Hagek a Liboczan Annales Bohemorum e Bohemica editione latine redditi et notis illustrati a P. Victorine a S. Cruce nunc plurimis animadversionibus historico-chronologico-criticis nec non diplomatibus, literis publicis, re genealogica, numaria, variique generis antiquis aeri incisis monumenti aucti a P. Gelasio a S. Catherina.* 6 vols. Prague, 1761–86.

Dobrovský, Josef. *Ankündigung eines deutsch-böhmischen Lexicons.* Prague, 1798.

————. *Ausführliches Lehrgebäude der Böhmischen Sprache, zur gründlichen Erlernung derselben für Deutsche, zur vollkommenern Kenntniss für Böhmen.* Prague, 1809.

————. "Beyträge zur Geschichte des Kelchs in Böhmen." *Abhandlungen der königlichen böhmischen Gesellschaft der Wissenschaften* 5 (1818-19): 1–27.

————. *Die Bildsamkeit der Slawischen Sprache an der Bildung der Substantive und Adjective in der Böhmischen Sprache dargestellt.* Prague, 1799.

————. *Böhmische Biegungen.* Prague, n.d.

————. *Böhmische Litteratur auf das Jahr 1779.* Prague, 1779.

————. *Böhmische und Mährische Litteratur auf das Jahr 1780–81.* Prague, 1780–84.

————. "Geschichte der Böhmischen Pikarden und Adamiten." *Abhandlungen der böhmischen Gesellschaft der Wissenshaften zu Prag* 4 (1788): 300–43.

————. *Geschichte der Böhmischen Sprache und Litteratur.* Prague, 1792.

————. "Kritische Versuche, die ältere böhmische Geschichte von spätern Erdichtungen zu reinigen. I. Bořiwoy's Taufe." *Abhandlungen der königlichen Böhmischen Gesellschaft der Wissenschaften* 1 (1803), 1–111.

————. "Kritische Versuche . . . II. Ludmila und Drahomir." Ibid., 2 (1807): 1–87.

————. "Kritische Versuche . . . III. Wenzel und Boleslaw." Ibid., 6 (1818-19): 1–119.

————. *Litterarisches Magazin von Böhmen und Mähren.* 3 vols. Prague, 1786–87.

————. *Litterarische Nachrichten von einer auf Veranlassung der böhm. Gesellschaft der Wissenschaften im Jahre 1792 unternommen Reise nach Schweden und Russland. Nebst einer Vergleichung der Russischen und Böhmischen Sprache.* Prague, 1796.

————. *Neues Hülfsmittel die Russische Sprache leichter zu verstehen, vorzüglich für Böhmen, zum Theile auch für Deutsche. Selbst für Russen, die sich den Böhmen verständlicher machen wollen.* Prague, 1799.

————. *Slawin. Bothschaft aus Böhmen an alle Slawischen Völker, oder Beiträge zur Kenntniss der Slawischen Literatur nach allen Mundarten.* Prague, 1806.

————. *Slovanka. Zur Kenntniss der alten und neuen slawischen Literatur, der Sprachkunde nach allen Mundarten, der Geschichte und Alterthümer.* 2 vols. Prague, 1814–15.

————. "Über den Ursprung und die Bildung der slawischen und insbesondere der böhmischen Sprache." *Vollständiges Wörterbuch der böhmisch- deutsch- und lateinischen Sprache.* By František Jan Tomsa. Prague, 1791.

————. *Über die Ergebenheit und Anhänglichkeit der Slawischen Völker an das Erzhaus Österreich.* Prague, 1791.

————. "Wie man die alten Urkunden, in Rücksicht auf verschiedene Zweige der vaterländische Geschichte, benutzen soll. Ein Versuch über die Břewniower Stiftungsbrief Boleslaws des Zweyten." *Abhandlungen der böhmischen Gesellschaft der Wissenschaften zu Prag 1* (1785): 178-200.

Dobrovský, Josef, and František Martin Pelcl. *Scriptores rerum bohemicarum.* 2 vols. Prague, 1783–84.

Durych, Václav Fortunát. *Bibliotheca Slavica antiquissimae dialecti communis et ecclesiasticae universae Slavorum gentis.* Vienna, 1795.

Hanke von Hankenstein, Johann Alois. *Empfehlung der böhmischen Sprache und Litteratur.* Vienna, 1783.

Jungmann, Josef. "O jazyku českém. Rozmlouvání druhé." *Hlasatel český* 1, no. 3 (1806): 321–53.

————. "O jazyku českém. Rozmlouvání první." *Hlasatel český* 1, no. 1 (1806): 43–49.

Kinský, Franz Joseph Graf von. *Erinnerung über einen wichtigen Gegenstand, von einem Böhmen . . . in Des Grafen Kinskýs, gesamelte Schriften.* vol. 3. Vienna, 1786.

Kramerius, Václav Matěj. *Církulární spis pána z Háje, biskupa královéhradeckého, na duchovenstvo osady jeho strany tolerancí.* Prague, 1782.

————. *Ezopovy básně spolu s jeho životem.* Prague, 1791.

————. *Historické vypsání, kterak čtvrtý díl světa, Amerika, od Kolumbusa vynálezená byla.* Prague, 1803.

————. *Jana Mandivilly, znamenitého a vznešeného rytíře Cesta po svetě.* Prague, 1795.

————. *Kniha Josefova.* Prague, 1784.

————. *Krátká historie o válce židovské.* Prague, 1806.

————. *Letopisové trojanští, to jest vypsání desítileté války řeků s Králem Priamem, též obležení a zrádného dobytí, a vyvracení přeslávného v světě města trojanského pro Královnou Helenu.* Prague, 1790.

———. *Obzvláštní zprava veškerému národu českému, moravskému a slovanskému.* Prague, 1789.

———. *Patentní ruční knížka pro měšťana i sedláka.* Prague, 1781.

———. *Příhody Václava Vratislava svobodného pána z Mitrovic.* Prague, 1807.

———. *Přítel lidu.* 2 vols. Prague, 1806–07.

———. *Šimona Lomnického z Budče, Krátké naučení mladému hospodáři, kterakby netoliko sám sebe, manželku svou, i čeladku, i své všecko hospodářství užitečně zpravovati, a živnost svou vésti: ale také jakby býti, v moudrosti a jiných ctnostech prospívati, a čeho se kdy varovati měl.* Prague, 1794.

———. *Večerní shromáždění dobrovické obce.* Prague, 1801.

———. *Xenofonta, mudrce athenského, život a skutkové Cyra staršího.* Prague, 1809.

———. *Zrcadlo šlechetnosti pro mládež českou.* Prague, 1805.

Meinert, Georg. *Český poutník.* Trans. Jan Nejedlý. Prague, 1801.

Melezínek, Václav. "Dar nového léta 1787, všem pánům jazyka českého horlitelům, pánům Thámům, pánům vlastenského divadla milostivě obdařeným hercům a šlechetným pánům a pannám, spolu pánům hudebníkům." Prague, 1787.

Nejedlý, Jan. *Akademische Antrittsrede gehalten den 16. November 1801.* Prague, 1801.

———. *Hlasatel český.* 4 vols. Prague, 1806–08, 1818.

———. *Homerova Iliada.* Prague, 1802.

———. *Kritische Revision der Thamischen Grammatik.* Prague, 1798.

———. "O lásce k vlasti." *Hlasatel česky* 1, no. 1 (1806): 3–5.

———. *Smrt Abelova.* Prague, 1800.

Neuere Abhandlungen der königlichen Böhmischen Gesellschaft der Wissenschaften. 3 vols. Prague, 1790–98.

Palacký, František. *Dějiny národu českého v Čechách a na Moravě.* Prague, 1848, rpt. 1908.

Pelcl, František Martin. "Abhandlung über den Samo, König der Slawen." *Abhandlungen einer Privatgesellschaft* 4 (1779): 18-70.

———. *Akademische Antrittsrede über den Nutzen und Wichtigkeit der Böhmischen Sprache.* Prague, 1793.

———. *Apologie des Kaisers Karl der Vierten der allgemeinen deutschen Bibliothek entgegengestellt.* Prague, 1782.

———. "Biographie des Adauct Voigt, a S. Germano." *Abhandlungen der böhmischen Gesellschaft der Wissenschaften zu Prag* 3 (1787): 15–20.

———. *Böhmische, Mährische und Schlesische Gelehrte und Schriftstellern aus dem Orden der Jesuiten von Anfang der Gesellschaft bis auf gegenwartige Zeit.* Prague, 1786.

———. "Das Edikt des Kaisers, Karl des Vierten, wider die Ketzer, vom

18. Sept. des 1376ten Jahrs, wird in Zweifel gezogen." *Abhandlungen einer Privatgesellschaft in Böhmen* 5 (1782): 55–65.

———. *Grundsätze der böhmischen Grammatik.* Prague, 1793.

———. *Kaiser Karl der Vierte, König in Böhmen.* 2 vols. Prague, 1781.

———. *Kurzgefasste Geschichte der Böhmen.* 1st ed. Prague, 1774.

———. *Lebensgeschichte des Römischen und Böhmischen König Wenceslaus.* 2 vols. Prague, 1790.

———. *Nová kronyka česká.* 3 vols. Prague, 1791–96.

———. "Píseň pro český vojenský výbor." In *Naučení, jak se ma dobře česky psát,* ed. František Jan Tomsa. Prague, 1800.

———. *Příhody Václava Vratislava svobodného Pána z Mitrovic, které on v tureckém hlavním městě Konštantinopoli viděl, v zájetí svém skusil, a po šťastném do vlasti své navrácení sám Léta Páně 1599 sepsal.* Prague, 1777.

———. "Über das Vaterland des Jacobus de Misa, genannt Jacobellus." *Abhandlungen einer Privatgesellschaft in Böhmen* 6 (1784): 299–312.

———. "Wann ist Kaiser Karl IV. Markgraf in Mähren geworden." *Abhandlungen einer Privatgesellschaft in Böhmen* 4 (1779): 71–82.

Pelcl, František Martin, and Mikuláš Adaukt Voigt. *Abbildungen Böhmischer und Mährischer Gelehrten und Künstler.* 4 vols. Prague, 1773–82.

Prager gelehrte Nachrichten. Prague, 1771–72.

Procházka, František Faustyn. *Biblí česká, to jest celé Svaté Pismo starého a nového zákona, podle starého obecného Latinského od svaté Římské katolické církve schvaleného výkladu, opět s obzvláštní pilnosti přehlednuté, ponapravené, vysvětlené a znovu vydané.* Prague, 1804.

———. *De saecularibus liberalium artium in Bohemia et Moravia fatis commentarius.* Prague, 1784.

———. *Erasma Roterodámského ruční knížka o rytíři křesťanském, nyni podruhé vydaná, a na mnoha místech opravená.* Prague, 1787.

———. *Kniha Erasma Roterodámského, v kteréž jednomu každému křesťanskému člověku naučení i napomenutí se dává, jakby se k smrti hotoviti měl.* Prague, 1786.

———. *Kronika Boleslavská, o posloupnosti knížat a králi českých, a slavných národu českého činech, od založení téhož národu až do Jana Lucemburského, vypravující.* Prague, 1786.

———. *Kronika česká, od Přibika Pulkavy z Tradenína na poručení Karla IV. latině sepsaná, potom pak v i češtinu uvedená, a nyni v též řeči české z starožitného spisu poprvé vydaná.* Prague, 1786.

———. *Miscellaneen der Böhmischen und Mährischen Litteratur, seltener Werke, und verschiedenen Handschriften.* 3 pts. Prague, 1784–85.

———. *Pismo svaté nového zákona, podle českého přeložení od jeho knížecí milosti arcibiskupa pražského léta Páně 1778 na světlo daného, v nově vydané, a však s řeckým textem, s starým latinským výkladem, též podobně s východními přeloženími &c. naskrze srovnané, na mnoha místech opravené, i obšírným liberního smyslu výkladem vysvětlené.* Prague, 1786.

————. *Příkladné řeči a užitečná naučení vybraná z knih hlubokých mudrcův, ukazující pravidlo vezdejšího života, jakby se každý rozšafně držeti na světě měl.* Prague, 1786.

————. *Výtahy z kroniky Moskevské někdy latině od Alexandra Gvagnína sepsané, potom v český jazyk přeložené od Matauše Hosia z Vysokého Mýta. Přidaná jest Zygmunda z Herbersteina dvojí cesta do Moskvy.* Prague, 1786.

Puchmajer, Antonín Jaroslav. *Chrám Gnidský. Báseň.* Prague, 1804.

————. *Sebrání básně a zpěvů.* Prague, 1795.

————. *Sebrání básně a zpěvů. Svazek druhý.* Prague, 1797.

————. *Nové básně vydané od Antonína Puchmajera.* Prague, 1798.

————. *Nové básně. Svazek čtvrtý.* Prague, 1802.

————. *Nové básně. Svazek pátý.* Prague, 1815.

————. *Pravopis rusko-český.* Prague, 1805.

Riegger, Josef Anton Ritter von. *Archiv der Geschichte und Statistik, insbesondere von Böhmen.* 3 vols. Dresden, 1792–95.

————. *Materialen zur alten und neuen Statistik von Böhmen.* 12 vols. Prague and Leipzig, 1787–94.

————. *Skizze einer statistischen Landeskunde Böhmens.* Leipzig and Prague, 1795.

Rokos, Václav. *Důkaz, že kazatele Augspurského a Helvetského vyznání nejsou knězi, ani řádní služebníci církevní.* Prague, 1785.

Rulík, Jan Josef Nepomuk. *Boženka, veselého Kubíčka manželka.* Prague, 1802.

————. *Cesta z Moskvy do Číny, kterouž s ruským vyslancem Isbrandem, skrze krajiny Ostiku, Siberii, Taursko,a MogoskauTartarii šťastně vykonal Jiří z Drachova, Čech a rytíř vznešený Léta Páně 1693.* Prague, 1800.

————. *Cvíčení dítek jednohokaždého stavu.* Prague, 1792.

————. *Gallerie, aneb vyobrazenost nejslovutnějších a nejznamenitějších osob země České, spolu s vypsáním důležitých, zvláštních pamětních věcí, jenž se v Čechách za časů starobylých, tak y pozdnějších, zběhly.* 5 vols. Prague, 1803–10.

————. *Kalendář historický, obsahující kratké a summovní poznamenání všechněch proměn, příběhu, válek, nejvyšších nařízení, a t. d. jak v slavném národu a království Českém tak i na díle v jiných narodech a zemích, zběhlých.* 6 vols. Prague, 1797–1810.

————. *Kastonova užitečná naučení o dobrém zvedení mládeže.* Prague, 1794.

———. *Krátce obsahnutá pravidla k správě hospodářů.* Prague, 1801.

———. *Krátký spísek o stavu sedlském, aneb voráčském.* Prague, 1798.

———. *Laciné, a vpravdě hojící dobytka lekářství.* Prague, 1810.

———. *Památky starožitného a veleslávného kláštěra Sedleckého bliž Hory Kutné v království Českém, od leta 1142 až do roku 1807.* Kutná Hora, 1807.

———. *Sláva a výbornost jazyka českého.* Prague, 1792.

———. *Učená Čechia.* 3 vols. Prague, 1807–08.

———. *Velmi užitečná historie o slovutném národu Českém.* Prague, 1793.

———. *Věnec pocty k poctivosti učených, výborných a statečných Čechů.* Prague, 1795.

———. *Veselý Kubíček, aneb v horách Kašparských zaklený dudák.* Prague, 1799.

———. *Vesnického faráře rozmlouvání se svými osadníky.* Prague, 1805.

———. *Vlastenský mladý rekruta.* Prague 1808.

Schönfeldské císařské královské pražské poštovské noviny. Prague, 1786–92, 1796–99.

Šedivý, Prokop. *Krátké pojednání o užitky, kterýž ustavičně stojící, a dobře spořádané divadlo způsobiti může.* Prague, 1793.

Seibt, Karl Heinrich. *Kniha katolická, obsahující v sobě naučení a modlitby.* Trans. František Jan Tomsa. Prague, 1780.

———. *Vyučující a modlicí kniha pro mládež.* Trans. František Jan Tomsa. Prague, 1784.

Stach, Václav [Václav Petryn, pseud.]. *Historie velikého sněmu kostnického.* 2 vols. Prague, 1785–86.

———. *Kniha mravů křesťanských pro měšťana a sedláka.* Prague, 1786.

———. *Přiručka učitele lidu.* 2 vols. Prague and Olomouc, 1787.

———. *Počátkové k veřejnému v c. k. zemích předepsanému výkladání pastýřské theologie.* 2 vols. Prague, 1787.

———. *Psaní školního místra Petra Záchodského z Slevízu k obraně evangelických ucitelů a svobodného učení evangelického proti nedůvodnému důkazu, že učitelové evangeličtí nejsou knězi.* Prague, 1786.

———. *Rozmlouvání mezi otcem a dítětem o věcech náboženství se týkajících.* Prague, 1785.

Stach, Václav, Václav Thám, and Karel Hynek Thám. "Svátek českého jazyka, na den druhého provozování Stefanového Odběhlce v pražském vlastenském divadle od Bondynské společnosti německých herců, den 25 ledna 1785." Prague, 1785.

Thám, Karel Hynek. *Deutsch-böhmisches Nationallexikon.* Prague, 1788.

———. *Dritte und Letzte Antikritik und Abfertigung des Joseph Dobrowskys mit allen seinen Zehenden etc. zur Beurtheilung unpartheyischen Lesern vorgelegt.* Prague, 1798.

———. *Erklärung über die jüngst erschienene falsche Revision meiner Grammatik.* Prague, 1798.

————. *Makbeth, truchlohra v 5 jednáních od Shakespeara.* Prague, 1786.

————. *Obrana jazyka českého proti zlobivým jeho utrháčům, též mnohým vlastencům v cvíčení se v něm liknavým a nedbalým.* Prague, 1783.

————. *Über den Karakter der Slawen, dann über den Ursprung, die Schicksale, Vollkommenheiten, die Nützlichkeit und Wichtigkeit der böhmischen Sprache.* Prague, 1803.

Thám, Václav. *Básně v řeči vázané.* 2 vols. Prague, 1785.

Tomsa, František Jan. *Böhmische Sprachlehre.* Prague 1782.

————. *Grössere čechische Orthographie, gemeiniglich böhmische Orthographie genannt; mit zwei Anhängen, der erste enthält zehn alte čechische Fabeln, der zweite aber eine Probe, wie nach der hier vorgeschlagene und grösstentheils eingeführten čechischen Orthographie alle slawische Dialekte geschrieben werden könnte.* Prague, 1812.

————. *Laciný prostředek, jak i ze špatných a suchopárných polí živá a dobytku příjemná píce v hojnosti dostat se může.* Prague, 1787.

————. *Malý německý a český slovník.* Prague, 1789.

————. *Měsíční spis k poučení a obveselení obecného lidu.* Prague, 1787.

————. *Naučení, jak se ma dobře česky psát.* Prague, 1800.

————. *Šimon Lomnický z Budče, Tobolka zlatá, aneb lakomá žadost peněz nenasycená, a proti hříchu lakomství, kteréž nyní v světě velmi panuje a mnohé lidi oslepuje, výstraha prostá a věrná.* Prague, 1791.

————. *Tejné rady Šubarta dobře miněné volání na všecky sedláky.* Prague, 1785.

————. *Über die Aussprache der čechischen Buchstaben, Sylben und Wörter nebst Leseübungen.* Prague, 1801.

————. *Über die Bedeutung, Abwandlung und Gebrauch der čechischen Zeitwörter.* Prague, 1804.

————. *Über die čechische Rechtschreibung mit einem Anhange, welcher dreizehn čechischen Gedichte enthält.* Prague, 1802.

————. *Über die Veränderungen der čechischen Sprache, nebst einer čechischen Chrestomathie seit dem dreizehnten Jahrhunderts bis jetzt.* Prague, 1805.

————. *Verzeichniss der russischen Wörter und Redensarten, die im gemeinen Leben am häufigsten vorkommen als Hülfsmittel, um sich Russen leichter verständlich zu machen.* Prague, 1813.

————. *Vollständiges Wörterbuch der böhmisch- deutsch- und lateinischen Sprache.* Prague, 1791.

————. *Von den Vorzügen der čechischen Sprache, oder über die Billigkeit und den Nutzen, die čechische Sprache zu erhalten, empor zu bringen, und über die Mittel dazu.* Prague, 1812.

————. *Život Karla IV.* Prague, 1791.

————. *Způsob, jakby se vyplemenil všechen hmyz bez jedu.* Prague, 1810.

Ungar, Karel Raphael. *Allgemeine böhmische Bibliothek.* Prague, 1786.

———. *Bohuslai Balbini ... Bohemia docta, opus posthumum editum, notisque illustratum ad Raphaele Ungar.* 3 vols. Prague, 1776, 1778, 1780.

———. "Neue Beiträge zur alten Geschichte der Buchdruckerkunst in Böhmen." *Neuere Abhandlungen der königliche Böhmischen Gesellschaft der Wissenschaften* 2 (1795): 195–229.

———. "Versuch einer Geschichte der Bibliotheken in Böhmen." *Abhandlungen der böhmischen Gesellschaft der Wissenschaften zu Prag* 1 (1785): 234–71.

———. "Žižka's militärische Briefe und Verordnungen." *Neuere Abhandlungen der königliche Böhmischen Gesellschaft der Wissenschaften* 1 (1790): 371–72.

Voigt, Mikuláš Adaukt. *Acta litteraria Bohemiae et Moraviae.* 2 vols. Prague, 1774–83.

———. *Beschreibung der bisher bekannten Böhmischen Münzen nach chronologischer Ordnung, nebst einem kurzen Begriff des Lebens der Münzfürsten, und anderer, auf welche sie geprägt worden; mit eingestreueten historischen Nachrichten von dem Bergbaue in Böhmen.* 4 vols. Prague, 1771–81.

———. *Effigies virorum eruditorum atque artificum Bohemiae et Moraviae.* 2 vols. Prague, 1773–75.

———. "Nachricht von merkwürdigen böhmischen Mäcenaten, und einige ihnen sowohl von einheimischen als auswartigen Schriftstellern dedicirten Bücher." *Abhandlungen einer Privatgesellschaft in Böhmen.* 6 (1784): 325–63.

———. *Über den Geist der Böhmischen Gesetze in den verschiedenen Zeitaltern.* Dresden, 1788.

———. "Untersuchung über die Einfuhrung, den Gebrauch, und die Abänderung der Buchstaben und des Schreibens in Böhmen." *Abhandlungen einer Privatgesellschaft in Böhmen* 1 (1775): 164–99.

———. "Versuch einer Geschichte der Universität Prag." *Abhandlungen einer Privatgesellschaft in Böhmen* 2 (1776): 287–391.

———. "Von dem Alterthume und Gebrauche des Kirchengesanges in Böhmen." *Abhandlung einter Privatgesellschaft in Böhmen* 1 (1775): 200–01.

———. "Von der Aufnahme, dem Fortgange und den Schicksalen der Wissenschaften und Künste in Böhmen." *Abbildungen Böhmischer und Mährischer Gelehrten und Künstler.* Vol. 1. Prague, 1773.

———. "Vorrede von dem Gelehrten Adel in Böhmen und Mähren." Ibid. Vol. 2. Prague, 1775.

Zima, Antonín Josef. "Na den provozovaní české původní hry Břetislava a Jitky pro věčnou památky jazyka českého." Prague, 1786.

————. "Znamení vlastenské vděčnosti na den prvního provedení české hry na pražském novoměstském divadle dne 8 července 1786." Prague, 1786.

Secondary Sources

Books and Monographs

Amort, Čestimír. *Ruská vojska u nás v letech 1798–1800. Příspěvek k dějinám česko-ruského a slovensko-ruského přátelství.* Prague, 1954.

Anderson, Perry. *Lineages of the Absolutist State.* London, 1979.

Banac, Ivo. *The National Question in Yugoslavia: Origins, History, Politics.* Ithaca and London, 1984.

Banac, Ivo; and Bushkovitch, Paul, eds. *The Nobility in Russia and Eastern Europe.* New Haven, 1983.

Berls, Janet Wolf. *The Elementary School Reforms of Maria Theresa and Joseph II in Bohemia.* Ph.D. diss., Columbia University, 1975.

Bernard, Paul P. *Jesuits and Jacobins: Enlightenment and Enlightened Despotism in Austria.* Urbana, Ill., 1971.

Bosl, Karl, ed. *Handbuch der Geschichte der böhmischen Länder.* Vol. 2. Stuttgart, 1974.

Brandl, Vincenc. *Život Josefa Dobrovského.* Brno, 1883.

Brock, Peter. *The Slovak National Awakening.* Toronto, 1976.

Brock, Peter, and H. Gordon Skilling, eds. *The Czech Renascence of the Nineteenth Century.* Essays presented to Otakar Odložilík in Honour of his Seventieth Birthday. Toronto, 1970.

Československá akademie věd [ČSAV]. *Dějiny českého divadla. II. Národní obrození.* Prague, 1969.

————. *Dějiny české literatury. II. Literatura národního obrození.* Prague, 1960.

————. *Dějiny česko-ruských vztahů, 1770–1917.* Dějiny československo-sovětských vztahů nové a nejnovější doby, vol. 1. Prague, 1967.

————. *Češi a Poláci v minulosti.* 2 vols. Ústav dějin evropských socialistických zemí. Prague, 1967.

Dlouhý, Jindřich, ed. *Václav Fortunát Durych.* Prague, 1952.

Ernstberger, Anton. *Böhmens freiwilliger Kriegseinsatz gegen Napoleon 1809.* Veröffentlichungen des Collegiums Carolinum, 14. Munich, 1963.

Eymer, Wenzel, ed. *Pädagogische Schriften des Grafen Franz Joseph Kinsky.* Vienna, 1892.

Florovskii, A. V. *Chekhi i vostochnye slaviane: ocherki po istorii cheshsko-russkikh otnoshenii (X–XVIII vv.).* Vol. 2. Prague, 1947.

Fueter, Eduard. *Geschichte der neueren Historiographie.* Handbuch der mittelalterlichen und neueren Geschichte, ed. Georg von Below and Friedrich Meinecke. Munich and Berlin, 1911.

Gagliardo, John G. *From Pariah to Patriot: The Changing Image of the German Peasant, 1770–1840.* Lexington, Ky.: 1969.

Hanuš, Josef. *František Faustyn Procházka, český buditel a literární historik.* Rozpravy České akademie císaře Františka Josefa pro vědy, slovesnost, a umění, třída III, číslo 39. Prague, 1915.

———. *František Martin Pelcl, český historik a buditel.* Rozpravy České akademie . . . , číslo 38. Prague, 1914.

———. *Mikuláš Adaukt Voigt, český buditel a historik.* Rozpravy České akademie . . . , číslo 32. Prague, 1910.

———. *Národní museum a naše obrození.* 2 vols. Prague, 1921–23.

Hanuš, Josef, Jan Jakubec, Jan Máchal, and Jaroslav Vlček. *Literatura česká devatenáctého století. Díl první. Od Dobrovského k Jungmannově škole básnické.* 2d ed. Prague, 1911.

Haubelt, Josef. *Studie o Ignaci Bornovi.* AUC, Philosophica et historica, Monographia XXXIX–1971. Prague, 1973.

———. *České osvícenství.* Prague, 1986.

Havránek, Bohuslav, and Julius Dolanský, eds. *Josef Dobrovský, 1753–1953. Sborník studií k dvoustému výročí narození.* Prague, 1973.

Horák, J., M. Murko, and M. Weingart, eds. *Josef Dobrovský, 1753–1829. Sborník statí k stému výročí smrti Josefa Dobrovského.* Prague, 1929.

Hrabák, Josef, Dušan Jeřábek, and Zdeňka Tichá. *Průvodce po dějinách české literatury.* Prague, 1976.

Hroch, Miroslav. *Die Vorkämpfer der nationalen Bewegung bei den kleinen Völkern Europas.* Acta Universitatis Carolinae, Philosophica et Historica, Monographia 24–1968. Prague, 1968.

Hroch, Miroslav, ed. *Úloha historického povědomí v evropském národním hnutí v 19. století.* Acta Universitatis Carolinae, Philosophica et Historica 5, 1976, Studia Historica 15. Prague, 1976.

Jakubec, Jan. *Dějiny literatury české.* 2d ed. 2 vols. Prague, 1929.

Jedlička, Benjamin. *Dobrovského "Geschichte" ve vývoji české literární historie.* Archiv pro badání o životě a díle Josefa Dobrovského, vol. 1. Prague, 1934.

Jelínek, Jaroslav. *Nástin dějin vyúčování českému jazyku v letech 1774–1918.* Prague, 1972.

Johanides, Josef. *František Martin Pelcl.* Prague, 1981.

Jungmann, Josef. *Historie literatury České.* 2d ed. Prague, 1849.

Kačer, Miroslav. *Václav Thám: Studie divadelně historická.* Prague, 1965.

Kalousek, Josef. *Děje král. české společnosti nauk spolu s historickým přehledem publikací jejich z oborů filosofie, historie, a jazykovědy.* 2 vols. Prague, 1884–85.

Kerner, Robert Joseph. *Bohemia in the Eighteenth Century. A Study in Political, Economic, and Social History with Special Reference to the Reign of Leopold II, 1790–1792.* New York, 1932.

Kimball, Stanley Buchholz. *Czech Nationalism. A Study of the National Theater Movement, 1845–83.* Illinois Studies in the Social Sciences 54. Urbana, 1964.

Klimeš, Vladimír. *Počátky českého a slovenského novinářství.* Prague, 1955.

Kočí, Josef. *České národní obrození.* Prague, 1978.

Kohn, Hans. *The Idea of Nationalism.* New York, 1944.

Kraus, Arnošt. *Pražské časopisy 1770–1774 a české probuzení.* Rozpravy České akademie císaře Františka Josefa pro vědy, slovesnost, a umění, Třída III, číslo 31. Prague, 1909.

Krbec, Miloslav, and Miroslav Laiske. *Josef Dobrovský. I. Bibliographie der Veröffentlichungen von Josef Dobrovský.* Facultas philosophica et Paedagagica Universitatis Palackianae Olomucensis, Series Slavica 1. Prague, 1970.

Kubka, František. *Dobrovský a Rusko. Počátky vztahů česko-ruských a názory Josefa Dobrovského na Rusko.* Prague, 1926.

Kučera, Jan, and Jiří Rak. *Bohuslav Balbín a jeho místo v české kultuře.* Prague, 1983.

Kudělka, Milan. *Spor Gelasia Dobnera o Hájkovu kroniky.* Rozpravy ČSAV, Řada společenských věd, Ročník 74, sešit 11. Prague, 1964.

Kutnar, František. *František Jan Vavák.* Prague, 1941.

———. *Obrozenecký nacionalismus.* Prague, 1940.

———. *Přehledné dějiny českého a slovenského dějepisectví: Od počátků národní kultury až po vyznění obrodného úkolu dějepisectví v druhé polovině 19. století.* Prague, 1973.

———. *Sociálně myšlenková tvářnost obrozenského lidu: Trojí pohled na český obrozenský lid jako příspěvek k jeho duchovním dějinám.* Prague, 1948.

Laiske, Miroslav. *Časopisectví v Čechách, 1650–1847.* Prague, 1959.

Lemberg, Eugen. *Grundlagen der nationalen Erwachens in Böhmen. Geistesgeschichtliche Studie, am Lebensgang Josef Georg Meinerts (1773–1844) unternommen.* Reichenberg, 1932.

———. *Nationalismus.* 2 vols. Hamburg, 1964.

———. *Wege und Wandlungen des Nationalbewusstseins. Studien zur Geschichte der Volkwerdung in den Niederlanden und in Böhmen.* Münster i. W., 1934.

Macura, Vladimir. *Znamení zrodu: České obrození jako kulturní typ.* Prague, 1983.

Machovec, Milan. *Josef Dobrovský.* Prague, 1964.

Mejdřička, Květa. *Listy ze stromu svobody.* Prague, 1989.

Muk, Jan. *Po stopách národního vědomí české šlechty pobělohorské.* Prague, 1931.

Myl'nikov, Aleksandr Sergeevich. *Epokha prosveshcheniia v cheshskikh zemliakh.* Moscow, 1978.

————. *Vznik národně osvícenské ideologie v českých zemích 18. století. Prameny národního obrození.* Prague, 1974.

Novák, Arne. *Czech Literature.* Trans. Peter Kussi; ed. with a supplement by William E. Harkins. Ann Arbor, 1976.

Novotný, Jan. *Matěj Václav Kramerius.* Prague, 1973.

Osvald, Václav. *Vychovatel lidu Matěj Václav Kramerius.* Prague, 1943.

Pražák, Albert. *České obrození.* Prague, 1948.

————. *Národ se bránil. Obrany jazyka českého od nejstarších dob po přítomnost.* Prague, 1945.

Pribić, Nikola. *Studien zum literarischen Spätbarock in Binnenkroatien. Adam Aloisius Baričević.* Munich, 1961.

Prokeš, Jaroslav. *Počátky České společnosti nauk do konce XVIII. století.* Prague, 1938.

Przedak, A. G. *Geschichte des deutschen Zeitschriftenwesens in Böhmen.* Heidelberg, 1904.

Renner, Hans. *Studien zum tschechischen Frühnationalismus. Motivationen, Anfänge und Initiatoren der tschechischen Wiedererweckung.* Inaugural diss., Faculty of Philosophy, Friedrich-Alexander University, Erlangen-Nürnberg, 1974.

Robek, Antonín. *Lidové zdroje národního obrození.* Acta Universitatis Carolinae, Philosophica et Historica, Monographia 48-1973. Prague, 1973.

————. *Městské lidové zdroje národního obrození.* Acta Universitatis Carolinae, Philosophica et Historica, Monographia 69. Prague, 1977.

Rogger, Hans. *National Consciousness in Eighteenth-Century Russia.* Cambridge, Mass., 1960.

Roubík, František. *Počátky policejního ředitelství v Praze. Sborník archivu Ministerstva vnitra Republiky československé.* Vol. 1. Prague, 1926.

Rybička, Antonín. *Přední křísitelé národu českého.* Vol. I. Prague, 1883.

Schamschula, Walter. *Die Anfänge der tschechischen Erneuerung und das deutsche Geistesleben, 1740–1800.* Munich, 1974.

Shafer, Boyd C. *Faces of Nationalism: New Realities and Old Myths.* New York, 1972.

Slavík, Bedřich. *Od Dobnera k Dobrovskému.* Prague, 1975.

Šmid, Luděk. *Lidoví kronikáři středního Polabí. I. Franěk Jan Vavák—typ selského autodidakta a regionálního kronikáře.* Práce oblastního muzea v Poděbradech, Řada B, číslo 1. Poděbrady, 1967.

Šťastný, Vladislav, ed. *Slovanství v národním životě Čechů a Slováků.* Prague, 1968.

Strakoš, Jan. *Počátky obrozenského historizmu v pražských časopisech a Mikuláš Adaukt Voigt. Příspěvek k historii protiosvícenské reakce v národním obrození.* Prague, 1929.

Svobodová, Zdeňka. *Dobrovský a německá filologie.* Prague, 1955.

Szyjkowski, Marjan. *Polská účast v českém národním obrození, I.* Práce Slovanského ústavu v Praze, Svazek III. Prague, 1931.

Thompson, James Westfall. *A History of Historical Writing.* Vol. 2. New York, 1942.

Vávra, Jaroslav. *Osvícenská éra v česko-ruských vědeckých stycích. Ignác Born, Česká společnost nauk a Petrohradská akademie věd v letech 1774–1791.* Studie Československé akademie věd, 10. Prague, 1975.

Vlček, Jaroslav. *Dějiny české literatury.* 3d ed. Vol. 2. Prague, 1940.

Volf, Josef. *Dějiny novin v Čechách do r.* 1848. Prague, 1930.

Vondráček, Jan. *Dějiny českého divadla. Doba obrozenská, 1771–1824.* Prague, 1956.

Žáček, Václav, ed. *Češi a Jihoslované v minulosti. Od nejstarších dob do roku 1918.* Prague, 1975.

Articles and Chapters

Agnew, Hugh LeCaine. "Enlightenment and National Consciousness: Three Czech 'Popular Awakeners.'" In *Nation and Ideology: Essays in Honor of Wayne S. Vucinich,* ed. Ivo Banac, John G. Ackerman, and Roman Szporluk. Boulder, 1981.

———. "Josephinism and the Patriotic Intelligentsia in Bohemia." *Harvard Ukrainian Studies* 10 (1986): 577–97.

Baťha, František. "Dva dokumenty k historii počátků českého divadla v Praze." *Divadlo* 9 (1958): 750–57.

———. "Nejstarší obrozenecký divadelní překlad." *Sborník národního muzea v Praze, Řada C, Literární historie* 8 (1965): 54–55.

———. "Václav Thám, zakladatel českého divadla v době obrození." *Slovesná věda* 5 (1952): 127–57.

Bechyňová, Věnceslava. "Adam Alois Baričević a Václav Fortunát Durych." *Slavia* 37 (1968): 129–36.

———. "Ruská literatura v díle V. F. Durycha a její význam pro Durychovo slovanství." *Slavia* 24 (1955): 248–68.

———. "Vaclav Fortunat Durych a jeho Bibliotheca slavica." In *Študie z dejín svetovej slavistiky do polovice 19. storočia,* ed. Jozef Hrozienčik. Bratislava, 1978.

Daňková, Mirjam. "Dobrovského práce k dějinám českého knihtisku." Introduction to *Josef Dobrovský, O zavedení a rozšíření knihtisku v Čechách.* Spisy a projevy Josefa Dobrovského, 19. Prague, 1954.

Dostál, A. "Práce Josefa Dobrovského o tvoření slov." In *Josef Dobrovský, 1753–1953.* Prague, 1953.

Drabek, Anna M. "Die Desiderien der böhmischen Stande von 1791. Überlegungen zu ihrem ideelen Gehalt." *Die böhmischen Lander zwischen Ost und West.* Festschrift für Karl Bosl zum 75. Geburtstag. Munich, 1983.

320   Bibliography

Dukat, Vladoje. "Dobrovský i Hrvati." In *Josef Dobrovský, 1753–1829. Sborník statí k stému výročí smrti Josefa Dobrovského,* ed. J. Horák, M. Murko, and M. Weingart. Prague, 1929.

Franta, Ondřej. "Po stopách Dobrovského v deníku hraběte Eugena Černína z Chudenic." *Bratislava* 3 (1929): 868-91.

Graus, František. "Die Bildung eines Nationalbewusstseins im mittelalterlichen Böhmen (die vorhussitische Zeit)." *Historica* 12 (1966): 5–49.

Hanuš, Josef. "Dobrovského časopisy: Böhmische Litteratur auf das Jahr 1779; Böhmische und Mährische Litteratur auf das Jahr 1780; Litterarisches Magazin von Böhmen und Mähren." *Bratislava* 3 (1929): 373–493.

———. "Josefa Dobrovského Geschichte der Böhmischen Sprache (1791), Geschichte der Böhmischen Sprache und Litteratur (1792), Geschichte der Böhmischen Sprache und ältern Litteratur (1818)." *Bratislava* 3 (1929): 494–574.

———. "Počátky kritického dějezpytu v Čechách." *Český časopis historický* 15 (1909): 277–302, 435–463.

Hanzal, Josef. "Jazyková otázka ve vývoji obrozenského školství." *Československý časopis historický* 16 (1968): 317–25.

Haubelt, Josef. "František Joseph Kinský." *Věstník Československé akademie věd* 78 (1969): 560–77.

———. "František Palacký a Gelasius Dobner." *Československý časopis historický* 24 (1976): 885–916.

———. "Ignac Born." *Věstník Československé akademie věd* 78 (1969): 98–111.

———. "O Gelasiovi Dobnerovi." *Přednášky v XXIII. běhu Letní školy slovanských studií, 1974.* Prague, 1976.

———. "Počátky historiografické práce Gelasia Dobnera. (Příspěvek k dějinám čs. historiografie)." *Československý časopis historický* 22 (1974): 717–22.

Havránek, Bohuslav. "Vývoj spisovného jazyka českého." *Československá vlastivěda,* 2d ser. Prague, 1936.

Hemmerle, Joseph. "Der Josephinismus und die Gründungsmitglieder der Gelehrten Gesellschaft der Wissenschaften in Prag." *Zeitschrift für Ostforschung* 31 (1982): 208–22.

Heymann, Frederick G. "The Hussite Movement in the Historiography of the Czech Awakening." In *The Czech Renascence of the Nineteenth Century,* ed. Peter Brock and H. Gordon Skilling. Toronto, 1970.

Horálek, K. "K poetice A. Puchmajera a jeho škola." *Slovesná věda* 2 (1948–49), 160–69.

Hýsek, Miloslav. "Bürgerovy ohlasy v české literatuře." *Listy filologické* 25 (1908), 106–21.

Jedlička, Alois. "Dnešní stav a úkoly studia spisovné češtiny v národním obrození." *Slavica Pragensia* 14 (1972): 7–22. Acta Universitatis Carolinae, Philologica 2–4, 1972.

―――. "Josef Dobrovský a jeho význam v procesu českého (a slovanského) jazykového obrození." *Slavia* 47 (1979): 151–58.

Kapras, Jan. "Národní vědomí české šlechty." *Národnostní obzor* 1 (1931): 9–12.

Kleinschnitzová, Flora. "Josefa Dobrovského řeč 'Über die Ergebenheit und Anhänglichkeit der slav. Völker an das Erzhaus Österreich.'" *Listy filologické* 45 (1918): 96–104.

Kollman, J. "Obrana Čech v letech 1796 a 1800." *Sborník archivních praci* 5, no. 1 (1955): 77–158; ibid., no. 2: 26–204.

Krbec, Miloslav. "Soupis korespondence Josefa Dobrovského." *Sborník Národního musea v Praze*, ser. C, 4 (1959): 45–96.

Krejčí, Karel. "Obrana českého jazyka ze stanoviska literárního druhu." *Slavica Pragensia* 12 (1970): 81–87.

Krofta, Kamil. "F. Pubička, předchůdce Palackého v zemském dějepisectví Českém." *Časopis Společnosti přátel starožitnosti* 51–53 (1943–45): 1–24.

Kučera, Jan. "Příspěvek k problémům lidového náboženství v 17. a 18. století." *Sborník historický* 23 (1976): 5–34.

Kutnar, František. "Mikuláš Adaukt Voigt, profil historika a vlastence." *Věstník Československé akademie věd* 79 (1970): 75–84.

―――. "Národně obrozenecká společnost a její skladba." *Dějiny a současnost* 6, no. 2 (1964): 22–25.

―――. "Povaha obrozeneckého vlastenectví." *Dějiny a současnost* 6, no. 9 (1964): 12–16.

―――. "Reakce státu v Čechách na Velkou revoluci francouzskou." *Český časopis historický* 43 (1937): 323–42, 520–42.

―――. "Velká revoluce francouzská v naši soudobé critice." *Český časopis historický* 40 (1934): 33–79.

―――. "Život a dílo Ignace Cornovy." *Český časopis historický* 36 (1930): 327–50, 491–519.

Lemberg, Eugen. "Der deutsche Anteil am Erwachen des tschechischen Volkes." In *Die Deutschen in Böhmen und Mähren: Ein historisches Rückblick*, ed. Helmut Preidel. Gräfeling bei München, 1950.

Lisický, Alois. "Z dějin zápasu o české slovo." *Osvěta* 49 (1919): 475–78.

―――. "Jan Václav Pohl v zápase o české slovo." *Osvěta* 50 (1920): 39–46, 160–69, 214–22, 285–93, 345–52, 415–23, 459–67.

Mukařovský, Jan. "Dobrovského 'České prosodie' a prozodické boje jí podnícení." *Česká literatura* 2 (1954): 1–29.

Myl'nikov, Aleksandr Sergeevich. "Ideino-politicheskie predposylki prosveshcheniia v cheshskikh zemliakh i ego rannii period." In *Istoria, kul'tura, folklor i etnografiia slavianskikh narodov*. Moscow, 1968.

———. "Vozniknoveniie ranneprosvetitel'skikh ob"edinenii v cheshskikh zemliakh." *Razvitie kapitalizma i natsional'nye dvizheniia v slavianskikh stranakh*. Moscow, 1970.

Mysliveček, Zdeněk. "Duševní choroba Josefa Dobrovského." *Bratislava* 3 (1929): 825–34.

Němec, Jaroslav. "The First Austrian Learned Society." *Kosmas: Journal of Czechoslovak and Central European Studies* 3, no. 1 (Summer 1984): 149–55.

Nesvera, Rudolf K. "Zásluha Františka Jana Tomsy o český knihtisk." *Sborník Národního technického musea* 1 (1955): 72–82.

Novák, Arne. "Klopstockův vliv na poesii českého obrození." *Listy filologické* 30 (1903): 205–13; ibid., 31 (1904): 31–42.

———. "Ohlasy Klopstocka v literární činnosti Václava Stacha." *Listy filologické* 30 (1903): 31–42.

Novák, Jan Bedřich. "Války osvobozovací a naše obrození." *Časopis Musea Království českého* 88 (1914): 19–29, 113–25, 256–83.

———. "František Faustýn Procházka. (Hrstka zjištění a poznámek)." *Slovesná věda* 3 (1949–50): 193–200.

Novák, Mirko. "K problematice nacionalismu a národního vědomí." *Československý časopis historický* 18 (1970): 609–20.

Novotný, Jan. "Příspěvek k otázce úlohy některých lidových buditelů v počátcích českého národního obrození." *Československý časopis historický* 2 (1954): 600–32.

Páta, Josef. "Josef Dobrovský a Lužice." In *Josef Dobrovský, 1753–1829. Sborník statí k stému výročí smrti Josefa Dobrovského*, ed. J. Horák, M. Murko, and M. Weingart. Prague, 1929.

Pekař, Josef. "Naše šlechta a jazyk český v 18. století." *Český časopis historický* 20 (1914): 80–82.

Prokeš, Jaroslav. "Osudy prvního vydání Balbínovy 'Obrany jazyka českého.'" *Časopis Matice moravské* 35 (1925): 245–59.

Robek, Antonín. "K otázkám lidových zdrojů národního obrození." *Studia Ethnographica* Vol. 2. Acta Universitatis Carolinae, Philosophica et Historica, 5. Prague, 1974.

———. "Názory vesnické společnosti na úloha Ruska při porážce Napoleona v roce 1812." *Československé-sovětské vztahy* 2 (1973): 27–43.

Rossos, Andrew. "Czech Historiography, Part 1." *Canadian Slavonic Papers* 24, no. 3 (1982): 245–60.

———. "Czech Historiography, Part 2." Ibid., 24, no. 4 (1982): 359–85.

Roubík, František. "Ohlas francouzské revoluce na českém venkově roku 1793–94 v světle úředních zpráv." *Časopis pro dějiny venkova* 10 (1923): 177–81.

Schamschula, Walter. "Der slowenische Kirchenhistoriker Kaspar Royko (Rojko) und die tschechische nationale Erneuerung." In *Geschichte,*

Kultur und Geisteswelt der Slowenen: Studia Slovenica Monacensia, in honorem Antonii Slodnjak septuagenarii. Munich, 1969.

———. "Der tschechische Anteil an den 'Österreichischer Biedermanns-chronik' (1784)." *Die Welt der Slawen* 16 (1971): 262–82.

———. "Dobrovský's und Pelzel's Beiträge zu den 'Lieferungen für Böhmen von Böhmen.'" In *Aus der Geisteswelt der Slawen. Dankesgabe an Erwin Koschmieder.* Munich, 1967.

———. "Sprachreform und Sprachpflege bei den Tschechen im Zeitalter des Josephinismus." *Zeitschrift für Ostforschung* 31 (1982): 200–07.

Shirokova, A. G., and G. P. Neshchimenko. "Vozrozhdenie cheshskogo literaturnogo iazika kak neobkhodimyi komponent formirovaniia cheshskoi natsii." In *Slavianskie kul'tury v epokhu formirovaniia i razvitiia slavianskikh natsii XVIII-XIX vv.* Moscow, 1978.

Šimeček, Zdeněk. "Počátky osvícenského dějepisectví v českých zemích a studium dějin slovanských národů." *Slovanský přehled* 56 (1975): 303–29.

———. "Studium českých dějin, slavistika a austroslavismus. (K vývoji státní ideologie v Čechách v 18. a na počátku 19. století)." *Slovanský přehled* 63 (1977): 115–42.

Šťastný, J. "Krameriovi 'Noví čeští zpěvové pro krásné pohlaví ženské.'" *Listy filologické* 27 (1900): 23–30.

Štěpánek, Vladimir. "Dobrovský a Gottsched. K významu jazykové teorie Dobrovského." *Slavica Pragensia* 14 (1972): 23–34. Acta Universitatis Carolinae, Philologica 2–4, 1972.

Sugar, Peter F. "External and Domestic Roots of Eastern European Nationalism." In *Nationalism in Eastern Europe,* ed. P. F. Sugar and Ivo J. Lederer. Seattle and London, 1969.

Sussex, Roland. "Lingua Nostra: The Nineteenth Century Slavonic Language Revivals." In *Culture and Nationalism in Nineteenth-Century Eastern Europe,* ed. Roland Sussex and J. C. Eade. Columbus, Ohio, 1985.

Švankmajer, Milan. "Počátky českého rusofilství. K problematice jejich studie." *Slovanské historické studie* 7 (1968): 181–93.

Teich, Mikuláš. "The Royal Bohemian Society of Sciences and the First Phase of Organized Scientific Advance in Bohemia." *Historica* 2 (1960): 161–81.

Teplý, František. "Z lidové četby konce XVIII. a první polovice XIX. stol." *Časopis pro dějiny venkova* 17 (1930): 232–46.

Thomas, George. "The Role of Calques in the Early Czech Language Revival." *Slavonic and East European Review* 56 (1978): 481–504.

Thon, Jan. "Vydávání českých knih v době Krameriusové." *Slovesná věda* 4 (1951–52): 132–37.

Urfus, Valentin, "Osvícenství a ekonomická ideologie v Čechách." *Právně-historické studie* 14 (1969): 201–20.

Vávra, Jaroslav. "Böhmen und Russland in 18. Jahrhundert: Zur Bedeutung der wirtschaftlichen, politischen, und kulturellen Kontakte." *Canadian-American Slavic Studies* 13 (1979): 510–44.

———. "K počátkům rusko-českého slovníkářství." In *Rusko-české studie. Sborník Vysoké školy pedagogické v Praze, Jazyka a Literatura*, vol. 2. Prague, 1960.

———. "Podstata a problemy česko-ruských kulturních vztahů za pozdního feudalismu." *Slovanský přehled* 59 (1973): 255–75.

———. "Tschechisch-russisches Zusammentreffen auf dem Gebiet der Aufklärungsgeschichtsschreibung." *Historica* 19 (1980): 171–94.

Vodička, Felix. "Neznámé svědectví o vydavatelské činnosti Fr. F. Procházky." *Slavica Pragensia* 4 (1962). Acta Universitatis Carolinae, Philologica 3. Prague, 1962.

Volf, Josef. "Na obranu dobré pověsti pražské university." *Časopis Národního musea* 107 (1933): 75–85.

———. "Vyšetřování vlivu novinářských zpráv o francouzské revoluce na selský stav v Čechách roku 1789." *Osvěta* 43 (1913): 565–83.

Zacek, Joseph F. "The French Revolution, Napoleon and the Czechs." *Proceedings of the Consortium on Revolutionary Europe* (1980): 254–63.

———. "Nationalism in Czechoslovakia." In *Nationalism in Eastern Europe*, ed. Sugar and Lederer (Seattle: 1969).

———. "The Virtuosi of Bohemia: The Royal Bohemian Society of Sciences." *East European Quarterly* 2 (1968): 147–59.

Zeil, Liane. "Die Bedeutung des tschechischen Josefiners František Jan Tomsa (1751–1814) für die Entwicklung seiner Muttersprache." *Zeitschrift für Slawistik* 14 (1969): 597–608.

Zeil, Wilhelm. "Das Russlandbild der böhmischen Aufklärung im letzten Drittel des 18. Jh." *Jahrbuch für Geschichte der sozialistischen Länder Europas* 20 (1976): 97–115.

Index

Pitt Series in Russian and East European Studies

Jonathan Harris, Editor

That Alluring Land: Slovak Stories by Timrava
Norma L. Rudinsky, Translator

Troubled Waters: The Origins of the 1881 Anti-Jewish Pogroms in Russia
I. Michael Aronson

The Truth of Authority: Ideology and Communication in the Soviet Union
Thomas F. Remington

Varieties of Marxist Humanism: Philosophical Revision in Postwar Eastern Europe
James H. Satterwhite